315 shell
1:00

D1169095

DEATH OF THE GUILDS

Claud

908 492 4713

Tenure

DEATH OF THE GUILDS:
PROFESSIONS, STATES, AND THE
ADVANCE OF CAPITALISM, 1930 TO THE PRESENT

Elliott A. Krause

Yale University Press
New Haven and London

Published with assistance from the Mary Cady Tew Memorial Fund.

Designed by Wendy Mount and set in Bembo type by Rainsford Type, Danbury, Connecticut.
Printed in the United States of America by Edwards Brothers, Inc., Ann Arbor, Michigan.

Library of Congress Cataloging-in-Publication Data

Krause, Elliott A.
    Death of the guilds : professions, states, and the advance of
capitalism, 1930 to the present / Elliott A. Krause.
        p.   cm.
    Includes bibliographical references and index.
    ISBN 0-300-06758-5 (cloth: alk. paper)
            0-300-07866-8 (pbk.: alk. paper)
    1. Professions—Sociological aspects. 2. Power (Social sciences)
    I. Title.
    HT687.K68   1996
    305.5'53—dc20   96-1040
                                                                CIP

A catalogue record for this book is available from the British Library.

The paper in this book meets the guidelines for permanence and durability of the Committee on Production Guidelines for Book Longevity of the Council on Library Resources.

10   9   8   7   6   5   4   3   2

FOR THEODORA

CONTENTS

PREFACE

It came to my attention many years ago that the study of professions was only a part of a much wider field: the study of the arrangements people have made, in many historical periods, to get the services that are vital for their survival. I began to work within the narrower field of medical sociology and eventually on the political sociology of work, but a new field grew up in the meantime, that of the sociology of states. I made a mental note to turn to this wider field some day, with the knowledge of professions that I had developed. Another motive impelled me—the knowledge that many of us, as consumers of services, were facing a much uglier world, one in which professionals, instead of operating "on their own" as they had in my own childhood and youth, were being increasingly limited by forces quite alien to the professional ideal.

We have always known, from sociological and general literature as well as from everyday experience, that professionals and the professions act with a dual motive: to provide service and to use their knowledge for economic gain. Few, certainly not I, would begrudge them this. But what has begun to change is that professions and the work that professionals do have increasingly become the focus for actions by states, working with sectors of capitalism. For professional work can be profitable if it is organized in capitalistic forms, forms that no longer place the person who needs the service as the first priority. This trend seems to be leading to a redefinition of what professions are, from something special to just another way to make a living.

This book is an attempt to understand how and why and when this change took place, from the beginning of the modern form of established professions, in the 1920s and 1930s, to the end of the twentieth century.

But this effort grew wider as I thought about it, and it also took more time to complete than I had ever dreamed. First, it was necessary to do the work comparatively, and this meant looking for studies of professions (and their relations with states and capitalism) in nations besides the United States. Because the literature on professions in France, Italy, and Germany was just becoming available, and because I could read the languages of those countries tolerably well, I chose to involve these nations in my study, with the addition of Britain as a second English-speaking nation. (Translations in the text, unless otherwise noted, are mine.) Looking at these western European nations would allow me to trace changes from the turmoil of the 1930s to the 1990s in a limited geographic region, one where postwar economic and political ties directly affect the professions.

Finally, it took quite a while to settle on the key concept of *guild power*. I had to go back to the medieval guilds and understand them in depth, comprehending what they were and were not—and in the process realizing that guild power is a concept that is as applicable to modern occupations as to medieval ones. The term as I use it is not a metaphor but rather an operationally defined term that tends to grasp in complex ways the phenomena with which we will be concerned. In any century, a group that has guild power exercises it primarily for its own ends. The issue that I shall address—whether the consumer of professional services benefits by the loss of guild power by major professional groups or whether he or she is falling out of an uncomfortable frying pan directly into the fire—cannot be answered definitively. But I certainly can point to directions and consequences of the decline of guild power, both for the professional and for the consumer.

Many people in many nations have been helpful in the preparation of this book. Some made invaluable bibliographical suggestions, some of them read chapters of the book, a few read the whole manuscript. I would particularly like to thank the following for their help, while absolving all of them from the inevitable errors that result when one as error-prone as I goes tramping across national boundaries in search of evidence: Marzio Barbalgli, Michael Boyd, Maria Pia Camusi, André Grelon, Claudine Herzlich, Terrence Johnson, Stephen Kahlberg, Thomas Koenig, Louis Orzack, Massimo Paci, Geneviève Paicheler, Aldo Piperno, Gian Paolo Prandstaller, Michael Saks, François Steudler, Alain Tinayre, Giovanna Vicarelli, and an anonymous reviewer from Yale University Press. I would like to thank the reference staffs of the following libraries: Northeastern University library, Widener Library, Countway Medical Library and the Law School Library at Harvard University, Mugar Library at Boston University, O'Neill Library at Boston College, the library at Ecole des haute études en sciences sociales/Maison des sciences de l'hommme in Paris, the main library at the University of Cambridge, and the library at the Institut für Freie Berufe at Freidrich-Alexander-Universität, Erlangen-Nuremberg. The time to begin this work was provided by Northeastern University as part of the provisions of my initial award as Matthews Distinguished University Professor; travel funds were provided at various times by the Provost's Travel Fund and the Department of Sociology and Anthropology. I would also like to thank Gladys Topkis, my editor at Yale University Press, for her encouragement and her patience, Dan Heaton, also of the Press, for his careful copyediting, and my wife, Theodora, to whom the book is dedicated, for her support and understanding throughout the long struggle to complete the work.

DEATH OF THE GUILDS

1 | GUILD POWER AND THE THEORY OF PROFESSIONS

Is the organized political power of traditional professions—medicine, law, engineering, and the university professoriate—slowly fading in the West? Are some professions losing their guild powers—to control their association, their workplace, the market, and their relation to the state—faster than others? And if so, why? Is this loss of power happening faster in some nations than in others and to some professions more than others? And is it happening now for the same reason that it happened hundreds of years earlier, when early capitalism and the newly forming nation-states singled out *other* areas under guild control for rationalization? Have capitalism and the state finally caught up with the last guilds?

Just to ask these questions involves us in the developing field of "the sociology of states," bringing the state back into the study of such social institutions as professions. A new generation of sociologists and social historians have developed case studies of single professions in particular periods in specific nations. New large-scale approaches in the sociology of professions have been concerned with the broad sweep of historical change in the last century. But no studies ask, as a basic question, how a particular state acted over a period of time vis-à-vis a number of professions and how different states approached the same problem.

Visualize a triangle, with the state, capitalism, and the professions at the corners. The state influences and shapes capitalism and professions, capitalism influences and shapes both the state and professions, and the professions

1

act to influence and confront the power of both capitalism and the state. Who eventually gains or loses power in these relations will eventually depend upon the particular profession and state studied, and upon what the relevant sectors of capitalism are doing, directly or indirectly through the state, to influence the power of each profession.

Marx, Weber, and Durkheim each had an interest in this problem. Marx's understanding of the transition from guild economy and guild control of the workplace to capitalist control is instructive (Marx 1976, 284–85, 423, 439, 479–80), but it will not be our only guide. Also relevant is Weber's concern that the "iron cage of bureaucratization" will imprison all of us, and that to some extent this process might already be weakening the traditional professions (Weber 1978, 2:1097–98, 1241–60). Weber's concern with the conflict between the politics of class and the politics of status is also central to the question (Weber 1978, 1:303–6). And I share Durkheim's concern that there need to be strong intermediate institutions between the isolated individual and the state (Durkheim 1957). These processes are central to the theme of the death of the guilds, whether those guilds be ancient or modern. Finally, beyond the contributions of these three social theorists, there is a major literature on professional power, professionalization, and deprofessionalization, as well as on the development of states and state-society relations.

Ultimately, there is also the consumer's question: who controls the services critical to our lives in the modern period? If the doctors, the lawyers, the engineers, and the professors lose their power over the delivery of health care, legal service, applied science, and knowledge itself, and they lose it to capitalism and the state, what will be the implications for all of us? But we need to begin at the beginning. What is guild power? What did it mean for craftsmen and knowledge workers then, and what does it mean for them now?

Guild Power: Historical Institution and Modern Reality

Guilds are social groups, institutions created by groups of workers around their work, their skill or craft. The same questions are at the heart of the growth and loss of guild power in any era. If we briefly review the history of the craft guilds in the Middle Ages and the Renaissance, we can develop a model of the specific dimensions of guild power that can be applied to any occupational group, at any time and place. With this model we can investigate how two other social forces arising at the same time as the craft guilds—early capitalism and early, localized states—challenged the power of this social institution. In some social and historical contexts, the formation of craft guilds was prevented. In others, where the early state took a more sympathetic view or capitalist forms of organizing work had not yet developed, guilds thrived. The story, from the start, depends on which craft or skill and which local state we are considering, and on how far early capitalists had gone in rationalizing each area of work and destroying the power of a guild to control it.

Antony Black (1984, 7) provides a good preliminary definition of guild power: "In the craft-guild, the 'mystery' of craftmanship is joined with the dynamic of the pressure-group; skill and endurance, on which life and progress depend, are powered by a specific social bond." Black reminds us that guilds varied in size, status, and wealth and that they did not develop in all areas of Europe. In some areas merchant guilds (capitalist in nature) set up their workplaces themselves before craft guilds organized. In some places, craft guilds formed in reaction to early capitalist activity. The guilds, Black continues,

> "were primarily characterized by a concern for economic and above all artisan manufacturing interests and policies. They were formed specifically to oversee and regulate the activities of all practitioners of a given craft in the region controlled by the town. . . . It seems clear that they in fact combined juridical, political, religious, and social aspirations, but that the economic motive of establishing corporate monopoly was primary; it was this which specifically brought together all those engaged in a single craft" (Black 1984, 7).

A model of guild power—any model—has to be abstracted out of the complex reality from which the guilds, with their tremendous variation, arose. The model, as I propose it, should have the following dimensions: power and control over the *association,* the *workplace,* the *market,* and the relation to the *state*. These dimensions are interrelated, and the degree of power and control can vary widely.

The first of these dimensions of power—association—is basic. When the first guilds were established, the power of association was counter to the feudal system, under which power was given or lent by the feudal lord. In many European cities and towns from about 1150 to 1400, guilds became the main way of organizing work. Underlying the power to create an association of equals, a *universitas* in the medieval Latin, was the principle of self-organization and self-government of the group by the group itself. Ullmann (1966) contrasts this principle of self-rule or local control, which he calls the "ascending" principle, with what he calls the "descending order" of rule by princes and feudal lords, with the church legitimating the feudal order and the hierachical society that resulted. The descending principle usually, but not always, prevailed in the countryside, the guild order in the towns.

Associations of craftsmen took upon themselves the right to create all their own rules—on who might enter the association, on how an initiate would be trained and progress from apprentice to journeyman to master craftsman, on how the workplace would be controlled and the product and skill monopolized, and so on. An association's right to control who would join as new apprentices, to determine the moral suitability and family legitimacy of a new recruit, was especially important. The association claimed the right to determine the required length of apprenticeship in each guild in each town and to prescribe the behavior expected of journeymen who had completed apprenticeship but not yet been accepted by the guild as masters. The association had the power to levy dues and assess fines for breaking guild rules. The dues would go for widows' pensions, for health insurance payments to local hospitals, for burial expenses, and for the costs of the meetings, feasts, and celebrations that each guild held at least annually. Members were required to use special guild courts to settle disputes before approaching the town and its courts. The guild courts could assess fines and had the ultimate sanction of expulsion of a master, which in a tightly controlled guild town meant loss of livelihood for the offender. All of the rights and obligations of the guild rested in the masters, who were required to be equals and colleagues, responsible for the group and for the behavior and activity of the apprentices and journeymen. After due time some of the latter would become self-governing guild colleagues or brothers as well (Black 1984, 12–29).

But this dimension of power could be, and was, abused. Especially in the 1400s and 1500s, special exemptions to the rules on entry and length of training time were made for the sons of guild masters, giving them a greater chance to break into the carefully limited number of master positions in each guild in each town. This nepotism often produced a permanent second-class status group of lifetime journeymen. As their numbers grew they began to form journeyman's associations or *compagnionages*. Associational powers may have protected guild colleagues from competing against one another, but when this power was unfairly applied against the far greater numbers who they eventually trained, guilds began very early, and certainly before 1500, to appear elitist to many working craftspeople, especially to the many apprentices and journeymen who could not reach the master rank.

The second dimension of power—control over the workplace—existed because guild masters owned the means of production: the tools and the workshop. As a group, the masters deliberately limited production to a pace that all could maintain and that would not debase the quality of the product. Only a set number of products were produced per week, and the number of employee journeymen was also restricted. The number of apprentices, who worked for room, board, and experience, was also strictly limited to a few per guild master. The pace of work defined by the guild was a humane one, with no night work and with frequent holidays, religious and otherwise. For one guild master to profit at the expense of another, by charging more or less for the product than the guild price, by hiring more employees than the guild maximum, or by upping productivity above guild standards—thus "overproducing" and creating a factory instead of a craft workshop—was in theory prohibited. But of course the history of guilds does show much circumvention of the rules. As the power of the guild as an association weakened, as it did early in some nations, guild masters not only hired nonguild labor but also hired more than the maximum number of employees, paid less than the guild-set wage, and in effect became capitalists themselves (Black 1984, 123–28).

Control over the market, through the guild's monopoly over the product made or the skill provided, was the third power, and of course it was intimately interrelated with the fourth, power over the relation between the guild and the state. (The "state" was at first the town, later one of the developing regional governments.) Someone had to grant the guild a monopoly, and guilds threatened by nonguild production constantly had to lobby, beg, or bribe the local powers to protect and preserve their monopoly. Then as now, however, the right to control the availability of an item meant the ability to set the price—at a level that the guild always called fair but that consumers, or states, often felt was too high. Monopoly also meant control over the training of skill in the field, over its secrets or "mysteries." Yet the literature of the time often aptly refuses to distinguish between the power to control the association and the monopoly over the required skill. If others not in the guild can learn the secrets and train those not in the guild, the skill monopoly is broken, and with it control over the market. Sounding much like the United States Federal Trade Commission of the 1970s or Thatchers' Monopolies Commission in the 1980s, early town governments complained of "restraint of trade" and price-rigging by the guilds—unless the guilds controlled the town governments, as they did in some parts of Europe (Thrupp 1965; Kramer 1929, 185–210).

The skill and the group possessing the skill were thus equated. Without solidarity in the guild training system, the skill would no longer be a mystery. Without sole possession of the skill and the tools to use it (which often meant fighting closely related crafts over turf) the guild had no power. Compromises between guilds fighting over an area of work might involve amalgamation, subordination of one guild to the other, or even dissolution of the monopoly, with the state selling the rights to the highest bidder. Just as in interprofessional jurisdiction battles in modern times, the craft guilds fought over the skill monopoly, over the market, over who could control and employ whom in the workplace. Then as now, power of association plus power over the workplace could lead to market control—if local or national government would agree to grant it, or protect it, instead of challenging it.

Power over the relation to the state evolved variously according to the century, region of Europe and the kind of local or national government the guild was confronting. The aim of an early guild in formation was to obtain a written charter from the local power. In such centralized governmental regions as early France or England, this meant a royal charter or state approval, with state-set fees to be collected by royal tax collectors. Loss of monopoly was the price for nonpayment of fees, and there was usually an agreement to let the king decide on boundary disputes and monopoly squabbles between guilds. The stronger the state, the more it exacted from the guilds. In less politically centralized regions of Europe, particularly in regions where towns were not controlled by rural aristocrats or where merchant princes and merchant guilds did not control the town, craft guilds actually helped form the local government. In some areas of northern Italy and southern Germany, where states were weak and decentralized, guilds had much control over the town, elected the mayor, and were strong in all four of the key dimensions.

Of course it is impossible to speak of one dimension apart from the others, for the guild powers constitute a system of control. The powers can shift somewhat independently of one another in the short run, but in the long run a change in one necessitates change in the others. Without group associational solidarity the guild rules cannot be enforced, nor can a craft group have real power and control over the workplace or hold a market monopoly; the craftsmen, acting singly instead of with solidarity, have little effect on the state at any level. Clearly, though, the evolving elitist nature of the guilds as they developed from 1100 to 1500, the continuing limitation on the number of masters and the growing army of journeymen without hope or future, the abuse of the monopoly privilege to limit production below demand and inflate the price beyond community standards—all of these factors provided fertile ground for the attack on guild powers by early capitalism.

The "free market" ideology, increasingly supported by early states, viewed guild power as the enemy and limitation of production as a plot against the consumer; capitalist rationalization of work was regarded as more efficient and agreements between guilds and governments as subject to challenge. Early capitalists and capitalist associations promised to pay towns and states more to dissolve a monopoly than the guild would to preserve it. Increasingly, towns and states accepted such offers. Slowly, except in areas where either states or capitalists were weak, the craft guilds lost their powers, except for the scholars' guilds, the "universitas" of *studies,* which came under local and national protection and subsidy. This profession, which was the generator of the other learned professions, continues to have some guild characteristics even today.

It is striking to see how each of the four developing European nation-states on which we shall focus dealt with the guilds and how their approaches anticipated the ways these states acted in the modern period, especially after 1930, vis-à-vis the guild power of the traditional professions. For example, England's craft guilds faded early, in the mid-1500s in many regions, as local governments began to sell monopoly rights to outsiders or competitors, while the king stayed out of the fray. London, the home of craft guild power in the 1300s and 1400s, was constantly in turmoil because of turf battles between guilds over the division of labor (Kramer 1929, 52). The Civil War, and then the Restoration policy of letting veterans do work previously reserved for guild members—a form of state support for guild breaking—helped to weaken guild power in the 1600s. By the early 1700s the London guild masters themselves were selling the right of guild membership to the upper class to co-opt them in support—and perhaps to exercise their own status striving. Guild solidarity broke down as ordinary craftsmen masters found themselves unwelcome in their own guilds while lords and even the royal family itself were accepted as members. Guildhalls stand today in London, but most are essentially drinking and feasting clubs for the upper class and wealthy finance and production capitalists. The central state did not actually suppress the English guilds. Rather, local governments subverted the monopolies while local guild masters broke their own rules and hired nonguild help, losing the will after about 1600 to police their own monopolies or to look over the shoulder at the employment and production practices of their own guild brothers (Brentano 1870; Kramer 1929; Lesson 1979).

France's early centralization of power, even before Louis XIV, created a strong central state and left a weak set of local community governments. The power to tax was primarily reserved for the central state, and the state's ability to administer local government made the development of a strong relation between guilds and the town bureaucracy difficult to achieve. If the town was not free to work with the guilds, the guilds would have difficulty controlling the town government to protect their power and monopoly (Coornaert 1968). Although there were pockets of guild power, and journeyman's associations survived the death of the guilds to become the ancestors of labor unions, the state had a well-developed control over the economy. The revolution of 1789 further centralized state power; under the Jacobins, those guilds that still survived were immediately made illegal by the Allarde law of 1791. Shortly thereafter the LeChapelier law mandated express state approval for all groups and institutions mediating between the individual and the state. By the early 1800s, when De-

Tocqueville toured the United States, he commented on the vigor of the private associations, and particularly on the elite status of the legal profession in politics and government as compared with the weak institutions of his own France (Desmaze 1975; Sewell 1980; Tocqueville 1838).

Italy had neither the strong central state nor any national language throughout the Middle Ages and the Renaissance, and it still had no central government until well into modern times, becoming a nation only in 1876. Such coastal trading cities as Genoa and Venice developed strong merchant guilds, which quickly controlled the politics of the city and prevented the development of craft guild power. Inland, especially in the north, guilds developed early and grew strong. The skilled craftsmen from some cities, such as Florence, became famous throughout Europe. The Italian craft guilds never held exclusive power, however, even during periods in given towns when the government was more "popular" than "aristocratic."

Both Martines (1968), in his study of the lawyers' guild of Florence in the 1500s, and Park (1985), in her study of the Florentine doctors' guild in the same period, show that the university degree was a qualification for guild entrance but that practice was controlled by the guild—with the lawyers far higher on the prestige ladder of the guilds than members of the doctor-grocer-pharmacist guild. Family ties, personal relations, and allegiances by marriage and friendship, as well as sponsorship, added to the power of a guild master or an entire guild. Knowledge-based guilds were organized similarly to handicraft-based ones or ones that required both knowledge and handwork, as the medical groups were sometimes classified.

In Italy in the later Middle Ages, the Renaissance, and even today, the locality of institutions is a major theme. Guilds could be strong in one town and weak in the next. At first no central government existed to force conformity of economic arrangements—to work for or against increasing capitalist rationalization of the nation—and even after nationhood, the government would make no such attempt until, perhaps, after World War II. But conversely, a weak central state allowed guilds a foothold in controlling local government. They might thus maintain guild structure and power far longer than in, for example, France.

Finally, Germany is an example of the late development of capitalism in any form, late central state development (except in Prussia) and the preservation of guild organization and guild power almost to the middle of the nineteenth century. In many parts of Bavaria and southwestern and central Germany, guilds not only continued but grew strongest precisely when they were losing power in England, France, and even to some extent Italy—from 1650 to 1800 (Walker 1971). The "corporatist" model that we will see in post–World War II West Germany, which gives the professions greater relative power than elsewhere, was born in the guild/society model of this period in Germany. Local values remained strong and anticapitalist. Walker, considering the reasons why guilds did not develop everywhere in a region that tended to support them, lists the universal enemies of guild power: a strong centralized state (and a professionalized civil service), capitalists, aristocratic elites (feudal in 1400, state connected in 1850), and rurality (Walker 1971, 90–92). His summary suggests how and why guilds lost power or never developed it, and also what to make of the exceptions: "In the countryside, in professionally governed or mercantile cities like Hamburg and Nürnberg, and in the Prussian centralized country, incorporated craft guilds either did not exist or their structure was used as the channel for government regulation of the economy. But the guilds within the hometown communities could not be reached by that kind of legislation or control because the civic communities of uncles and brothers lay between, and because the guilds themselves were part of the communal system of authority" (Walker 1971, 79).

The University: Guild Survivor and Profession Maker

One guild—the scholars' guild—built its institutions in the same period as the craft guilds. But unlike the others, it survives to the present day. During the great wave of formation of craft guilds in Europe, from 1100 to 1200, scholars in small numbers at little schools attached to cathedrals and local churches organized themselves in almost independent fashion as a *universitas magistribus et pupillorum,* or "guild of masters and students." Early on, such associations in Paris demanded rights and guild powers, as when they wrote in 1253 to Pope Innocent III, himself a former master scholar at Paris, that he should not interfere with the university at all, because:

> "1. . . . according to the civil law the society ought not to be compelled to do anything which it has not voluntarily affirmed to do and 2. Apostolic authority does not extend itself except to that which is relevant to the Cathedral. This includes student societies, except for providing scholarships, administering the sacraments, and other things of this sort" (Rashdall 1936, 302n).

The early university was portable, for buildings were rented; the masters and the apprentices *were* the university. Their mobility gave them leverage over the towns, which could profit from the presence of an established university. In an early town-gown battle, for example, scholars left Paris in 1229 in protest against the failure of the local government and the church to support the guild unequivocally. The majority went to Oxford and Cambridge, where they helped to turn little collections of church schools into genuine Paris-style scholars' guilds. When some of the scholars returned to Paris two years later, it was with written agreements clearly spelling out their guild powers (Rashdall 1936, 336).

Latin was the language of studies everywhere, and thus instruction and guild fellowship; and student bodies as well as faculty were international from the start. Most early universities grouped their students for residence and other purposes in rough linguistic groups or "nations." But all were instructed and were expected to converse in Latin. Bologna's students, displaying the ideology of local control and the democratic values that still characterize that region of Italy, organized first into a students' guild. It hired and sometimes harassed the professors, who reacted about 1200 with the formation of the masters' guild and then slowly took control over the students. Most universities modeled themselves after Paris, where the masters were in control from the start. As with all other guilds, the student was in apprentice status as an arts candidate (the preparatory or "undergraduate" program); upon successful completion of that curriculum he entered the upper faculty as a student of medicine, civil and/or canon law, or theology. Achieving master status was a matter of satisfying a committee by examination, then publicly defending a thesis, often in the town square and with local grocers and shoemakers asking questions along with the scholars. The pattern remains essentially the same today, minus the grocers and shoemakers (Rashdall 1936, 87–283).

Economic and political factors allowed the scholars' guild and the guild model of the university to survive while all the others fell. The early university was not an economic rival to the growth of capitalism, as were the craft guilds, and universities from the beginning came under local government sponsorship. As nation-states gradually formed, the sponsorship and funding became national; endowments were founded with some royal support and supplemented by private donations. In addition, those graduates in the 1300s and 1400s who did not marry often left their books—and scholarship funds—to their university.

Because of the sources of the funding, the scholars' guilds had to deal with interference from both the church and the state. But early popes, especially Innocent III, supported the idea of guild independence and self-determination and in general supported this right for scholars' guilds as well, giving them official recognition and bulls or charters of independence from the local clergy. The guild itself often negotiated with local governments for secular power over its members. Like the other guilds, the master scholars won the right to their own guild courts to discipline students independent of the local police and courts. The four European nations in our sample differ in their history of state-profession guild power relations, usually in parallel with state-university relations, for each profession we will consider.

Both the classical works of scholarship and recent study show that most education, even in the high Middle Ages, was secular or semisecular in nature (Haskins 1923; Rashdall 1936). That is, even though technically most were clerics, many had not taken vows. The vast majority would never preach from the pulpit. The university was primarily a producer of arts graduates, of physicians, of lawyers both civil and canon, far more than it was a producer of theologians. The record shows clearly that the professions were not a product of the Industrial Revolution. The universities created a professoriate (with groups of scholars leaving Paris and Bologna to colonize Oxford and Cambridge, other Italian cities, and eventually Germany). They created as well a medical profession and two kinds of legal professional—experts in civil or administrative law and canon lawyers destined for legal careers in the growing international bureaucracy of the church itself.

By the late medieval and early Renaissance period, the graduate doctors and lawyers had begun to develop their own practitioners' guilds in the community. The two excellent studies cited earlier of the late medieval period in Florence, by Martines and Park, indicate that the graduates organized in guild fashion, on their own or in combination with related guilds. The students were usually middle to upper class in origin; scholars who lacked funds were always welcome and were supported in some locations, Paris, for example. The upper-class class background (and thus family influence) of many students and at least some of the faculty protected the scholars' guilds and the growing institution of the university from the early nation-state. Those in control of the early nation-states supported the scholars' guilds and limited state interference at the same time these new states were working with capitalism against the power of the craft guilds. The prestige of scholarship, the early university, and the developing knowledge in law and medicine gave towns and early states a reason to support "their" universities, even though the professors and students were actually an international group (Martines 1968, 41–61; Park 1985).

How did the early professional guilds of doctors and lawyers relate to the scholars' guild or to the university itself? Although Florence did not have a strong university—in much of the period covered by Park and Martines many professionals had studied medicine or law at Bologna, Pisa, or Padua instead of at the smaller and less prestigious University of Florence—there was a clear relation, and it was essentially the modern one. Scholarly training was essentially the "apprenticeship" period, and "journeyman" status— further training with established community professionals—followed graduation from the university. Although in many locations it may have been possible to practice with the degree alone and without further training, in Florence the legal guild (comprising notaries and advocates) and the medical guild (doctors, pharmacists, and grocers) conducted their own entrance exams or otherwise made their own decisions on membership. The guild had an effectively enforced monopoly on practice, and applicants who did not have an ally in the guild would not likely be approved for master status.

Both Park and Martines show in striking detail that the early professions were internally stratified. Some lawyers with noble families and connections did well, others without such family and connections just scraped by. Some doctors with the same connections did well for the same reason, but they by no means served the upper class only: in fact, they practiced across a broad socioeconomic range, attending publicly paid-for poor clients, as well as craftsmen and the upper class. A doctor with no connections might make a good living by combining his practice with that of a pharmacist (often a guild brother), but an upper-class background helped ensure a medical professorship and a stable of wealthy patients. Clearly family background was related to the length of one's training (more money was required for longer training) and to one's prospects after graduation—much as it is today. One difference, though, is that we know concretely more about these dimensions in fifteenth-century Florence than we do about the same ones today in any nation in my sample. Park and Martines studied the universe of all doctors and lawyers, respectively, in their period and researched all the relations between family backgrounds and practices. We would do well to repeat this work today on modern professions.

Guild position in all guilds depended on family status. Because guilds were brotherhoods—social clubs as well as economic organizations—the mix of family backgrounds in a guild would determine its position in a town's guild hierarchy, and perhaps the amount of political clout the guild could muster in support of its monopoly. For example, doctors tended to come from lower social origins than lawyers. Doctors mixed with the lower craftsmen of the pharmacy and even with grocers in their mixed guild. And because the work of doctors inevitably involved handwork, their guild was not far removed from a regular craft organization. What ultimately linked doctors with lawyers in the elite group of guilds was their university background.

Monopoly power varied along with status in early Florence. The legal guild clearly controlled all practicing lawyers, for example, yet many types of informal medical care were provided by nonphysicians. The relation of the guilds to political power differed, as well. Lawyers were close and notaries closer to state power, even before Florence evolved from a city-state with some craft guild (popolo) power toward one with a greater concentration of power in the hands of the aristocracy and merchant-princes. In contrast, Park shows how the sons of the aristocracy deserted medical training for careers in law and the physicians' guild lost power as doctors proved helpless in defeating the bubonic plague. Once the sons of the elite no longer dominated the guild, the guild itself lost status (Park 1985).

One thing is clear from the Florence cases: both professions were well established institutions in the 1500s. Recent historical studies have thus demolished the stereotyped ideas of Carr-Saunders and Wilson (1933) and of Reader (1966), who quotes them as authorities, that the bulk of professional group activity was a creature of the industrial revolution after 1860 (Carr-Saunders and Wilson 1933; Reader 1966). Instead, we now see that universities, and thus the professoriate, developed with differing degrees of guild power vis-à-vis the state, and well before the modern era. I will consider this premodern difference in each case study, though I concentrate on the period since 1930.

England is a deviant case. Whereas the professions and the professoriate developed on the Continent and in Scotland in continuity from the Middle Ages to the present, England's universities, in the period of Henry VIII, ejected or suppressed the professional faculties. With civil and canon law abolished, the Inns of Court in London trained the barristers, and the London hospitals trained the doctors. Before 1800 universities in the United States offered no professional training, instead copying the post-1600 Oxbridge model of liberal arts alone, but starting in the mid-1800s they recreated, with some modifications, the Continental model.

Until recently the sociology of professions was an Anglo-American field, using English and American models. Carr-Saunders and his followers wrote before the latest generation of studies of professions in late medieval periods, in Augustan England, and in the early modern period, and before the recent work on professions in Italy, France and Germany. All of these studies show the dangers of generalization without historical background or on Anglo-English models. Only in England did the professional associations proliferate, from 1850 on, outside the university, because only in England were efforts to increase group status attempted without university training. Elsewhere enhancement of professional guild power has always involved the university. Ironically, when "pure arts and sciences" universities have come under attack, as they have in Britain, they have suffered from the lack of powerful alliances that professional groups provide when they are within the university as well as without (Kogan and Kogan 1983, 37–54).

In general, then, the answer to the question of why the scholars' guild survived when all the others failed is complex, but it is consistent with the overall history of guild power that we have developed thus far. Craft guilds lost their power of association and training, their control of the workplace, their market monopoly, and control over their relation to the state to early capitalist forces, by a historically well-understood process. The university and scholars' guilds held onto their power over membership, training, and workplace because early capitalism was not interested in it (there was no product that the capitalist wished to produce) and because the state, which was not yet controlled primarily by capitalist interests, was the university's primary sponsor. Various forms of sponsorship have contributed to divergent histories of professional guild autonomy by academics in the nations of our study, even into the modern period. State sponsorship predominated on the Continent, for example, while a disengaged state allowed private upper-class sponsorship in England. Some universities in the United States received regional governmental funding, others had private upper-class or denominational religious support, plus heavy capitalist funding involvement in the U.S. case, give different histories of professional guild autonomy by academics in our different nations, even into the modern period. In each society, however, the cultural prestige of knowledge itself helped keep the scholars' guild and the university alive while all other guilds failed. The professions trained in it borrowed its prestige and made their own arrangements with the state. Only after about 1930 did capitalism reenter as a force, affecting each of our professions and the state's relation to them.

Guild Power and the Theory of Professions

Before proceeding to a detailed discussion of the analytical model to be used in the book, we must assess some of the previous models for analyzing professions and their work. My approach, like all others, emphasizes certain features and deemphasizes others in the complex world we are considering. In part, my choices are related to the questions I am asking as well as the analytical approach. Perhaps the best way to begin is to consider some of the dimensions that theories dealing with professional life survey. Then we can outline some of the major approaches, the questions they ask, and the way my approach relates to theirs.

Parsons, in a series of articles, posed a general question about professions' functional role in modern society and made a series of observations on the nature of profession-client relationships. Professional power was a functional requirement for the use of expertise, and clients were treated equally by "affectively neutral" professionals (Parsons 1954a). Parsons also concerned himself with the concept of "role strain" in general terms (Parsons 1952). But it was Field, in a series of studies of the medical profession in the Soviet Union, who used Parsons' concepts to greatest effect. Field showed the nature of the medical profession's work in pre- and postrevolutionary times, especially how it lost its guild autonomy as a consequence of revolution, even having its authority over workplaces curbed when excusing workers for illness (Field 1957, 1988). Both Parsons and Field concentrate on the workplace, showing how professional action there is shaped by training and, in Field's case, by the actions of the state. The primary criticism of Parsons (less true of Field) has been that his concepts are too general, too focused on the workplace, and that the functional approach he posits demands an ideal, perfect situation and not the reality of particular professions in particular nations.

A second group, the "trait" school, asked this question: "What characteristics classify an occupation as a profession?" These authors differed first over what characteristics to use, second over how or whether to order the appearance of particular characteristics, and third over how to interpret the results. Caplow (1954) suggested that a profession begins by establishing an association, then changes its name and asserts its monopoly, then sets up a code of ethics, then works to obtain legal recognition, first to monopolize the title to the work and later to criminalize others working in that field. It soon became apparent that this sequence was not universal. Wilensky (1964) presented a similar version but added the observation that although certain key traditional professions had indeed gone the route to full professionalization, the many semi-professions attempting this route seemed unlikely to succeed. His era, the early 1960s, did not allow most groups to monopolize workplaces, eliminate competition from other groups, or prevent subordination to other groups in the workplace. Millerson (1964) used a greater number of variables to assess the foundation of each major British professional association. He found no consistent sequence for the appearance of the various traits. That could have meant either that the whole trait approach was wrong or that the English case differed from that in the United States. Indeed, Abbott (1983) found a definite order in the American sequences but not in the British ones. In general, all trait approaches were concerned with the externals of the process of professionalization. That, not the experience in training or control over the workplace, was what they were trying to explain. These approaches also lacked any overall theoretical framework beyond a vague, unstated version of functionalism.

A third school, beginning with Hughes (1958) was concerned with professions as institutions, and with the extent of their community acceptance. He and his coworkers (Becker et al. 1961) focused on the educational process in professional training and on professional activity in professional workplaces. Relying on interviews and participant observation, the group traced the attitudes of an entire class of medical students. The researchers wished to study the differences between the student culture and that of the faculty—particularly changes in their attitudes toward "mastering the literature" or choosing a specialty. This large group of researchers also studied surgeons in operating rooms (Goffman 1961), interns (Miller 1970), patients and staff in a tuberculosis sanatorium (Roth 1963), nurse-patient interaction (Glaser and Strauss 1965), and polio as a process of doctor-patient interaction (Davis 1963). The participant-observation school continues to make a major contribution to our knowledge of how professions actually behave on workplaces. This, they believe, is the question to investigate, for professionals interact with clients in real locations. Their work has tended, however, to be ahistorical, U.S.-centered, and primarily based on the medical and nursing professions in the health-care setting.

With the work of Freidson (1970a, 1970b, 1975, 1986) we come a little closer to the approach I shall use. Freidson's basic approach appears as the subtitle of his first book: the sociology of applied knowledge. Coming primarily out of the Hughes tradition, Freidson has been concerned with the problem of professional medical dominance in the workplace (1970a, 1970b), with the way that professionals resist others' attempts to define their work (1975), and with the way that professional control over the workplace relates to control over credentialing, the court system, employers, and the overall political economy (1986). In many different ways, he shows how a dominant profession in a state that exercises limited oversight (medicine in the United States, 1950–1965) can define the terms of its work, hand off "dirty work" to subordinate groups, and define problems as its own rather than a competitor's by a combination of language and resources. Freidson (1986) shows how some professions—especially doctors and lawyers—can present their views outside the workplace. He shows how federal and state courts and regulatory agencies in the United States protect professional powers even while limiting them somewhat. His asserts that in spite of all recent changes, professions remain dominant even while in employee status (Freidson 1986, 109–33, 185–208).

It is critical to note that Freidson works on an abstract, deductional level, that he does not approach his work historically, that almost all of his corpus is based on one profession in one nation—U.S. medicine from about 1950 to about 1965—and that he does not work comparatively. Thus he cannot explain why medicine's role is different in France or Great Britain, or how the history of U.S. medicine differs from that of other nations. Many of the people who have studied nations besides the United States showed how and why Freidson's thesis did not really apply in their nations, while others debated its relevance to the medical profession in the United States in the 1980s and 1990s (McKinlay and Stoekle 1988). What Freidson accomplished was to reinstate power as a variable in explaining how professions work. He showed how the U.S. workplace is related to the power of the association, to power over the state, and to power over the market. But he did not focus on any of these variables in terms of understanding professional group action, and he deemphasized capitalism as a force.

Approaches that adopt this wider perspective on professions are the Marxist views (which themselves cover a broad spectrum) and the work of

Larson (1977). I will consider them in that order, while noting that Larson owes much to the overall Marxist model. The Marxist approaches include at least two kinds of focus—class analysis and the analysis of workplaces, with each containing the other as a subsidiary concern. One type of class analysis, the kind favored by Navarro (1976), looks at the class allegiances of various factions of health workers and of sectors of the medical profession, with special attention to the differences between the academics and the mass practitioners. Attempts to provide health care for all, he finds, run up against the class biases of the doctors, the capitalists, and all those who work to profit from the current system. But this type of analysis, while valuable, is still centered on the United States. It fails, in fact, to distinguish between the class structure of this nation and that of other capitalist nations. The dynamics of capitalism in the past twenty years tend toward a rationing of health care in the United States and toward a diminishing of the power that doctors had been handed during the period considered by Navarro. Finally, he does not consider lawyers or other professional groups, as his focus is on health care only.

Other forms of class analysis have centered around the concept of the "professional-managerial class" (PMC), on the concept of "contradictory class locations," or on analyses of the workplace. In terms of my model, these approaches focus on the role of capitalism as it takes from the professional association the power to control workplaces; the PMC argument sometimes deals with the issue of professional markets as well. Barbara and John Ehrenreich (1979, 11) define the professional-managerial class as "salaried mental workers who do not own the means of production and whose main function in the social division of labor may be described broadly as the reproduction of capitalist culture and capitalist class relations." The characteristic embodiment of the PMC is the professional, whom they define as does the trait school, as having a "specialized body of knowledge, ethical codes, and a measure of autonomy from those outside the profession" (Ehrenreich and Ehrenreich 1979, 12). The subgroup that most interested them were the "radicals in the professions," that subgroup of late 1960s and early 1970s undergrads in the United States who became the radical doctors, lawyers, and social workers of the seventies. The Ehrenreichs suggested that these workers would be a revolutionary vanguard.

Intellectually, the PMC argument was criticized both within the Left and without for its naïveté. The idea that a key group within the PMC—engineers, for example—would take a position of technocratic independence from capitalism instead of working within it was unrealistic. The vast amount of evidence indicated that the possibility within capitalism of upward mobility into management kept all but the technicians quiet. In Wright's version, members of the PMC were in "conflicted class locations," sharing the employee status of the proletariat but the values, and to some extent the income, of managers and even lower-level or petit bourgeois capitalists (Wright 1978).

In the more specific workplace-centered version of the Marxist approaches—Derber (1983) and McKinlay (1982), for example—the emphasis was on the "proletarianization of the professional." Although there is much evidence that medicine and other professionals are under pressure, and that doctors in particular are working harder and harder in stress situations similar to those encountered in industrial work, the workplace-centered approach needs to be modified and studied comparatively, outside the United States. While capitalism is clearly an important factor in understanding professional development, these studies do not show that the phenomena observed are due to capitalism per se, or rather to bureaucratic pressure to produce. In fact such pressure—which also thrived in Eastern Europe without capitalism—is due in the United States and several other nations to pressure from capitalism to reduce the costs of health care. This economizing pressure then affects resources and working conditions on the setting, as well as generating new bureaucratic procedures and programs that decrease workplace autonomy of physicians. Most of the workplace-centered studies fail to recognize this dynamic. Finally, most studies of this sort in the United States have been done in nonprofit workplaces, where effects studied are necessarily indirect. Larson (1980) agrees that the trend is toward speedup and increased control by nonprofessionals, but she refuses to call the process proletarianization. Spangler (1986) has found the same current in different segments of the U.S. legal profession, especially among corporate staff counsel, the civil service, and legal services attorneys.

Larson's 1977 approach is even closer to the approach of this book. Although Larson is broadly informed by Marxian perspectives, her perspective, compared with those of her colleagues, is more historical and more concrete in its focus on different kinds of professions, and she also contrasts the American case with the British. She is concerned with how professions control markets by gaining a cognitive monopoly over education, inside or outside the university, a process that involves the professional association's ability to use the (American or British) state as a tool to build that monopoly. She considers workplaces, positing an ahistorical classification of bureaucratic and nonbureaucratic professions. But her focus is on the market and the way professions control it through their control of the theoretical base of a profession and displacement of rival groups. Larson suggests that professions go from a "premodern" phase to a "laissez-faire capitalist" phase to a "monopoly capitalist" phase. She goes astray, however, when she attempts to show how the traditional professions were formed in the laissez-faire stage; as we have seen, they were formed much earlier. Likewise,

Larson is mistaken when she states that the "bureaucratic professions," such as engineering, were formed later, in the monopoly capitalist phase of her model, though it is true that later specialties were formed in the 1920s and 1930s (Larson 1977, 137–45, 178–207).

Larson's terms demonstrate a desire to include capitalism as a factor in understanding professions, as well as a perception that capitalism and professions evolved at the same time. But she does not consider the precise details—the differences between capital-state-profession relations in Germany, France, and the United States, for example. The details of the groups she does consider are also sometimes sketchy. For example, the fact that laissez-faire capitalism occurred at time A and monopoly capitalism occurred at time B may be associated with the birth dates of certain professions. But Larson does not consider as central to her analysis the fact that a given profession, say medicine, emerged in the 1100s, declined in subgroup status from elite to mass at different times in different nations, and became predominantly, in her terms, a bureaucratic profession in Britain and France but not in the United States or Germany in the 1960s and 1970s. Why it changed at the time it did and who changed its status—these matters are not her concern. Further, Larson's model is based on the Anglo-American professional model, not that of the Continent. When I look at France, Italy, and Germany, the danger of underestimating the role of the state becomes clear. Finally, Larson's approach is only partly time-bound. Although she gives foundation dates of professional associations, she does not give major emphasis to particular historical eras and their politics, parameters that are basic to my approach. In a sense, Larson takes professional groups to a vaguely defined "present," whereas I begin in the 1930s and proceed decade by decade to the 1990s.

Abbott (1988) presents another perspective that bears on my analysis. His focus is on professional jurisdictions. He shows that the boundaries between professional groups are often contested, with solutions ranging from domination of one group by another to sharing of the work or the clientele through division of labor by task or client group, to consultant status for one group to the disappearance of groups entirely. Legal and public jurisdictions tend to be firmer than workplace ones. By placing the workplace at the center of analysis, Abbott works in the Freidson-Hughes tradition. But he deemphasizes the stability of the traditional professions to concentrate on fields whose professional status is contested. The strength of the approach, which is not the study of particular professions in particular nations (though a range of such material is considered) is that Abbott's analysis goes consistently from the workplace toward the association, the state, the market, and even capitalism. By taking a more historical perspective than Larson's, and by studying France as well as the United States, he is careful to show the strong role of the state in Continental professions. But Abbott puts too much weight on the fights between professions. Although this is clearly a way of understanding professional life, it works much better for professions that are less well established than medicine, law, engineering, and the university professoriate. His analysis stands much in the spirit of this book, though the focus is on interprofessional struggles rather than on the professions themselves. But I do not agree that the only way to understand professions is through the struggles between them.

To conclude this listing of the major approaches to the sociology of professions, there are a group of scholars who are beginning to focus on the state as a key actor in professional life. Early work was done by Ben-David (1984), who investigated the differences in the education systems of the United States, Britain, France, and Germany to see their different effects on the growth of science. A series of monographs—Reuschemeyer (1973) on German versus American lawyers, Stone (1980) on German doctors and the health insurance system, Immergut (1987) on French, Swedish, and Swiss doctors and their respective states—have all shown that professional autonomy and guild power cannot be studied without studying the state as well. Theoretical articles and books by Fielding and Portwood (1980) on "bureaucratic professions," Johnson (1972) on corporation patronage and state mediation as alternative forms of professionalization, and Reuschemeyer (1986) on the role of the state in the legal profession are examples of a new literature to be drawn on in the coming chapters. Skocpol (1985, 27) presents this perspective when she states that "Important new work is now examining relationships between state formation and the growth of modern professions as well as related concerns about the deployment of 'expert' knowledge in public policy areas." The present work will do just that with a series of key professions, while bringing capitalism back into the picture as both employer and influencer of state action vis-à-vis professions.

From Guild Power to State and Capitalist Power

To what extent does the model I plan to develop here have a more general application, beyond the focus occupational groups of doctors, lawyers, engineers, and academics? The alternatives to guild power over workplaces are capitalist power, state power, or some combination of the two. For each of these alternatives, not only does the amount of guild power differ at the beginning of our period (depending on the nation), the dimensions also vary depending on which occupational group we are considering. During the periods I have chosen, furthermore—the Depression, World War II, the postwar recovery, and the 1970s and 1980s—each of our three rivals for power, in each of our five nations, develops and changes along the dimensions of our interest. Consequently we have one general question to ask, along with a series of specific ones. The general question—to what extent guild power characterized each group at the beginning of the era and then grew or waned by the end of the century—will involve us not just in the history of professions but also to some extent in the history of states and the history of capitalism as well. The relations among these actors, in a set of nations whose histories are disparate in some respects but similar in others, will lead us to tentative conclusions on this basic question.

That general question established, it might be useful to acknowledge some questions that will not be addressed in detail here. For example, the occupational groups that most writers call semi-professions merit some attention, but that segment is outside the scope of this book. A major difference between semiprofessions and the professions considered here is that they have developed very little guild power, at any time, either because of their dominance by one of the professions considered here or because states and/or capitalism prevented them from developing such power. In fact, our consideration of engineers can be viewed as a case study of a profession of this type. There is also the question of the proliferation of bureaucratic professions in recent years. I will assess two of the most important—engineering and academia—in that regard. Another important question not considered in detail here is that of the class action—or lack of it—among doctors, lawyers, engineers, and academics. It is not that these groups have not taken positions on general political issues or formed allegiances with others in society, or even that their work in some cases necessarily supports, on the whole, one class against another. But describing aspects of that, as I will below, is not the same as testing whether professions as a group did or did not, in some period, join the working class or the bourgeoisie. In fact, in most eras, elements of each group did both. My aim, though, is to establish patterns, trends.

Why these four groups? Precisely because most people, whether social scientists or not, consider them to be central to our understanding of modern professions. Quantitatively, they constitute between half and three-quarters of those people that most sociologists call professional. Their history is long, and even engineers were well established by 1930.

We will not consider the employment status of each group as a simple issue. For one thing, we cannot talk about what percentage of doctors or lawyers are self-employed, compared with other statuses, until we consider each nation, for the concept of self-employment varies in meaning and consequences from nation to nation. Engineers vary, too—from primarily capitalist employment in the United States and Britain to a mixture of capitalist and state employments in France and Germany. Academics, except in the United States, are primarily state employed, but that status, too, has different meanings in each nation. So this book will make no easy assumptions on this key variable, on what working in bureaucratic state or bureaucratic capitalist employment means. We will look at the content of the case studies to observe changes and what they mean.

Finally, a word about the levels of analysis used in the book. I am really operating on two levels—the level of case analyses and that of the comparative work in Chapter 7. In the case analyses, I focus on individual differences in the histories of professional development in five nations: the United States, Britain, France, Italy, and Germany. In the comparative chapter I stress what is common among all doctors from one nation to the next, for all lawyers, all engineers, and all academics. I focus there on three issues: the relation of supply to demand of professionals, the national contexts of states and capitalism as these have increasingly affected the professions in individual states, and finally, the international context of states and capitalism, as epitomized by the European Economic Community and its relations with professional groups.

But what may not be obvious is that in considering how workplace activity relates to a profession's organization and professional groups, to the role of market factors, and to the role of states and capitalism, I am not saying, even as a hypothesis, that any given profession "dies." What I do suggest is that guild power—the control of these factors by professions—is declining as state power and capitalist power encroach upon it. Where state and capitalist power have won out, they and not the profession control the aspects of professional life that we call "the workplace" and "the market" and determine to a large extent how much associational group power the profession has left vis-à-vis the state and capitalism. Subgroups play an important role here—in some cases, the elite remains in some kind of guild control while the mass has succumbed to capitalist or state control, or to a mixture of the two. But that is just one of a variety of outcomes. In this approach we will need to scrutinize, in historical depth, the individual states and the corporate capitalist sectors in each of these states, in order to understand the precise nature of their interactions with particular professions over time.

States as Actors

States in our approach are defined as bodies that possess a monopoly over the means of force, as well as most of the means of sustaining the society through education and professional training. Capitalism is a political-economic system with organized corporations in production and finance. States intervene in and support capitalism to different degrees and in different ways. In a system founded on capitalist principles the state may intervene in the economy to help or disadvantage a particular sector but is constrained from "hurting" the broader capitalist process. Professions are important to both the state and capitalism, but the degree of importance varies according to the profession and the to roles of the state and capitalism in a particular nation at a particular time.

Skocpol notes that "a complete analysis . . . requires examination of the organization and interests of the state, specification of the organization and interests of economic groups, and inquiring into the complementary as well as conflicting relationships of state and societal actors" (Skocpol 1985, 20). Professions are the societal actors of concern here. Capitalism is a force with which states deal at the same time as professions. States affect patterns of politics, like the ways in which professions can or cannot influence social policy. "The investigator looks more macroscopically at the ways in which the structures and activities of states unintentionally influence the formation of groups and the political capacities, ideas, and demands of various sectors of society" (Skocpol 1985, 21).

Poggi, in an overview of the development of the Western state, discussed the stages of institutional differentiation of the state out of the matrix of feudal society. First, most nations underwent a transition from the pure feudal system to the *Ständestaat*—a status state, where the nobility, the clergy, and the towns as corporate entities constituting the "third estate," had representative bodies that worked out their grievances and petitions with respect to a king or emperor. During this period the nobility and church had more power than the towns. But Poggi notes that in some regions, such as southern Germany or northern Italy, the system never developed or did so only in rudimentary form because states were weak and guild power—in the medieval and early Renaissance sense—was strong. As a system, the Ständestaat was also transitional in terms of geographical areas, for modern nation-states had not yet developed (Mitteis 1975, 400–401; Poggi 1978, 36–59).

The next stage—the rise of absolute monarchs and their own court-centered bureaucracies—is central to the development of the modern state. The king gradually took power away from the nobility and replaced their local agents and tax collection systems and courts with agents of the king and a bureaucracy centered in the capital. This period, roughly 1450–1600, was also when lawyers, working for the king and his court, first gained entrée as servants to power (Poggi 1978, 60–85). In France this was the period when the "bourgeois gentilhommes," ancestors of the modern French avocat and gentlemen of the robe instead of the sword, first came into their own (Huppert 1977). Regimes varied in their degree of centralization and according to whether the old feudal aristocracy was brought into the central bureaucracy, as in Prussia, or replaced by the new group, as in France.

In the next period, roughly 1600–1800, the slow growth of parliamentary representation at the expense of royal and central power occurred at different rates in different new nations—somewhat peacefully in England, violently in France. The nineteenth-century parliament in the liberal state generally served as a transition to the present system, under which capitalism's important role is combined with elections. The masses won the right to vote at the precise time that the most important decisions shifted from the electoral sphere to the sphere of the state or to state–capitalist alliances. The blurring of the line between state and society, characteristic of the later nineteenth century and the twentieth, was caused by working-class agitation and eventually resulted in the welfare state. Such nations as France and Italy fostered joint ventures between state and capitalism, with the state itself owning and operating large public and semipublic corporations. Poggi notes that bureaucracies gradually gained power at the expense of parliamentary bodies between the nineteenth century and the late twentieth. But he concludes that the modern state is not all-powerful: capitalism is a force to be reckoned with in every nation, and each state has a different set of relations with it (Poggi 1978, 127–49). Clearly Poggi deemphasizes the English experience and the American in favor of French and German models. But his is a step in the direction of our concern.

Marxist approaches work primarily at the society-wide level and emphasize class struggle. Unlike these analyses, we will look at the stances that states take toward such categories as professions, while at the same time looking at the ways that states politically work out their relations to capitalism. Unlike Marxist analyses, I will not make assumptions either that the state owns and controls capitalism or that capitalists own and control the state. Instead I recognize that power relations between the state and capitalism vary from one nation to the next, and that such power relations govern such matters as institutional arrangements for economic planning, organization of the banking system (Hall 1986: 258–83), and the degree of professional autonomy over training and practice. Nor will we ignore the issue of capitalist rationalization of the workplace and capitalist attempts to control the way the state relates to given professions.

Badie and Birnbaum present a perspective on the state that is closest to that of this book. They show the ways in which different patterns of state-society relations characterize the nations of France, Prussia, Great Britain, and the United States. France displays the state-dominant model: "From Hugh Capet to Louis XIV, from the French Revolution to Napoleon III and the Gaullist regime, the state without stopping has extended its grip on civil society, autonomized itself to form a closed space, an immense administrative machine for the purpose of dominating all the peripheries" (Badie and Birnbaum 1982, 173). In contrast with the French model, the Prussian state was forced to recruit its members from both the Junker nobility and the middle class. Top posts in the Prussian state were reserved for upper-class army officers. These practices compromised the independence of the Prussian state and led to the slow development of industry (in which the nobility was uninterested) and also to the lack of citizen values to accommodate capitalism. The Prussian bureaucracy began here, however, with its professional civil servants, and this bureaucratic model would have an impact on the professions in Germany (Badie and Birnbaum 1982, 188–95).

The English model was different. The state was not fully institutionalized and was underdeveloped in comparison with France and Prussia. England, and later Britain, would never develop the kind of professional bureaucrat found on the Continent. Instead, the nation was ruled by a class: the "Establishment" of Oxford and Cambridge graduates from upper- and upper-middle-class families (Badie and Birnbaum 1982, 196–210). The United States also differed, combining the informality of the centralized but amateur British system with a decentralized form of government in which decisions were made at three levels—federal, state, and local—by three cross-checking branches of government, the executive, legislative, and judicial. Nevertheless, the U.S. system is marked for the percentage of its elected and unelected officials who come from the economic elite or the capitalist class (Badie and Birnbaum 1982, 206; Domhoff 1979, 160–61). The different patterns of state development will have major implications for forms that professions take in different nations.

Different state-society patterns can also affect the development of political ideologies (Birnbaum 1988, 68–80). In addition, the way that classes and interest groups, such as professions, mobilize politically depends on the kind of state that they are facing (Birnbaum 1988, 81–105). Similar factors govern the development of corporatism, a form of state-society relation involving de facto government by such peak associations as capitalists, labor, and the professions. Corporatism has succeeded in West Germany but not such societies as France, whose state is too strong to allow such arrangements, or Britain, whose state, for much of its history, was not well organized enough to act as a body vis-à-vis outside groups (Berger 1981; Birnbaum 1988, 106–27;). In general, the lessons of Skocpol, Birnbaum, Badie, and of their colleagues is that we must make distinctions between nations according to the kind of state and the nature of state-society relations over time. Professions are a critically important part of each society and an excellent place to look at these different kinds of relations.

The Analytical Questions

I conclude this introduction with a brief presentation of a set of general questions that I will use to analyze the historical development of state-profession-capitalist relations. Note that essentially the same questions are relevant to each of the three main actors in our model. We must first be concerned with the degree of centralization of each of the actors: is the state centralized or decentralized, is the profession unified or split, are the capitalist sectors reasonably united politically or do they constantly work against each other? How does the degree of centralization relate to the degree of power-effectiveness, the ability of one of the actors to proceed independently of the will of another? How powerful is the state with respect to the professions, and vice versa? What role does capitalism take with respect to a given professional group? To what extent are the state, a given professional group, or capitalism accepted and considered legitimate, or to what extent are one or more of the actors considered illegitimate, to be routinely ignored and worked around? To what extent are the state, the professions, and even capitalism involved in a full welfare state? How have developments from the 1930s to the 1990s affected the nature of the relations among the actors?

Related to these questions, what are the size, strength, direction of gain or loss of influence of parties of the Left (socialist, Communist, Social Democratic) and of the Right (Tory, Christian Democratic, Gaullist)? Political parties have a complex effect on state policies affecting the professions, and they also affect the degree of unity or conflict within the professions themselves. Parties of the Left tend to be against fee-for-service practice and guild power while usually favoring the expansion of professional positions in a welfare state. Conversely, parties of the Right often uphold guild values while cutting back on the resources of the state—usually to benefit the capitalist taxpayers who have a large influence over these parties. In fully developed welfare states, such policies put great pressure on publicly employed professionals.

Finally, to what extent is the educational system centralized? Is it state-run and state-funded, or one of these, or neither? Although most European nations have ministry of education with a budget for professional training in universities, the professions in different nations have different degrees of leverage over these state decisions. And whether the professional training is within or without the university can influence whether the politics of funding the universities are the same as the politics of the professions themselves.

A second series of questions addresses the professional workplace—whether the majority of jobs are within control of the professions themselves, or are in the public sector, or are within capitalist corporations. Often the obvious answer is misleading. The guild power of the Italian professoriate, for example, though fully within the public sector, is quite strong, sustained by such factors as the disunity of the Italian state, the extent to which the professoriate has co-opted the public organs charged with regulating it, and cultural traditions quite specific to this nation (Clark 1977). Generally, a group that has always worked for capitalists, such as engineers, will have a different employment pattern than a group, like doctors, that has gone from private fee-for-service practice to state-controlled or capitalist-owned systems. The changes in the working conditions of the different branches of the legal profession will merit particular attention in the following case studies. We will throughout resist the assumption that employee status is necessarily less autonomous for a group than self-employment, but we will search out what these statuses have actually meant for given groups in given nations.

A third set of questions will deal with the control of the market for services: to what extent is it under the control of the profession itself, of the state, or of the capitalist corporations? What interrelations among the three have been established in each nation? What is the role of licensing boards, qualifying associations, *ordres, ordini,* and *Berufskämmer* in these nations? Do they act as the state's representatives with professions or as co-opted bodies serving the aims and goals of professional groups in their attempt to gain or maintain market control against the wishes of the state? What is the history of the ability of a given professional group, in a given nation, to control its own numbers of graduates—a factor of central importance in any attempt to control the market? Has the profession worked out relations with the state only to have the professorial branch of each profession, working within the university context, demand more graduates than the practicing profession can bear, to satisfy its own ends rather than that of the overall professional group?

Finally, what is the history of the ability of a given profession to control its own relation to the state? We will be particularly interested in documenting the ways in which professional control of the relation has been giving way to state and capitalist control. Even further, four of the five nations of concern to us here, by joining the European Economic Community, now have a superstate, working primarily for the capitalists and against the interests of professional groups of the member nations. To what extent have the individual and cross-professional lobbying groups, set up to counter attempts by the EEC to control professional matters within individual nations, been successful? What are the long-term trends here?

In the case studies that follow, I will show the ways in which professional group powers have always involved the professional context, but in particular how the context has increasingly become an active rather than a passive partner. Whatever else the studies establish, they will definitely demonstrate the impossibility of understanding the function of professional groups independent of their social context. How that context changes, how the professional groups change, and the evolving nature of the relations between professions and state and capitalist concerns, is the story of the pages that follow. Whether the contexts of the professions in the different nations are also becoming more similar since the 1930s is an issue reserved for the comparative chapter.

2 | THE UNITED STATES: CAPITALISM DOMINANT, PROFESSIONS PRESSURED

Coming together out of a group of separate colonies, the United States reserved certain powers for individual constituent units in a federal system. Professions were then, and are now, licensed to practice state by state. Yet the overall governmental system has gradually changed from one of domination by the individual states—for the entire historical period up to the 1930s—to the great centralization in the 1990s of power and decision making in Washington. Capitalism too, from the 1930s on, has increasingly become centralized. But the professions have not. Thus leading professions have increasingly become subject to a more centralized locus of power. At the same time the guild powers that some professions developed have been partially stripped away from them by the state, by capitalist interests, or by the two working together.

Historical Dimensions of the Change in Context

During the colonial period the initial foundations were laid for the U.S. system of profession-state relations. Each colony developed informal methods for distinguishing between trained and untrained practitioners in medicine and law (Haskins 1960). After the revolution and up to the Jacksonian era, laws were enacted to create an elite profession of medicine and an elite profession of law—the practitioners to be trained by apprenticeship, with the better-known professionals if possible (Kett 1968; Horowitz 1977).

For medicine, the best path after that was further training in Edinburgh, or later in Paris—the leading settings of the time (Ackerknecht 1967). Old World training was more difficult for lawyers, however, as study at the Inns of Court became suspect and American law gradually began to deviate from English law. American professions from the beginning never observed the English class divisions between physicians and surgeons or between barristers and solicitors.

From the Jacksonian era, starting in 1840, through the end of the century, states required no certification for either medicine or law. Monopoly laws were repealed as being inconsistent with the new, more democratic political ideology. In fact, when the medical profession lost its monopoly (never an effective one except in certain major eastern cities), almost anyone could practice "medicine," and many did. Cults and theories and approaches warred with one another (Calhoun 1965, 20–58). Would-be lawyers typically read cases and helped a senior attorney as a clerk. But law could be studied at home. Judges accepted new lawyers upon personal recommendation. Up to the era of reprofessionalization (from about 1880 on) those with a formal apprenticeship were found mainly in the major cities in the East and near Middle West. Elsewhere, formal apprenticeship was rare.

The foundation of the first national professional societies—the American Medical Association in 1848, the American Bar Association in 1868—did not mean that at these early times the majority of doctors or lawyers were either formally trained in universities or belonged to these very exclusive societies, made up of the leaders of the profession. But the establishment of state universities, especially after 1865, gradually led each state to establish professional schools as well as undergraduate faculties for arts and sciences and for agriculture. The creation of model university-based programs at the end of this period, in medicine at Johns Hopkins and in law at Harvard, established a new way to train professionals (Brown 1979; Seligman 1978). From the British system of training by apprenticeship in the community, under the control of community professionals, America gradually developed a more Continental European system of professional training in universities. But like Britain and unlike the Continent, the states left accreditation of these programs in the hands of the profession.

Capitalism went through stages of growth and development that paralleled, but did not necessarily overlap with, the stages of professional development, until the end of this period, with the second professionalization of medicine and law in 1880–1920. Essentially agricultural from colonial times until the 1860s (except for the eastern cities), the United States rapidly caught up with the industrialization of Europe after the Civil War; the war itself may have provided an impetus. Political power began to pass from planter aristocrats and urban merchants to capitalist industrialists—to the robber barons of coal, oil, and railroads. "Laissez-faire" was the philosophy of the age: government should refrain from regulating industry, commerce, and banking. When the first regulatory agencies were created, capitalists quickly perverted them and ran them in the interests of private profit (Fellmeth 1970).

American professions found the ideology of laissez-faire congenial as well. The "culture of professionalism" became popular in the rising middle class, and its bounds exceeded the narrow ones of the key professions considered here (Bledstein 1976). In the decades following the Civil War, for example, the concept of the professional baseball player and the professional social worker also first appeared—even if in most cases no real guild power, as we have defined the term, was involved. As a result of the organized political action of the professional societies, new licensing laws were enacted, state by state, for medicine and law, in the 1880–1920 era, and they were accompanied by requirements that those who had completed the university-based training programs obtain new credentials and undergo examination by the new licensing boards. Several generations of professionals trained under the older system would continue to practice in the new era, however. Not until the 1920s or even the 1930s was the modern university degree–plus–license exam system firmly established nationwide. And then it was established state by state, for under the American system the licensing of professions is not a function of the federal government (USDHEW 1971).

The failures of capitalism and the onset of the Depression made the 1930s a turning point for the United States. Laissez-faire as an ideology no longer remained unchallenged. Roosevelt attempted to create, in his administrations of 1933 and 1937, a centralized set of programs to reform the nation's economy and to create the first elements of a welfare state. True, his program did not succeed, except for the founding of the Social Security system and the more general start of the growth of the federal government in Washington. In his battle for Health Security, Roosevelt was opposed not only by capitalism but also by labor, and by the American Medical Association (Hirschfield 1970). He nevertheless joined the battle with American capitalism for the first time.

More important than these skirmishes were the arrangements Roosevelt fostered between corporations and the federal government for war production, which also co-opted the labor movement. This joint planning process did not survive the war. But it did let large capitalists work with government in a way that led to the military-industrial complex of the Cold War years, defined by a growing military spending program with strong ties to certain industries and quite insulated from citizen control. Truman, Eisenhower, and succeeding presidents, Republican and Democratic alike, found that it was easier to work with this combination of corporate and congressional power than to oppose it. The legislative veto power that capitalism developed after the war was possible in part because neither political party was willing to oppose capitalist interests. This reticence has been seen in general, not just in military affairs (Mills 1956).

Professional associations, and the overall guild power of American medicine and law, grew from the 1930s to the early 1960s. Although World War II led to a closer working relation between large corporations and the central state, it did not disturb, in this time period, the essentially private model of American professions, nor their private power to control and accredit their training programs. Lobbying in Washington, professional associations repelled new federal threats to their autonomy. Many new semi-professions established licensing between 1930 and 1960, but most never developed a fraction of the guild control of medicine and law to control all workplaces, expel competitors, and build a private market for services. What did grow in scope and importance after World War II was the role of the "fourth branch" of the federal government—the regulatory agencies. By the late 1960s, they would begin to affect the power and activities of professions. But in the immediate postwar period these activities were defined by the professions themselves.

From the mid-1960s on, the role of the federal government in limiting the independence of the professions rapidly began to change. First, the postwar expansion of universities and the rapid rise in the federal funding support for them, as well as the increasing percentage of students pursuing college and postgraduate education, gave the central government a new and important role in the operation of the universities that trained most American professions. Research grants in medicine, science, and engineering made a major difference in the size, shape and function of the American university. By the mid-1960s Kerr's phrase "the multiversity" described almost all centers of professional education (Kerr 1967). Although most research grants were awarded at this through a colleague-based referral system, contracts in defense—often far larger—were not. The growth of universities also led to greater leverage and guild power for academics themselves, peaking about 1965–1970.

Gradually, however, the key professions in the United States began to lose guild power, and in the years since 1970 their control has increasingly been shared with capitalism and the state. We will review this process for each of our key professions. In general, however, the erosion of professional control over the association—a loss of control by the profession over the numbers trained, in particular—has coincided with precipitous increases in the costs to both capitalism and the state of the services provided by professions. This has increasingly led capitalism and the state to new working relations with professionals and further challenges to professional group

guild power. The regulatory agencies, especially the Federal Trade Commission, have redefined professional work and professions as equally susceptible to regulation as all other forms of commerce, rescinding a long-held
exemption (Kissam 1983). The payout agencies for professional services,
especially the Department of Health and Human Services for health work,
have taken on a new role in shaping practice by professionals. Three of our
four groups—doctors, lawyers, and academics—have massively overex-
panded their ranks since 1970 in the past twenty years, compared with
population ratios of the previous era. The guild power of engineers, never
comparable with that of the other three, is further threatened by changes
brought on by new technology. The clear trend is for the key professions
to lose guild power, while the marginal professions never developed any to
begin with, except for some control over their training programs.

How has the role of the state evolved in the United States? And how has
this evolution affected the development of U.S. capitalism and U.S. professions? The first factor to consider is the diffuse nature of the state, compared with the others in our sample. First, the constitutionally separate
federal branches of the executive, legislative, and judicial can all act at cross
purposes. This is so especially when, as is common in the United States,
the president and thus the executive branch is from one party and the
legislative branch is dominated by the other party. There is a separate and
parallel system of executive, legislative, and judicial branches in each of the
fifty states. The professions in the U.S. system are licensed by executive
state agencies in Massachusetts, New York, and so on. But they appeal their
decisions, and all problems about funding of services, to a state and then a
federal judiciary system. Many cases involving professional autonomy are
judged in the state courts, but they can also be reviewed by the federal
regulatory agencies and the federal courts.

The trend is for licensing to remain at the state (New York) level but for
regulation of payment (for public programs) to become a more national
concern, and for regulatory agencies, which are part of the federal system,
to become more important, especially as forums for approving and supporting new ways of deploying and paying professionals, thus continuing
to diminish their power to control workplaces and markets. Also, universities have become even more enmeshed in recent decades with the government, not only because of the way professional training programs are
funded but also because of state and federal legal actions that affect how
universities do business.

State unity is rather poor in the United States, compared with the French
or the German systems. First, the state at each level, including the local,
both has and hasn't the ability to act, depending on the issue. Second, with
the existence of regional state government (comprising jurisdictions within

states, usually at the county level) as well as regional national government (groups of states considered together under a federal aegis), much policy action can be taken by circumventing one level of government for the next, which affects the ability of the state as a whole to act with unity (MacMahon 1972). Third, given the nature of the American judicial system—the case-law method by which policy is finally approved in the courts if established by government action and then challenged by, for example, a professional group—decisions about professional behavior can be made at different levels, again depending on the issue. When the U.S. Supreme Court handed down decisions on restraint-of-trade issues by the medical profession in the 1960s, or when the Federal Trade Commission nullified rules about professional advertising in the 1970s, the state affected only one area of a profession's autonomy, but it was an important one. There is no central body in the U.S. system like the French Cour de Cassation to decide all basic legal issues involving the rights and obligations of French professions.

Does the average American hold strong views toward the U.S. state, taken as a whole or broken down into different levels of government? Research since the 1960s reveals a complex of mostly ambivalent attitudes. Since Roosevelt's time the majority of citizens have expected the state to act as something of a safety net under all. Yet these same citizens have often expressed resentment or refused to pay additional taxes for state services, not simply because they don't like the people who will receive them but also because they mistrust state employees and the size of government. This, rather than the Republican ideology of a minimal state, inhibits the creation of many elements of a continental European welfare state. Such attitudes also prevent the creation of a truly professional civil service. In some eras—the reformist era at the turn of this century, for example, when civil service was set up in the United States as an alternative to the spoils system, or in Roosevelt's time, or during the Kennedy-Johnson years—public service jobs gained social acceptance. But even though the public sector has continued to expand gradually at local, state, and federal levels, the creation of a systematic welfare state, with defined roles for each of the professions, never has been a feasible alternative in the United States. Nor do Americans expect, or generally desire, their professionals to be state-employed, except for those that naturally are based in this sector.

The absence of a political Left is critical in understanding the special nature of U.S. society and the U.S. professional system. Not since the late nineteenth century has a socialist Left seemed capable of exerting significant influence in the United States (Foner 1972–1975). Even in the 1930s the socialist-communist Left was very weak, and by then the American labor movement had long since thwarted the socialist challenge to Gompers. The absence of a Left has made the politics of universities different from those of Europe until the Vietnam era. Roosevelt's aims were to save capitalism, not to replace it. But the New Deal co-opted many on the near Left; in the McCarthyist fifties the remaining Left was driven underground, or at least out of government and the universities. Thus the story of the politics of professional groups is especially simple in the American case. Only in the late 1960s was any sizable Left visible on professional campuses and in the ranks of American professions—and even then that Left received very little support from the general population or from their fellow professionals (Hoffman 1989, 186–89).

Capitalism's role vis-à-vis the U.S. state structure and vis-à-vis professions varies according to the part of the state and the profession considered. After World War II, the top five hundred or so corporations became a kind of policy-making sector involved in state affairs, apart from the medium-sized and small companies (Galbraith 1967). The executives in the first group often circulated in and out of government, a process accelerated by Roosevelt during the war and continued by all succeeding administrations. This involved not only the corporate sectors of the military-industrial complex (aerospace, weapons, technology, electronics) but many other sectors as well. This government by lower-level bureaucrats, with temporary bosses appointed from capitalism, has, through the years, hindered the full professionalization of our civil service as well as encouraging the ideology that the state could never be good at providing any service.

Indirectly, capitalists and capitalism shape the direction of the American university, or influence the ways the state pays for, or does not pay for, professional services. Directly, capitalists are the employers of many professional groups. The characteristically privately practice of the American medical and legal professions of 1930 has given way, especially since 1970, to employed physicians and an elite segment of lawyers working directly for big corporations either in legal firms or, increasingly, as "house counsel" within the corporation itself (Spangler 1986). We will consider the ways that engineers in the United States have always had low guild power because of their relation to capitalist employers. And we will consider how the model of the university changed from an emphasis on arts and sciences in the 1930s to the much more vocational curricula of the 1990s, again because of capitalist influence and its effect on both students and faculty.

In a more general sense, capitalism in the United States did not usually act as a political bloc vis-à-vis professions, except in the general sense of vetoing approaches to professional services that capitalists considered liberal or socialistic. Increasingly since the 1970s, though, capitalists have moved to employ professionals, including doctors and lawyers, more directly, to take ad hoc action to control the costs created by professionals, and to work with the state toward constraining the remaining guild power of professions.

This process has occurred in different ways for each of our professions, which we will now consider in turn.

American Medicine: The Fall of a Giant

No profession in our sample has flown quite as high in guild power and control as American medicine, and few have fallen as fast. The particular forces that accounted for the rise of the profession in 1930–1965 have all contributed to the decrease of professional autonomy and group guild power since that period. The history of the rise and fall of medicine's guild power falls naturally into four eras: the 1930s under Roosevelt, World War II, the immediate postwar period to 1965, and the Medicare/Medicaid fight and the decline in power from 1970 to 1990.

The 1930s to World War II

When Roosevelt took over the White House from Hoover, the medical profession was in the process of formalizing the internship-residency system under the supervision of the American Medical Association. This would be the first full decade of medical students that could truly be characterized, nationally, as fully modern physicians. But economic conditions were terrible. The AMA began to grow in membership during the late 1920s and the 1930s, when it professed to act as the spokesman for all physicians. But membership, after rising from 57% of all physicians in 1920 to 64% in 1930, declined during the Depression years, falling to 60% in 1935. Doctors, if not out of work, were often unable to collect fees in a nation with massive unemployment and with very poor health services in many regions (Garceau 1941, 131; Murrow 1963, 185–204).

In the 1930s the AMA pushed for voluntary health insurance (such as Blue Cross/Blue Shield plans) as a method favorable to and consistent with the private fee-for-service practice of medicine. The group opposed Roosevelt's plans for a national health insurance that would cover everyone, for this coverage would be compulsory; even in the 1960s the AMA continued to call such plans "socialized medicine." The "Blues" would be run by the doctors and hospitals and would address their crisis of uncollected fees. Although AMA leaders have often been medical specialists in private practice, the mass of the membership has been general practitioners and office-based specialists (Murrow 1963, 228–51).

To win AMA approval voluntary health insurance plans had to meet a very strict set of criteria, including noninterference with the doctor-patient relationship (freedom of patient choice) and a fee-for-service basis. Physicians participating in groups—like Dr. Michael Shadid's prepaid group health plan in Oklahoma—earned the enmity of the AMA. Often, the physicians in such plans were driven out of the local medical societies, the constituent units of the AMA. (Each state medical society was made up of local units and sent delegates in turn to the national association.)

The AMA recommended plans with local sponsorship by physicians, like Blue Shield, which was under physician control and based at the local county medical society. Because the group did little or nothing to address the medical needs of the working class or the poor, however, the Roosevelt administration began a long-term effort to create two parallel programs: Social Security and Health Security. The AMA waged a national campaign against the latter, succeeding because only a few progressive academic physicians endorsed it. (The academic wing of the profession was on the whole neutral.) American labor, an important constituent in the support for Social Security, officially opposed a national health bill, and older people were not yet organized politically. Roosevelt, faced with the opposition to a major bill in 1940, accepted defeat. The AMA, successful in defeating a popular president, won more members among physicians and became a formidable force, a veto group in Congress. The nation prepared for war under a climate in which government involvement in health care, except for public health areas and the military itself, was not acceptable. The AMA, with its executive officers in Chicago and its national network of county and state medical societies, guaranteed that that climate would prevail in a nation that respected the doctor over anyone else as an expert, not only in diagnosis and treatment but also in the methods of running hospitals and paying for the care (Hirschfield 1970).

During World War II the profession was divided. Some doctors remained at home, manning a very doctor-short system, but the majority volunteered for military service. Some enlisted to avoid being drafted and denied officer status. The federal government and the Departments of the Army, Navy, and Air Force provided universal health care for the services. Up to 80% of medical students were drafted, though they were allowed to finish school before reporting (Murrow 1963, 281–305).

Even at the height of the war, with all those in uniform receiving government medicine, the AMA fought proposals by Roosevelt that might have led to a postwar national health insurance system. The AMA also opposed government health care for the dependents of servicemen. When the revised Wagner-Murray-Dingell bill came up for a vote in 1943—a last attempt to create a national health insurance system—Congress caved in to the opposition of not only the American Medical Association but also the American Bar Association. The Physicians' Forum (the majority of whom were in academic medicine) was no match for the AMA and its Bureau of Medical Economics. When, at the conclusion of World War II, it became obvious that because of the war millions of young Americans visited a doctor or a dentist for the first time because of the government's medical program, most Americans were still not organized to push for this care in peacetime. The AMA's hold on Congress at war's end was stronger than ever.

The Peak of Power

During the Truman and Eisenhower administrations the American Medical Association reached its peak as a symbol of the power that an independent profession could reach. It was almost universally respected. Capitalism had yet to decide that the power of the profession was a menace to its own survival. Those sectors of capitalism that made money from health care delivery—the hospital industry, the construction firms and banks, the drug and medical supplies fields—worked with the medical profession and guaranteed large profits for all.

The role of the state during this period was twofold: at the level of individual states, the licensing boards in medicine, working under the complete control of state medical associations, carried out the policies of those professional bodies. Each state licensing exam was slightly different and protected the turf of each state association. The acceptance of foreign medical school graduates and the grades they would be required to have to pass a particular state exam were determined at each state level with AMA advice. Often the foreigners were allowed to practice provisionally in such settings as mental hospitals, rural areas, or poverty-stricken neighborhoods where American graduates would not go. Federal attempts to regulate the profession, except for Supreme Court rulings on early restraint-of-trade cases, did not threaten the primarily local power of the profession. The AMA's effectiveness in Washington nullified legislation that threatened the autonomy of the profession as a whole.

Power over the association was the first aspect of the profession's guild power. The AMA's policy of limiting the number of doctors graduated each year slowed to a crawl the growth of medical school populations and the accreditation of new medical schools. As a result the ratio of doctors to the population changed hardly at all from 1931 (126 per one hundred thousand) to 1949 (135:100,000) to 1961 (131:100,000). Underserved areas remained underserved (Fein 1967, 16). The Hill-Burton hospital-building program, the large federal-state effort after World War II, built hospitals in rural areas, but then often had to close them because the doctors didn't arrive. The government could not employ them, for the AMA vetoed any major expansion of the public health system. The AMA Council on Medical Education was the supreme body for accrediting medical schools, and it seldom approved a new one. It also vetoed progressive approaches to education, such as more social science or public health in the medical school curriculum, in the programs that did pass inspection.

In addition to controlling its own profession, the medical profession during 1945–1965 gradually consolidated a pyramid of power over most other health professions (except dentistry) by using its monopoly powers at the state level and its national Council on Medical Education as an accreditor and sponsor of nonmedical programs in universities. Most common was the strategy of helping subsidiary occupations in the health field—nursing, X-ray technology, physical therapy, occupational therapy—lobby state legislatures to get their licensing laws passed, but with one proviso: inclusion of the "supervision" clause, under which practitioners of the occupation would do their work "under the supervision of a licensed physician." In practice, this meant that most other health occupations, arriving later on the scene than doctors and without their local political power, had little or no chance to get their limited licensure approved without AMA support, for the national and state medical association would lobby against occupations that insisted upon independence. In addition, with many of these occupations, the AMA Council on Medical Education acted jointly with the accreditation organization of each group in accrediting university programs, and physicians often joined occupation members on the licensing boards (USDHEW 1971, 11–12).

Power over the workplace, the second area of guild power, was almost unchallenged in this period for medicine. The hospital was under the doctor's control. Each department in a hospital was effectively run by a chief, who was usually a privately practicing physician and not a hospital employee. The chiefs together hired the hospital administrator, who reported primarily to them. Nursing was always defined by doctors and almost always also by its own licensing laws as subservient to and under the direction of the medical profession, on the model of the other health professions (Reverby 1987; Melosh 1982). In office settings the auxiliary health professionals almost always worked on salary for physicians. In the hospital, though most of these occupations were employed by the hospital, they nevertheless worked directly under the doctor's orders.

Nurses complained, especially during this era, that they might be given conflicting orders by the administrative side of the hospital (head of nursing and head of hospital) on the one hand and the doctor in charge of a patient on the other. But the general rule was to follow the doctor's orders. As Freidson noted, the doctors also had general authority to define illness and to challenge any other occupation's right to do so. Medical societies often prosecuted chiropractors and osteopaths in this era, and usually won (Freidson 1970a).

Training in the workplace was the province of the medical school and was carried out, as it is today, in medical school–affiliated hospitals. During this era, the dividing lines between the different occupations in the hospital were rather strictly observed. For medicine, third- and fourth-year students were rotated through the different specialty areas of the hospital, under the supervision of interns (first-year graduate physicians), residents (specialists in training), and senior physicians affiliated with the medical school but usually in private practice, as well as the actual medical professors based at each hospital. Mumford observed that training after graduation differed somewhat between community hospitals and the hospitals of the academic medical elite, affiliated with the leading research-oriented medical schools. In the former, where the majority of medical students took internships, the goal of community practice was primary, and some deference was paid to the patient, especially if he or she was middle class and important in the community. In the elite teaching hospitals, which represented the top third of the American hospital status system, the goal was research, and two kinds of settings were available: the most prestigious hospitals in the area, where the interns and residents would work under very close supervision, and the public city hospital, where poor people gave their bodies for free treatment, often under the hands of the same medical students, interns, and residents, but under far less supervision (Mumford 1970). Some of these settings, like the Harvard Teaching Service of Boston City Hospital, were a proving ground for the leaders of academic medicine in the 1950s and the 1960s— regardless of how callous they were in treating the poor, who in any case had no other alternative (Miller 1970).

In more general terms, there was a division of labor in the postwar period between the academic, research-oriented wing of the profession on the one hand and the private practice wing on the other. The academics tended to be less active than before the war in the politics of the AMA but had yet to become the AMA's opponents. The practitioners controlled the majority of medium-sized and small general hospitals across the country and became more active in the AMA. Practitioners, especially such specialists as surgeons and radiologists, were often much more wealthy than their academic counterparts. But the academic wing, from the war's end to the late 1960s, not only gained in prestige compared with the private practice wing, but also got a lot of research funding. The 1950s and 1960s were the great era of the foundation and expansion of the National Institutes of Health. The top thirty medical schools, and especially the top fifteen, created a vast research empire. Although the money was federal, it was supplied through a system of peer review committees, where one's colleagues in other medical schools decided which proposals to fund. A pragmatic stratagem grew out of this system. Tuition funds had become insufficient to train medical students, and the AMA had vetoed most scholarship plans. As a consequence, medical schools gradually began to use the overhead for their research grants for training, and the schools thus became partially dependent on Washington for operating funds (Richmond 1969).

After medical school, depending on the placement of a particular medical school in a well-established pecking order of prestige, a medical student could choose a career in academic medicine (if he had earned outstanding credentials at a major medical school) or a career in practice. Those who became specialist practitioners had a third alternative: courtesy appointment at a local medical school, which would combine a little teaching with a primarily private practice.

The growth of specialty medicine, as detailed by Stevens, began in the 1930s and accelerated rapidly in 1945–1965 (Stevens 1971, 173–290). Each specialty established national standards, and administered a national exam, certifying expertise beyond the degree. All doctors can do specialty work, though often at their peril, so this extra certificate was not required, just recommended. By the late 1960s, more than three-fourths of American physicians were calling themselves specialists, and about two-thirds of that number actually had board certification in their specialty. But this trend to specialization and specialty practice, and the expansion of specialty associations, soon engendered differences of opinion between the AMA and generalists, on the one hand, and the new groups, with more narrowly defined interests and often their own positions on social issues, on the other.

In the U.S. system, this fractionalization of interests did not lead to deep divisions in the medical profession. There were enough jobs for all graduates, and many areas of the nation had shortages. A good student could choose a career of high prestige and moderate income in academic medicine or a career as a specialist in private practice, with less prestige but higher income. But this pattern—and the overwhelming choice of a specialty instead of general practice—did not meet the needs of most consumers. By the end of this era, studies commissioned by the federal government showed that the profession needed to change its habits. Medical economists like Fein, in his pivotal work on the doctor shortage, pointed to the drastic maldistribution of physicians and the need for an increased number to meet increasing demand—especially by the poor, who often did not demand health care yet whose need was obvious. Fein also was one of the first to recommend major reorganization of the system for providing health care: group salaried practice, for example, instead of the fee-for-service model in totally private settings, and the training of more general or family practitioners and fewer specialists. His views were those of academic medicine, however, not those of the AMA and the practitioner wing, which ignored them (Fein 1967).

The market for services was clearly controlled by the medical profession during the first twenty years after the war. Physicians controlled most health care and marginalized not only chiropractors (branded as quacks by the profession) but osteopaths as well, a dissenting sect within medicine itself, who then set up their own hospitals and medical schools. Private practice and fee-for-service medicine were jealously guarded by the AMA as uncompromisable principles, and only a very few group health plans were set up in this era.

In 1950, the vast majority of U.S. doctors were in private practice, in control of their hospitals and governing the division of health work as well, with the state neutralized at the national level and co-opted in state licensing boards. But things were about to change.

Activism and the Fight over Medicare and Medicaid

The Kennedy-Johnson years (1961–1969) were years of activism on the part of a more liberal state and increasingly defensive action by the medical profession, especially its practitioner wing. But the reaction, when the Nixon administration took over, did not include a return to AMA domination. The Kennedy-Johnson era was the turning point for American medicine, as its solidarity began fell apart in the wake of its defeat over the Medicare-Medicaid Act. We will consider the activism briefly, then the problems that began to arise in the administration of Medicare and Medicaid. Various regulatory approaches to control the rise of health care costs were tried in this period, but they all failed.

When Kennedy was president, certain programs became the hallmarks of his approach. But in the wake of his assassination, it was President Johnson who put the majority of them, including Medicare-Medicaid, through Congress. The Community Mental Health Centers Act of 1963, a Kennedy program, would build a nationwide network of mental health centers; and as a part of the Economic Opportunity Act and the Office of Economic Opportunity (OEO) Neighborhood Health Center program, general health centers were established in urban and rural poverty areas. The Johnson administration gradually began to realize that these programs, advances though they were, raised issues of two kinds: who defined professionalism, and what approach would work best for the poor and the old?

The definition of professionalism was challenged in this period by a new emphasis on community participation in social programs. As Hoffman shows, community boards began to demand control over hiring of staff at clinics. They began to fight with the medical schools with which the programs were affiliated by the grant system from OEO. Health activists, though less elitist than medical school professors, did not share the community perception that expertise in medicine was nearly irrelevant. Special clinics began to be developed at this time for blacks (usually through the Black Panthers), for women, and for gay and lesbian clients. The very model of expertise inherent in medicine (for that matter, in all health occupations) was challenged. But most efforts in this area came to little, as funding rulings from Washington favored the professional model (Hoffman 1989, 93–106, 191–204).

Johnson's interest shifted from community action programs (which were a political headache) toward the Democratic Party's goal since Roosevelt's time: the creation of a national health insurance system. But Johnson was a realist, recognizing that a partial system, serving those over 65 (Medicare) and the "medically indigent" (Medicaid) would be an achievable intermediate step. Thus the 1965–1966 Medicare-Medicaid Act was born (Stevens and Stevens 1974; Marmor 1970).

From the initiation of the planning for the Medicare-Medicaid legislation the AMA fought against it with all the weapons at its command. AMA membership peaked in the years just before passage, reaching 73% of all doctors in 1963 (AMA 1990). Extra assessments were made of the membership for a multimillion-dollar fight against the passage of "socialized medicine." But academic medicine, which had been neutral in the Roosevelt era, favored the new bill, and a new and powerful lobby supported it: older Americans. When it passed in 1967 the AMA had a clear defeat on its hands, and the organization has never since held the commanding position it had before. More important, community sentiment, which had generally been in favor of the medical profession, began to change. People still trusted their own doctors—if they had one—but they began to view the profession as a whole as greedy and heartless.

As is often the case after the passage of a major piece of legislation, it was necessary for the victors to get the opponents "on board." Practitioners were won over to participation in Medicare (administered through the Social Security system) by generous fees, or "usual and customary charges." Overnight, charity medicine disappeared in the United States, as all doctors and hospitals not only began to charge for their services to all patients, but charged the maximum that the law allowed. The result was an immediate giant increase in the cost of serving the old and the poor. The Medicaid portion of the program was for the poor of any age—and it was administered by the welfare apparatus of each state. Within one year New York and California, for example, placed strict limits on the eligibility of the poor. In spite of low rates of participation—only 15–25% of those eligible signed up, in part because registration was a complex procedure—and drastic new limits of eligibility, costs rose precipitously. By 1968, Johnson's last year, costs were double or triple what had been predicted at time of passage. And they would go still higher (Stevens and Stevens 1974, 156–82).

The cost of health care gradually began to mobilize American capitalism. Capitalism entered the health political arena on the side of the state cost controllers—and with the support of the salaried doctors in schools of medicine and public health, the groups lumped together by Alford as "corporate rationalizers" (Alford 1975). The Washington Business Group on Health, established by the Washington Business Roundtable, which in turn represents the two hundred largest corporations in the nation, worked with government and academic cost controllers and researchers of the problem to recommend solutions.

All of the solutions, however else they differed, involved the end of fee-for-service medicine, which was blamed as a major incentive to increase care past the point of need (Krause 1977b). The expense of health care, from the Johnson years onward, was becoming critical for capitalists. They did not want to pay the extra taxes for those who were not their employees (the old and the sick poor), and they were especially resistant to the large increase in costs for their employees through their contributions to Blue Cross/Blue Shield plans or private insurers. These plans operated as cost-plus arrangements, which meant that all costs could be charged up to employees and to American capitalism itself. But by the late 1960s, American capitalism was getting into stiffer competition with capitalism in western Europe and Japan and could see its profits being eaten up by health expenses. The doctors now had a powerful and well-organized opponent in Washington at precisely the time that their own lobby was falling apart.

State and Capitalism vs. the Medical Profession

The loss of guild power by the U.S. medical profession can be understood only by the interaction over time of the profession with the state and capitalism. Previous models of the American profession's loss of power agree with my approach about what happened but have made theoretical assumptions that do not hold up given the variety of forces at work. Models of "proletarianization" are primarily workplace- and profession-centered, and they do not recognize that the state, not capitalism directly, pushed for the regulation and restriction of the profession (McKinlay 1982; Derber 1982). Also, because many salaried doctors are working in nonprofit settings, the term *proletarianization* is metaphorical, if one wishes to preserve the Marxist meaning of the word. Nor can the defensive actions by the profession be strictly encompassed within the term as "resistance to proletarianization." Rather, the profession's ability to control the association, the workplace, the market, and the relation to the state itself were attacked by the federal state, by changes in the mode of producing health care, by court decisions, and by divisions within the ranks of doctors themselves. And the federal government gained in weight and effectiveness as the power of each individual state became less relevant in controlling the profession.

The AMA's defeat over the Medicare-Medicaid Act was not complete. As a condition of complying with the bill, the association had a hand in writing generous provisions into it (Stevens and Stevens 1974, 90–187). But those generous awards were precisely what caused the state to react, and soon, against the rise in cost. Within a year, Congress called for cost control, especially for Medicaid. The new era of regulation and then more direct forms of cost control had begun.

Power over the association concerns both membership and who controls the training. If the percentage of doctors in the AMA rose from 51% in 1912 to a high of 73% in 1963, the numbers decreased as more liberal and younger physicians, repelled by the AMA's stance on services to the poor and old, quit or never joined. By 1970, AMA membership had fallen to 65%, and one year later, the figure fell to 61%. Membership was less than 50% in 1990, below the level of 1912 (AMA 1990). Any organization that speaks for only half of its profession cannot have the same political influence as one that speaks for nearly three-quarters. Membership in specialty associations has risen, but each of these has its own interests—in part because the American state has fixed different rates of reimbursement for different specialty groups. By the late 1980s the specialties were often working against each other. Academic medicine took a much more active stance against the interests of the AMA after 1970, working with the state on a variety of measures to control costs that did not affect its own interests as much as those still in the fee-for-service private sector.

A second source of association power was control over the numbers graduated. Through the mid-1960s, AMA policy kept the ratio of doctors to the population fairly constant, in the range of 126:100,000 in 1931 to 132:100,000 in 1962. This ratio then jumped to 151:100,000 in 1970, 180 in 1975, 202 by 1980, 252 by 1986, and almost 300 by 1990—more than twice as many as in 1962 (AMA 1990). The reason for the increase is critical. Precisely because medical schools were dependent on government research grants from Washington and under pressure from state legislatures, they were vulnerable to demands to increase the number of graduates (to serve the unserved, the argument went). Also, money was made available to aid the medical schools in expanding. Furthermore, many schools were threatened with loss of federal research funds if they did not expand. In addition, after years of stability, the number of new medical schools grew—from 87 in 1959 to 126 in 1978. In the 1960s most of the growth was in the number of new students at existing schools; the 1970s and 1980s were characterized by both higher enrollments and new schools. The proliferation of students had little impact on the medical schools and the faculty, but the numbers of new graduates deeply affected the practitioner wing. And as the AMA lost power, it lost the ability to control, or even bargain with, the academic wing of the profession, the members of which were increasingly not even members.

The control of the AMA and the medical school over the nature of the association was further diminished by a mandated shift in the sex ratio of medical students. As Walsh made clear in a historical study, after a slight rise in females in the profession during the era of activism near the turn of the century (peaking at 18% in 1900), women's representation consistently regressed, even into the mid-1970s. From then on, though, the numbers have gone up steadily. Antidiscriminaton laws and increased female applications resulted by 1990 in medical school classes that were at least one-third female all over the nation, even in the face of considerable resistance by some professors and practitioners. Almost all female graduates eventually choose office specialties and are more likely than men to work on salary (Walsh 1977).

Medicine's control over the workplace has eroded along with control over definition of the profession. The rationalization of the medical workplace rapidly proceeded after 1970, and the percentage of doctors on salary rose. The workplace has been increasingly controlled by business administrators (the heads of health maintenance organizations providing group practice), or by groups of salaried physicians in freestanding for-profit clinics or by for-profit hospital chains. By 1990 more than half of all U.S. physicians were practicing in salaried positions, and the oversupply of new physicians in the 1980s and 1990s had begun to affect their salary levels. Practically all current medical students can expect to start and remain on salary. And in these settings, medical values are less likely than the "bottom line" of cost control to dictate behavior. McKinlay and Stoekle (1988, 192) describe the changes:

> Doctors used to occupy a privileged position at the top of the medical hierarchy. Displaced by administrators, doctors have slipped down to the position of middle management where their prerogatives are also challenged or encroached upon by other health workers. Clearly, managerial imperatives often compete or conflict with physicians' usual mode of practice. Increasingly, it seems, administrators, while permitting medical staff to retain ever narrower control of technical aspects of care, are organizing the necessary coordination for collaborative work, the work schedules of the staff, the recruitment of patients to the practice, and the contacts with third-party purchasers, and are determining the fiscal rewards.

A vast literature exists on this topic, Freidson's insistence that it is not happening to the contrary. (His work describes the peak of power, not the downslide of the 1970s and 1980s.) Almost all medical writers, in their own journals, complain of the loss of autonomy and control, even over such major medical decisions as when to discharge patients from the hospital.

Control over the market is the third guild power that the American profession is losing. In the 1930–1960 era, fee-for-service medicine and doctor-controlled hospitals put the profession in control of the American market. But the private third-party payment plans, originally under the doctor's control, began to declare their independence from their medical founders in the early 1970s. Capitalist firms, which paid the balance of the fees to such plans, exerted pressure to hold the line on costs. Because the vast majority of doctors now receive these payments, whether public or private, the plans are in a position to draft policy and to undermine physician influence on decisions. State regulatory programs to address public costs are paralleled by programs to control private, third-party costs.

A second aspect of a profession's market control is authority over competing professions. The AMA is losing its places on the state licensing boards and national accrediting boards of other professions in health care. The physical medicine and rehabilitation specialty (physiatrics) no longer controls the physical therapy programs in universities or the licensing process (Gritzer and Arluke 1985). Psychiatry no longer commands a pyramid of other mental health occupations. As several states have revised their practice acts, clinical psychology and social work not only can practice in competition but also, in many states, can collect payments from Blue Cross—all without medical supervision, and against the express advice and lobbying of the medical profession (Abbott 1988, 311–14). Administrators of salaried staffs in for-profit hospitals often prefer to have nurses do admission, diagnosis, and treatment, reserving doctors for serious and complicated cases. In the 1950s, this would have been called the "unauthorized practice of medicine" and would have been prosecuted as such. The same would have applied to pharmacists prescribing drugs, which was permitted in twenty-one U.S. states by 1995. And in the Reagan 1980s, under the guise of competition, such practitioners as osteopaths and chiropractors began to be paid for their services by Medicare and Medicaid—the former group now formally included by the state in statistics on "the medical profession."

But the U.S. medical profession has found its strongest opponent to be a federal government whose role has changed, allied with large American capitalist firms in pursuing cost control. The federal government's hospital-building program of the 1940s and 1950s (Hill-Burton) and a small movement to foster community action and neighborhood health centers in the

1960s have been replaced by major programs in the 1970s and 1980s to control costs. Attempts at reorganizing patterns of service—through programs such as the Comprehensive Health Planning Program, the Regional Medical Program, and the 1974 National Health Planning Act—failed (Krause 1977). Attempts to construct rational systems of care were replaced with much more brutal programs to control costs through rationing service—accompanied by accusations that doctors perform too many tests and keep patients too long in the hospital.

Two products of these cost-cutting programs are particularly important: professional review organizations, which review a doctor's decisions regarding hospitalization and treatment, and diagnosis related groups (DRGs), which pay for hospital stays based on a fixed amount for a given diagnosis. This latter system awards money to hospitals for publicly paid patients— often up to 40% of their clientele—and encourages the hospitals to discharge them "quicker and sicker," after the number of days that are actually paid for. Heavy pressure on physicians from the hospital accounting department is the result. By the late 1980s fee schedules for office visits were being established as well. The federal government's Health Care Financing Agency, working with academic medical-cost analysts, have devised new scales that will pay more for office practice and less for surgery. This plan, which has enlisted the AMA on the side of the government and against the specialists who do invasive, high-risk medicine, further divides the practitioner wing, to which both the office-based pediatricians and the surgeons belong. What remains of medical group solidarity is evaporating as the state acts to set one group of doctors against the other, and as each group lobbies to get a larger share of federal funds at the expense of the others.

Finally, capitalism is having a variety of effects, both direct and indirect, on the medical profession in the United States. Capitalists are organizing health services, especially in the western and southern parts of the nation. Overall, 30% of all hospitals in 1990 were in the for-profit sector, as well as nearly all of the nursing home industry. In these settings, the industrial production model is completely appropriate, even though a few physicians also own stock in such ventures. But the latest generation will go to work on salary at such institutions and in the profit-making free-standing clinics.

Capitalism itself is divided, though, between the few sectors that make money as costs rise—medical technology, drugs, hospital supply—and the majority, which suffer increases in health coverage costs. The state acts with the majority of capitalist sectors and is gradually restricting for-profit medicine. Doctors thriving as owners of for-profit settings are already beginning to lose their advantage as regulation tightens. And to make matters worse, doctors are increasingly being sued for malpractice, and thus order more tests and procedures to protect themselves against legal action. But as the state closes in, working with U.S. capitalism to cut costs, it begins to ration precisely the tests that the doctors must do to avoid lawsuits. The crossfire between cost control and malpractice cases is profoundly demoralizing to the profession. Still retaining some of its guild power, medicine is increasingly on the defensive on all fronts.

American Lawyers: Two Half-Professions, Similar Fates

In Puritan Massachusetts, lawyers were banned. According to the Puritan elite, lawyers would argue either side of a case, and since only one side could be "correct" and therefore "moral," lawyers took the side of the Devil as often as the side of God. Magistrates, lay judges, carried out the legal work, much as they had in the small towns in England from which the Puritans came. They worked under the consultative supervision of preachers in dealing with complex moral issues. As Puritanism faded and commerce increased in the early 1700s, the lawyer came into his own, drafting the contracts that governed much of the trade in early Portsmouth, Salem, Boston, New York, Philadelphia, and Charleston (Haskins 1960, 186).

Training by apprenticeship, with an elite, semiprivate bar structure only for the leading practitioners and only in the major cities, was the main form of the "profession." The leaders of this early bar, as de Tocqueville noted, were very important in framing the U.S. Constitution. But outside the early cities the legal profession in general, both before and after the Revolution, was primarily involved with disputes over land use, indebtedness, and contracts. In the Jacksonian era, all monopoly licensure was abolished (Wiebe 1984). One could study law on one's own, or part-time (Lincoln did both). One-person law schools, such as Judge Litchfield's in Connecticut, sprang up in many locations. Although the American Bar Association was founded in 1868, it did not have the early effect on legal education that the American Medical Association had on medicine. When C. C. Langdell came to a moribund Harvard Law School in the 1870s, he had to revise the curriculum, establishing the "case method" of Socratic dialogue with students on the essential principles behind the law, and in so doing he used federal appellate court decisions. This narrow and nontheoretical method of teaching became, gradually over the next seventy years, standard pedagogy in every American law school (Seligman 1978, 20–46).

The legal profession in the United States took far longer than the medical profession to establish its current educational requirements. While Langdell was busy at Harvard, the majority of lawyers were still being trained by apprenticeship. Not until the 1940s or 1950s—about fifty years after American medical education was standardized—could it be said that a legal education was really possible only in law schools. And the requirement of some college before law school was established only through a painstaking lobbying effort by the American Bar Association. Most students in 1900 did not go to college before law school, and only some college was the norm in the period 1900–1930 (Abel 1988a, 192–94; Abel 1989).

States, not the federal government, were (and remain) the locus for qualifying for the U.S. legal profession. Only a few leading law schools before World War II had full-time faculties; the majority preferred to use leading practitioners to prepare the students for the bar exam and practice. Gradually, though, the professoriate separated itself from the practitioners. The American Bar Association supervised the bar examinations in each state, acting with the participation of the local bar associations in each major city. The ABA produced a rather steady supply of graduates with respect to the population by increasing or decreasing the failure rate of the bar exam as economic conditions warranted. Members of ethnic or religious minorities, particularly Jews, were discriminated against in the testing, as the personal interview part of the exam was used to weed out those who did well on the written section. The result, except in New York City, was a primarily white, Anglo-Saxon Protestant male profession. Political radicals were also unwelcome, no matter what their grades or background (Abel 1988a, 200–205; Abel 1989, 69–70).

The Flexner report in 1910 led to the disappearance of smaller and less well-qualified U.S. medical schools, but equivalent reports on the legal profession (the Root report, the Reed report) did not find acceptance in the legal profession. A two-class system of schools developed—elite schools with gradually limited enrollment and more selective entrance criteria, and a much larger set of smaller schools, most but not all approved by the American Bar Association, where practically anyone could study for the bar, including those who were poor or working full-time and could afford only an evening education. By 1930, the current system of a two-class profession was well established. The elite law schools (Harvard, Yale, Columbia, Chicago, Stanford) prepared their primarily upper-class white, male, Protestant students for corporate law work in private firms. The mass of the profession was trained in the schools of lesser status. Here were the great majority of the lawyers from ethnic and religious minorities doing personal-problems practice: divorce, small-business, auto accident, and small-claims work for clients much like themselves. Most of the great bar associations were city-based, filled with the corporate sector of the profession, and elitist; until well after World War II most had quotas or firm rules against the acceptance of women, blacks, Jews, and Catholics. Only slowly did the local and state bars democratize themselves. By that time, beginning in about 1960, many of the excluded had already formed their own associations, as had specialty groups. Far from representing justice and fairness in their own ranks, the American legal profession was a model of exclusion and prejudice well into the modern period (Auerbach 1976, 3–13).

Legal work can be generalized and given to one group—as in the U.S. model—or parceled out among several groups, as in England and especially on the Continent. The American legal profession is inclusive, practicing in all areas: legal advice to businesses, advice to individual clients, representation in court cases, consultation on financial problems, and counsel of clients, especially corporate ones, before governmental regulatory agencies. This inclusiveness was established early, well before 1930. The two spheres of individual and corporate practice divided the labor. Also established early was the common-law system of England rather than the Continental civil (Roman) law system. The former built on a combination of legislation and previously decided cases by judges and regulatory agencies, the latter rested on a code and general principles and gives less weight to previous decisions (Reuschmeyer 1988, 289–321). Lawyers slowly—but never completely—established their dominance over this broad domain of work.

The profession also established itself as the source of the judiciary. In the American system politically appointed judges are chosen from lists of candidates of state and local bar associations, and the ABA has some consultant power over the federal judiciary. Yet judges are still, ultimately, appointed from among lawyers who are generally active in politics, and who thus have allegiances and debts not just to the legal profession but also to those who have appointed them. We will return to this issue below, when we look at the complex relations between the U.S. legal profession and both capitalism and the American state.

American lawyers, at least since the rise of corporate capitalism and perhaps even before, have never been viewed as a profession that serves most people—though the need for lawyers in times of trouble has long been recognized. By 1870 or 1880 the division was already clear between the elite bar, serving corporate capitalism, and the mass bar, serving the needs of small businessmen and helping wealthy and upper-middle-class individuals with their wills, estates, lawsuits, and divorces. Only a tiny group of the profession has ever devoted practice to the needs of the poor and lower middle class; even the mass personal service bar seldom works with this group (Abel 1989). The details of practice and the expansion and contraction of the profession's guild power can be considered from three vantage points: the historical periods of 1930–1960 and 1960 to the mid-1990s, and evolution across both periods of the complicated relations among the legal profession, capitalism, and the U.S. state.

Establishing Control: The Two Sectors, 1930–1960

By the 1930s, the modern law school and the demand for some college education before law school had been established as the norm. But college *graduation* was not required for most law schools, and law school was by no means the only forum of preparation for the bar exam. By the end of this period all that was generally true, for the vast majority of the candidates. Also essentially unchanged—since 1900, in fact—was the ratio of lawyers to the population. Supply was regulated by the profession through the failure rate on the bar exam. During this period, what were the characteristics of the association, the workplace, and the market?

Entry into the legal profession was monitored by bar exam committees in each state, rather than by the law schools themselves. Given what we already know about the philosophy and prejudices of the lawyers in control of local, state, and national bar committees, the demographics of the profession in this era should not be a surprise. A few segregated law schools were virtually the only source of black recruits to the law. The American Bar Association refused to admit blacks until 1943. In a relatively liberal state like New York, in 1930 blacks accounted for only 0.4% of the profession, and in 1940 just 1.1% of the lawyers in the nation were black. This figure decreased further to 0.7% in 1950 and was still only 0.8% in 1960. Women, meanwhile, made up 3.4% of the profession in 1934 in liberal New York City. In 1940, national statistics showed that 4.3% of students in ABA-approved law schools were women. As with blacks, by 1950 the percentage of women, too, had declined, to 3.1%; it remained at 3.5% in 1960 (Abel 1989, 285). Ethnic and religious statistics were parallel, except that Jews, Catholics, and ethnics from central and eastern Europe had been accepted into the profession. But the route for most of them was the non-elite law schools and such night and part-time law schools as Suffolk in Boston, which were unapproved by the ABA. Suffolk advertised itself with a large neon sign above its quarters on Beacon Hill in Boston. With 4,000 students in 1930, Suffolk was, the sign proclaimed, "the largest law school in the world" (Koenig and Rustad 1985).

We have noted that the profession was divided into sectors of corporate and personal practice. More important than this division, though, is that the formal association of the profession—the American Bar Association, the state bar associations, and the important big city bars, such as those in New York, Chicago, Boston, and San Francisco—were strictly under the control of the WASP male corporate practice elite, with only token membership, if that, for religious and ethnic minorities and women. Because the power was handled in this way, only the corporate wing of the profession could be said to enjoy power over the association—*their association*. In about twenty states, where all bar-qualified lawyers were nominally included in the state bar association, the distribution of power was no different. Although the legal profession did not have the direct pyramidal and representational structure of the AMA, the result for lawyers was scarcely different. Policy made by the elite WASPs was the same whether it was made at local, state, or national levels.

Power over the legal workplace during this time period varied in the profession according to sector. The practicing lawyer had some autonomy with respect to individual clients, most of whom, though somewhat skeptical about lawyers, had little alternative but to use one, especially if they were in trouble. As Carlin (1962) made clear, however, the lower-level mass practitioner, hard-pressed to make a living, may have descended to ambulance chasing and wake visiting to drum up malpractice cases. Solo practice, with large numbers of clients and large numbers of routine case appearances in court, was at the low-status end of the profession, even if in a technical sense the lone attorney had workplace autonomy.

In contrast, the large law firms doing corporate work were far more bureaucratic—though the bureaucracy itself was autonomous—with staff and assistants to help. Status, along with quite a lot of money, was accorded to the firms in the corporate-practice sector; lawyers in the other sector felt inferior to the corporate bar. Each major capitalist firm usually had one big law firm to represent it. Although at the time these corporations already had small in-house law departments, the big law firms were chosen for the most important work. Technically the capitalist corporations had more control over their law firms than small clients had over their mass-practice lawyers, given the relative prestige of client and lawyer. But the corporate lawyers in private practice shared with their corporate sponsors a WASP upper-class view of the world, and they often belonged to the same social clubs as well (Smigel 1964).

Professional control over the U.S. legal market probably reached its peak during this era. Bar associations successfully prosecuted nonlawyers for the "unauthorized practice of law." Jail, fines, and cease-and-desist orders discouraged laymen from providing self-help manuals and advice about divorces and wills. Accountants, themselves important to the finance work of corporations, ran afoul of legal claims when they encroached into fiscal consulting. To clear up jurisdictional questions, responsibilities were divided among the various practitioners. In some states documents on the division of labor were drafted and approved by both lawyers and competing professional associations—but the lawyers got a substantial share of the work. The mass practitioner tried to establish a monopoly over the thousands of title searches required in real estate transactions, and many state bar associations got this monopoly written into the law. Automobile accidents, in the era before no-fault insurance, were another major source of profit. Finally, lawyers established a near monopoly over family law—wills, estates, divorces, and so on—and volunteered their services for criminal work, though only a few found this last area profitable (Abel 1988a, 205–10).

The split in the profession underlies another important element of the profession's ability to control relations with the market: self-policing. Or, rather, not self-policing as such—which has never been effective—but rather who does the self-policing. Most cases of ethical misconduct have involved the behavior of the mass practitioner and the individual client, and such cases were brought before city and state bar associations, run by the elite corporate sector of the bar. Misconduct in the corporate sector itself was seldom investigated during this period by the profession, the state, or the press. Thus self-regulation, to the extent that it existed at all, involved the elite of the profession investigating the rank and file—on cases of judge bribing, ambulance chasing, and all the dodges that the mass profession has used to survive in a competitive atmosphere (Abel 1989, 147–50). The behavior of the two sectors—their social characteristics, their workplaces, and their shares of the market—remained essentially constant from the beginning of this period to its end.

The State Intrudes, the Profession Loses Control, 1960–1990

Even in a profession as privately run as American law, the outside world had ways of intruding. The 1960s were a decade of civil rights demonstrations, antiwar activism, and the rise of feminism. Naturally, social institutions that were outstanding examples of racism, sexism, and political conservatism came under attack—including the American legal profession. At the same time, university professors in law, just as in medicine, began to declare independence from the practitioners who ran the credentialing system. The Civil Rights Act of 1967 directly concerned, among other things, admissions to college and graduate education. The ABA and state boards began to find that the professoriate was not only expanding in size—to more than twice its size in the previous periods—but that more and more of the professoriate disagreed with the ABA and the bar associations about the composition of the student body.

Halliday, who has studied these trends for the U.S. legal profession over the longest span, found that the ratio of lawyers to the population ratio was steady for the period 1930–1960, even a little lower after 1950. But beginning about 1970 the numbers of lawyers rose at a furious rate, from 125: 100,000 in 1960 to 150:100,000 in 1970 to 300:100,000 in 1980—more than double in twenty years—and they have continued to multiply, though not as rapidly (Halliday 1986, 57–58). Curran (1986, 24) provides the next piece of the puzzle. The vast majority of the new students after 1970 are due to increases in the size of law school classes to admit women. Student bodies were expanded to include the new group, and many new law schools were founded as well. From the insignificant ratios that were observed in the past, women were soon making up from 35% to 40% of each new law school class. The ratio of blacks rose, too, though at nowhere near the same rate as for women. Blacks benefited less than women from new enrollment policies because the standard of four years of college plus three years of law school—not a difficulty for the predominantly upper- and upper-middle-class female candidates—has been a major hurdle for blacks and other minorities, even before the Reagan administration stopped enforcing the Civil Rights Act (Abel 1989, 99–108). Because of the better college background and the better law school training of candidates, the bar exam has ceased to be a significant force for limiting the size of the profession.

What of the bar associations themselves? Some big city bar associations, such as Chicago's, changed their rules to welcome the new graduates. Others, such as New York's, did not, giving rise to counter-bar associations. The solidarity of the profession, always undermined by the elite nature of most bar associations, was shaken even more. The newer groups violently protested against the discrimination of the older generation in control of these bar associations. And far more specialized associations—for trial lawyers, malpractice specialists, civil-rights attorneys, and others—grew from tiny fractional groups to national associations with conflicting professional interests.

How did the massive increase in new lawyers affect the legal workplace? Minority and women graduates of elite schools got jobs as salaried associates in the larger firms, others practiced on their own. Even though solo practice is considered a last-resort option for a lawyer (as it seldom is for American physicians, who face higher costs), 67% of the nation's lawyers were in the private sector in 1985. Yet as Spangler (1986) has shown, both the private and the public practice of law have more routinized and rationalized workplaces than in the pre-1960 era. Increased numbers in the corporate law firms and in the in-house offices of corporations have led to closer administrative observation of the work being done and have produced more permanent associates with no chance of partnership. Most government work has always been routinized and poorly paid. Poverty law, in legal clinics for the poor, has been the most harassed and unstable work of all, even before the Reagan administration cutbacks of the 1980s.

With major growth in numbers of lawyers came growth in firms, both in larger staffs on existing firms and in the creation new firms, as well as branch offices in different cities. Long-standing relations between a given corporation and a given corporate law firm are now collapsing, as the competition between firms grows. Instability plagues the corporate law sector, as firms split and former partners take clients with them, much in the manner of the American advertising industry. More important, the ratio of associates to partners has risen, especially in the prestigious law firms that have long been the primary goals of elite law school graduates. But competition cuts profit margins at these firms, which respond to worsening economic conditions by using more paraprofessionals—often at the expense of associates. Medium-sized firms in medium-sized cities are affected by these trends less than big-city firms, but they suffer, too, for they tend to combine some corporate work with some client work. Small-town firms, as in the earlier period, resemble the mass bar in large cities in their overwhelming occupation with individual client work.

Markets are shaped by professions in competition with one another. The federal government and state supreme courts have begun in this most recent period to reconsider the legitimizing of certain areas of work as the monopoly of lawyers. This shift affects the mass bar in particular. The Federal Trade Commission has ruled, for example, that legal services may use mass-media advertising (Kissam 1983). This has led to competition, including price wars, between the solo practitioners and large, multistate and capitalist-rationalized law firms that use large numbers of paraprofessionals, salaried lawyers, and computer equipment. The two sectors increasingly fight over small clients. Because the profession has done such a poor job in policing itself, regulation of lawyers has been taken over in some states by the state supreme court or by independent commissions (Abel 1986). Crime in the large law firms is also coming under investigation: the savings and loan scandal is just one of many in recent years that have involved lawyer misconduct.

Arrangements between professions to carve up an area of work—say between lawyers and accountants in California—have been thrown out by the U.S. Supreme Court, as have lawyers' fee schedules (Abel 1989, 201). The Federal Trade Commission has removed the general exemption under which professions protected their work. Much legal work—and many aspects of the legal profession's monopoly—have thus now been reinterpreted by the FTC as restraint of trade (Kissam 1983). More generally, corporations in some areas, such as real estate and insurance, are redefining work—real estate transfer, for example—so that it can be done by nonlawyers or creating no-fault auto insurance systems that deprive lawyers of business and therefore increase capitalist profit while rationalizing the area. Often the trial lawyers' associations object, but the corporate bar remains indifferent.

Has this shrinking professional control over the association, the workplace, and the market led to the same kind of direct bureaucratic rationalization by capitalist or nonprofit firms that has happened in American medicine? Has the legal profession in the United States lost as much ground as the medical profession? This does not seem to be the case, for the majority of American lawyers still have the option of practicing privately. But the quality of life in legal positions has definitely diminished since 1960, and nearly 50% of all lawyers were beginning in salaried positions by 1995. And the conditions of work will not improve, for the profession cannot reimpose the autonomy it once enjoyed. Both sectors suffer—corporations and corporate law firms from greater pressure to produce, and the public sector from declining manpower. And regardless of sector, it is no longer the profession that sets the rules. As Spangler (1986, 64) summarizes the result for American lawyers: "To some degree, therefore, lawyers are selling their services in a buyer's market. They are in no position to challenge or subvert their client's goals, even if they have a clear agenda that motivates them to do so. . . . A client who has any questions about his firm's loyalties replaces the firm. A firm that has any questions about an associate's loyalties replaces the associate."

State, Capitalism, and the American Legal Profession

Lawyers as a profession help to preserve the present U.S. system of overwhelming capitalist domination over state policy. But the role of the profession differs according to the level of state activity—the local judiciary, the state supreme courts, the federal judiciary and the Supreme Court, the regulatory agencies, and the employees of the profession who work as lawyers and not as judges in local, state, and federal settings. In some cases, the question is whether the judges at a particular level really share the interests of the lawyers, even though in most cases they were formerly members of the bar. On the other hand, with the low salaries on the bench, the judges may increasingly be contemplating a return to private practice, and may wish lawyer help to do so.

In other cases, as with the regulatory agencies, the powerful law firms of the corporate bar defend their clients' interests against a much less effective—and understaffed—set of government attorneys, usually much more burdened with work and without the resources of those who work in the corporate law firms. They work in the federal system, before federal judges who are much more likely to have a background in those same corporate firms than in governmental lawyer roles. We will consider U.S. judges first, as representatives of the state with a background in the profession, and then consider the issue of the corporate bar and its influence on general capital-state relations.

The complex character of the American state, with its systems of local, state, and federal courts to parallel the executive and legislative branches at each level of government, affects the nature of the judiciary differently depending on the level. Generally trained as mass-practice lawyers first, the judges in the local courts in many parts of the nation are required to run for election and reelection and thus need political patronage from parties and even from some individuals—lawyer and laymen—who might appear before them. Local and state bar associations often work for the reform of laws in states that have elected judges. But the civil service judiciary, especially at local and some state levels, is more a goal than an accomplished fact. In most states, only supreme court judges are appointed for life.

Halliday shows that the Chicago bar worked during the period 1950–1980 to give judges in the state system civil service status—against the will of some judges, who preferred to take their chances (and perhaps money on the side) under the patronage system. The lawyers' agenda was to increase the predictability of the local and state judges, but they portrayed it as being in the general interest and part of the profession's wider professional role. At the same time, the bar campaigned for higher salaries for these judges. Yet regardless of what the bar did at this level, it is clear from Halliday's findings that political considerations are as important as legal qualifications for judicial appointments—especially the desire of ethnic and racial groups in Chicago and elsewhere to have "one of their own" on the bench. But once on the local or state bench, most judges find even worse conditions than at the bar—massive caseloads and bureaucratization, with little administrative help (Halliday 1987).

The federal judiciary operates on a slightly more elevated level. Judges are appointed by the president for life and are far more likely to be corporate lawyers, with an occasional professor. Names are submitted by state bars and the ABA—though some presidents are more likely than others to choose from those lists. A distinguished record as a jurist is usually required for a federal appointment, though there are exceptions. Once appointed, federal judges are more likely to be independent of the bar, though most share its economic and political bias, and are more likely, in the most recent period, to work to discipline the bar through committees and actions. The decisions of judges in the appellate federal courts are recorded, and in the U.S. system are law and precedent, carrying as much legal weight as the laws passed in legislatures. So much more care is taken in appointing these judges.

Even more care is taken with appointments to the Supreme Court. Here an appointee is chosen by the president and reviewed by the legislative branch before taking his or her seat. The political coloration of this top court can change over time—from the procapitalist bent of the court before Roosevelt to the generally liberal courts from Roosevelt to Johnson to the restoration of a conservative, procapitalist majority since the start of the Reagan administration. When the Supreme Court is conservative, progressive legislation—such as civil rights and abortion right laws—can be narrowed from its original intent. Anticorporate laws that get through Congress can be nullified or at least gutted by the lower federal judiciary and the Supreme Court.

In front of the court, in every part of the system, appear lawyers in private practice and those in government. In the local and state systems, the antagonists are often an overworked assistant district attorney opposing a practitioner from a small law firm, or a public defender opposing his opposite number, also publicly employed, from the prosecutor's office. Federal courts are more likely to be the scene where corporate capitalism fights for relief from regulation or laws affecting it adversely, though most legal business is carried on out of court, by lawyers who advise corporations on ways to avoid such appearances. In state and local settings the judges are almost as overwhelmed, though they are getting some relief in the latest period through the use of magistrates, lawyers functioning as parajudges (Seron 1988). In federal settings the large firms, working for their corporate clients, often overpower the government lawyers with motions to drag out the trial, to make things more complex—all of which helps to keep the corporate profits continuing while justice is delayed, sometimes for years. This is the center of legal work in the corporate sector: to represent firms before the federal judiciary, or even better to settle out of court beforehand, but in any case to preserve for these firms their freedom of action. It is not that the government lawyers are unskilled, but they tend to have less time to spend on each case, and they are usually not in permanent career commitments—unlike the lawyers in the big firms.

There has been a hypothesis, by some journalists, lawyers of the District of Columbia bar, and functional sociologists, that lawyers, especially in Washington, act as mediators between capitalism and the state (Mayer 1966; Horksy 1952; Parsons 1954b). Yet the extensive study by Nelson and Heinz (1988) of legal representation in the nation's capital suggests that much of this is mythology. Whether lawyers are working for a Washington law firm or for a branch office of a firm located elsewhere or for a pressure group, they are primarily technicians, working in narrowly defined areas to advance the interests of their clients, much as they do elsewhere, and they are not usually in a position to make policy for these organizations. Most Washington practice is conducted before such regulatory agencies as the health cost divisions of the Department of Health and Human Services, the Federal Trade Commission, the Federal Aviation Agency, the Food and Drug Administration, and so forth. Lawyers develop expertise in these areas and can defend their clients' point of view quite effectively. But they are hired guns far more than policy makers.

In general, the role of the legal profession in the United States is to advance the interests of large capitalist firms (the corporate bar), or the interests of the middle-class businessman as individual or group client (the mass bar). Lawyers—especially those aspiring to a judgeship—can and do get active in politics, but when elected to office in legislatures, either state or federal, they vote much like their colleagues who are not lawyers. Lobbying at all levels is more likely to be done by nonlawyers than by lawyers.

Critical legal studies, a movement among radical professors at some elite law schools, suggests that the law as well as the lawyers is procorporate (Hutcheson 1989). Certainly much of the legislation is, but that reflects the legislative process, which is controlled overwhelmingly by corporate interests. Many judges, given their biases and origins, do not uphold the law or interpret it equally for small client and corporations. And because very few American attorneys provide services for the poor, and there is no major government legal services program, the profession clearly provides unequal justice. This was true in 1930, and it is true today. The only real changes are the increase in the numbers of lawyers, meaning that those working to advance corporate interests are more likely than they were before to experience some of the job stress of other workers under American capitalism. The small practitioner's autonomy has decreased with the competition for clients, while the large firms and the corporate in-house practitioners have much more pressure to produce for their more important clients.

American Engineers: Middle-Class Employees of Capitalism

Unlike American medicine or American law, there never has been much question about the status of American engineering: engineers were and are the middle-level employees of capitalism. Since the beginning of this century, this has not changed. Neither theories of professionalization—which either found engineers wanting from the start or changed their criteria to differentiate them from other groups—nor more recent theories of proletarianization grasp the essential reality of the group in the American context. It is a category of work but not, in most of its essentials, an occupation acting in its own interest (Larson 1977, 190–207). I have included it here and in the other case studies precisely for that reason, for in the groundlessness of its claims to guild power, it is similar to many other occupational groups that are basically employee categories rather than potent political entities.

The concept of guild power can nevertheless be applied to engineering—if only as negative example. In addition, the picture is not altogether negative everywhere; in France and Germany, for example, engineers wield limited guild power. But in the United States the profession has never had, much less controlled, any central association, and it trades its lower-level control of the daily workplace for capitalist control of ends, projects of work chosen, and even the decisions to hire and fire. Engineering is not in control of the market for services, except for a tiny group in consultant status, and it has no essential relation to the state because it is not a licensed group. Only a small proportion of its workers are in public employment. Finally, although I do not intend to abandon my historical approach, the changes in engineers' professional status have not been marked in the United States from 1930 to 1990. So, citing historical changes where relevant, we will inspect rather each dimension of guild power over the entire period.

Control Over the Association

From the beginning of the nineteenth century training of engineers evolved in two contexts: the workshop, which imparted mechanical skills to the unschooled, and the school, which taught basic and applied science. Gradually, the school won out over the workshop, especially in newer fields like chemical and electrical engineering, but all engineers continued to learn much on the job, no matter what their formal training. Capitalist employers, rather than groups of engineering graduates, were the force behind the development of the American training system and the creation of modern college programs. Capitalist firms dictated the curriculum, adding specialties as they developed in private industry, and supplied the basic value system in every engineering course. Engineering would be, and still is, defined as applied science in the pursuit of profit. Engineers overwhelmingly agree that "their work is inherently economic in character; *cost is itself a criterion of technical efficiency.* Cost is a parameter of their work, no different in principle from the physical properties of a metal. They do not experience a tension between the logic of efficiency and the logic of profitmaking precisely because their very conception of efficiency is shaped by considerations of profitability (Zussman 1985, 121)." This basic difference, between pure science (which disregards the economic dimension) and engineering as applied science, lies at the heart of the American profession, and to some extent at the heart of the profession in other nations as well.

Engineering schools in the United States, whether private and elite like MIT or Caltech or public in the state college and university systems, have been established directly in response to the needs of American capitalism, with direct fiscal support from that source (along with government research funding after 1950) and with the corporations hiring about 85% of the graduates. Although some industry-based labs such as General Electric's and the Bell Laboratories originally trained some of their own workers, they evolved by the 1930s into institutions that hired the graduates of the better engineering schools (Noble 1977, 73–83). Corporate sectors in manufacturing hire the majority of the graduates. Although most of the hires are graduates of four-year college programs, it is employers, not the training profession, that determine who is given the job title of engineer. In 1969 Perucci and Gerstl cited national surveys showing that those practicing as engineers did not necessarily have a college education, and in 1985 Zussman studied a high-tech engineering firm and a traditional metalworking firm in the Northeast and found that the percentage of engineers with no college degree was 25% at the former firm and 28% at the latter (Perucci and Gerstl 1969, 75; Zussman 1985, 94).

Because neither the colleges of engineering, the corporations, nor most engineering specialty societies support a monopoly licensure system, there is no "engineering monopoly." Although promotion into management is usually reserved for the college graduates, especially in the last twenty years, that is an individual decision made by managers. Nor do the 10–15% with higher degrees have a better chance of getting promoted into management than do college graduates. There is a small consulting sector of engineers in private practice, mostly in civil engineering, but again the majority of engineers who work for one of these firms do so as employees and not as partners. Because few engineers have direct contact with the public, the licensure issue is neither relevant to the general population nor a source of professional group action.

Engineering students in the United States have varied little in social background and demographic characteristics throughout our entire period. Overwhelmingly, they are white males of working-class or middle-middle-class backgrounds, from small towns and medium-sized cities, and they are usually more interested in machines than in people. The majority are pre-socialized toward accepting a subordinate, though middle-level, role in American industry. Kept apart from most arts and sciences students and given heavy, vocation-relevant course loads, they develop attitudes toward work and the corporate world that will last a lifetime. The majority do not belong to the national associations in their specialty, although they occasionally attend local meetings of these groups, mainly for social and career purposes. The absence of any overall unitary shape to the profession prevents the development of any oppositional group consciousness. In 1930, in 1969, and in 1995 they are a "profession without community" (Perucci and Gerstl 1969).

Capitalist firms were in control of each major sector of the profession from the start. Successful engineers, promoted into management and with the procapitalist values of management, were always the officers of each engineering society, such as the American Institute of Electrical Engineers or the Engineers Council for Professional Development. Leadership was *defined* by the mass, and by the corporation, as promotion into management;

the alternate career of "senior engineering scientist" has never caught on as an alternative. As Noble (1977, 243) puts it, the Wickenden report of 1930, which defined professional engineering education, "signaled the complete triumph of the corporate engineers and their particular brand of professionalism. Success in the profession now officially meant promotion up the corporate ladder, and education for the profession now officially meant education for both subordinate technical employment in and responsible management of corporate industry."

A brief attempt on the part of some engineers to form an association "for themselves" in the 1880–1920 period was studied by Layton (1971). But it foundered because the employers of engineering graduates opposed it and because most of the engineering professoriate (already committed to capitalism and often its consultants) were uninterested. Then as now, employer opposition, either to unions or to professional associations that would take an anticapitalist position, meant that joining either automatically meant forgoing chances for promotion into management itself. Brief periods of unionization, in the 1930s, and the 1960s, did occur in a few selected industries affected by job instability, but these associations are either no longer in existence or are organizing only a tiny fraction of the profession.

Control Over the Workplace

Engineers present a classic case of a bureaucratically situated profession, one that controls some aspects of its work but not others. The sociological studies of scientists within bureaucracies, such as the work of Kornhauser in the 1960s, are only partly relevant, for scientists in some settings have roles different from engineers (Kornhauser 1963). Regarding engineers per se, we find a dearth of studies that are observational in nature as well as using questionnaires. Fortunately, Zussman's work is recent, it is thorough, and it combines these approaches in two engineering settings— a high-tech company and a more traditional one. There were minor structural differences between these two companies, but the role of the engineers was similar in both and clearly differentiated from both blue-collar assembly work and upper management. Briefly, engineers circulated, they made rounds of the different parts of the organization and did not remain chained to a desk. They were in control of their work, and acted collegially with both engineering supervisors and engineering technicians, rather than in a strictly authoritarian manner. But upper management set the parameters and decided on the projects (Zussman 1985, 33–58).

Career lines seemed to be the best way of understanding the vexed question of whether the engineers were labor or management. In the clearest way possible, Zussman showed how they start in the lower levels of a middle-rung area of authority in most plants, accepting the legitimacy of being in a chain of command, and even complaining if this chain of command is unclear. Conversely, supervision is loose, often confined to picking the projects a given engineer is to work on and then giving him relative freedom to find solutions—within cost constraints, the profit dimension, which all understand. Senior management works with middle-level engineers, who are in most plants carefully graded by ability and seniority in a many-stepped hierarchy. Management, not engineers, decides on general issues concerning whole departments (including whether to relocate them in another city for general corporate reasons), on salaries, bonuses, step raises, even promotion into management—and they do these things with the consultation of an intermediate level of senior technical managing engineers (Zussman 1985, 124–39).

Career progress lies in moving up the hierarchy in almost imperceptible steps from junior project engineer to senior project engineer to technical management to full-time management work, first in the engineering department and then possibly at the company level. The operating rule for a successful career in U.S. engineering is to reach technical management by age 35 and management itself by 40 or, at the latest, 45. Depending on the industry, about 40 to 50% of engineers make it into technical management and about 10–15% of that group go on into the company's general management, though in the last twenty years that last step finds them in competition with MBAs in many industries. And for those who do not reach general management, there really is no precise point at which an engineer leaves "line" work behind and enters "management."

Engineers also have the option of switching companies to advance faster—especially to go from direct engineering to engineering management. In areas where there are many engineering and manufacturing firms, such as New England, parts of the South, Southeast, and southern California, an engineer can keep his home and switch from one company to the next within the same geographic area. Upward mobility does seem to have something to do with the amount of education, though, according both to Perucci and Gerstl and to Zussman (Perucci and Gerstl 1969, 135; Zussman 1985, 154–55). Having an advanced degree in an engineering field does not lead to faster promotion into management, however—though it might help in the few, highly specialized industrial research labs where it is possible to have a research career. Rather, the interpersonal skills and experience on the job—neither stressed in school—tend to separate those who succeed from those who do not. Those who remain lower-level engineers after ten to fifteen years define themselves as failures, and success is defined as moving out of direct engineering into management.

Failure to advance is almost always internalized by the individual as his problem rather than a structural one, unless a whole industry goes sour. In such periods, advancement is blocked both internally and in terms of movement to other firms. But regardless of the outward economy, most engineers burrow in and go through the motions after the age of forty-five if they have not made it into management. Given the speed of technological change, it is highly unlikely that they can compete with those just out of school.

Professions, in theory, are supposed to have codes of ethics. Not so in engineering. One thing that engineers almost never do, given their values, is to complain when they work on projects that maximize profits through cutting back on safety. Whether the area is nuclear engineering or the O-ring seals on the space shuttle, whistleblowing on the company will lead to being fired, and usually also to being ostracized by other companies working in the same field. The moral is not lost on U.S. engineers: do not question the safety aspects of your work if you want to remain employed. The codes of ethics of engineering societies are mere pieces of paper, and the officers of the associations that have drafted the codes are practically all in corporate management.

Capitalist Control Over Market and State

Given engineers' lack of control over their functional specialty associations, and given the lack of real power in the accrediting associations for engineering schools compared with the power of corporate capitalism to designate specialties in the field, and given the willing acceptance of capitalist values on the workplace by engineers, it should not be surprising that engineers have no control over the American market for engineering services. And given that only 10–15% of engineers in the United States work for the state at any level, the private corporations far outweigh the state in control of the profession. The market for engineering services does exist, however, even though it is moderated by corporate employers, and the state has taken an increasing role in funding engineering education, working with the corporations to supply manpower where the needs are strongest. But again, it is not primarily engineers but corporations in charge of this activity. The state plays a minimal, consultative role in the American system, and there primarily in education, except for the state's involvement in the military-industrial complex.

Market considerations are determined by the ratio of supply of engineering manpower to demand by the corporate sectors. Using the same dimensions as for American doctors and lawyers, the ratio of engineers to the general population was 184:100,000 in 1930, 186 in 1940, 344 in 1950, 487 in 1960, 618 in 1970, and 610:100,000 in 1980 (Abel 1989, 281). This figure reflects the overall rise in number of students in higher education generally after World War II, and especially in the last thirty years. The slight decline from 1970 to 1980 also reflects demographic trends. But trends in higher education affect the engineering group less than the medical and legal because a significant proportion (approaching 25% in many companies) are only high school graduates or junior college technicians who, after many years' experience, have moved up to the role of engineer by management.

Areas of specialty directly relate to the needs of the economy, which in the United States is not directed in any way by the government. Electrical, chemical, and mechanical engineering are always favorites, joined after 1950 by aerospace, not as popular as the others but strong. Remembering that a firm can hire whomever it wants, regardless of these specialist groupings, and that records are kept on at least fifteen major specialities in engineering, the width of skills is impressive, even if the amount of training possible in a few years in school makes this learning shallow, and possibly rather topical and dated.

Cutbacks in defense spending have an effect on specialties chosen—the popularity of aerospace and electronics, for example. Defense-related specialities are very susceptible to decreases, as occurred immediately after World War II and more recently with the post–Cold War cutbacks in the late 1980s. But the figures are not complete enough to tell whether a great mass unemployment will result. At no point have the college educated had more than a 5–7% unemployment rate. This relative job security, when compared with blue-collar workers, is a major factor for engineers. It tends to confirm the wisdom of their promanagement and antilabor stance. Because there are no significant professional groups, or professional-managerial unions, as in France, or a strong labor union movement, the options really do not exist for cross-corporation political and economic action.

American capitalism, compared with capitalism in some western European nations, strongly influences the direction of state policy. Nor does the American state fund production directly in areas outside of the military-industrial complex. Thus state policy regarding engineering in the United States can be stated rather simply. A small part of the profession (no more than 15%) work at engineering jobs in local, state, and federal government, in the latter especially in the Bureau of Standards and the branches of the military. Military-industrial complex work, in those areas that are particularly labor intensive, involve about 20% of engineers in the private sector, working for the companies that have direct contracts or subcontracts with the Pentagon. But state funding, and thus state control of private sector work, is absent from the remaining sectors of American capitalism. Though the Federal Reserve system has an indirect effect on lending rates for financial capital, there is no direct relation between a government-owned bank or banking system on the one hand and corporate decisions on the other.

Because government is not directly involved, the fortunes of particular corporations, or of given capitalist sectors as a whole, change only because of their competitiveness (or lack of it) in the world economy. Between the immediate postwar era, from 1945 to 1960, when American firms were dominant, and the present era, when there is far more competition from western Europe and Japan, the overall situation has become more difficult for the American firms. But this does not necessarily cause industry to fire engineers—rather the reverse. As the market gets more sophisticated, the role of engineers becomes more central. Thus even if there is some displacement due to continued military spending cuts, there does not seem to be a glut of engineers due to a downturn in demand.

In conclusion, engineering in the United States is a very poorly organized, middle-level employee group, with a series of scientific societies for each specialty, usually run by capitalist engineers-turned-managers. Production and development are controlled by the corporations, with a high proportion of engineers sharing the corporate values, the loose supervision of middle-level employees, and the possibility of promotion at least into technical group management. With practically no action as a group across work settings, engineers are an example of a group that has never had guild powers. Capitalism controls the market and its own relation to the state in the American case. Engineers provide an important stratum of middle-level employment within this picture.

The American Professoriate: United or Divided?

Out of the schoolmasters and tutors of the nineteenth century a new profession emerged: the university tenured professor. Many studies have been done in recent years on aspects of the profession—some on the history of individual universities, some on the development of particular disciplines (Metzger 1987). It is important to recognize from the beginning, however, that the main professionwide national association, the American Association of University Professors, was founded in 1915, during an era when each of the disciplinary associations in the field (American Economics Association, American Sociological Association, etc.) also began to meet regularly. It is also significant that such disciplinary leaders as Richard T. Ely, E. R. A. Seligman, and John Dewey were also the founders of the AAUP (Metzger 1987, 167–68).

American professors are members of an occupation with a complex structure. They are hired by university presidents and their boards of trustees (both public and private universities use this model), they work as almost autonomous employees with a set of prescribed freedoms and responsibilities (of which tenure and freedom of scholarly work are prominent examples), and they can have, in addition to their relations with their colleagues at the place of employment (usually but not always in the specific discipline in which they were trained), a relation to a partial profession, to specific regional and national associations in their field or discipline. These associations, operating across universities, are groups of colleagues who judge professors in terms of their contribution to research and to the health of the academic discipline as a whole. But, as Metzger (1987, 163) notes, "there are good empirical and logical reasons why full professional faith and credit should be extended to the comprehensive as well as the partial entity. The fact remains that while all or nearly all academics teach, only a quarter of them account for what may deservedly be called research, and only a tenth of them account for nine-tenths of all scientific and scholarly publication."

In our considerations thus far, we have included both the academic wing and the practitioner wing of medicine, law, and engineering. We must note here that in considering all academics we must again include these professional academics as well as those in arts and sciences faculties—for all are lumped together and then differentiated in historical and demographic approaches. It will be important to see how these different professional groups relate to the overall American university structure (Halpern 1987). Furthermore, any academic can choose, within the limits of the institution within which he or she works, whether to be a "cosmopolitan," with an eye primarily on the disciplinary group, or a "local," with a career based not on moving elsewhere but on moving up, possibly out of the professoriate and into administration. Obviously whole segments of academia—especially research universities—have more individuals of the cosmopolitan sort than do community colleges, both because of the difference in talent and because of the enhanced opportunities to do research in the latter kind of setting.

In general, we find that the U.S. professoriate rose in guild power of a specific and limited sort from 1930 to about 1965, and since then there has been a parting of the ways between locals and cosmopolitans. The research faculties at major research universities have kept their power, while those at lesser-prestige universities and colleges have lost ground, especially in terms of job security for the untenured and in general benefits and aid—salary, travel funds, secretaries, summer grants, and so on. The pattern is complex, and it varies both by type of university and type of discipline. But it can be inspected with our model by looking at the historical role of guild control (or lack of it) in shaping the association, the workplace, the market, and the relation to the state.

The Association and the Discipline

Professors, more than most other occupational groups in America, live in two different worlds: that of their campus and that of the discipline in which they were trained, as represented by the disciplinary associations or learned societies in which research results are presented. The primary association that has represented all professors as a group, and which was instrumental in developing the policy of academic tenure, has been the American Association of University Professors. Each discipline, each departmental field in the structure of an American university, has at least one national association—the American Economic Association, the American Sociological Association, the Modern Language Association. The disciplinary association often acts not only as a forum at which to deliver academic papers but also as an informal employment association for each disciplinary field. Professional fields have their own disciplinary associations.

But as we have already noted for doctors, lawyers, and engineers, the percentage of academics active in these disciplinary associations varies. In some fields not even a majority belongs, though the concentration is higher in elite universities and elite liberal arts colleges. Also common are specialty societies, which deal with the development of a subfield, such as solid state physics or cell biochemistry or phenomenology, and some of these societies are interdisciplinary in nature. In addition to having national and regional meetings, most disciplinary societies also publish journals, which in the United States are usually "refereed"—contributions are read by one's colleagues in the field at other universities, often "blind," with no name attached to the article, to provide a more objective judgment of the value of the work. Leaders of the disciplinary associations are usually chosen from the leading researchers in each field, who are typically the leaders of the main Ph.D.-granting departments. But academic papers are given at disciplinary association meetings by a wider variety of participants, even graduate students in some fields—a much more open system than in most western European nations (Bowen and Schuster 1986; Martinelli 1978).

Neither the AAUP, as the society representing the whole, nor the disciplinary societies, enroll the majority of professors, for membership is compulsory in neither group (Slaughter 1980). Furthermore, except in the professional schools, professors are not licensed and therefore do not need to belong to such associations in order to teach. But after 1970 the Ph.D. degree is almost mandatory for being hired everywhere but at a community college. And in the manner of the medieval guilds, the Ph.D. is awarded by a department to its own graduate students, but not to all of them: only about half of those who begin graduate courses complete the degree.

Until the 1970s, most Ph.D.-granting departments in each field were located in a restricted number of research elite universities. They granted the majority of the degrees in each field. With the growth of faculties and departments elsewhere, the number of these Ph.D.-granting departments has risen to double or even triple their numbers of 1950. Because of this proliferation, more and more departments are giving degrees to students precisely at the time when the number of jobs is shrinking. And although this process creates serious employment problems, American education, including Ph.D. programs, is not centrally planned. The federal government is not directly involved in education, though individual state governments, through the appropriations process, can "starve" new or old academic programs.

The AAUP was founded in 1915 by elite professors in leading research universities. Its aim was to establish the university professorship as an institutional body, separate from the administration and lay boards of trustees (usually successful businessmen) that had the power and control over the American university. It worked to establish goals and eventually the reality of academic tenure. The original goal statement of the AAUP, revised several times since, set procedures for review of nontenured faculty and mandated a defined probationary period to be followed by a tenure decision to be supported or rejected by the administration and board of trustees of each university. Tenure brings lifetime job protection, though with some limitations: controversial public speech that brings embarrassment to the university, political bias in lectures, and "moral turpitude" are grounds for dismissal, even for the tenured. But without formal power, the AAUP has always sought an advisory role with university administrations.

Only a minority of faculty have ever belonged to the AAUP. Furthermore, as with engineers, "management" members—former academics who have gone into academic administration—belong to the group and sometimes run its major committees. Partly as a result of these demographics, the AAUP has had a mixed record in achieving its goals and has always caved in before wider political pressure, such as in the protection of pacifists and antiwar professors during World War I, in the McCarthy period of the 1950s, and during the Vietnam war. The organization succeeded first in building tenure in at the elite universities and liberal arts colleges in the period from 1920 to 1950 and then advised the growing university systems during the 1950s and 1960s to emulate their elite brethren in establishing the same tenure rules there. But the AAUP has abhorred controversy and often sacrificed individual professors—especially those accused of Communist Party membership. The association agreed with university boards that such people were disqualified from teaching. It declined to vigorously defend even those "fellow-traveling" leftists or those who pleaded the Fifth Amendment before congressional committees (Schrecker 1986).

In terms of actual members, the academic profession in the United States grew steadily until 1960, doubled in the next decade, and has grown moderately since. There were approximately 82,000 academics in 1930, 100,000 in 1940, 165,000 in 1950, and 236,000 in 1960. The steady growth rate exploded in the next decade to produce 474,000 academics by 1970, then tapered off again to 628,000 in 1975, 678,000 in 1980, and about 695,000 in 1985 (Caplow and McGee 1958, 18; Bowen and Schuster 1986, 179). The composition of the faculty has changed as well. Although in 1930 the modal job was in arts and sciences, medicine, or law at an undergraduate liberal arts college or a large university, the expansion since then of engineering programs, undergraduate business programs, education programs at both undergraduate and graduate levels, and such fields as nursing, allied health, pharmacy, and so forth has led to a far more varied group using the title "professor."

This proliferation of disciplines has led to a continuing struggle on college campuses to expand the areas and fields of instruction—far beyond the definition of the university in western Europe. Unlike European systems, where such programs are often offered at vocational institutions, in the United States they compete for the university dollar (sometimes quite successfully) with the more classic arts and sciences departments. When Kerr (1967) described this new form as the "multiversity," he was speaking about the elite research university with its multiple ties to capitalism and the state. Since the 1960–1970 growth period, this model is now being replicated among a whole range of nonelite universities (Ruscio 1987).

What is the social character of the professoriate? Since the period when the key elite research universities awarded Ph.D.s primarily to White Anglo-Saxon Protestant males of upper-middle-class background, the composition has begun to change, especially as a result of the decades of expansion after 1950. Growth in size of the professoriate occurred at the precise time of the Civil Rights Act and the rules prohibiting discrimination in hiring. The growth period thus led to major opportunities for Jews (15–20% of the faculty now at leading research universities), Catholics (a wider representation, but not necessarily concentrated at the top), and those of working-class background. Women, almost completely shut out of academia except for the junior colleges before 1960, have made major gains since the 1960s, though they are still underrepresented at the tenured ranks and in the higher-level universities. But women are well organized, and in certain fields (sociology and history, for example) they have set up women's studies programs that not only employ new faculty but also critique sexism in the academy as well as the society. Blacks, however, are quite underrepresented in American academic life, except for the black colleges and universities. The requirement of a college degree and then a graduate degree to join a nonlucrative field has discouraged most blacks who graduate from college (a percentage on the decrease since 1980). Recent surveys of American universities in the 1980s show that the problem is mainly one of supply, not racism on the part of hiring universities, though of course there may be a little of that, too. With medical and legal and business careers paying so much more than academic ones for those blacks with college degrees, it is not a surprise that there is a shortage of applicants for academic posts (Bowen and Schuster 1986, 30–54).

In general, the American model is increasingly inclusive, both as to numbers of academics and to titles. The turning point for the career is the achievement of tenure. But with the passage of the years the transition from apprentice to true "guild member" is being determined not only by the candidate and the department, but also by the stringency of budgets, as perceived by university administrations. Tenure can also be broken if financial exigencies require it—according to the administrative definition of "requirement" rather than the faculties'. These developments are affecting the nature of academic work in the nation—our next consideration.

The American Academic Workplace, Then and Now

In understanding the impact of the changes since 1930, two dimensions are critical: the increasingly difficult process of obtaining tenure in the American university, and the nature of the workplace in which the academics work, before and after tenure. During the years from 1930 to about 1950, the supply of new recruits to academia in the United States was just about matched by the number of new openings. Not all achieved tenure, of course—but that was never promised. Then, with the expansion of existing universities and the creation of new ones, possibilities existed for the candidate who had not achieved tenure at one place to try again at another. This was an opportunity during the expansion of the 1960s. But this "second chance" came to almost a complete halt about 1970. From then on, the inability to get tenure in the university where one took one's first tenure-track job usually meant leaving academia completely. This has not meant, however, that those who fail make no use of their academic training. Natural scientists and even some social scientists have been increasingly finding that private-sector employment, while not giving as much freedom as academic work, can sometimes pay better. In addition, learned society membership, in the work of the discipline, is also open to those outside the university who want it. But the tenure "crunch" since the 1970s has led to the departure from academia of many talented people.

Most universities and all community colleges are on tight budgets. Public school budgets are set primarily by state legislatures, while enrollments determine budgets in most private universities. Cutbacks in state funding (due to tax revolts) or enrollment (because of demographics) will have major consequences for the professoriate. The majority of universities grew because of increased funding and demand. With funding tight and enrollments leveling off, all schools suffer, except for the elite research institutions that have major endowments.

In the American case, these budget decisions are made far above the level of departments, and the faculty are usually not consulted. As a result of continuing crises, the administrators of individual universities have told their department chairs to hire more part-timers and non–tenure track faculty, who can be dismissed or rehired on a year-to-year basis. Part-time faculty went from 82,000 in 1960 to 220,000 in 1980; in percentage of all faculty from 35% in 1960 to 22% in 1970 to 32% in 1980. But the reasons were different—in 1960 there was a shortage of credentialed faculty, but by 1980 there was a surplus. The universities, less and less certain of funding from year to year, are unwilling to commit to new tenure-track positions (Bowen and Schuster 1986, 61).

The result has been the growth of an "academic proletariat" on the American scene. Although elite universities (but not elite liberal arts colleges) usually use their own graduate students in undergraduate teaching, other schools employ academic "gypsies" for that purpose. With degree in hand but unable to land a tenure-track job, these teachers hang on from year to year and go from place to place to survive in the overcrowded market (Wilke 1979; Abel 1984). After a few years of this nomadic existence, they become typed, rather cruelly, by the nature of their vitas. When a job does open, a new Ph.D. from a good department is more likely to be hired than a "gypsy." Fully 28% of part-time faculty in 1995, in fact, were formerly full-time at institutions that either didn't keep them or didn't keep the "slot" that was formerly theirs in a department (Tuckman et al. 1978, 24). The effect of this phenomenon on those who do stay in their jobs, working toward tenure, has been extreme. While all U.S. universities expect faculty to teach well, even institutions of medium and low rank have come to expect publication, even though the junior faculty carry teaching loads that allow little time for research. Promotion and tenure are also setting senior faculty who have not published much against junior faculty who have, and who get turned down anyway. "Publish or perish," the rule in first-rank departments in the 1950s, is being replaced today in many places, definitely not of the first rank, by the slogan "publish *and* perish."

Working conditions have worsened as well, for all faculty. As the majority of universities cut back on funding maintenance of buildings, on general upkeep, they also have restricted such amenities as travel funds, extra summer teaching, supplies, secretaries, and even, in some places, the toilet paper in bathrooms. The result, for those who have managed to survive and stay, has been a degenerating work environment, one in which major decisions affecting all faculty are made at the administrative level, for budgetary reasons, often in state-college system offices remote from the campus. The rise of unionism, especially in state colleges and junior colleges, is a reaction to all of this. Bowen and Shuster (1986, 118) conclude:

> Often the failures of maintenance and the inability to increase building space have offended the sensibilities and dignity of faculty members confined to quarters that are inadequate, crowded, ugly, uncomfortable, and lacking in privacy. It has reduced the proportion of the faculty on permanent and full-time appointments and increased their responsibility for the operation and continuity of their institutions and the advising of students. It has changed and increased the rigor of the standards for faculty promotion and mobility, thus diverting their efforts to research and scholarship, while at the same time demanding excellent teaching. It has increased the time and effort devoted to accountability.

Academics, the Market, and the State

To what extent do American professors, as a group, control their own relation to the market and the state? Not very much at all—except for an elite group of professors, in a small number of elite universities, who can switch universities at will, even after tenure and in bad times, for the right offer, and who have formed close relations with the state (through success in the federal grant system) or with private industry. The mass of the professoriate can do neither. It is thus at the mercy of the market except in years of major expansion, and subject to the ways the American state or capitalism favors or does not favor their skills and their disciplines.

In the 1930s, the Depression led to a slight growth in faculties, not a diminution, because many unemployed workers decided that a university degree was something to pursue in the absence of a job (Caplow and McGee 1958, 18). At the end of the 1930s, émigrés from Europe, most fleeing Hitler's persecution, found a home in this growing market, though usually not at major universities. Sometimes they worked for a while in such special settings as the New School for Social Research in New York before finding jobs in American academia (Fleming and Bailyn 1969; Heilbut 1983). Though World War II brought temporary interruptions in classrooms, the postwar G.I. Bill, which provided scholarships for a whole generation of veterans, led to the expansion of the professoriate (Jencks and Riesman 1969, 94–95). Salaries, however, did not keep pace with inflation throughout this period.

Only in the 1960–1970 decade, when universities were desperate for more Ph.D.s, was the normal academic buyer's market—with the universities usually deciding how much they would pay—replaced by a seller's market and a rise in real income, after inflation. After 1970 and especially after 1980, however, the usual condition of an underpaid faculty returned. Those institutions that have consistently remained the lowest paying—secondary branches of state universities, state colleges, and junior or community colleges—have in fact been the only ones where this discontent has given rise to unionization. By 1977, about 18% of faculty, mostly in these markets, had joined unions (Wilson 1979, 164). By 1981 the figure was 25% of all faculty units (Metzger 1987, 70). But the majority, including those at virtually every first- and second-rank university, public and private, had not, even though their salaries, too, were rising slower than the cost of living. Most preferred the relative security of tenure, even with worsening salaries and surroundings, to the risks of the nonacademic market.

All professors and fields were not equally affected, of course. The humanities and the social sciences tended to suffer more than natural sciences or the professional schools. In the U.S. university systems, individual capitalists or corporations sometimes fund departments or academic chairs, and they tend to support engineering and business faculties disproportionately. In the 1960s, especially as student antiwar protests increased, it became obvious that faculties were often politically divided depending in part on the presence or absence of external sponsors for their field. Faculty who had sponsors involved in war work prospered and were often prowar. Departments without such support tended to be antiwar. As the university has become more and more a model of the wider society, it has succumbed to corporate priorities at the expense of basic educational ones.

One example of this shift has been in science research. Up to about 1970, the National Science Foundation and the National Institutes of Health gradually increased the amount of funding of basic science. Basic science departments and medical schools benefited. Although the state (the federal government) paid for the research, it did not dictate which grants should be funded. That was determined through referred panels of experts in each discipline. Although this process was biased toward the elite universities, where most research was carried out, it was still somewhat under the control of the experts in each field and led toward the advance of basic knowledge. But starting in the 1970s and escalating in the 1980s, the Republican Party and the major corporations changed the method of funding. Instead of the traditional system, Republican leaders have pressured for a decrease in direct governmental funding, under academic control, toward direct funding of research by the corporations themselves. The corporations work with entrepreneurial faculty who share their values and goals and who often agree to keep findings secret to protect corporate profits. This latter development is changing the nature of science and knowledge from free inquiry and professional journal publication to private property. Meanwhile, those who cannot or do not want to work directly for corporations in their academic jobs are deprived of much new outside funding and compete with increasing numbers of colleagues for a shrinking federal dollar.

In the last decades of the twentieth century, therefore, the politics of universities have become more polarized. Departments and schools that receive funding from corporate work—in engineering, medicine, business, law—become more politically neutral or conservative, while those left out or who want no part of the corporate connection are more likely to be liberal or even radical. Administrators, while always paying lip service to liberal arts, expand the schools and departments that "pay"—and that pay increasingly involves corporate and not government support. The job market follows the trend.

At the same time, the complex American state has been changing its role as well—receding in some areas as capitalism advances, growing more powerful elsewhere. Originally, in the colonial period, such elite schools as Harvard, Yale, and Columbia were partially supported by the colonial treasury, but they grew independent and became more strictly "private" (Whitehead 1975). Public support of education became much more active after the Civil War with the Land Grant Act, providing for the development of the great state universities. A large number of small, private colleges also were founded for a great variety of ethnic, racial, and religious groups, as well as for women, but it was the state systems that proliferated, before and especially after World War II. They now clearly constitute the majority of settings and include within their ranks great research systems, such as Berkeley and UCLA, or the Texas system, or Michigan and Minnesota (Jencks and Riesman 1969, 263, 267, 271–79).

During World War II, American universities worked with the state in two ways. First, scientific research, especially as it related to the Manhattan Project and the atomic bomb, led to greater prestige and funds for such fields as physics (Kevles 1971, 302–72). Second, leading figures in the social sciences worked for the Office of Strategic Services, doing various kinds of spy work during the war, and in some cases after it. Elite universities, especially Yale and Harvard, were headquarters for recruitment. Area studies programs, involving different disciplines, were directly funded by the OSS and then by the postwar Central Intelligence Agency. When the antiwar movement of the 1960s began, universities were forced to acknowledge their ties. The CIA, it should be noted, was far more politically conservative in the fight against communism than the wartime OSS was in its fight against fascism. Continuing contact with the CIA brought most leading American universities into the conservative, procapitalist camp more than working with the OSS in wartime ever did (Winks 1987, 60–114, 439–69).

To what extent has the gradual change from a system of private universities and colleges (already a minority by 1930) to a primarily public system in 1990 affected the academic freedom, tenure, and guild power of the U.S. professoriate? In a general sense, the growth, due to spending by state governments for larger systems and by the federal government for research, has left more universities and their faculties dependent on these funds to the point of vulnerability. By 1975 some city college systems (such as the City University of New York) were laying off faculty. Some campuses of state systems also disappeared (SUNY-Brockport, for example), and their faculty, tenured or not, were let go. Because tenure clauses allow universities in the United States to fire for financial expediency, fiscal trouble meant trouble for the faculty. Moreover, unionization as a response to these conditions does not necessarily work. The federal court system and the U.S. Supreme Court upheld in 1980 a decision of the National Labor Relations Board that private university faculty did not have the right to unionize because they are a part of "management" (U.S. Supreme Court 1980). Unrealistic though this is in fact, given the trends we have reviewed here, this ruling has the force of law and will prevent any unionization in private American universities in the future. The state, while never decisive, is everywhere, and in its different branches and its different methods, it works primarily in one procapitalist direction.

In conclusion, the U.S. professoriate has some guild power of a limited sort to choose its own successors and colleagues in fields, but that power has always been subject to university approval. Tenure provides job security and some freedom from harassment. But the university hires, promotes, or fires the professoriate. Only in a limited number of universities, in 1990 as in 1930, have certain persons—well-known senior professors with national reputations in their fields—had the power to play the market instead of being subject to it, to work with capitalist firms or the state, on the terms usually of these firms or the government. That they have usually shared the capitalist values of both the firms and those running the government is beside the point—if they did not, they would not have been called on for service and expertise. The majority of the profession trades a form of job security for worsening real wages and a deteriorating work environment. All work within the highly individualized model of American universities and colleges, where the state has no planning role and even the university not much of one. Areas of supply and demand are increasingly determined by the capitalists who endow the universities, support or frustrate state taxes for university expansion, fund the academic chairs, help to hire the faculty in the departments they care about, and increasingly determine the direction and nature of research.

3 | Britain: Class-Divided Professions and an Amateur State

Class position is a critical factor in understanding the past, present, and future of individuals, families, or whole professions, everywhere. But the degree to which it explains behavior depends on the nation. In Britain, class is clearly the most important dimension on which the entire analysis must be based. According to Goldthorpe (1980, 327), "the net association between the class position of individuals in the present day [British] population and their class origins remains essentially the same as its extent in the interwar period and even, it seems likely, as that which would have been found at the start of the century."

Graduates of the British elite private preparatory schools—Eton, Harrow, Winchester, Marlboro—and then of Oxford and Cambridge universities constitute the leadership of each of our professions and of both the Conservative and the Labor parties (especially the ministries of each government). They also constitute the majority of the civil service's "administrative class" (Sampson 1971, 1982; Fry 1985, 9–35). British capitalism and the British empire were built in an era before this model was established. But beginning in the period 1870–1910, the elite educational system created an establishment that remained in power until the era of Margaret Thatcher. An appreciation of how this form of class rule came to be and how the Thatcher government tried to turn back the clock to a previous period is critical in understanding the class-divided nature of British professions, and their fate under the governments of the 1970s and 1980s.

Capitalism, the State, and the Professions

British capitalism was already in place in the early to mid-1800s. Although by this time the "public" schools and Oxbridge were more than finishing schools for the gentry or training grounds for the ministry, they were certainly not where capitalists learned to form and to manage corporations. The civil service was small, and more important, it was full of incompetents and rife with nepotism (Kearney 1979). By the mid-1800s, however, the split between the landed aristocrats and capitalists in industry was disappearing, and some landed aristocrats were investing in manufacturing, railroads, and real estate. By 1900 the practice of awarding knighthoods to highly successful capitalists without "social background" was well established.

What led to the change in the role of the universities, and thus of the private preparatory schools, was a desire to reform the civil service so as to better serve the needs of the Empire. The university system was revamped, and full-time scholars or "dons" replaced the young clergymen who had served as tutors while they awaited assignment to a permanent ministry (Rothblatt 1981, 16). This improvement was matched by a new seriousness on the part of the public schools, which in turn brought the schools a greater role in the development of the leaders of professions, especially medicine and law (Reader 1966, 127–45). Leaders of the bar, the medical profession, and the professoriate itself began to take the place of nonuniversity men in politics and government. The result, by 1930, was a system that combined the principle of amateurism in government—rule by those with the right public school and Oxbridge connections—with a professional world stratified by Oxbridge background or the lack of it (Fry 1985, 10–13).

We can deal with the civil service and politicians—the heart of the British state—first, then with the background of the professional system as it existed in the early years of the twentieth century. Finally, we will examine the ways in which the system has evolved since the 1930s, beginning with the cooperative relation between state and the professions under which private professional bodies or "qualifying associations" were granted all major regulatory functions, and proceeding through the post-Thatcher era, with the state working more closely with capitalist interests and against preserving professional group power and independence.

The relation between the civil service and the government of the day is critical in understanding the operation of the British state. The majority parliamentary party designates a prime minister, who in turn chooses a cabinet. Each cabinet minister is in charge of a department of the permanent state, and the leading permanent bureaucrat of each department—the permanent secretary, who has worked his way up the ranks of the civil service—is obliged to carry out the policy of the elected government. In reality, however, swings in policy are often moderated by the service, especially its administrative class of top-level experienced bureaucrats, in part because the service prefers continuity from government to government, in part because few ministers are as expert in their fields as are their corresponding permanent secretaries. Since World War II, service bureaucrats have also often been the initiators of policies, which a prime minister then presents to Parliament. Both during the creation of new legislation and in its passage and implementation, the permanent service has wide latitude to work with the "affected interests," such as the professions, in designing conciliatory changes. (An example is the creation and enactment of the National Health Service, to be discussed below.) Lobbying by interests—which is expected, and almost required, as part of the process—focuses, therefore, primarily on the administrative process rather than the legislative one, as in the United States. (Birch 1967, 134–46, 212–39).

Britain is a unified nation-state, centralized in London but with some institutional variation (including in professional training and practice) in the historically different countries of Scotland and Northern Ireland; Wales is usually on the same model as England, especially in our area of research. In terms of our comparative perspective, Britain is halfway between such almost totally centralized regimes as France and the decentralized federal systems of the United States and West Germany, but it has tended toward more centralization since World War II. Wartime experience did not change the essential nature of the British state, but it did expand it markedly, and it also sped up the transition from an aristocratic society toward a more meritocratic one.

Power is shared in Britain between center and periphery. For example, though the health budget is administered centrally, once the parameters are established most decisions are carried out regionally and locally, with local government in control of much welfare provision. Even nationalized industries are run far more as private corporations than as state-run businesses. The central state is not well unified, either, as various ministries war over funding. The predominant national spirit of Britain is a combination of tolerance and skepticism: each government proceeds without much input from the citizens at large, though with much special-interest lobbying by those working with the ministries. If the government's approach doesn't work, the electorate replaces it with another, presumably with a new set of policies. Yet this deference, this "give them enough rope" philosophy, has been less common in recent decades, with more groups than in the past adopting activism and intervention. The heavyweights—capitalism and the professions—usually intervene with more success than do smaller interest groups.

The welfare state has developed fully in Britain, beginning as early as 1910 (Wrigley 1976). But expansion slowed in the 1970s, and Thatcher, starting in 1979, tried to begin to roll it back, though without much success, except in the nationalized industries and the universities (Krieger 1986). The permanent party before World War II, the Conservatives, gave way immediately after the war to the Labor Party, then to a succession of Conservative and Labor party governments that shared many social policy assumptions though they differed on small details. Since 1979 only the right-wing Thatcher government has broken the consensus and attacked not only the Labor Party and the unions but also the professions and the universities (Leys 1989, 101–28). Labor could not fight back successfully because it became divided between Left radicals who wanted to replace Thatcher with overt socialism and liberals who thought the leftist position even more unrealistic than in the 1960s and 1970s. The unions themselves, meanwhile, dwindled in membership and influence. The polarization within Labor, and thus its increasing inability to fight back against the Thatcher and Major governments, have continued to increase (Leys 1989, 213–41). The educational system is, with only the partial exception of Oxford and Cambridge, totally state-funded through the University Grants Committee and its successor. But much professional training takes place outside the university, so state control over the university is not necessarily state control over the professions.

Dominant regulatory mechanisms of the state invoke the advice-and-consent model, with the relevant state ministries consulting with the "affected interests"—the professions, for example. The "qualifying associations" that register the professionals in each field are in the private sector, performing what are public functions in most other nations, and they also act as lobbies (Millerson 1964). The state does not control the training slots of professions, except indirectly through funding to some university programs, and does not control professional performance at work except, again, indirectly through the impact of funding decisions. Parliamentary commissions—usually with elite, establishment, upper-class members, including some in the specific profession—recommend changes in professional conditions and behavior. But such recommendations, at least until the Thatcher government, have never been extreme, and even then not were usually not acted on by Parliament itself.

One such commission report was the Northcote-Trevelyan report on the reform of the civil service in 1854. But unlike many of its successors, it was acted on, and it has continued to shape the British state, the professions, and the university, to the present day. Parliament acted on the Northcote-Trevelyan report to change the way the British civil service administrative class is staffed. Candidates must pass civil service examinations after completing university studies (usually in classics, humanities, or history), and they must commit to a lifetime career, for which they are rewarded with full security. Civil servants are recruited for general work, on the assumption that brilliant amateurs, with first-class degrees from Oxford and Cambridge, can learn any task; such generalists are preferred to those with scientific and technical backgrounds, whose expertise might be limited to their specialties. This principle of amateurism—that "superior men of general ability" are preferable to technicians—and the belief that all those with science and social science background *are* technicians—still prevails; since the 1970s there have been many more appointments for midlevel science and technical graduates, but not in the administrative class (Fry 1985, 16). In spite of attempts to liberalize standards in World War II and recommendations for further reform by the Fulton report of 1968, the principle continues to govern recruitment. A minor and unimportant training college for new civil service appointees does now exist, but it is nothing like the elite technocratic training in France given to those at the Ecole nationale d'administration (Fry 1985, 9–25, 36–71).

Why was this reform so important in shaping the modern British university system and the grammar and public schools that fed it? First, scholarship became a priority at Oxbridge after these reforms in a way that it had not been beforehand, leading to the replacement of clergymen by academically dedicated experts and the revival of the tutorial system. Although the majority of those actually qualifying for the civil service through the exams were upper middle class (not upper class), the professionalization of the university changed the experience for nearly all students (Rothblatt 1981). Second, as Oxbridge gradually began to demand performance and ability instead of simply upper-class background as criteria for admission, Eton, Harrow, Winchester, Marlboro, and the other Clarendon schools— those with foundation dates in the fourteenth, fifteenth, and sixteenth centuries—began to reform their own curricula and to emphasize character and team sports, as well as putting a higher premium on scholarship (Reader 1966, 157).

It was in this era, 1850–1900 or so, that training for the professions of medicine and law began to differentiate between the elite, who received an Oxbridge education, and the rest of each profession, who did not—and in fact often had no college at all, though most had gone to private or grammar school first. The reforms did not require a college degree before training for medicine or law, however, and engineering was not viewed as an activity for which advanced education was necessary; "engineer" described a mechanically gifted working-class factory expert. When the University of London and the other early municipal universities were founded in the late nineteenth century, they were not viewed as being on the same level as Oxbridge, and their graduates almost always failed the examinations for the civil service; yet these schools and not Oxbridge held the first profession-relevant training programs, for solicitors and for some kinds of engineers. The University of London began to act as a kind of "holding company," a degree legitimizer for the hospital-based medical schools in London. Their graduates were likely to staff the lower level of a profession, or the lower branches of a divided one—to become solicitors, for example, but not barristers (Reader 1966, 136).

What was unique in England and Wales (less so in Scotland) was the disassociation between the university on the one hand and both the professions and capitalism on the other. After about 1600, Oxford and Cambridge changed their function. Up to this time, they were similar to such Continental universities as Bologna or Paris in being primarily professional training bodies. After this time, the universities gradually became finishing schools for the men of the British upper class. These upper-class students came originally from the landed aristocracy (along with a few destitute scholars), but when students of merchant banking or capitalist industrial background began to enter, the universities' aims did not change (Kearney 1979). Only in the later 1800s did the concept of competitive university education begin to take hold. By then the professions, in effect ostracized by the university, had long since established their own traditions and their own licensing bodies, primarily in London. The state, for its part, accepted the professions' rulings as to who was qualified to practice (Engel 1980).

In medicine, for example, it gradually became acceptable after 1900 for those who had studied medicine at Oxford and Cambridge to qualify for practice on those grounds, or at least to receive several years' credit toward qualification. Barristers were registered as students in the Inns of Court in London, and although one did not have to go to Oxford or Cambridge first to become a student, graduates of these universities had first choice for the training positions in barristers' chambers that were important to qualify for the bar. Others had a much harder time finding apprenticeships and far less likelihood of success in the practice of law if they did qualify. Solicitors, the less prestigious half of the profession, who dealt with clients first, usually had no college or took some courses at the municipal universities while carrying out the apprenticeship period that constituted their main training. In other words, an Oxbridge degree was helpful to those who could afford it and who did not have to directly begin training after preparatory school, and it was necessary for a leading future role in the professions (Reader 1966, 197). But until the 1970s, a college degree as part of the training program was not mandatory in most professions. The university was in one place, the professional training in another (Monopolies Commission 1970).

Great Britain is a nation of many exceptions to any rule, a collection of historical particularities and survivals in many social institutions, and the professions provide many examples. So in summarizing in advance the main dimensions of analysis for the professions in our study, it is important to note that the individual case studies will deal with these exceptions in greater detail. In general, some professions have high political solidarity (the barristers and solicitors are examples, as were professors until recently), some, like the medical profession, usually have solidarity over pay issues but split between generalists and specialists. And some have low solidarity and a whole series of different qualifying associations—the different types of engineers, for example. By definition, a professional belongs to his or her qualifying association in order to be registered to practice but usually remains inactive in it except on pay issues. There are marked hierarchical differences in most British professions—more so than in any other nation in our sample except Italy—the elites leading a style of life quite different from the mass in each line of work. The class distribution of nineteenth-century Britain inspired the split on class lines within each profession. Yet professional solidarity is increasing vis-à-vis the government as paymaster, especially since 1960. Public employment in the 1990s includes nearly all doctors, many barristers, and all university professors, but not most solicitors and only about a quarter of the engineers. In any case the public-private split has not led to the formation of different bargaining groups to the extent that it has in, for example, France.

Politically most professions, including the doctors in the National Health Service, are to the right of center. Yet each profession has some representation on the Left, especially medicine, with the Socialist Medical Association (Navarro 1978, 31–32). Engineers, still being mostly working class and lower middle class in origin, are more likely to vote Labor than their compatriots in the United States or France are to cast liberal or leftist votes (Whalley 1985, 158–87). Yet these differences within professions have not politically fragmented them to the point where, as in Italy, the different political wings do not speak with one another and professors in a field go to different national meetings and publish in different journals based on their politics.

Training need not be university based in professions and still is not in law. Yet there have been major changes in this direction since the 1970s. Many of the more business-oriented professions have built training programs into the provincial universities. Traditionally, each qualifying association decides for itself whether university training or a university degree is necessary, or whether those with a degree can shorten the time period of apprenticeship necessary to qualify for full status in the field. And some qualifying associations do not even administer the examination that a candidate must pass before registration as a professional. That test can be given by a university, or it may be replaced by an apprenticeship, or both may be needed, or neither, depending on the group—and the most relaxed rules are often those of the oldest professional groups (Millerson 1964). Solicitors, for example, started university courses in the late nineteenth century, whereas barristers began only in the 1980s. And although the qualifying association, not the state, decides whether there will be a maximum number trained every year, many simply register the training carried out elsewhere, so they often have no effective power over numbers. There are some relations between the state, the university, and the qualifying association concerning the numbers in training, but no one has the power to force changes. Universities, as they have become increasingly important since 1970 in professional training, always have a tendency to overtrain, to justify their programs and their expansion by the number of students in them—against the wishes of practicing professionals who fear a glut on the market.

Membership is by definition in the qualifying association of each profession. Yet no one must belong to a bargaining association such as the British Medical Association, though the majority do. In recent decades the BMA, the Law Society, and the National Union of Teachers (university professors) have all registered as unions with the Trades Union Congress (TUC) to fight against an increasingly cost-cutting and aggressive state. Many professionals belong to specialty associations, and most elites within each profession still belong to the honorific Royal Societies, which are quite hierarchical, and which give extra prestige beyond the qualifying training (Clark 1966–1972). Yet each profession still goes its own way, and there is very little cross-professional associational activity in Britain. Each profession lobbies the relevant ministry, some, such as the doctors and barristers, with success, others, such as the professors, with much less. Even Britain's membership in the EEC, where such cross-professional associations have now emerged for defensive purposes against the massed and coordinated power of nation-states and international capitalism, have not led to their development or strength in Britain.

Capitalism, at least the modern form of industrial capitalism, also grew apart from the British state. In the early years of the Empire, the state was much involved in the creation and the administration of the colonies, and the great colonial fortunes were built with state support. But industrial capitalism grew on its own. The state treasury and the Bank of England paid little attention to this growth and development and certainly did not fund it. Even in the period from 1900 to 1980, the British state remained aloof from manufacturing and merchandising. Control over funds in the financial system, unlike in France, where the state plays a major role, is not strong in Britain. As Hall (1986, 52) notes, "This sort of instrument has not been available to the British state, partly because successive governments have shied away from the nationalization of the banks, and partly because the Bank of England, which has some influence in this sector, retains considerable independence from the government." Private finance capital—the "City"—grew in importance and remains so. But its investments are primarily not in British industry but rather in international money flows and international investing and takeovers.

As Britain began to lose its colonial empire, the government might have developed a policy of supporting industry with government funds, for much of Britain's prosperity has been based on trade with the Empire and then the Commonwealth. But neither Conservative nor Labor governments wished to pursue that option. This is an important part of the background for understanding the uniqueness of the British economy. When Keynes' theories began to gain acceptance in the 1930s and immediately after World War II, they were adopted to build the postwar welfare state and not to help British industry. Thus the nation did not build an economic base to replace its lost Empire (Hall 1986, 69–99).

Politically, the leading party of the latter half of the nineteenth century was the Liberal Party of Gladstone, which tried and to some extent succeeded in mediating between an old Tory (Conservative) aristocracy and a new and gradually more militant working class, which, once it had the right to vote, formed the Labor Party. In reaction to the growing militancy and power of the Labor Party, the new capitalists joined the landowners in the Conservative party, and the "middle," the Liberals, virtually disappeared (Leys 1989, 279–91). Yet the Labor party never became Marxist, though some of its organizers were. Rather, the Labor Party became enmeshed with and primarily supported by the various unions, most of them craft based and not industrywide, that formed the Trades Union Congress. A rather conservative Labor position on government finance of industry always has opposed government involvement to help capitalists by directing industry. Labor has always maintained a rather obstructionist position, claiming that help for capitalists does not necessarily translate into better conditions for workers (Hall 1986, 64–65). This antiplanning position, briefly suspended in World War II and in one postwar period in the 1960s, has reinforced the position of the Conservative governments, creating a state-capitalist distance that parallels the distance between state and professions.

World War II was a turning point for Britain and for the professions within it. Total mobilization for war, and a wartime, state-run and state-directed economy proved to many in Britain that the laissez-faire system should be replaced by a more integrated, if not corporatist, model, in which planning (or at least consultation) should increase between the great actors of capitalism, labor, and the state. Labor won the first postwar election and put the National Health Service into place, with much support from Conservatives and opposition primarily by the leadership of the general practitioners in the British Medical Association, although they eventually went along as well (Perkin 1989, 346–50). The welfare state—social insurance against unemployment, pension schemes for most workers, the National Health Service, and even a right to one's existing job—all resulted from the understanding that "things should be better after the war." Perkin (1989, 418) observes: "The quarter-century after the Second World War saw the culmination of the trends leading to professional society: the rise of an affluent, permissive, more homogeneous society with greater equality between the classes, the sexes and the generations, the completion of the welfare state run by professional administrators and experts, and the creation of a mixed economy controlled on both sides by professional managers."

Ignoring for the moment Perkin's very broad use of the term "professional," which conflates groups organized by occupation and acting as such with occupations of professional status, the growth of the welfare state, in his terms, primarily benefited public-sector professionals, where he places medical and social workers, barristers (who performed a large amount of legal aid work after 1945), and university professors.

Britain had an extremely elitist educational system in the early postwar period (1% in universities in 1930, only 4% in 1960), and even with full scholarships and maintenance grants for all accepted, only a tiny fraction of the working-class youth attended. Thus in the late 1960s the Robbins Commission report and an immediate favorable response in Parliament led to a rapid expansion in British universities: eight new campuses on the Oxbridge model, plus a major expansion of the municipal universities, the upgrading to university status of such older large polytechics as Manchester, and the creation of a whole new set of polytechnics. This expansion would produce a much-enlarged university professoriate, whose numbers, if not prestige, dwarfed Oxbridge by 1980. But all of this growth in the public sector, with nearly half of all Britons working in the public professions or the nationalized industries, did not mean that Britain was keeping up in percentage of college students with France, West Germany, the United States or Japan (Perkin 1989, 405–71). Finally, the stagnation of the economy, and the long-term cultural bias of the universities and most of its graduates against private business, led to a different kind of government under Thatcher.

The Thatcher government, beginning in 1979, was not a traditional Conservative regime interested in planning and consultation of labor unions and professions but rather sought to confront them. In many ways, Britain since Thatcher's rise has turned backward as much as forward. In addition to declaring war on universities and unions, Thatcher declared war on British professions. She tried, without much public support or much success, to create a competition between the National Health Service and a tiny private medical sector. She recommended, through a Monopolies Commission staffed by her supporters, the removal of many professional monopolies in areas of their work. A similar effort failed in 1970, but EEC rules that demand more of it since 1992 helped Thatcher.

Finally, Thatcher declared war on the university professoriate, abolishing academic tenure for those who did not already have it, cutting operating budgets expanded as recently as the Robbins era, and not sparing Oxbridge. If Thatcher favored any group, it was the polytechnics supposedly close to industry. British industry, however, is still not financed to any great degree by the state, at least directly, and public corporations under the theoretical control of the state actually are fairly autonomous. Corporations still prefer to recruit Oxbridge graduates to industry rather than polytechnic graduates, especially for managerial jobs, and do not usually promote scientists or engineers into management. Nor has Britain generally become more economically competitive in the 1980s. What has changed is the cozy relation between government and the professions. The civil service is now unionized and in a mood to fight (Fry 1985, 122–45), and the professions can no longer count on a delegation of trust and support by the government. In many ways, the plan was to take Britain back to 1850, in the hope of making it more efficient, and to centralize power in the hands of the state to make it possible. We can now consider these historical changes in greater detail for the professions of medicine, law, engineering, and the university professoriate.

British Doctors: A Two-Class System

In Victorian times, there was a slow transition from the centuries-old hierarchical model of physician, surgeon, and apothecary to a model of specialists in hospitals (consultants, in modern British terminology) and general practitioners in the community. The trend accelerated in 1858 with the establishment of the General Medical Council, a new registration agency for all physicians that replaced in part the separate licensing of the Royal College of Physicians, the Royal College of Surgeons, and the apothecaries group. But as with much else in Britain, the surface change had little effect on underlying class differences. The general practitioners pushed for this "reform," but the result was continuing control of the profession by the Oxford- and Cambridge-trained specialists, who also ruled the new GMC (Peterson 1978, 35–39).

Before the creation of the General Medical Council, the vast majority of physicians were men of the upper class, often second sons, who were not primary heirs. After taking nonmedical degrees at Oxford or Cambridge, they trained at London hospitals and were then accepted by the Royal Society of Physicians because of their Oxbridge background and not because of the degree of their medical skills (Peterson 1978, 198–99, 233). After a short period of work they were made fellows. Most surgeons in this period were not graduates at all but were trained by apprenticeship, working for other surgeons and taking classes at the larger hospitals. (University education for surgeons became routine in Scotland earlier than in England.) Apothecaries were general practitioners, training by apprenticeship in offices of senior practitioners. Social background—the class of one's parents— determined which medical profession one entered. Except for an occasional star surgeon, only the physicians, most of whom practiced in London, did well financially. Many others took joint training as surgeons and as apothecaries and practiced as general practitioners in London and especially in the provinces. Only physicians were "gentlemen" (Peterson 1978, 194– 243).

The passage of the General Medical Council Act was the first major change in the hierarchical system—and it was designed not to break the hierarchy, but rather to rearrange it under different principles. Nominally one profession after 1858, British doctors still were fragmented. The new factor was the beginning of the modern hospital. In the early 1800s the elite physicians and surgeons worked in hospitals but did not control them. They seized power from the lay social elite on hospital boards in the latter half of the century; their influence over the growing and increasingly important medical schools that they ran in these hospitals was of primary importance in gaining overall control of the hospital setting. The hospital specialists gradually accumulated more degreed students and maintained a large distance between themselves and the primarily working-class general practitioners. Even after the 1858 reform, only physicians with Oxbridge backgrounds could become Fellows of the Royal Societies, and only fellows had voting privileges. When general practitioners began to be examined by the Royal Societies and then registered by the GMC as members, they were not even allowed into the buildings where the fellows met. Peterson (1978, 243) concludes: "For general practitioners, corporate distinctions between physicians, surgeons, and apothecaries had lost much of their meaning. What now divided them from their own professional elite was their powerlessness in the face of growing elite authority, their ignoble status in the face of the consultant's high prestige, their poverty in the face of wealth, and their dependency in the face of the consultants' growing independence. . . . While they all belonged to one profession, they did not belong to the same social class."

By the turn of the twentieth century, both branches of the profession were in trouble. Elite physicians and surgeons were earning good livings, but most other physicians and surgeons in ordinary hospitals were not, for a large percentage of patients could not afford to pay their fees, and many hospitals were just breaking even, or worse. General practitioners, lacking hospital connections, were in even worse shape. So when Lloyd George and the Liberal Party passed a national health insurance bill in 1911 for the poorer members of the working class, the conditions for general practice began to improve. Over the years from 1911 to the late 1930s, the benefits of health insurance were slowly extended to more of the workers and then to their families and to some members of the middle class. By the outbreak of the war in 1939, about 75% of British citizens had partial coverage, though usually more for general practice than for hospital expenses, and no system covered everything. There was also no clear pattern of responsibility between the community and the hospital doctors. The Dawson report of 1920, written in the moment of victory after World War I, died on the vine, as neither the general practitioners nor the specialists were ready for the massive state involvement that the report recommended. And the Depression of the 1930s was not a time for innovation (Navarro 1978, 3–24).

World War II was the turning point for British medicine and for the relation between British doctors and the state. During the war, a coalition government of Conservatives and Labor found that the health of the British people was abominable. Both parties promised—even before the success of the Normandy invasion guaranteed victory—that after the war health and social services would be much improved. In addition to the development of a joint policy by Conservatives and Laborites, wartime Britain had its first full-scale and direct experience with an expanded state and a state-run health care system. During the war the state nationalized and ran most of the economy, including the food industry, and the state created an emergency national health-care system, in which the Ministry of Health directly employed all doctors, nurses, and other health personnel and ran all hospitals. The nationalization of health care affected Britain as a whole, not just the military, as in the United States (Gill 1980, 95–98). For the first time specialists, formerly based at elite London hospitals, were assigned to small provincial hospitals, where they found practically no equipment or supplies. Only when the extent of the difference between elite facilities in London and those elsewhere struck home to the elite branch of the profession did they begin to advocate a postwar national service. As Navarro (1978, 31) concludes, "Millions . . . were better fed in wartime than in peacetime. In the health sector, war planning meant state direction of the medical and hospital sectors through the Emergency Medical Service, with the need for (1) coordinating (but not integrating) all hospital facilities in Britain, and (2) distributing hospital resources, including human resources—to hospitals not previously attended."

In the later years of the war, after it became clear that the Allies would win, the British working class, along with many in the middle class who had not had health coverage before the war, determined that nationalized health care must continue after the war. The Beveridge report, commissioned by the Churchill government, was one early blueprint of a future British society that would "[provide] social security from the cradle to the grave, and [call] for the maintenance of full employment and the provision of a national health service for everyone" (Eckstein 1958, 1960).

But the Beveridge report was only partially responsible for the future National Health Service; the Conservative-Labor coalition government had already gone further before the war ended. With the 1945 victory of the Labor Party, the stage was set for the creation of the NHS. Different studies of the period produce different versions of who were the most powerful actors, depending largely on the politics of the authors. But all agree that the important actors were the state (with Aneurin Bevan as health minister), and the two wings of the British medical profession (the specialists, represented by the Royal Colleges, and the general practitioners, represented by the BMA). There was no representation of, or broad discussions with, other health professions or the general public—reflecting a major difference between the British political system and that of the United States.

The first draft of the NHS proposal, calling for a continuation of the nationalized hospital system, had been developed at the outset of the war. After the wartime changes had been put into effect, Arthur MacNalty, a physician-bureaucrat in the civil service and the chief medical officer of the health ministry, proposed the strategy by which the state should approach the medical profession: "The time is ripe that we should approach the medical profession in this way, not as seeking to impose a national system upon them, but taking them into council, saying, for example, these are our difficulties. Will you help us find a way out of them? On these lines it might be possible to get a National Hospital Service established by negotiation with the general agreement and support of the medical profession" (Klein 1983, 8). This first version also contained a bias that would continue throughout the creation and existence of the Service: it cared about the specialists or consultants in hospitals and would confer with them in planning the new service, but not with the general practitioners.

The key actors during the stages of revision, the proposal in 1946, and the enactment in 1948, took positions on the shape of the Service according to their special interests, but all acknowledged that *some* national system would be created after the war. Bevan worked to divide the specialists from the general practitioners; he "stuffed the specialists' mouths with gold" by offering them salaried positions in a nationalized hospital system that would continue the wartime mode but pay far higher salaries than had prevailed before the war. He also offered special status under the NHS to the teaching hospitals (which were the medical schools), thus meeting objections by the Royal Colleges. He also allowed some private practice in the NHS beds, though this was never in Britain to surpass 4% of the patients seen (Klein 1983, 1–25).

The British Medical Association, which at that time was primarily the voice of the practitioner mass, was offered a continuation of the prewar insurance model, with the state providing the funds. All patients would be covered, and each practitioner would be contracted by the NHS to treat a panel of patients. The BMA leadership protested initially and even called for a strike by the membership just before the NHS was put into effect in 1948, but the majority of the practitioners saw that they would be better off under the change, rebelled against their own leadership, and supported the Service almost unanimously. Public health functions were left under the control of local area governments. All other elements of the system, including all funds, were to be administered centrally (Eckstein 1960, 132; Klein 1983, 31–38).

Although Bevan had omitted the profession from any consultation on the broad outlines of the NHS during its early planning, he took almost all their suggestions in the details of the act. From the start, National Health was very popular among the British citizenry, and it remains so decades later, even after the cuts of the Thatcher years. In the early years of the NHS the consultant elite benefited the most and had the most influence, while the BMA got much less and had less input in either the broad system development or the details. But the worst fears of general practitioners—that they would be working for local government laymen—were not realized.

The 1950s and 1960s were the period Klein (1983, 62–99) calls the "era of consolidation and technocratic change." The National Health Service promised far more than it could immediately deliver. Although the basic principle of free health service at the point of delivery remained, the Service soon began to charge for some drugs, eyeglasses, and so on. Because the very poor could not afford these charges, they did not use the new NHS at the rate the working class and the middle class did; this pattern still held in 1990 (Klein 1983, 95). Doctors also found early on that health care had to be rationed, for global budget caps limited the expenditure in each health area or hospital. The expansion of the Service in the 1950s and 1960s was not at first matched by increased incomes for doctors or other health-care workers. Strikes in the early 1970s by groups of junior consultants and nurses, and even a threatened general strike by all consultants, led to a change in the nature of British medicine (Klein 1983, 58–62, 95).

The British Medical Association gradually increased its political solidarity by attracting a higher percentage of doctors to join—from about 50% in 1930 to a high of 85% in 1950, and the medical profession began to behave more and more like a trade union, eventually joining the Trades Union Congress. But BMA membership plunged again to 55% by 1973 as specialists and general practitioners jockeyed for position vis-à-vis the state (Jones 1981, 49). Increased solidarity on issues of pay, as a result of all working for the Service, did not help the profession increase—or even maintain—its overall status during this period. The monopoly on advice and consent, for example, which the profession had enjoyed during the formative years of the Service, was gradually lost. In reorganizations of the NHS in 1974 and especially in 1982, other health professions were given advisory roles in the new and more complex structure of the Service (Klein 1983, 92–99). Furthermore, from the start of the NHS, bargaining committees had to be set up with more than fifty occupational groups working in the health-care field. Each bargained with the state, and the interests of one were not necessarily those of another; there was never any cross-occupational solidarity until the unions became more involved in the early 1970s.

Doctors lost ground financially as a group in the 1950s with respect to other major professional groups not in public service, gained in the 1960s, then lost ground again in the 1970s and 1980s (Jones 1981, 32–43). With the exception of some equalization between general practitioners and consultants, all doctors fell behind relative to the cost of living. And even though the NHS was not cut when the British economy lagged in the 1970s and 1980s—not even under Thatcher—doctor's raises were not in line with those in comparable professions.

In the 1974 reorganization of the National Health Service, the state gained greater control over the profession, although technical decisions were still left to the profession. The centralization of state power was marked. For example, in the early years, the teaching hospitals (the home of most prestigious consultants) were in a separate structure within the NHS. In 1974 this separate structure was removed: "The prestigious teaching hospitals lost their special independent status. Boards of governors disappeared; teaching hospitals were integrated into the administrative structure of the NHS. . . . The contrast between 1948 and 1974 was striking. While Bevan had had to make extensive concessions to the leaders of the specialists, [Keith] Joseph was able virtually to ignore the special pleadings of the consultant élite" (Klein 1983, 87). The consultants were themselves now more divided between the London teaching elite and those in the provinces; there was division as well between senior consultants and the juniors who struck in the mid-1970s, between doctors and nurses over control of hospital policy (an old grievance reinvigorated with new NHS advisory roles for nurses), and of course between general practitioners and consultants over the former's newfound equality (Klein 1983, 95; Gill 1980).

After Thatcher came to power in 1979, private and even for-profit medicine was encouraged in Britain in an attempt to weaken the NHS, which she viewed, somewhat simplistically, as the last monument of the Labor Party. In spite of Thatcher's efforts, the NHS remains popular with an overwhelming majority of British citizens, but the introduction of American for-profit medicine and the growth of private health insurance (now covering about 8% of the population) have led to a further split between consultants and general practitioners. Consultants, under Thatcher's revised regulations, can participate in private medicine as well as holding full-time appointments in the NHS, while general practitioners usually cannot add to their income in this way (Higgins 1988). The added income for specialists is usually not great (typically about 10%), but it highlights the philosophy of the government: for private medicine and against the NHS. The rising costs of drugs and technology also penalize the Service disproportionately. NHS hospitals often cannot buy the new technology that the private sector can afford. Thus the future in Britain may hold a two-class hospital system on the American model in place of the generally classless system of the NHS. Although there are differences in quality and equipment between major teaching hospitals and community ones, both are deprived in comparison to the new, more expensive, for-profit institutions. The moral stance of the NHS—of key importance before Thatcher—was questioned by her government's laissez-faire "buy the health you can afford" approach, which was the complete opposite of the philosophy of care for all that underlay the NHS (Higgins 1988, 237).

In sum, how has the British medical profession changed in terms of our variables of guild power between 1930 and 1990? First, British doctors have never acted as a politically united action group, for the consultants and practitioners have always had different interests and methods of medicine. The advent of the NHS codified this schism into law, requiring the general practitioner to refer patients to the specialist and making the former a permanent second-class citizen. All British doctors are registered by the General Medical Council but are in fact graduates of university or hospital medical schools—typically a university school *in* a hospital—and the exams are given by these schools or by the Royal Societies, not by the GMC. The British Medical Association, which had represented primarily the general practitioners from 1930 to about 1970, now represents a greater percentage of the consultants as well on pay issues but does not hold them together on other issues, and membership in the Royal Colleges is more important to most physicians. Furthermore, membership in a professional organization is not the same as real activity within it. For the vast majority of BMA members, the journal subscription is their only contact with the association unless they are represented by it in a pay settlement (Jones 1981, 114). Specialists prefer the specialty meetings of their group to sessions of the BMA. Public employment, however, keeps the profession from being divided between a "free practice" sector and a public sector; almost all are in the public employ.

It is also nominally one profession, unlike the two British legal professions, which have separate and quite different training pathways. Still, the distinct class origins of the specialists and the general practitioners continue to divide British doctors. The upper-class and upper-middle-class Oxbridge background of state health administrators in the civil service enables them to understand the consultants, to work well with them, and to understand their point of view. Both groups are separated by a gap of manners and attitudes from most general practitioners, who are of working-class and lower-middle-class background to a far greater degree, in 1990 as in 1930. In recent years foreign-born and foreign-trained general practitioners have also become more common in a nation that is concerned with these national differences.

Politically, most doctors are moderate (though not Thatcherite) Conservatives, which is not in their minds incompatible with a public-sector job and even with unionlike activities. A significant minority were socialist in the 1930s and involved in the Socialist Medical Association; the younger physicians in the 1990s are quite militant and somewhat to the political left of their elders, though few tend to join leftist associations. But political membership per se does not divide the profession as much as class differences and the split between specialist and general practitioner.

Medical training takes place in university-linked teaching hospitals, but the link to the university is rather weak. The only important difference is that between, on the one hand, Oxbridge and the better teaching hospitals in London and, on the other, hospitals connected to the provincial universities. Most specialists train at Oxford, Cambridge, or an elite hospital like Guys, or Hammersmith, while those who train elsewhere usually become general practitioners (Robson 1973, 421). The actual number of graduates each year is controlled by the medical profession, working with the University Grants Committee; the profession still has some guild power in this dimension, for it has not allowed a runaway growth in numbers in the 1970s and 1980s, as happened in the United States. The decisions on numbers and types of graduate medical training—specialist training—are made by the Council for Postgraduate Medical Education (with its members from the Royal College of Physicians, the Royal College of Surgeons, specialist associations, and teaching staffs), but it has its non-Council staff members from the Department of Health and Social Services (the updated and expanded Ministry of Health).

This body also allocates specialists after training, and they are thus more fairly spread around the map than are the general practitioners, who are less involved with the state in training—though regions can be designated by the Council as off limits if too many general practitioners practice there. In spite of state attempts to control placement, however, there are two National Health Services—the overstaffed one in London and certain other locations and the understaffed NHS in both general practice and hospitals in Wales and the industrial North of England and Scotland. These areas of staffing surplus and shortage correspond, of course, to the wealthy and poor areas of Britain, and the NHS has not succeeded in equalizing access to care in these two regions (Hart 1971; Navarro 1978).

Control over the workplace, the second dimension of guild power, is complex within the British medical system and can best be conceived in two areas, one of technical decision making and another of budget control. As the latter area assumes more importance, it begins to affect the former. The broad-scale budgetary area is controlled by the state, the narrow technical dimension—which the medical profession effectively widens to cover much that is determined in other countries by state policy—is shaped by the profession. Until the Thatcher era the role of professional autonomy was quite broad within this system, but even then it had limits. The state told the regions and they in turn told the hospitals and the doctors what the broad parameters and the fiscal limits were, and the doctors were allowed to make all decisions within these parameters. These included the decision not to treat someone, for the NHS guaranteed treatment but not a specific procedure; it was up to the doctor to decide a specific course of action, or whether action would be taken at all. Thus a patient over a specified age could be denied certain care, kidney dialysis, for example, and any patient needing nonurgent surgery, as for a hernia, could be put on a long waiting list (Higgins 1988, 189–92).

The private sector, for those who can afford it, allows private operations, usually in private and for-profit hospitals. Yet here, though the doctor is not constrained by the state, he is often constrained by management (usually not physicians), who encourage certain operations but discourage others on profit grounds. If a physician is in a specialty where operations are likely to be profitable, then he will often try to get into this small but expanding sector. Still, no more than 10% of care in Britain is in the private sector. Most patients, and most physicians most of the time, remain in the NHS (Higgins 1988, 227–39).

British doctors do not control the market for services; the state does, through the NHS. The Service is available for all Britons, regardless of income, and many who could enjoy private insurance and hospitals choose not to. By not having to compete for patients, the average doctor in Britain feels at an advantage with respect to the American physician, though he may envy the American salary. And to some degree doctors can control changes in policy within the NHS—to encourage the Service to pay for some procedure demanded by many patients, for example—through medical representation on the complex set of advisory committees.

Thatcher was the first British prime minister since World War II to try to build a private-market sector in health care, to offer competition to the public sector, to go from a state-controlled to a market system like the United States'. Yet these Conservative attempts have faltered in the 1980s because as more middle- and working-class patients with higher bills patronized the private market, the cost of services skyrocketed and health insurance premiums were adjusted upwards. This in turn has led to decreased numbers of subscribers to private plans—only about 7–8% of the population at their peak in the mid-1980s (Higgins 1988, 117). Private medicine simply is not attractive enough to most patients, except for members of the upper class and managers who predominantly use it. Although there are new incentives to doctors to practice privately (all consultants may now do so even while remaining full time within the NHS), it is the patients who ultimately choose—and they are still, after more than a decade of government encouragement of private practice, faithful to the NHS.

The imposition of the NHS cost the British medical profession some measure of the final dimension of guild power, control by the profession over its relation to the state. Then, as the NHS has been called upon to do more and more with essentially the same resources as in the early years—and with far fewer resources than are available in France or Germany—the profession has lost yet more control. Until Thatcher, the state had generally deferred to the profession on many details of the running of the NHS, including numbers of students, numbers of hospitals, and even to some extent geographical concentrations of doctors. Yet this latitude was a gift that has been taken back in recent years, and the Royal Colleges and medical schools have lost some of their influence over the state. Doctors in Britain are well on their way to being expert employees on the model of engineers.

It is in the nature of the British compromise that the state delegates power to groups outside its borders, but it can renege on this delegation. Unlike most solicitors in law or other private-sector professions, the status of most physicians vis-à-vis the state—no matter how special and privileged that status might seem to be at a particular time—means that they are vulnerable whenever the state changes its philosophy about decision making, or even about the value of a large public sector. Thus the trend to more control over the NHS by the central government, (as in the last two Service reorganizations), the rejection by the Thatcher government of the old "consult the interests" model of previous Labor and Conservative governments, and the slow death of the old popular philosophy that citizens were "all in it together" suggest a return to the days before the NHS.

An example of the new Thatcherite philosophy came with the recommendations of a parliamentary committee of her supporters and with the state's new contracts with the general practitioners and specialists in 1989–1990 (Johnson 1990). The Thatcher government rearranged the nature of the payment of general practitioners, paying them primarily under capitation instead of under a fee system that maximizes treatment for need. Under the revamped system, each general practitioner is conceived of as a "budget center" and is paid under a system that tends to deemphasize the treatment of the elderly and others chronically ill. The government, in other words, now intervenes in what previously were technical medical decisions. This changing of the boundary between what is professional and what is policy, and the accompanying shift toward a free-market model within the system, has been fought by the medical profession, which has continued to campaign against the Thatcher changes. Yet they signed the contract, showing the power and leverage that the British state can exert against the power of a profession—in this case against doctors' guild power to control their workplace—when government leaders reject the course of collaboration with the profession that all previous governments have chosen in setting up the system.

Hospital care would also be affected by the shift toward a for-profit model; if taken to their logical conclusions, the Conservative policies would so change the nature of the Health Service as to make it unrecognizable to those who set it up in the 1940s. Although the hospital changes had not been realized by late 1995, any changes in the setup of the Service would exacerbate the existing inequity. The gaps between the richer specialists and the average general practitioner will increase—and the state will sit by, or even cheer, the changes. And these gaps and arguments within the profession will continue to weaken it precisely when it needs solidarity to fight back.

The Thatcher government redefined the nature of professional autonomy in medicine not by absenting itself from the process but by enforcing greater bureaucratic regulation of what Freidson called the heart of the medical game: diagnosis and treatment of the patient by the physician. Starr and Immergut (1987) note that the boundaries between professional and political decisions are always in a process of change. Johnson observes that in Britain the state's intervention into previously neutral or nonpolitical areas of professional function may ultimately prove self-destructive, for states require professional expertise to function, and such extreme intervention—in effect publicly disparaging that expertise—can ultimately destabilize the state (Johnson 1990, 57–63). But as we shall see, Thatcher's moves against the legal and academic professions, if not her health intervention, had popular support, so the "destabilization of the state" argument seems extreme. As our comparative work will show, there are ways besides the traditional British model before the Thatcher era for professions and states to relate to one another.

British Barristers and Solicitors: From Gentlemanly Autonomy to State and Bureaucratic Dependency

The British barrister, in his or her powdered wig, conjures up an image of an earlier day. British solicitors, the business wing of the legal profession, recall another image, that of Dickens's considerate, stout man of all affairs. Yet both images, significantly, are of the past, a past that the British legal professions have tried to protect through their ancient institutions. The present, especially since the 1960s, has brought major changes to both legal professions, which remain on the verge of still more. What are the continuities and discontinuities of this history? How have the British legal system, and the state that lies behind it, influenced the development of guild power in these groups? How have the legal professions influenced, or failed to influence, the state in return?

We can begin with the first form of guild power, power over the association. But even describing the nature of the barristers' professional association is a complicated matter. Although British barristers have a continuous history that goes back several centuries, their central association, with power to represent the profession to the state, was founded after World War II. At first, the Bar Council was dependent on the Inns of Court for support. The Senate of the Bar, which represents all barristers and includes about 80% of them as members, grew out of the Bar Council in 1966 (Abel 1988b, 59). Before then, each of the four Inns of Court, to which a barrister must belong and from which he is called to the practice of law, constituted his major professional frame of reference. The four Inns practically never agreed to act in common on any topic. And only occasionally did the Inns formally train lawyers. The Inns were self-perpetuating oligarchies, with senior barristers and judges, in the role of "benchers," acting as the primary decision makers for each subguild. Decade after decade, they acted to veto practically any attempt to modernize the bar. How could a profession so recently organized become so powerful without a strong association? How could it develop a monopoly on representation in the higher courts and have a monopoly in supplying higher court judges? The answer lies in the lack of challenges to the profession's legitimacy, its sound harboring within the British class system, and, until recently, the secure division of labor between barristers and their colleagues, the British solicitors (Abel 1988c; Podmore 1980).

Long before the twentieth century, British barristers were expected (though not formally required) to be graduates of Oxbridge, but they were not expected to study law there. Rather, an aspiring barrister applied to an Inn, with letters of reference from two barristers and a statement of his family's social position. Once a candidate was accepted into the Inn, his social position and the network of relationships that accompanied it gave him the contacts with which to arrange a pupilage—a one- to three-year training period with a barrister—as well as the wherewithal to withstand a further period after completing training during which he could expect at best to break even. The Inns have resisted all attempts to change this system, stressing its importance in ensuring an upper-class bar. In recent years the British legal aid system has made it possible for more young barristers re-gardless of class to make a living in their earlier years of practice. Still, half of those who complete pupilage (which is now required) and take the bar final exam leave the bar to work in private employment, which disqualifies them from the barrister profession, or leave the field of law altogether (Abel 1988c, 74–76).

Only with strong social contacts, including a family willing to support one for a period that can last up to seven years after college graduation, can the average student make a career in this field. This situation has long created dissatisfaction—but little action—within the bar. Only when the state took a role in the sponsorship of the younger members of the profession, through the financing of legal aid, did younger barristers have a chance to act as an interest group without jeopardizing their future earnings (Abel 1988c, 96). They worry about this because of the conservative structure of the bar, with junior barristers deferring to senior barristers, senior "juniors" deferring to Queen's Counsellors (Q.C.s), and all deferring to judges before whom they try cases, some of whom may even be benchers of their own Inn. With the creation of the Senate of the Bar, all of the members of all of the Inns, including the previously disenfranchised junior barristers, were finally represented by a single agency. Among other functions, the Senate of the Bar now acts as a union, bargaining with the state for higher legal fees in the court system, especially for legal aid cases. It has also worked to create more favorable conditions for apprenticeship.

Note, however, that formal training did not become a responsibility of the bar until the 1980s, with the establishment of the Inns of Court Law School. And this law school is not required for all candidates. The majority study law at a university or attend a professional "cram school," which is actually affiliated with their competitors, the solicitors. The Senate of the Bar also acts as a disciplinary agent, but a very weak one, prosecuting about 1% of those accused of wrongdoing. Finally, it acts as the general representative of the bar with respect to the state (Abel 1988c, 50, 133–36).

The Senate of the Bar has apparently not taken over the role of determining how many barristers are to be produced each year, for such control would require decisions that the Bar Council, as a complex representational body, cannot make. This does not mean that there have not been trends of major importance. Before 1950 records were extremely poor, especially concerning the numbers of foreign students who, while training to be barristers in London, never intended to practice there upon completing the requirements. In 1959, 75% of those admitted to the Inns of Court were foreign students (Abel-Smith and Stevens 1967, 360). According to Richard Abel (1988c, 67), membership in the bar fluctuated widely during the first half of the century. Each World War was costly to the British bar, both in terms of men lost and in shortfalls in production for periods after the war. Half the bar served in World War II, for example, and many were wounded or killed. All of the fluctuations produced no net change in the size of the bar: virtually the same number of barristers were practicing in 1951 as in 1891 (Abel 1988c, 68–69).

The bar admissions rate plunged between 1951 and 1961, and the number of barristers entering practice fell 57% from 1947 to 1960. Yet the numbers turned around again in 1969—according to some, because nearly all candidates by this time were studying law on scholarships to universities or polytechnic institutions, which exempted them from part of the bar final. Both university instruction in law and candidates for the bar shot up in the 1970s. As Richard Abel observed, "All of this signifies that the expansion of undergraduate law teaching and the provision of government grants reduced or even eliminated any obstacle posed by the Bar examination (although entry to law faculties might be a new bottleneck). At the same time, however, the cost of pupillage, the scarcity of tenancies, the importance of personal contacts in obtaining both and the difficulty of making a living during the early years of practice remained significant hurdles and may even have grown in magnitude" (Abel 1988c, 69).

Solicitors had a different professional approach from barristers, both to recruiting and to training, and have more consciously developed an associational strategy. Theirs is the more "modern" of the legal professions and was by the 1990s almost the equal of the barristers' in prestige, with a major role in shaping legal opinion. This has been a long, hard battle, one that has counterposed professional training focused on skills and testing against the status-locked system of the barrister. Solicitors, who are about ten times as numerous as barristers, were not originally required or even encouraged to earn a college degree in law—or in anything else. Rather, their primary education consisted of a five-year apprenticeship, for which they paid two hundred pounds—a considerable sum before the Second World War. But solicitors' offices were more spread out on the map than barristers, so students outside of London could live at home while serving apprenticeships (Abel 1988c, 41).

Solicitors, because they envied the status of barristers, took an aggressive approach to professionalization, establishing educational hurdles earlier and taking them more seriously than barristers did, and giving more weight to tested competence than to inherited rank and social position. They were for many years viewed as the junior legal profession, for in the established division of labor in British law work, they cannot argue cases in the higher courts, nor are they eligible for most court appointments. The only avenue of upward social mobility for a solicitor is by generating business for himself and his firm. (Barristers always practice as individuals, but solicitors, like American lawyers, can join firms). The solicitor's main areas of expertise have been "conveyancing" (real estate transactions), family law work, including wills, trusts, and divorce, and cases of injury on the roads or in the workplace. When court appearances are necessary, the solicitor briefs a barrister, who would then discuss the case with the solicitor and then argue it in court. The solicitor is thus the client's counselor, the barrister their hired gun in court—although the barrister, who is forbidden from approaching clients directly, would resist that characterization.

The Law Society represents the associational interests of solicitors. This organization—to which a vast majority of solicitors belong—has had a long history of fighting for the rights of the junior branch. It has also been in the forefront, since the 1970s at least, of efforts to combine the two professions into one lawyer group—a position that the barristers have resisted successfully. Evidence of the latter group's continuing power was found in the 1979 Royal Commission on Legal Services Summary Report (1979, 13), which recommended against combining barristers (or any other professions) and solicitors in interdisciplinary firms. The Law Society protected its existing power by successfully lobbying the same commission to recommend against the representation of solicitors in pay negotiations by the British Legal Association, a more radical group of younger lawyers. In recent years, however, the Law Society has had less support from the rank and file membership. Only two hundred solicitors out of the roughly sixteen thousand who belong to the association attended its national meeting in London in 1994, for example, a grim sign for the future.

To assess our second dimension of guild power, control over the workplace, in the British case, we must view the legal aspect separately from the sociological aspect. Legally, a barrister who quits private practice to work on salary for anyone, be it the state or a private concern, ceases to be a barrister by that act. Representing the state—for the foreign service, for example—disqualifies one from arguing before the bench, though one can, of course, still use one's legal training. In contrast, a solicitor may offer advice from such a post and remain a member of his profession (Abel 1988c, 41). In practice, however, the carefully protected autonomy of the individual barrister is imperfect. The role of the state has grown, for example, as the percentage of public funding has increased for barristers' services. Furthermore, barristers must practice in chambers—officially designated settings, usually connected to one of the Inns (though space here is in short supply) and headed by a chief barrister, in whose premises other barristers are practicing "on sufferance."

All work goes through a barrister's clerk. Until very recently, these were lower-middle-class or working-class entrepreneurial "fixers" in the hierarchy, who intervened between the solicitors firms on the one hand and the individual barristers on the other hand. These individuals have tremendous power over the career of a young barrister, for the convention remains that barristers are not to look for work themselves but that they are obliged to accept every brief given to them by the barrister's clerk in chambers. The clerk also assigns work to complete the court schedules of the barristers in his office, sometimes even trading cases with clerks in other sets of chambers. The court caseload of a group of barristers is analogous to the musical commitments of a rock group, and the barrister's clerk is their handler or agent. Because he earns a percentage of the bookings of his barristers, he is inclined to maximize the caseload of each barrister in his office. But woe betide the young barrister who falls afoul of the clerk in his chambers; he or she can be starved out of the profession (Flood 1983).

The everyday work of barristers encourages conformity. Much has been reported of barrister's clerks who have refused to brief young female barristers on the grounds that they might charge less than a man for a case. Some of this generally conservative crowd also let political prejudice get in the way of fair assignments. The growing feminization of the barrister's clerk role—they have been called "legal executives" since the 1980s—can be expected to redress some of the discrimination (Kennedy 1978, 148–67). But the conformity goes further. To succeed in the profession means to go from the role of barrister (or "junior") to the elite group of senior or Queen's Counsellors, who are required to have accompanying juniors at each trial and to charge more for their time, among other perks. One must be nominated for the role by the lord chancellor—the highest legal official of the Queen—and recommended for the post by one's fellow barristers. Needless to say, barristers who have made a career of complaining about the customary rules of the bar do not usually receive such nominations.

The typical pose of the barrister before the judge—who may be a bencher in one's inn, or connected in some way to someone in power—is humility, and a marked unwillingness to criticize the system. Judges, in contrast, can reward or punish not only lapses in courtroom behavior but any opposition to the status quo in the legal profession (Hazell 1978, 99–129).

Solicitors work in a different kind of workplace, and under a different set of rules. Unlike barristers, who have a monopoly over arguments in the higher courts, solicitors do not have a monopoly over legal advice. The de facto monopoly they enjoyed in the early 1900s, especially over the conveyancing of land that was a major part of their practice, has been challenged by the new profession, approved by the British government, of "licensed conveyancer." Banks and trust companies compete with solicitors for wills and trust work, and psychological counselors and arbitrators compete with them in the area of divorce (Abel-Smith and Stevens 1967, 377–405; Abel 1988c, 218–34).

The development of large solicitors firms in London, like Freshfields, with more than eighty partners, makes the position of solicitor highly dependent on the firm for which the individual works. The use of many junior solicitors, plus associates who are in training or otherwise nontenured, further threatens the livelihood of solicitors. The solo practitioner in the countryside can ill afford the chipping away at his customary monopoly in conveyancing work, though the senior partner at a large firm dealing with corporate law and other commercial matters of a specialized nature does not seem to mind. In many ways, the British solicitors are coming to resemble the American profession: an elite bar for corporation work, and a mass bar of solo practitioners dealing with the specific problems of the middle class (Abel 1988c, 190–203).

Autonomy in the workplace, however, is not parceled out according to that hierarchy. While senior solicitors in large firms clearly have more autonomy than their juniors, they do not have the autonomy of the small practitioner in an English village. That solo solicitor retains some of the general capacity to advise the client that has been lost by those working in the larger firms, almost exclusively as consultants to specific businesses (Abel 1988c, 119–203). That autonomy has a price, though: the large solicitors firms pay much better than life in the country, whatever its nonmonetary rewards.

Both barristers chambers and solicitors firms are growing in size, and adopting the more bureaucratic working conditions that characterize the larger firms. Although technically barristers are all solo practitioners, in London the average size of a set of barristers practicing together, sharing a clerk and offices, grew from 7.5 barristers in 1939 to 16.7 in 1984; in the provinces the growth was from 5.6 to 12.6 barristers per chamber (Abel 1988c,

103). Barristers have also adopted computer technology for word processing and scheduling—all of these work better with groups of barristers. The large solicitors firms, and to some extent barristers chambers, have developed areas of special expertise, and will come together to work in certain areas. A solicitors firm specializing in admiralty law, for example, will work with a barristers office experienced in arguing such cases in court, or a divorce firm of solicitors will brief an office of barristers known to be good at this kind of work in court.

More generally, however, control over the British legal profession is exerted by those who write the check. Both barristers and solicitors are evolving from professions for which individuals and their needs are primary into professions with large bureaucracies, public and private, as their primary clients. These larger clients are more likely to interest themselves in the conditions of production of legal work—as the Thatcher government has with the rising cost of legal aid—or in the private sector. Private firms that in the past have hired solicitors firms to represent them will increasingly hire their own house counsel, who will work under much more closely controlled conditions. In general, because of needs to bargain against the state for salary increases or efforts to serve their business clients better, both barristers and solicitors enjoy less autonomy than they did in the 1930s. That solicitors are the more popular profession—even among honors graduates of Oxbridge in the late 1970s—probably indicates that the professions' relative positions have changed. Because of the role of the state in supporting legal services, barristers can be assured of a low-level income, while for solicitors, the rewards are much higher, though more likely to be in large bureaucractic settings, dealing with the problems of British (and foreign) corporations (Abel 1988c, 280).

Barristers and solicitors each had a strategy for the third element of guild power, control over their markets. But the state, since 1965, has interfered with these strategies. A Labor government increased the scope of legal aid markedly, to the point where the senior branch of barristers has become dependent upon it for support. Then a more Conservative government entered the politics of payment, certain that the money would be better spent elsewhere. These cutbacks forced the barrister profession to reunite, and, due in part to this shock, barristers have shown greater strength in recent years. On the other hand, increased state spending on legal services expanded their market.

To understand the interrelation of the state and the market, it is necessary first to assess how the division of labor shapes the market. Barristers can only take cases in court that have been given to them by solicitors. Solicitors, meanwhile, have traditionally only given a small percentage of their time to arguing criminal cases or preparing them for a barrister. (The profits for this kind of work are usually minimal). Thus to enlarge the role of the barrister in legal aid without increasing the support for solicitors the state became a major de facto referrer of cases to barristers, without the intervention of a solicitor. The flood of new legal aid cases constituted 91% of a junior barrister's criminal practice in 1971. Most junior barristers depended on this kind of work regardless of their ultimate specialty. This in turn changed the relation between the class system and the barrister profession (Abel 1988c, 117–18). Not only were growing numbers of Redbrick university graduates joining the products of Oxbridge at the bar, but the legal aid scheme gave the market for barristers' services a new lower-class component. The fees from this practice gave barristers of middle-class status a livelihood through training and the earlier years of practice. A more middle-class bar served a more lower-class clientele. Conversely, the solicitors moved up the scale, losing some of their conveyancing work, but gaining—in competition with the accounting profession—more and lucrative work for corporations.

Solicitors have never enjoyed monopoly conditions on their market, although they have had strong informal control. For fifty years the solicitors had a de facto monopoly on conveyancing work, for example (Abel-Smith and Stevens 1967, 382–89). The government Monopolies Commission, along with action in the 1980s by the Department of Labor and Commerce, finally struck the monopoly down by giving a wider role to licensed conveyancers. This strategy—breaking the monopoly of a group by creating a competing group—will probably not destroy the solicitor's dominance in this area. But the state has set a precedent of ending a de facto monopoly of solicitors over legal service. Chartered accountants, who are beginning to challenge the rights of business lawyers in the United States, have challenged the British solicitors in business law (Abel-Smith and Stevens 1967, 401–2). Solicitors may not have seen these challenges coming and also may have underproduced their numbers, encouraging the division of the market with other groups (Abbott 1988, 275–78). But it must be noted that they never had an official monopoly over any part of their market.

Finally, however, it is important to consider the role of the legal profession with regard to the British state separate from market conditions. It is important to return to our concept of the British state as an amateur one— one that does not require specific professional training, as do the French and German states, in engineering or law, respectively, as a condition of employment. The amateur state grew primarily from the British class system, under which all professional work, except that by Queen's Counsel barristers, is beneath the uppermost level of prestige. There is as well a desire, since the foundation of the civil service, to have those responsible for the state be able to write and think in good, clear English. Because the state did not specify legal skills as central to policy-making positions and thus did not create a state-based market segment, the market for lawyers was much smaller than such a market in France, Italy, and Germany.

Furthermore, although there has been a growth of administrative courts, on the European model, to handle the problems of the welfare state, these have not used professional judges trained in the law. Rather, Britain since the war has expanded its justice of the peace system to include special courts for workers' compensation, welfare provision, and so on—all of which are conducted by laypeople, not lawyers. The justices of the peace prefer to have people appear without counsel; the result is a system of justice run by amateurs, who even pass sentence for lesser crimes. The administrative courts provide a major source of jobs for law graduates in continental Europe. The justice of the peace system in Britain has not made the administration of justice less fair than if professional judges, trained in law, were used, though there have been complaints about the age and values of some of these lay judges. Some are considered by the British people as too young, while others are thought too old and conservative.

The most recent proposals for changes in the two legal professions, stressing the increased role of the market in professional affairs and made within the context of the Common Market changes of 1992, will be the focus of our final observations on the increasing role of the state in controlling the market for legal services. In the British case, the Thatcher initiative in changing the role of the state vis-à-vis professional groups was a matter not of deregulation but rather of reregulation, in which the boundaries between state control and professional control of practice were rearranged (Johnson 1990). In 1989 the Thatcher government proposed new procedures for licensing professional lawyers, which would have effected radical changes in the relation between the two legal professions and the relation between the professions and the state. The existing regulations, under which barristers alone could argue cases in the higher courts and solicitors had to refer all clients to barristers for higher court work, were to be replaced by steps toward effective fusion of the two professions. Also, the solicitors' partial monopoly over conveyancing, which had been attacked since the mid-1980s, was to be ended. Finally, the prohibitions were to be eliminated against advertising by barristers and against their appearing in court as employees.

The Law Society, representing the solicitors, and the Bar Council, representing the barristers, responded differently to these proposals. The solicitors, who are the majority profession—and the one that after 1992 would be able to practice and argue cases in any court in Europe—were generally favorable (Johnson 1990). But the barristers, especially the Law Lords— the judges who members of their Inns and who sit in the House of Lords— were overwhelmingly opposed to these proposals of the government, especially the proposal that the bar lords or a committee advisory to them constitute a new licensing agency for lawyers in Britain. The barristers complained that this step would subvert the judiciary's independence from the state (Johnson 1990, appendix 2, 3–6). The compromise legislation of 1990 was a step toward the fusion of the professions.

Under the pressure of the bill, the barristers relaxed their professional rules. As Johnson (1990, appendix 2, 7) observed,

> In order to strengthen its position the Bar also acted rapidly to remove virtually all restrictions on advertising by barristers (this only two months after rejecting advertising as "inappropriate for a consulting profession"); to allow barristers to open new chambers, thus creating more places for pupils; to allow barristers to practice without a clerk (a traditional limitation on professional expansion) and to appear in court without a solicitor. In an effort to ward off legislation, then, the bar eradicated within months many of the restrictive practices that it had successfully defended for a century or more.

The new legislation has another and more important pressure working in its favor—by 1992, all of Britain's legal workers are to be under European Common market rules. Why, then did the bar resist for so long, only to surrender in the face of legislation that would only readjust the British professions in line with those of the Continent? Johnson suggests that the professions could thus maintain that it was not the supra-British state that was dictating the changes but rather the professions and the British government itself (Johnson 1990, appendix 2, 8). The field of effective forces was in fact wider. The consumer movement allied itself with a Conservative government, worked against two long-standing professions, and under the gun of the changes in professional services inherent in the Common Market union in 1992, began a long-desired reform.

In summary, the British legal professions are examples of incomplete professionalization in a nation that still is open-minded about the necessity for professional monopoly. Their haphazard attitude toward credentials, their many pathways for reaching professional status, the degree to which that status continues to be challenged by a Conservative political party all lend strength to the idea that professions cannot be understood separate from their immediate social context. Clearly the autonomy and guild power of the British legal professions, well established in the 1930s, are under strong challenge in the 1990s.

British Engineers: A Profession with Dirty Hands

Perhaps nowhere do class origins of a group play as important a part in the group's ultimate role as for engineers. Britain's profession of engineering is, in fact, a collection of individuals with differing levels of training—most of it on the job—and educated mostly in programs affiliated with local polytechnic institutions. The polytechnics, not on the same level as universities, serve student-engineers hired by corporations out of grammar school; through alternate periods of work and study, successful students achieve a slightly higher status within the corporation. Just who is designated as an "engineer" is, in fact, up to the management of a given corporation, with little or no relevance to a candidate's credential (or lack of one). Although the statistics vary according to nebulous definitions about 80% of British engineers are of working-class background (Whalley 1985; Glover and Kelley 1987).

The state's sponsorship of polytechnics since 1965 has not changed these demographics. The state designated the polytechnics as a distinct educational forum, inferior in the minds of most Britons to the universities. British engineering qualifying associations have no power vis-à-vis employers and do not bargain collectively with them. Unlike the members of the British Medical Association or the Law Society, the engineers are employees of the companies that hire them. And only a about a third of engineers are members of the qualifying associations. A significant minority are members of trade unions. The largest union—TASS—is affiliated with the Trades Union Conference and the Labor Party. The "professional" union—United Kingdom Association of Professional Engineers—which requires chartered status for membership, represents only the top division in a three-division pattern of professional (chartered), technical, and nonprofessional engineers. Loosely affiliated with the Conservative Party, the professional association is considered very weak and of little help on the workplace (Whalley 1985, 181–82).

Most engineers pay little or no attention to the activities of professional associations that represent a minority of British engineers at most and are in fact run by engineers who have become de facto managers (Whalley 1985, 190–94). TASS, which does not respect the fine distinctions between classes of engineers, is the only one with any power in British industry. Engineers belong to unions for pragmatic purposes rather than ideological ones—to try and keep their salaries higher than the manual workers in their own workplaces, for example. Yet no researcher considers British engineers to be a "new working class" in Mallet's sense for French technicians, for they are on management's side when it comes to progression through the ranks, and they tend to distance themselves socially from the workers—and the physical setup of the typical British company tends to foster this kind of separation (Whalley 1985, 190–94).

The structured methods of training engineers firmly place each individual in a corporate setting, defining his work program and role in terms of company actions and company need. In addition, studies of the profession since 1960 have agreed that the profession is not a primary pathway into management in Britain as it is in the United States or on the Continent (Whalley 1985, 39–65). The antitechnological bias of existing managements—most of whom received arts or business degrees from universities—includes the assumption that all engineers are technicians, not capable of managing. There are exceptions to this rule, of course, and actual studies of what British engineers actually do on the workplace reveal that management is part of their daily work. But the ideology continues to influence hiring and promotion policy in most companies.

The work-study pattern of progressing in the field might also contribute to corporate assumptions about engineers' unsuitability for management. But beyond the "subject" bias there is the prevailing class bias of Britain. Because a minority of engineers come from middle- or upper-class homes, most lack the social polish and vocabulary that comes from a university background. Many British companies have separate dining facilities for the various ranks of employees, for example, and engineers usually are prohibited from attending the management dining hall. This kind of social snobbery, of course, may be one of the reasons why British industry is so far behind: those who don't know production manage it, and those who do are cut off from management.

There is another related explanation, cited both by Whalley and by Glover and Kelley, of the British pattern of engineer employment: the overwhelming cultural bias of the British upper class, and thus of British institutions generally, against technical expertise, the very possession of which signifies social unacceptability, much as "going into trade" did a hundred years ago (Glover and Kelley 1987, 234). This bias makes training as an engineer a liability in itself. Most engineers are trained in the polytechnics, where the emphasis is on practical knowledge, not theory (though this is changing in recent years). Most studies have indicated that engineering students are somewhat deficient in basic science education and that engineering slots in these programs often are not filled, given the job future of most engineers after graduation.

Most engineers start out near the bottom of their company hierarchy, regardless of whether they have a degree, for most British companies, not attuned to academia and not involved in shaping the polytechnic programs, do not value the training that the students received. Engineers begin only one step up from the work floor, regardless of their background, and then most prove themselves practically, by demonstrating not book learning but expertise in the setting. They are advanced through a series of steps to the upper positions within the engineering divisions—research, development, and production—with somewhat more room for initiative in the first of these areas. Still, it is important to remember that British engineering does not emphasize profitability as much as American or Continental engineers do, for profitability is monitored by management. Nor is the engineer a natural scientist in any sense of the term. The latter have first-class degrees from universities. Still, in most British corporations, anyone with a science background would start even with the engineers in the workplace. Only a few large research divisions, like that at British Petroleum, have separate staffs of scientists, on which a "science-in-industry" career track can be developed (Prandy 1965; Sofer 1970).

The relation between the workplace and the polytechnic can, of course, be improved. But the basic problem is that British industry does not value credentials, and the polytechnic teachers value theory and research rather than the practical skills required by employers. Thus there is little encouragement by employers for engineers to go back to school, no automatic advancement after the completion of a work-study degree program at the nearby polytechnic, no payment of fees or other expenses for graduate education. (The British government used to pay all fees for students, but this is no longer true.) Many engineers have major problems moving within and between companies. Obtaining a degree or a (very rare) graduate credential helps one secure membership in the relevant qualifying association—to allow oneself to be called a chartered engineer. But because British industry refuses to value such credentials, this professional advancement does not accelerate progress through the ranks of engineering divisions, and with the exception of the minority who develop engineering as a consulting practice, it does not help one financially. It is true that in some older corporations with more finely graduated work situations—those in metalworking, for example—the credential may produce improved status within the plant. Surprisingly, however, the electronics and computer industries—in the United States the exclusive province of graduate engineers—seem to value credentials less than the older, traditional industries (Whalley 1985, 157). There is some indication that chartered engineer status is required for those who wish to leave engineering and enter management. But as long as few engineers are asked into management, the requirement of credentials for such advancement is moot.

In conclusion, the associational power of British engineering professional associations is nil. (Although most engineers in Britain call themselves professionals, they do not mean this in the sense of belonging to a profession but in terms of acting "professionally" on the workplace [Whalley 1985,

154–58]). Union activity is a defensive action, and of course belonging to a union puts one in the opposite camp from management. About 33% of British engineers do belong to unions, and about 50 to 60% do not oppose them on principle—perhaps a holdover from their working-class background. But the nation's engineers are not strongly unionized, either. So in terms of any collective power as a profession, their power would be negligible. The report of the parliamentary Finniston Commission in 1980 recommended changes in the field, in particular a greater reliance on credentials and the creation of technical grades. But this report was issued primarily by the leaders of the profession and had no binding power on employers, who have not moved far to implement it (Finniston 1980).

Control over the workplace, the second element of guild power, provides only a slightly different story. The most careful studies of what engineers actually do on workplaces put them in another category from those of the manual worker. In Whalley's terms, they are "trusted employees" (Whalley 1985, 124). In the British situation, education is company-based, and allowing a student to alternate terms of work and study requires the permission of the company. Furthermore, there is little or no concept of "technocracy"—the engineer as technocratic manager, in the French sense of the term. The practicality of the workplace education—which most engineers feel is superior to the polytechnic education that has become increasingly more theoretical since the 1970s—rewards practical "know-how" and "know-what" over theory. This means that, in actual studies by Whalley in the 1980s, of the pseudonymous Metalco and Computergraph, engineers' work was arranged to be project specific as it applied to research and task specific as it applied to monitoring or quality control of production.

Although the factor is probably exaggerated based on the companies that Whalley chose, costs do not appear to play quite the part in engineering work in Britain that they do in the United States. British engineers in both Metalco and Computergraph focused on process and let the managers—most of whom were accountants—set the financial parameters and veto the development of certain lines of work (Whalley 1985, 124). It is always within the control of British management to show how "market forces" preclude the development of a product. Because engineers, as employees, accept the basic right of management to make these decisions, and because management can subdivide a company and its units infinitely if it wants to subject any unit to the "market forces", the firing of whole divisions can result, or, less drastically, the transfer of engineers from one area of the company to another. Engineers have no control over what products are to be developed and the cost constraints on their development. Nor do most engineers even participate in the management decisions, for they are considered unskilled in areas of finance, even though they work with financial parameters every day (Whalley 1985, 124–39). In more general terms, "British engineers are characterized not by possession of a particular training or set of skills, but by occupancy of a distinctive place in the division of labor. The nature of that place, access to it, even the qualifications, are controlled not by engineers but by employers" (Whalley 1985, 87).

In summary, the strongly developed hierarchy of British companies, the lack of any real participation by engineers in the decisions that affect their working lives, and the lack of relation of the educational system to the workplace system all contribute to the lack of guild power for British engineers. (It does little good to have a work-and-study pattern of education if the education is not valued by the company and if the corporation cannot participate in defining what is to be taught in the polytechnics.) Engineers thus have little mobility. The result is a condition that has not changed significantly since the early days of the Industrial Revolution: engineers are viewed as highly specialized members of the upper working class, with loyalty to the companies, but not as management material. The absence of a professional tradition—engineers as a distinct class for themselves—combined with their lack of upward mobility in most companies, limits the further development of industry in Britain.

Another characteristic of most British corporations hinders the development of a market that engineers could control: the lack of much movement *between* companies. The typical engineer will make one or two moves at most in a lifetime. Because the companies do the real training, the kind that most engineers themselves value, and because company-bred skills are job and place specific, engineers are not likely to develop general skills that they can use to bargain for higher wages at another company. The shortage of engineers is real in Britain, but the companies do not generally want graduates of the technological programs at the polytechnics unless the students are already their own employees, in which case the employer controls the market.

Engineers do not control the production of engineering graduates, either. That is the role of the polytechnics, which are more closely allied to the world of education than that of the profession itself. Even in an applied field like engineering the training is far too abstract for the companies that hire the products (or lend them out for periods of education). Nor does the state play much of a role in getting industry to work more closely with the polytechnics. The Thatcher government has fostered more training in engineering, but has not been able to stop academic drift—a pattern wherein the polytechnics tend to teach progressively more like the universities, with an emphasis on research, while the students there are increasingly deficient in the basic math and science required to follow the lectures. Furthermore, the laissez-faire attitude of the Thatcher and Major governments toward intervention in industry prevented them from seeing whether a three-level program instituted in 1985 for certifying and training engineers has actually shaped criteria for promotion within the plant. According to Whalley, it has not. The employer alone controls the market for engineering services in Britain.

The role of the state in the profession in Britain has grown with time. Although in the 1930s the state virtually ignored engineers, it has slowly developed a concern with the performance of British industry and thus an interest in the engineering profession. But the late date of the state's real interest—the 1980s—has left Britain far behind in developing useful programs. The Finniston Report is a recent example of the state's interest and limited role. Because the British state is little concerned with the running of British industry, except in the public sector, it has little or no leverage with which to make any of its recommendations stick. What little evidence there is of formalization of engineering levels is found primarily in state-connected industry.

Although Thatcher, as we shall see, abolished tenure in Britain, she could not make the courses taught in individual polytechnics more practical and relevant to the workplace. Her pattern of funding higher education—cutting back on the funding for the universities and the older polytechnics—provided more money for the smaller and more applied polys—the ones more close to the interests of industry. But this trend was resisted by the polys themselves, which stressed that research and new products are the future of British industry and have a rightful place in the curriculum. They furthermore argued that practical training is not the function of a university or a polytechnic, regardless of the demands of British employers and the British state. On the the other hand, the most drastic of the wave of cuts to British universities in the early 1980s were to those with the most extensive relations with industry.

The underlying problem, which has great consequences for Britain, lies in the disassociated pattern of relations among the British state, the British professions, the British university system, and British industry. Because industry does not get involved in the funding or the endowment of the British universities or even the polytechnics, and because professional bodies (like the engineering qualifying associations) are isolated from the university and from industry, to get them all together to solve the problem is an almost impossible task—especially in an era when Conservative governments are cutting back on funding for education. Add to this the deeply elitist bias of the British establishment, as well as the bias against technical knowledge, and it becomes evident how much ground must be covered before engineering can be considered a profession with any guild power at all. Rather, a small, credentialed elite provides ineffectual representation while a mass of middle-level employees remain essentially immobile within their companies. In particular they are blocked from transition into management, which is the province of arts graduates and the accounting profession. As Glover and Kelley (1987, 187–88) summarize the group's plight: "Since the Second World War the status of engineers in Britain has not only not improved but has probably declined. In the same period engineers have tended to maintain their living standards compared with manual workers, but when compared with professionals like doctors, lawyers, and solicitors, and with middle managers in industry, their living standards have fallen behind."

British Academics: From Protected Elite to Harassed Mass

The British university system, and the role of academics within it, have changed drastically since the 1930s. In 1930, as for the previous fifty years, Oxbridge was the model if not the reality for British academics at the early Redbricks At this time, Oxbridge dominated the Redbricks in terms of the image and role for the academic (Halsey 1992, 57–88). Halsey and Trow (1971, 72) consider the effect of this dominance, at a time of great turmoil, forty years later:

> Oxford and Cambridge still stand in the public mind for the older social and educational ideals of the cultivated member of a governing class rather than the highly trained professional expert. They are thought to embody the pedagogical ideal of an intimate relation between the teacher and the taught through the tutorial method, through shared domestic life in a human-sized collegiate organization, and through the separation of the role of the teacher and examiner. They are held up as examples of democratic self-government by academics, where the administration is either subservient to or is itself the don, individually or in committee.

But by 1990 this was not the reality throughout most of the British academic sector. The history, through five consecutive periods, of the relations among the university academics, the Association of University Teachers, the state, and its semi-independent University Grants Committee will present the broad outlines of evolution, as the profession faded from a protected elite to a harassed mass. It is a story of professionalization, then unionization, then utter defeat, as the state managed not only to devalue the profession but to eliminate selected departments within universities, finally dismantling the profession's protected status, academic tenure.

In the period before World War II, British universities could be classified in two groups: Oxbridge and the Redbricks, including the University of London, with its constituent university colleges. Many of the academics at the other institutions had received their training at Oxbridge. As late as 1969, 44% of British university teachers either had studied or taught at Oxford or Cambridge at some point in their careers. Among those academics who wish to move, about half chose Oxbridge as their preferred destination (Halsey and Trow 1971, 224, 230). The nonprofessorial model of Oxbridge, with staff allotted to each independent college, contrasted with the more hierarchical model of London, the Redbricks, and the Scottish universities. In the second model, each department has one professor, along with a group of readers and senior lecturers (approximately equivalent to associate and assistant professors in the American system) and junior lecturers. In this system the professor controls virtually all research, rules the graduate students, and generally runs the department. About 10% of British academics are professors. Oxbridge, in the last thirty years, has begun to overlay the professor system on its more classic medieval guild model, but never to the same extent as the Redbricks; in every Oxbridge college, each fellow has a vote.

During this prewar period, the Association of University teachers, the union of the teaching staff, was in its infancy. Its headquarters was in the house of its director, who had one secretary (Perkin 1969, 50–52). The British universities were partly funded by the state. The government—specifically, the Treasury department—set up the University Grants Committee as an advisory body, composed primarily of senior professors still working at the universities, and with a representative or two from the schools and industry. Every five years the treasury gave a sum of money to the UGC, which distributed it among the universities. The awards in this period tended to be small, for the Redbricks were supported primarily by their communities, and Oxbridge was financially independent, with each college having its own endowment and funds.

After World War II the British university system began to grow, and the professoriate with it. Oxbridge professors gradually became a small fraction of all British teachers, although a significant percentage of them had some former connection to Oxbridge. Most of the expansion after the war was in science and technology faculties, and in the 1960s in social science. Academic staff grew from about 3,000 in 1920, to 5,000 in 1940, to 10,000 in 1950, to about 15,000 in 1960. Then, with massive expansion in British higher education after 1963, as a result of the Robbins plan, the faculty size doubled again, to about 30,000 in 1970 (Halsey and Trow 1971, 140; Halsey 1992, 91–110).

Lord Robbins, a liberal former academic, envisioned not a mass education system, as in the United States or western Europe, but rather an expanded elite system. The Robbins plan called for an exceptionally high teacher-to-student ratio of 1:8, virtually a tutorial system throughout (Committee on Higher Education 1963). The short British school year, the opportunities for each professor to do research, the understanding that tenure would come after a three-year probationary period all made for excellent academic working conditions. During the Robbins era funds were provided for eight new universities, built more or less on the model of Oxbridge, and for major expansion of the older Redbricks—Manchester, Leeds, Leicester, Birmingham, and so on. In fact, most of the growth of the academic system took place here, rather than in the new Oxbridge-style campuses.

The British pattern of generous funding for universities was combined with an equally generous scholarship program. Every student who achieved qualifying scores in the national entrance examination ("A-levels") received a full scholarship to attend the university that admitted him or her. During the Robbins era all the universities joined in an admissions system under which applicants could be matched against the places available in their fields of choice. Also during this period, roughly the 1960s, UGC grants became a primary source for funding universities, along with student maintenance grants (Carswell 1985).

Faculty salaries were arbitrated across the system, within limits set for each rank, and were set by the UGC after consulting with both the state (the UGC had begun by this time to answer to the Division of Education and Science rather than the Treasury) and the universities. The Association of University Teachers, which had about 60% of the academics as members, bargained with the UGC as well. The UGC, whose faculty members came disproportionately from the Redbricks, with the junior lecturers generously represented, usually held salaries in check but occasionally gave way before the pressure of the AUT. Certain groups, such as the medical faculties, did better than others. One thing was clear: the system was not a free market. As Halsey and Trow observed, "On the demand side it is arguable that though there are seventy-six colleges there is only one buyer; and on both the supply and demand sides there is a strongly and widely held conception of university teaching as a single vocation which stems from the medieval guilds but which now also reflects the hierarchy of professional expertise." (Halsey and Trow, 1971, 180). Academic salaries, outside of Oxbridge, were now fixed by the chancellor of the exchequer. "One effect of the financial dependency on the state has been to move the salary variations of independent guilds (or in terms of the Victorian foundations, local academic corporations) toward the uniformity of a national bureaucracy" (Halsey and Trow 1971, 181).

By British parliamentary rules, when more than half of an enterprise is funded by state money, the state has the right to investigate how that money is spent (Carswell 1985, 86–87). Thus increased state funding increased the government's managerial role over expanding institutions in a gigantic system of universities, polytechnics (a separate hierarchy, except for the seven Colleges of Advanced Technology, which had university status), and colleges of education. A second way of funding university research was set up: research councils. Lord Robbins himself was interested in setting up the Social Science Research Council, along with expanding the funds for the Medical Research Council, the Science Research Council, and others. These councils allowed grants to go to individual researchers for particular projects. But there were other, more ominous changes:

> By the end of the 1960s . . . all was turmoil and doubt. The government's acceptance of the Robbins report led to the transfer of the UGC from the Treasury to the Department of Education and Science; the Public Accounts Committee's special report for January 1967 led to the opening of the books and records of the UGC and the universities to the inspection of the Comptroller and Auditor General; and the report of the Prices and Incomes Board of December 1968 on academic salaries seemed to herald the possibility of direct intrusion into university affairs by an instrument of government which is outside the control of the DES. (Halsey and Trow 1971, 84)

Furthermore, British universities were often disturbed in the late 1960s by the student protests that swept through academia elsewhere in the world. The proximate cause in Britain was the raising of the student fees of non-British students (Carswell 1985, 119–30; Ashby 1970). Students eventually won places on the committees and councils of universities, although they did not vote on academic issues involving them or the staff. But the ultimate result of student protest was a cooling of the voting population, and thus of Parliament, toward British higher education. Remember that the percentage of the British population with any experience of the university was quite low in comparison with the United States or any country with a mass higher education system. The students' belief that the grants they received were a wage, not an opportunity and a privilege, added to the anger of the general population (Carswell 1985, 120–21). This soon translated, in the early 1970s, to the tabling of further growth plans and projections implicit in the Robbins proposals, a leveling off of staff in what was now an expanded system (which nevertheless enrolled no more than 4% of the eligible age group), and the beginnings of cutbacks by a harder, more intrusive UGC and DES. Professors were still in the majority on the UGC, but their role was now to say no rather than yes.

The period from 1969 to 1979 was characterized by little growth and some retrenchment. The bloom was off the rose. The UGC, whose function had been to stand at arms length from both the government and the universities, became little more than a cost controller for the system. It began to reject plans for all further expansion (Kogan and Kogan 1983, 37–54).

In the 1970s the major innovation in British higher education was not in the universities but rather in the second tier, the "public" branch of polytechnics. Here the student population, which did not need test scores as high as those necessary to enter the universities, expanded rapidly. As the universities began to tighten up entrance standards, the polytechnics took the overflow. Because school planning had not been coordinated with academic planning at the university level in the postwar era, and because students are accepted not simply in a faculty but also a subject area, an oversupply of qualified arts and social science candidates developed, along with a shortage of those qualified in science (Kogan and Kogan 1983, 126–33). The polytechnics had been set up primarily for vocational and engineering training, but they began also to take the thousands of students in social sciences and arts who could not get places at the universities. And while universities turned away qualified candidates in those disciplines, they began to lower their standards in the sciences to address that shortage. This created a problem for teachers in the polytechnics, for their science candidates—the few rejected by the universities—had barely enough science for their programs. The closing of university departments in social sciences and the arts in the 1980s exacerbated both problems.

Finally, the advent of the Thatcher administration threw the academic system into reverse gear. Thatcher concluded that the British university system had grown large and expensive, and she set about to reduce its size, between 1981 and 1983, by 10 to 15% (Kogan and Kogan 1983, 55–71; Halsey 1992, 124–46). Academic tenure came under attack—for the tenure that most British academics possessed was an obstacle to reducing the size of the British system. Thatcher's plan challenged students' status as a privileged class. She and the ruling right wing of the Conservative Party were also violently antiunion and made decisions to cut the universities without even consulting the AUT. As Kogan and Kogan (1983, 84) observed, "The universities were strapped. They could not simply break tenure. If they were to enforce redundancies, there would be painful internal conflicts about who was to go and which subjects were to be lost or reduced. They could lose large sums in the courts. But if they planned, as all did once government-backed compensation schemes were promoted, for reduction through voluntary severance, they risked losing their ablest employees or employees from subject areas which they had been told to preserve."

The Thatcher government, working with a now prostrate UGC, not only directed the size of the cuts to different universities (Oxbridge, London, and a few chosen Redbricks got the best deals, while others suffered larger than average cuts) but also the subject areas to be cut within each faculty. Social sciences and arts were particular targets, especially sociology. Only a year later, Thatcher introduced new positions into the mix, in fields where she thought that "new blood" would bring a payoff, such as DNA-related cell biology, computer science and information technology, and business studies (Kogan and Kogan 1983, 152). Finally, in the late 1980s, the Thatcher government passed a bill that abolished further academic tenure in state-funded British universities; those who already had tenure kept it, but could neither be promoted nor move to another university without losing tenured status. Only Oxbridge, which had its own separate sources of funds and its own system of tenure—lifetime fellowship to a college—remained relatively unharmed by the changes. And Oxbridge did not band together in solidarity with the other universities—especially with those hardest hit—for many at Oxbridge were against the original Robbins-era expansion. The cuts and the abolition of tenure have led to a mass exodus of many leading British academics, to the United States, to Australia, and to the Continent. The long-term consequences for Britain can only be imagined, but their magnitude was obvious to everyone but the Thatcher administration.

In general, British academics have gone from a medieval guild model, which to a small extent survives in the Oxbridge colleges, to a hierarchical, professor-centered academic model that relies heavily on state support. As the British economy worsened after a major expansion of the university system, capitalist pressures on the state, combined with a state very un-friendly to education and eager to replace it with training, led to a massive cutback of the funds on which the system had grown dependent. This led to a major and somewhat irrational cutback in staff, the abolition of tenure, the dissolving of entire departments and the near-disappearance of some fields, especially those, such as sociology, that had reputations for opposing Thatcher's politics and policies. Higher education was being reshaped, even more brutally than medicine and law, in the image of the new British state. The guild power of the profession was shown to be nil as Oxbridge did not come to the aid of its sister universities, and the AUT was a slender reed unable to resist the onslaught.

The British public essentially yawned as this happened. The universities were not part of their world, and so they did not care what happened to them. The lack of public support, the lack of alumni clubs, the lack of built-in boards of industrialists in each university with large contributions of their own to protect meant that political resistance was minimal. Britain began to get the kind of university system that the government really wanted: a return to the very elite systems of the past, transformed a little in a practical direction. On the other hand, because higher education had been the primary pathway for upward social mobility in British society, weakening the university and demoralizing the academic staffs assured the continuation of the stratified British social class system.

4 | FRANCE: STRONG STATE, CLIENTAL PROFESSIONS

In France, the state stands at the center of the society and makes many of the decisions that in nations like the United States or Britain are made in the private sector. The French state was built during the period of absolute monarchs, when the monarch gathered around him his own corps of bureaucrats, the noblesse de robe. These early lawyer–magistrates and tax collectors fanned out over the countryside, increasing the grip of the central state on all organs of local government and many aspects of what elsewhere would be considered private business (Huppert 1977). Tocqueville wrote that the revolution of 1789 did not change the essentials of the system: "Under the Old Regime, as in our time, one does not find a town, city, village, not even a small hamlet in France, nor a hospital, factory, convent, or school which has independent control over its own affairs, nor can administer its own property. Then, as now, the administration holds the French under its own supervision (tutelle)" (Tocqueville 1856, 122). In a word, after the revolution, the absolutist state took the place of the absolute monarchy.

State, Grandes Ecoles, and Capitalism: The Matrix

Although ordinary political parties always had a role to play in French history, they were always re-forming and reassembling and always had to be considered against the steady background of the central state.

Throughout the nineteenth and twentieth centuries, as regime succeeded regime, the only steady note was the central state bureaucracy. Its bureaucrats were educated, in the nineteenth and early twentieth centuries, primarily at one grande école, the Ecole polytechnique. The graduates of this small school in Paris, instead of those of the marginal and unimportant French university, ran the state (Kosciusko-Morizet 1973).

The Napoleonic era set the French state on its present course, with the establishment of the public system of high schools (lycées) whose graduates, especially those in the Paris region, competed in special competitive examinations for the strictly limited number of positions in the two major grandes écoles of the time: Polytechnique, whose graduates went from general education in science and engineering to positions in the higher reaches of the French administration, and the Ecole normale supérieure on rue d'Ulm, whose graduates would teach in the lycées and sometimes in the universities (Suleiman 1974, 1978; Bourdieu 1989). Napoleon did not envisage a major role for the university in France. Like generations of his successors in France, he preferred the applied and nontheoretical education given in the grandes écoles to the theoretical perspective and the questioning, often leftist, tone of the university, as the proper background for state service (Suleiman 1978, 51–56). Thus professors, and the education they give, have long been devalued in France, compared with the education given in the grandes écoles. After completing the lycée, students can attend the university if they wish (the lycée degree ensures admission), but this is a second choice for most. The grandes écoles—Polytechnique, Ponts et chaussées (bridges and roads), Mines, Normale supérieure, and l'Ecole nationale d'administration—educate most of the French governing elite. Graduation in the top fifth of one's class from these schools means a career in one of the grands corps of the state. These grands corps are the upper civil service level of each of the state bureaus—the Finance Ministry, the Cour des comptes, the Conseil d'Etat, the Ministry of Justice, the Ministry of Transport—all of the major levers of power inside the state (Bourdieu 1989, 428–81; Suleiman 1974, 239–84).

Nor do the advantages of this pathway end at state service. The better graduates of the grandes écoles, after a period of state service at the top of the most important state ministries, "parachute" into the private sector, to become the chief executive officers of most of the semipublic and private large corporations in France (Suleiman 1978, 226–29; Bourdieu 1989, 428–81). The field of French capitalism is thus divided between large corporations in each economic sector that are run by ex-state bureaucrats and grande école graduates, and the vast majority of small corporations, which are run by graduates of the less prestigious grandes écoles or by relatives of the founders (Bourdieu 1989, 191). Some medium-size corporations are run by the graduates of the business-oriented grandes écoles, such as the Haute école de commerce (HEC), which are less prestigious than the elite grandes écoles but which have gained status in recent decades (Bourdieu 1989, 482–87; Nouschi 1988). It is also true that the majority of the graduates of Ecole polytechnique do not follow the route of the top fifth of the class from state service into top private-sector jobs; still, they go directly into industry with a distinct advantage over those who are graduates of the university.

The system thus defines university education as socially second-rate. The university is where the vast majority of students go, those who did not do well enough in the lycée to enter the special post-lycée cram courses. These programs, given in certain Parisian lycées, provide two or three more years of preparation for the special entrance exam—the Concours—for the grandes écoles. Bourdieu notes that with every step—lycée, postgraduate cramming program, entrance to a grande école, entrance into a grand corps of the state—the social background of the applicants is increasingly upper class. Ostensibly a purely meritocratic system, the multiple levels of screening actually involve much social snobbery and prejudice posing as objective examination criteria. Professional training programs, meanwhile, are found only at the university—one reason why professions, too, have second-class status and limited rewards in French society (Bourdieu 1989, 50–51, 82–85).

One could wonder why a society accepts such a strict gradation system, in which the majority of students—even in the grandes écoles—are defined as "losers" rather than "winners." The answer seems to lie in the typical French acceptance of hierarchical relations, their political passivity, and their general acceptance of the large role of the state in their life. The state's legitimacy is taken for granted, and private complaints about unfair treatment are generally considered to be the special pleading of interest groups, suspect by definition. Also, the school system is very careful to breed into most French children a sense of the inevitability of the state's role in their lives. The socialist government of the early 1980s tried to get most citizens to participate in government, but its efforts generally failed, for the typical French response to the state is not to participate in it but to be passive before it—and to complain when it does not provide the paternalistic favors that they feel are due.

Professions were not always in a second-class position, nor was capitalism as restrained by state intervention as it has become. The turning point for both was probably World War II, when the Germans occupied much of northern France and the puppet Vichy regime controlled the rest of the nation. Under Vichy (1940–1944) the power of the unions was destroyed. At the same time, the regime helped the professions set up "ordres," which survived the war, but these were limited in function to carry out professional discipline under state supervision (Bezat 1987, 119–32). When the Resistance and the Free French set up the first postwar government, the capitalists (who had cooperated with the Germans and with the Vichy regime) were powerless to oppose the state intervention of the postwar planning system. The central banks of France were nationalized and directed to help develop certain sectors of the economy. This technocratic order depended on the graduates of the grandes écoles to run it and act as its agents (Kuisel 1981, 187–218; Hall 1986, 139–40).

Professions are classified as "interest groups" in France, as in the United States, but the French term has more opprobrium attached to it than the English equivalent. The state is said to represent "the general interest"— the interest of all the people—while the professional ordres (for professional discipline and control) and bargaining associations (which deal with the state on the fees charged for professional services) argue only for the interests of their members, just as the trade unions and the business interests do. This makes them somewhat suspect in the view of the state. The state and representatives of the larger corporations that work with the state are in theory "above politics" and concerned only with the general good, unlike the obviously self-interested professions (Suleiman 1974, 316–51). The professions, to counter these simplistic assumptions, have organized cross-professionally in groups that complain about increasing encroachment by the state, including unfair competition by state bureaucrats moonlighting in the private sector (Association nationale des avocats de France 1974).

This generally conservative and state-centered ideology is found in the governments of the Right and the Left alike, although the Mitterrand government of the 1980s tended to distrust the large corporations as well as the professional groups (Dagnaud and Mehl 1988). The power of the professions, such as it was, was centered in Parliament. In the nineteenth century, when the village "notable" was often the town's doctor or lawyer and often represented his profession as well as his local area in Parliament, the professions had some political influence. The governments of the late nineteenth century were called "les republics des avocats"—lawyers' republics. (Debré 1984). But with the increasing centralization of the French state, particularly under Vichy and in the postwar period of state-concerted economic planning, the power of professional groups weakened. This was especially true with the advent of the Fifth Republic in 1958. DeGaulle often ruled by decree and without Parliament, which in any case had much weaker powers under the Fifth Republic than it had under the Fourth, even though that postwar government had often been paralyzed by party strife (Becker 1988, 77–100; Immergut 1987). Powerful as an interest group in the period 1880–1930 and given special powers under the Vichy regime, the professions lost much autonomy as an ever more centralized and powerful state worked with capitalism to plan the future of France. Professions became viewed as a center of conservative resistance to this new order, as an impediment to progress.

Professional power in France has always depended on the specific cliental relations that a particular professional group or segment is able to establish with the ministries of the central state. These relations are primarily with the bureau charged with supervision of the profession: health professions answer to the Sécurité sociale, the Ministry of Health, and the Ministry of Labor, legal professions to the Ministry of Justice. But other ministries are also important. The Conseil d'Etat, for example, establishes rules and boundaries for each profession and can change them over the objections of a given profession (Rendel 1970; Abbott 1988, 158–60). If the professional group gathers money for the state, as the notaries do, then the Ministry of Finance can play a supervisory role. In general, because state power has existed far longer than professional power, a profession is far more often a supplicant to the state for power and control over its own affairs than a dispenser to the state of such power. Conversely, the state feels free to redefine professional boundaries when necessary, reassigning functions at will to serve "the public or general interest." Abbott (1988, 158) notes that "the old institutions governing medicine and law were reconstructed rapidly and firmly" after the revolution of 1789. Furthermore, as in the prerevolutionary period, "state authority over French professions affected professional jurisdictions and competition not only directly, but also through state control of the professional structures that secondarily determine competition—professional organization, professional discipline, and profession–client relations. This pattern, continuing to the present, makes the state by far the central audience for professional claims in France."

Professions in France as elsewhere are segmented into an elite and a mass. But in the professions that we are considering in France, the elite is the sector closest to the state, with the mass sector serving the community. Furthermore, because the important parts of the state remain centralized in Paris, the elite is primarily Parisian. In the the medical profession, for example, the professors at the medical schools (a branch of the universities, all of which are funded by the central state) constitute an elite group of teacher-practitioners. Working at the Parisian (and a few provincial) Centres Hôpitals-Universitaires (CHU) or teaching hospitals, they have some rights to practice privately and collect two salaries as professors and as members of the hospital staff (Steudler 1973). They are quite separate, as a group, both from the specialists in the community, who in larger towns have a reasonably high income but lack the prestige of the university professors, and from the general practitioners, who constitute a rather underprivileged mass, now an overcrowded branch with surplus graduates, with no rights to supervise their patients upon hospitalizing them.

The legal professions have a similar hierarchy. Before beginning their apprenticeships, all legal professionals must pass through university law faculties that are controlled in large part by faculty unsympathetic to the needs of the practicing professionals. Legal professions are all sharply delineated by the state and are changed from time to time by state edict. Notaries, for example, are tied to the state by virtue of their tax collecting function and their control over (and profit from) every exchange of property in France. The special legal officials or ministerial officers, on the other hand, are licensed to practice before the Ministry of Justice, the Cour de cassation (supreme court of appeals), and the Conseil d'Etat and sometimes become members of these bodies. Finally, the ordinary members of the bar are excluded altogether from the state-related elite.

Engineers follow a similar pattern. The top graduates of the Ecole polytechnique, as well as those who go from there to further training in the Ecole des ponts et chaussées or the Ecole des mines, never practice as engineers per se but as members of the state corps and eventually as the directors of private companies. This state-elite segment shares virtually nothing, certainly not political solidarity, with the majority of engineers, who since World War II and particularly since 1960 have trained in hundreds of programs in the petites écoles—schools with a more practical and industrial focus than most elite engineering schools—or in the new applied programs for engineering in the (primarily provincial) French universities. Management is reserved for grande école graduates, either in engineering, in business (Haute école de commerce), or in general administration (Ecole nationale d'administration) (Bourdieu 1989, 185–264).

Professors, our fourth group, are in a strange position in the French system. Because the teachers at each grande école generally are graduates of that school, the only grand école that employs professional academics in significant numbers is the teachers' own Ecole normale supérieure on rue d'Ulm. Here the best students who want an academic career are trained, and they generally have the first choice of the best teaching positions within the French university system. As ENS graduates they are set apart from ordinary students throughout their university graduate programs all the way to their position in the academic labor market. In an earlier era, a degree from the ENS was also useful within the state administration, but this degree is now useful only in academia proper; the greatest advantages within the state now belong to those graduating from Ecole nationale d'administration (ENA). And because any position within the French university system is by definition second-rate, the professoriate lacks the prestige that it enjoys in other nations without this two-tiered system of grandes écoles and universities.

Some graduates of the Ecole normale supérieure aspire to a full-time position in the Centre nationale de recherche scientifique (CNRS), a network of publicly funded national research centers. Research that in the United States or in Britain would be conducted at universities is performed at CNRS. (The grandes écoles do applied research for corporations, a source of significant funds for them in recent years.) A career in research is usually preferable to a strictly academic one, unless it is in the faculties of medicine or law, where professors may have both teaching positions and ties to the CNRS or the Vaucresson law research center. Note that most of the students in the university have little chance of a career in the professoriate—for the majority of those with these jobs graduated from a grande école and not from the university itself.

French capitalism, as noted, can be split into two main sectors: the large public and semipublic corporations, as well as the private ones that work closely with the state, and the sort of business run by the descendant of a patron, an old-fashioned boss who might nowadays have a degree from a petite école, usually a smaller business school. The large corporations are controlled by the same kind of people who populate the state bureaucracies with which they often interact: grande école graduates. There are structured relations between the state and the private sector as well. The major banks in France were nationalized after World War II and work in close collaboration with the Bank of France and the Ministry of Finance. Hall discusses the consequences of this relation. During the period from 1945 to 1975, "Key parts of the French state prepared to embark on a strategy of state-led growth. Over the course of the post-war period their approach was characterized by expansion of the nationalized sector, a highly interventionist industrial policy toward the private sector, the extensive use of diplomatic pressure in support of exports, and the development of a system of national economic planning (Hall 1986, 140)." In an already centralized state system, compared with other European nations, nationalization of the larger private banks was followed by nationalization of the gas, electrical, and coal industry, of Air France, and of the larger insurance funds. A government planning group (Commisariat General du Plan) was created, along with a national statistical agency to gather economic and sociological data (INSEE), and the Ecole nationale d'administration was founded. The banks, being public, could also serve as the center for credit control. In effect, the state's relation to capitalism paralleled its relation to the professions. But unlike the professions, capitalism had more resources to fight back, to use the state as effectively as it was used, especially after the mid-1970s, when the state planning system faded.

It should be noted that the governments, until Mitterrand's in 1980, were uniformly rightist and overwhelmingly statist. Under DeGaulle and his successors, the power of the state was identified with the good of France, which was to provide employment for all while preserving the capitalist system, though modifying it under state control. From this state-centered perspective, professional groups were more of an irritation than a major actor. The professions of medicine and law had established their separate beachheads within the French university in the mid-1800s and had enjoyed great prestige—and some power—before 1900. Informal but complex systems of dividing the labor in law and an elitist system controlled by the academic physicians in the Paris hospitals prevailed until World War II. Then the gradual imposition of a national payment system began to lessen the medical profession's autonomy, particularly after 1958, when the Fifth Republic was born. A similar change in 1971 rearranged the existing legal professions and reassigned privileges, all to make a more efficient instrument for serving capitalism and the state. The key elite of engineers slowly lost its privileged position within the state, which began to prefer the graduates of Ecole nationale d'administration to the graduates of Ecole polytechnique. After 1968 the universities were enlarged but not reformed, and the grande école system became even more important to the power structure of France.

We can now consider this system in greater detail for each of our four professions. In general, one must understand the shape and power of the central state vis-à-vis the professions, its relative power in comparison to that of the professions, and the nature of the client relations between each group and the central state. Especially in the French case, where the state plays such a central role, the political sociology of the professions cannot be understood without understanding the political sociology of the state.

French Doctors: A State-Shaped Profession

In the prerevolutionary period, French physicians were a small elite, educated in one of a few medical schools, the two most prominent of which were Paris and Montpellier. Most medical practice was carried out not by physicians but by surgeons or surgeon-apothecaries, who served the general public that could not afford the physician's fees. They shared this market with faith healers, maiges, witches, and empirics, each of whom could deal with one particular problem (sometimes with success) but had no general knowledge of medicine. The revolution, which abolished the corporations or guilds for medicine and surgery, established in their place a two-class system—officially trained doctors and surgeons, with full academic degrees in a national education system, and health officers, with far less training, who would compete with the folk practitioners in the countryside. Ramsey

(1988, 125) observes that "it was the revolutionary state that abolished the old corporations and joined medical and surgical training; and it was the Napoleonic state that reestablished the profession on new foundations. To a far larger extent than in Britain or America, the profession in France, somewhat like its German counterpart, was shaped from above." The medical elite was granted a large role in establishing the policies set by the state, but until late in the nineteenth century the profession did not enjoy the right to organization into associations to bargain with the state. The loi le Chapelier expressly forbade such organization, which, it was feared, might lead to a return to the prerevolutionary guild structure. The le Chapelier law did permit learned societies, and in Paris these were often informal centers of elite power. When the law was repealed in 1892, doctors set up a national medical association and a bargaining association. The latter worked to create a system of health insurance that doctors could profit from and control, rather than a national system that would put doctors on salary.

Not only did this fight ultimately tighten the hold of the physicians over health care and gradually drive out the nonphysicians, it produced the principles of French "liberal medicine": the free choice of doctor by each patient, direct payment (fee for service) between patient and physician, confidentiality, and the elimination of third parties from the relationship. The relations between the profession, the state, and the Sécurité sociale system went through at least six major phases: the failed attempt to impose a payment system on the physicians in 1929–1930; the Vichy period of World War II; the second unsuccessful attempt at creating a national system after the war, which did establish the part of Sécurité sociale not related to health; the early Fifth Republic period of 1958–1960, when DeGaulle imposed a national system placing the hospitals under direct state control; the political upheaval of 1968, which led to some reforms in the university system that had major implications for professional autonomy; and finally the growing cost crisis of the 1970s and 1980s, which led to more controls on the profession's basic decision-making powers. We will consider each of these periods in turn, and in each consider the difference between the hospital sector (run by the medical professors and the specialists) and the sector represented by the community general practitioners. The differences between these two sectors will show how the state slowly imposed its will on the profession, giving the hospital elite benefits in exchange for their cooperation while ruling by decree over the general practitioners.

Historical Perspectives on French Medicine

French doctors finally established their monopoly in 1892, a monopoly that provided, for the first time, strong legal penalties against the practice of medicine by folk practitioners and that also eliminated the occupation of health officer (Ramsey 1988, 123; Stephen 1978, 13–32). During the period 1929–1930 the Confédération des syndicats médicaux français (CSMF), the major French doctors' bargaining union, successfully blocked implementation of a national medicine system that would have restricted their freedom to practice. A much amended bill eventually passed, incorporating the four principles of liberal medicine and providing partial coverage of low-income patients without requiring doctors or patients to participate in any kind of plan. Because third parties were barred from the doctor-patient relationship, the patient paid the doctor a mutually agreed upon sum and was then reimbursed by the plan. The insurance covered just a fraction of the patients' cost (Stephen 1978, 32–58).

The elite medical specialists continued to practice fee-for-service medicine out of the teaching hospitals, as they had since the first golden age of clinical medicine in Paris of 1800–1848 (Steudler 1973). The general practitioners in the community and especially in the rural areas also practiced on a straight fee-for-service basis (Leonard 1977). These community physicians, dealing with less wealthy patients, were to some extent in favor of an insurance system, which might expand their clientele. But the Paris specialists were more likely to be active and influential in Parliament, and their views had more weight in political circles than those of the provincial physicians. The specialists were dead set against any restrictive form of health insurance and any arrangement that would control their fees. Nor were they alone in their opposition. At this time neither the labor unions nor the capitalists were in favor of a national health insurance scheme. The unions were opposed because they viewed the mutual societies that would administer the insurance as conservative political bodies; the capitalists opposed the system because their operating funds were threatened by the onset of the Depression. With physicians, unions, and capitalists resisting universal insurance, the scaled-down scheme insured no more than a third of all French citizens. The state was not involved in any major way in the administration of the system (Immergut 1987, 142–72; Herzlich 1982, 247–49).

Vichy France, under the leadership of the World War I hero Marshall Pétain, put the agenda of the French Right into place. Working closely with Nazi Germany but given some freedom to govern unoccupied France, the Vichy regime dissolved the union movement (which went underground), worked with the capitalists in supplying the wartime needs of Berlin, and set up corporatist alternatives to the interest groups to work with the state (Azéma 1979). Among these was an ordre for the French physicians, which to some extent replaced the disbanded CSMF. The new organization was to bargain with the French regime and police the profession in areas of ethical conduct, strictly enforcing, for example, the fee-for-service system, as before the war (Marrus and Paxton 1981, 18, 22). Vichy itself, meanwhile, imposed the antisemitic policies of its sponsor in Berlin, denying Jews membership in the Ordre des médecins, forbidding Jewish doctors from treating Gentiles, and establishing a quota system for the universities, with a maximum of 3% Jewish students (Marrus and Paxton 1981, 144; Azéma 1979). Furthermore, the few Jewish heads of clinical departments in the teaching hospitals were dismissed. Many of these physicians, however, continued to practice during the period, sub rosa. Most of the Jews who were deported from France were immigrants; many French Jews survived the war.

In the last year of the Vichy regime, when it became clear that the Allies would win the war, the Ordre des médecins published a statement reminding all doctors that the ethics of the profession protected the "secret" of the relationship between doctor and patient. In other words, doctors were not to betray resistance fighters who sought treatment. The timing of the statement renders it suspect, as does the fact that it had to be issued at all. Yet this statement was used for years after the war to vindicate the moral record of the profession (Bezat 1987, 124). Immediately after the war the CSMF was reconstituted by DeGaulle and the provisional postwar government, and the medical ordre was also reconstituted—stripped of its Vichy rules—as the ethics and licensing organization of the profession. It responded to the complaints made by consumers of services against practitioners in a three-level system of local, regional, and national ordres, with the right of appeal by an accused doctor to the central ordre in Paris. Here all case decisions would be reviewed by the Conseil d'Etat, which also had a legal representative on the disciplinary committee. Medical representatives of the ministries of labor, education, and public health are given seats on the national ordre, to further involve it in the actions of the state (Bezat 1987, 119–45).

The association of the Ordre des médecins with the discredited Vichy regime has continued to haunt the profession, as it has with other professional ordres set up as part of the Vichy program of corporatism. Most physicians are to the right of center politically, and the majority support the functions of the reformed ordre of postwar France. Yet this support is not complete—about one-third feel that its structure and function need revision or that it is totally illegitimate. Mitterrand made a brief and unsuccessful attempt in 1981 to abolish the ordre, as much for its contemporary politics as for its origins. For the ordre, which all practicing physicians in France must join and support, registers the conservative opinions of the regional and national leading members far more than those of the mass profession that it supposedly represents. It has dragged its feet on the issues of contraception and abortion, on the morality of group practice as a method for delivering service, and on other key policy matters, though recent reforms in the ethical code or *code de déontologie* have recently modernized its positions (Bezat 1987, 127, 131–32).

In sum, the Vichy period strengthened the profession through the creation of a national body to which all physicians had to belong. The immediate postwar period, under the provisional government of General DeGaulle, revised the ordre as an organization dealing with the individual aspects of French medical practice—moral conduct, professional licensing, and malpractice. All group cost and payment matters, on the other hand—salaries, health insurance, and so on—were to be the province of the CSMF. Yet this division of function, as Abbott has pointed out, separates professional functions that are joined in the United States: for the length of the period I have studied, the AMA has controlled education (the responsibility in France of the Ministry of Education), licensing (controlled by the ordre in France), and bargaining with the insurance system (handled in France by the doctor's bargaining association, either the CSMF or the FDF, the Fédération des médecins de France) (Abbott 1988, 159). Whether the French division of functions weakened the profession or strengthened it as a whole, however, is not really the point. The profession was unified in a narrow area, establishing a conservative lobbying body that, officially restrained from political action, lobbied effectively if informally at the national level. In the era between 1945 and 1958, the medical lobby was a bulwark in the professional resistance to change.

Immediately after the war, DeGaulle and the provisional government set up Sécurité sociale by decree. A private body, carrying out a public state function, it was to mediate between employers and employees (both represented on its governing board) and work under state supervision to create a system of retirement, unemployment, and health benefits for all French citizens (Immergut 1987, 197–219; Herzlich 1982). But the CSMF opposed the health insurance benefits in the package, as did both the small employers in the Confédération générale des petites et moyennes entreprises and the large employers. Together these groups had enough political power in Parliament under the Fourth Republic to block the creation of a system of health insurance that would constrain the doctor's ability to earn. This situation changed almost overnight with the creation of the Fifth Republic, with a strong executive branch that could rule by decree in areas of national importance. With DeGaulle returned to power, the ineffective parliamentary regime was replaced by a strong executive committed to far-reaching changes, including in health care. DeGaulle, working under the guidance of Dr. Jean-Louis Debré, issued a series of decrees from 1958 to 1960 that reorganized the French health insurance system and hospital system. Robert

Debré, the doctor's son, was DeGaulle's prime minister at the time, ensuring that the reforms would be implemented (Hatzfeld 1963; Immergut 1987, 197–200; 1992).

France thus set into place major health reform. The doctors in hospital practice agreed to work on salary. (Those who were medical professors got a second salary from the education ministry.) A small proportion were allowed to keep private beds and private practices in addition to their salaried position. Sécurité sociale's new system of "conventions" imposed maximums that doctors in the community could charge for specific services but reimbursed the clients for 80% of that fee. The "defeat" for doctors was that the state had assumed control of the rates for health care payments for a great majority of French citizens. While the average general practitioner resigned himself to this fait accompli, the leadership of the profession, especially the specialists who were not professors, opposed it bitterly, carrying out a brief administrative strike against it. A subgroup of physicians, unhappy with the CSMF's willingness to compromise over the issue, left to form the rival FMF. Eventually, however, 98% of French doctors joined in the system, and the ordre, given responsibility for disciplining doctors who practiced unprofessionally, was authorized to remove a doctor from the Sécurité sociale rolls, effectively cutting off his income. The mutual societies—private insurance companies—still existed, to cover the remaining 20% of the charges (Immergut 1987, 214–17).

The reform of the system extended to education well. In late 1958, as Immergut (1987, 199) points out, ordinances and decrees

> fused teaching hospitals and the biggest regional hospitals to create a new system of Centres Hospitals-Universitaires. They were to provide highly specialized medical treatment and a base for expanding the clinical portion of medical training. The new system established a rank-order among hospitals, important for coordinated planning because it established priorities for the distribution of medical equipment and defined more clearly the responsibilities of different types of hospitals. In the name of efficiency, hospital administrative boards were made more independent from local political entities.

Another aspect of the reform dealt with the process by which students were chosen for the internships that were necessary for a career as a specialist or a university professor. In the past, the "grand patrons" of French medicine made these choices by themselves, basing them as much on social class and background as on merit, virtually denying a Jew or a working-class student a career at the peak of French medicine. Only the change to a more meritocratic examination system could change this, although even with these changes it was still substantially more difficult for a minority to get a hospital internship.

The reforms of 1958–1960 divided the profession even more than before between the hospital elite, now essentially upper-level state functionaries, and the general practitioners, excluded from this world. As Steffen (1987, 204) observed, "The central position of the public hospital in French health policy is not necessarily a victory for the state over an originally liberal professional body. The growth of medicine occurred as the result of differentiation within the profession. The elite consolidated its position, based firmly on the state, to the detriment of another part of the profession, the liberal town doctors, and especially the general practitioners." In this reform, unlike the previous unsuccessful attempt of 1929–1930, the state was stronger and centered in the executive and not the legislative branch, the reforms were passed over the objection of the Ordre des médecins and the CSMF but with the support of the labor unions and—especially important—the large capitalist employers, who saw in the reforms a way of controlling the rise of health care costs.

The French Medical Profession in the 1980s and 1990s

At this point it is necessary to review the demographics of the French medical profession. Growth of the profession was slow early in the century, from 12,000 physicians in 1900 to 15,000 in 1920. The numbers doubled in the next ten years, to 30,000 by 1930. Problems related to the war slowed the increase, and in 1960 45,000 physicians practiced in France. The number rose to 65,000 by 1970, however, to 85,000 by 1976 (Bezat 1987, 54). The rapid increase in the rate of growth probably had two causes. First, the repeal of the numerus clausus in 1968, which opened the university to a far greater number of students, including medical students. Just two years later, changes in the hospital laws created a larger number of salaried positions and teaching slots in the nation's hospitals. Even though the numerus clausus was reinstated just a few years later, it was to deal with the flunking out of medical school of as many as 50% of the much expanded number of students who had finished the first year. Even though the percentage of students allowed to go on after the first year gradually decreased (to about 10% by the late 1980s, or only 4,500–5,000 students a year), the nature of the medical marketplace had changed permanently. For the 85,000 in practice in 1976 became 110,000 by 1980 and 150,000 by 1985, while the population grew at a far slower pace. Thus the doctor-patient ratio, which was one of the lowest in Europe in 1955 (90:100,000) grew rapidly to one of the highest (175:100,000 in 1976, 278:100,000 in 1987) (Doan 1984, 46).

The growth of specialty medicine and of salaried hospital practice was one of the first consequences of this medical population explosion, but in the later 1970s positions became unavailable in the specialties and hospitals. As a result of this radical change in conditions of supply and demand, a large part of the generation of medical students from the 1980s have had to enter general practice. According to some recent estimates, one out of every four general practitioners will eventually have to leave medical practice or will barely make enough to cover his or her retirement payments into Sécurité sociale. The rural general practitioner typically makes about a quarter the income of the specialist; some make no more money—and have less social protection—than the factory workers at the local plant (Bezat 1987, 101–13).

This is as much of an extreme, of course, as the physician at the teaching hospital who supplements his already comfortable income with a private practice. A considerable proportion of French doctors are in the middle: though specialists, they are tied not to the CHU system but rather to a network of smaller, sometimes nonprofit, hospitals, where they practice fee-for-service liberal medicine and make about three-quarters the income of their colleagues at the teaching hospitals (Herzlich 1973). A growing proportion of these midlevel specialists, and of the salaried general practitioners, are women. No more than one of every ten medical students in the 1950s was a woman, but the ratio in recent graduating classes is roughly one in three, clustered, as in other nations, in such specialties such as OB-GYN and pediatrics. The barriers are still up in the elite teaching hospitals in the high-paying specialties like surgery (with only 1.3% female representation in the mid-1980s) and cardiology (6.5%). Women in general practice have been far more likely to practice in clinics or other group practices than as solo physicians, and more likely than men to leave medical practice after years of barely surviving (Bezat 1987, 53, 55).

Recent developments have not shaken the profession as did the 1958–1960 reforms under DeGaulle, but the landscape has continued to change. About half of general practitioners in the mid-1980s practiced in groups of one to four physicians (Steudler 1986). Hospital practice in the 1980s was not as attractive as in previous eras, especially in those teaching hospitals that deal primarily with the underclass and the elderly, rather than patients needing acute care. In addition, the strict rules of Sécurité sociale were relaxed in 1980 and not retightened after the Socialist government of Mitterrand took office in 1981. In so-called sector II medicine—sector I is Sécurité sociale—specialists may charge more than the going rate for services. But sector II must compete with those in sector I, whose fees are controlled (Bezat 1987, 163–80). If too many physicians choose to practice in sector II, each will have a diminished share of the patients who are able to pay their legally inflated prices, only a fraction of which are covered by insurance. At the same time, if nearly all the specialists in an area choose to practice in sector II—as has happened in Paris—few are left to treat the patients of the working class and the poor (Bezat 1987, 166). Outside of the Paris area, only a small fraction of physicians choose sector II—10–15% in the late 1980s. And recent income figures indicate that in some specialties, staying with Sécurité sociale is still more profitable than taking one's chances in a new private market (Lebrette 1990, 54). It is, however, a sign that the specialists have regained some clout—and that the cost of Sécurité sociale has grown faster than expected—that the state allows some of the profession to practice outside of that system. Still, the centralized system dispenses the large majority of medical care, and the state reserves the right to restrict sector II practice should it threaten Sécurité sociale.

Guild Power and the French Physician: Increasing State Interference

We have seen that the French medical profession lost control, between the late 1960s and the late 1970s, over the numbers graduated. Given the expanded number of physicians beginning careers during that decade, it will be the year 2030 or so before the numbers in practice can be expected to decrease again. An overpopulation of doctors can significantly increase the health-care costs of a society, even while providing only a marginal living for the average new general practitioner. When the state and the medical professors finally cooperated in reimposing the numerus clausus on the second-year medical school students, the policy retreat was both a victory for the medical profession and a commonsense response by the state.

Control over the workplace, the second guild power, is still firmly in the hands of the profession. But the state made its first inroads on this power in the 1980s, as new forms of controlling costs were instituted. A review of the drugs prescribed by general practitioners was begun, for example, though protests of these physicians blocked, at least temporarily, full implementation of this plan. Medical audit procedures and patient profiles were established for the entire nation, using improved computer technology to highlight patient stays that exceed prescribed maximums, as well as hospitals and doctors whose rates are more than the norms. The medical elite led the way in adopting these cost-control features, which were then expected to be imposed on the practitioner mass. Economists, and to some extent demographers, have begun to play an increasing role in the development of the medical profession. The tentative return in the 1980s to a more liberal model of practice may be just a short respite before the state, working closely with Sécurité sociale, begins to tie payment for services to new statistical tools for measuring overcharging for patient care, and thus getting close to the heart of the medical act itself—the choice of the treatment. As of 1990, France had not proceeded as far in this direction as had the United States or Britain. But a formerly strong profession, using the state as a shield as much as it is regulated by it, medicine is being weakened by the oversupply of doctors and the controls of the Sécurité sociale system and other state regulatory bodies.

In 1930 French medicine was essentially autonomous and committed to a fee-for-service system. By the late 1980s, it had become a profession in which 64% were on salary, and were thus largely under the control of nonphysician administrators. A high-flying elite of state-based hospital-university professors and a second high-flying elite of specialists in private practice in major metropolitan centers, practicing in Sector II, has to be compared with the mass of the profession, working in hospitals and clinics, on salary, for minimal wages, and the mass solo and small-group practitioners in the countryside, many of whom, like their brethren in the non-university hospitals and clinics, are also barely members of the French middle class (Gilson 1990).

In terms of the market and the state, the French medical profession has gone from controlling the market for services to sharing this control with the state, through Sécurité sociale, though sector II medicine has reintroduced a small private sector. Because the market is ultimately affected by the numbers graduated, and the profession has lost much of its influence over that factor, its market control has declined since 1930, even as Sécurité sociale has increased the size of the market. Physicians have only an advisory role on the Sécurité sociale boards, which are dominated by employers, union executives, and representatives of the state. The role of the state is all-pervasive in French medicine, from overall control of the tutelle over the ordre, to the financing and running of the Ministry of Education (which controls the medical faculties), to the payment for most of the services, to the shaping of the market and the development of new methods of cost control in state-funded research bureaus and in organizations of the state itself.

The Legal Professions: State Control Over the Law

In France, the central state is essentially above the law. There are several reasons for this. The first and foremost is the legacy of absolutism—the centuries-old disinclination to give the judicial branch any real independence from the state, particularly the executive. Because the state dictates the division of the legal professions, which therefore cannot combine into a large American-style profession, there is no united forum for a campaign to change the French system. Law's subservience to the state is manifest in a variety of settings. The legal professions have little voice in the French economy, for example, because state decisions involving business usually involve no matters of law (Cohen-Tanugi 1985, 40). To the limited extent that the legality of state actions is an issue, cases are heard in a different set of courts, under a different set of laws, from those to which private parties have recourse. Judges who hope to rise in the hierarchy of positions in the courts of France must pay careful attention to decisions involving the state. A judge deciding against the state has signed his own career death warrant, for promotions are arranged on the basis of merit— as defined by the state. And finally, the state, not the legal professions, is the arbiter of the discretion and scope of the laws, including what state actions are even reviewable in courts (Varaut 1986, 59).

Thus the French live in a considerably different legal world from the Americans or the British. There is no law of habeas corpus in France, and the juge d'instruction, a major figure in criminal trials, has wide latitude to allow a suspect to be held before being charged (Romerio and Hervet 1977, 267–68). The French have no equivalent to the Bill of Rights, either, and only in the 1980s did the Revolution's Declaration of the Rights of Man begin to be applied in decisions of the three highest French courts, which seldom decide whether an act of the state is unconstitutional. This is particularly important, for in the Fifth Republic the president makes the majority of the laws, often by decree. There is thus no system of checks and balances as in the American tradition. The state can also set up special courts to invalidate a decision made by a lower court. State actions can be brought under review only by the courts that specialize in government law. These courts are typically staffed by magistrates who are grateful to the state for their well-paid jobs and unlikely to rule in favor of private citizens and corporations at the state's expense (Larivière 1987, 267–68). "Illegal" state action is more often handled by bureaucrats than by the courts, as happened in the recent case of the bombing of the ecology ship *Greenpeace* by French secret agents. The general in charge of the secret service was asked to retire and the investigation ended there; the question of who in the president's office ordered the Secret Service to bomb the ship was never officially asked. This was hushed up for "reasons of state"—in other words, because a full investigation might prove embarrassing for the state itself.

Again, the French system places the law above the individual but places the state above the law; all the different legal professions are therefore marginal to the central functioning of the state and the economy. Only the entrance of France into the Common Market is beginning to change this situation, as the Common Market nations have begun to adopt a more American-style understanding of the role of law in society. In contrast to the clear separation of powers in the American case, in France, as Cohen-Tanugi (1985, 137) observes

French statism frequently practices the confusion and the mixture of genres and sometimes tolerates ambiguous relationships between institutions. The hierarchical model which orders the functioning of the state, the society, and the relations between the one and the other in France substitutes for clearly defined relations with a horizontal division of competences of vertical authority relations. In this model, the juridical capacity to intervene, and certainly the "informal" manner of every decision, is uniquely a function of the rung occupied in the political hierarchy.

It is within this general context that we can discuss the French legal professions. In all "civil law" nations, as we will see in Germany and Italy as well as France, there is a much greater splitting of the roles that are combined in the American lawyer. But the centrality of the French state, as well as its power, has more consequences for the changes that the professions are capable of making in the legal system in France than in the other nations considered here. As we have seen, the French state orders the relations among these professions and, in essence, either originates or approves any changes in them. Before 1971, for example, the French had the *avocat,* a specialist in arguing cases in court (analogous to the British barrister); the *avoué,* who specialized in preparing these cases for court (similar to the British solicitor); lawyers who pleaded in special courts, like the *agréés* of the commercial courts; and the *avocats* of the highest French courts, who shared nothing with the ordinary avocats. These latter groups of lawyers, along with such minor court officials as *huissiers* (agents acting to carry out state decisions) and *greffiers* (court clerks), buy and sell their offices and have a monopoly on practice, as do the notaries in their monopoly over contracts and exchanges of property (Raguin 1972).

We will consider the three most important of these legal professions— the avocats, who practice privately with the autonomous status of a "profession libérale"; the notaries, who practice privately (in giving legal advice) but also serve the state (in authorizing documents); and finally the entirely public practitioners, the *magistrats,* including judges, state prosecutors, and the upper-court magistrates.

The Avocat: From Courtroom to Business Adviser

The avocats of the present day include the avoués, and the agréés of the commercial courts. The avoués of the higher courts have maintained their monopoly in the face of the 1971 reform. All of these professions may now do legal counseling, as may notaries and the new profession of fiscal and juridical counselors (conseils fiscaux et juridiques), as well as law school professors (Raguin 1972, 167–71).

The avocats began in the late Middle Ages, as court arguers who gradually developed a monopoly on the practice, working for private individuals as well as for the king. Centered primarily around the court, they began to develop their modern form after the Revolution. Avocats were important in the politics of the Third Republic and influenced the decisions of the governments of the later 1800s and early 1900s. They deliberately let the other legal professions—the avoués and the agréés—do the "dirty work" of the legal profession and were satisfied with combining law and politics. They also deliberately chose not to involve themselves in the legal matters of the capitalist corporations, maintaining a philosophy of "disinterested-ness." For ethical reasons they did not wish to be mixed up in trade. Gradually, as the lawyers lost their large role in the parliaments of France, they found that their remaining domains were insufficient to sustain a major profession, for the avoués had begun to monopolize the representation of businessmen in court. By 1960 the conseils fiscaux et juridiques were specializing in business advice (Karpik 1990; Boigeol 1988).

Because the avocats were by far the largest legal group, and because they still had some political clout by the early Fifth Republic, the commission that was set up to modernize the legal professions was staffed primarily by avocats. In the reorganized legal system of 1971, avocats assumed the "solicitor" role of the avoué as well as keeping their role as "barristers." The avoués and the agréés were almost completely absorbed into the new avocat profession. But the avocats did not have the power to force the state to accept the monopoly that they wanted most of all—over legal advice. The French state, in particular the Ministry of Justice, which has tutelle over all the French legal professions, believed that it was not in the economic interests either of the state or of French capitalism for one profession to monopolize that skill. With the support of the other legal professions, especially the conseils fiscaux et juridiques, the Ministry of Justice made its view prevail (Larivière 1982; Damien 1987, 239–54; Sialelli 1987, 197–219).

Most avocats today represent primarily either large businesses or small clients and small businesses. Although the caterogies overlap, Karpik found that one group of lawyers practices in the "domains of law" pertaining to fiscal matters: international transactions, corporate law and economic crime, and commerce, with intellectual property a prestige category but not a major source of funds. The other group practices the law of occupations and work, of construction, of rentals, of accidents and other personal issues, and ordinary criminal law. All lawyers, especially those involved today in the second group, wish to be involved in the first group, with its higher pay and prestige. Yet the intensity of that preference differs somewhat by generation. The oldest lawyers make the smallest distinction between these categories, while the youngest, almost all of whom are in the second group, attach the most significance to reaching the first (Karpik 1985, 572–76). Karpik's findings parallel those of Heinz and Laumann and of Halliday in the United States; essentially the same two fields of law exist—corporate and individual practice—though the differences are more nuanced in the French case and did not really take their present form until after the 1971 reform (Heinz and Laumann 1982; Halliday 1987).

The avocats are regulated by the legal ordres, attached to each of thirty-eight superior courts in France. These ordres are ultimately responsible to the Ministry of Justice (Boigeol 1988, 271–73). Each autonomous area bar arranges for the apprenticeships that each prospective lawyer must complete after law school. Each bar elects a council and a president (or *batonnier*). The bar council and batonnier share responsibility for discipline, which is usually limited to matters between lawyers and between the magistrates and the bar, not with such consumer issues as the cost of legal service or the competence of lawyers (Raguin 1972, 181). The national association of the bar, in a profession that resolutely refuses a national structure, is an ad hoc group, consisting of the conference of batonniers and the national bargaining associations. The National Action of the Bar brings together the Conference syndicale des avocats and the other lawyers' labor unions to bargain with the state over the legal limits of the fees which their members can charge, and more recently, over legal professions' role in the national legal aid system (Boigeol 1988, 274–75).

Karpik notes that individual bar councils are formally democratic, though in the larger cities they tend to be made up of successful upper-class practitioners. Only in Paris is there a sizable proportion of underemployed attorneys, many of them women, who do not vote in the elections for the ordres and the bar council. Elsewhere in France the democratic nature of the ordre is also suspect—few women are accepted to the bars at all, for example—but the majority of the members of the profession nevertheless vote (Karpik 1986, 496–517).

French legal education consists of two stages: the university years, which are shared with the notaries and the magistrats, and the postuniversity period, when the different legal professions diverge. The aspiring avocat pursues the Masters in Law (Matrice), which requires a *license* or degree plus a one-year period of intensive legal training, before which the candidate must pass an exam that four of five fail. This exam, rather than the entrance into law school, determines who becomes an avocat; those who fail often go into business, but not at the upper-level jobs reserved for graduates of the grandes écoles. Academic training concludes with a final exam—the Certificate of Professional Aptitude—which the overwhelming majority pass. The bar works with the state to arrange the apprenticeship period with the successful candidates (and pays for half of it). This extra year (two years after

1981) often has seminars and other legal activities as well. But not all candidates who pass the CAPA are welcome to apprentice everywhere; apprenticeship is a function of the prejudices of class, race, and sex of the private bar—leaving most members of the working class, women and nonwhites to chose apprenticeships in the Paris working-class suburbs (Boigeol 1988, 275–78). The profession is still almost as conservative politically as it was in the Vichy era. New law graduates, especially the women, nonwhites, and candidates of lower social classes who do get through the academic part and who pass the CAPA, often complain bitterly about this. The length of the education process—especially the increasing length of the apprenticeship—are perceived by French analysts as deliberate attempts by the bar to screen out the lower-income and female candidates who have gotten through the academic stage (Boigeol 1988, 276).

The bar is centralized in Paris, with 36% of the members practicing there in 1983. The number of avocats in the nation remained relatively constant between 1880 and 1950, grew slowly in the 1950s and early 1960s, then grew rapidly as a consequence of the general explosion of university education in the late 1960s and the 1970s—though not as rapidly as for physicians. The profession then grew by 65% between 1973 (when there were 8,307 avocats) and 1983 (13,757). Much of the increase in this period was due to the growing representation of women at the bar, from a tiny fraction in the 1930s to nearly 30% of the bar by the late-1980s (Boigeol 1988, 266). Yet the profession still has some control over its size—not at entrance to law school, for the laws of France dictate who is entitled to enter the university, but rather in the exam given before the last year of law school, just before the apprenticeship. The ability of upper-class students to navigate the hurdles and arrange the connections for apprenticeships gives them a great advantage, which carries over into the years of practice. Certain right-wing law faculties, such as the rue d'Assas, graduate a much higher proportion of practicing lawyers than the other branches of the University of Paris.

Associational power for avocats has somewhat faded since the 1930s. The Vichy regime confirmed their existing ordre, even granting them the long-sought right to practice in certain lower courts, but it also forced the avocats to remove all Jewish lawyers from the rolls—though to be sure, except for some academics, few avocats objected to this purge (Marrus and Paxton 1981, 144, 176, 228). As power has become increasingly concentrated in the postwar central state, divisions have left the avocats ever more fragmented. The National Action of the Bar—which links the Conference syndicale des avocats (and before that the Association nationale des avocats) with the Association des jeunes avocats and other lawyers' associations—is in the anomalous position of representing a profession of whose members about 70% remain in private practice, unaffected by the rates of legal fees in the national legal aid system. And the growing unionization of lawyers is a further sign of their defensive and weakening position in the job market. The elite of the bar, in Paris and other major French cities, are exempt from this trend, for they still depend on their social contacts for their business.

Control over the legal workplace is reasonably strong for the avocat—partly because until very recently, he was constrained to *profession libérale* status—independent practice—and very few even shared office staff. Many avocats, especially those in the provinces, still practice out of offices attached to their homes. In Paris the trend by the mid 1980s was toward group practice arrangements in "professional corporations" (Boigeol 1988, 266–67). As avocats have evolved from a late-nineteenth-century profession of local notables to a late-twentieth-century profession of business consultants, office logistics have assumed different meanings. Avocats who argue small cases for individuals are still likely to work in solo practice. Those who deal with large clients and corporations are much more likely to operate out of the larger group practices in Paris, Bordeaux, Lyon, and Marseilles. Gradually the profession is splitting in two, with the poorer lawyers in the lower sector increasingly dependent on the state for funding through the legal aid system and the elite increasingly dependent on corporate clients. Neither group is influential in national party politics, though they lobby at the Ministry of Justice in competition with the other legal professions (Karpik 1985).

Control over the market for services is clearly not a property of the French system, where aspects of legal work, especially legal counseling, are shared with other professions. The state not only designates which areas are to be monopolized and which are not but can change the rules against the wishes of given professions. The avocats' desire to take over all legal counseling in 1971 is a good example. The conseils fiscaux et juridiques, a more modern profession, clearly had their own friends in the Ministry of Justice. As a result of the 1971 changes they were officially recognized by the state, their title protected (Sialelli 1987, 164–66). Even the avocats' monopoly over advocacy in courts is limited to the lower and regional courts; the high court advocates are a separate group of sixty ministerial officers, who alone are allowed to argue cases before the Conseil d'Etat, the Cour de cassation, and the Conseil constitutionnel, the three French "supreme courts" (Bancaud 1989).

Finally, as is clear from their lack of autonomy in other realms, the French avocats are far from being in control of their relation to the state. Their influence at the Ministry of Justice is limited. Not only did the avocats fail to reform the system to create an "American-style" profession, they were not able to stop the expansion of the legal aid program financed by the state when it began to apply to all commercial and personal civil cases in 1972 and to criminal cases in 1983—though they stalled the legislation for thirty years (Boigeol 1988, 280). Now the state is in effect a third-party payer for the services to the poor and some of the working class, and it affords the lower-ranking members of the bar, particularly those in Paris, a chance to scratch out a living. The bar may ultimately have dropped its resistance to legal aid expansion because a growing number of impoverished lawyers became militant and unionist in the early 1980s. But the state did not need the permission of the bar to make these changes. From the republics des avocats of the late nineteenth century, the modern profession has developed and split, between a mass profession barely able to make a living in the personal service sector and an elite bar, centered in Paris but with elements in other major French cities, serving the needs of the corporate sector. And even this elite market must be shared with the remaining avoués, the avocats of the supreme courts, the notaries, and (until the early 1990s) the conseils fiscaux et juridiques.

Notaries: The Survival of a Venal Profession

Notaries in France represent a rare mixture of state and private professional control over the life of a profession. Unlike the vast majority of French professions libérales, notaries perform state functions, for which the state pays them a fee. However, they may also perform in the private sector, charging whatever the market will bear for legal counseling and accounting, in competition with other professions libérales that are allowed to work in these areas. It is this very arrangement—the performance of state functions for which the state has come to depend on the profession—that has nurtured notaries' solidarity and their willingness to oppose as a group any attempt to take any of their power and privileges away from them. They thus present an extreme example of the principle of clientalism—the capture of a public state agency by the private group that in theory the agency regulates. As Suleiman (1987) points out, the combined public and private legal status of French notaries affords opportunities not only for public security and monopoly of a public office but for private profit as well, and as a result they have more power than those either operating in the private sector alone, such as avocats or conseils fiscaux et juridiques, or those wholly in the public sector, such as magistrats. He continues:

The bastardized status carries with it remarkable advantages for the profession. The state grants the notaire a monopoly, fixes the prices of the services the monopoly obligates him to render, protects him in numerous ways, particularly against the hazards of the market, and helps create the conditions for lucrative gain. The state is thus placed at the service of the profession. The notaires depend on the state for the creation of conditions that allow them to improve their economic well-being. The profession may well be a conservative one, but the basis of its existence is the tutelle and it has ferociously clung to the protective umbrella of the state. (Suleiman 1987, 42)

The French state gives notaries a monopoly over legalizing all exchanges of property (both their sale and their purchase), whether that property is in land, apartments, homes, factories, or other businesses. When a marriage contract is desired, or a mortgage from a bank is sought, or an inheritance allocated, or any private agreement made between businesses or individuals, the transaction is not legal unless a notary draws up the contract. All of these legally required activities naturally give the notary access to the private affairs of individuals (to whom he often becomes the family legal counselor) and to businesses; he must answer questions raised by others regarding the family or business, because he is responsible for the accuracy of the contents of the contracts, not simply their legality. Publicly responsible for a limited role in contracts, notaries have used this position to build a powerful and privileged private profession, particularly in legal counseling.

The notarial profession is much more powerful in France than in either Germany or Italy, where the office cannot be either bought or sold, and the individual is primarily a civil servant. One exception in France is the province of Alsace-Lorraine, which still operates under a German-style definition of the notary's role. This right to buy and sell a state office and monopoly exists nowhere else in Europe and is a legacy of the Old Regime. Huissiers, greffiers, and the avocats of the supreme courts share this right, which has been jealously guarded for more than two hundred years. Napoleon restored the notarial monopoly after the Revolution abolished it. During the Restoration period the venality aspect—the sale of the office— was restored as well, for the state needed the money that a would-be notary paid for the position (Suleiman 1987, 33–59).

The profession was primarily rural in the nineteenth century, with the notary often one of the town dignitaries, along with the doctor and the avocat. Gradually the profession became centralized in the larger cities, especially in Paris, and it also shrank, from 13,900 practitioners in 1803, to 9,769 in 1855, and 6,323 in 1969 (Zeldin 1979, 43). The rural areas did not provide the notaries enough income, as they were very nearly restricted to their state fees, and notary offices went vacant, or ended in bankruptcy. Only in the metropolitan areas was there enough associated business to provide a living, and on these other activities the state did not set a limit. Thus the income gap widened between rural and small-town notaries on the one hand and urban notaries on the other, who often earned twenty or fifty times as much per year. Retirees usually sold their offices, sometimes to sons of notaries, and notaries who obtained their positions this way did not have to prove to the state that they had any necessary competence. By the late 1800s, corrupt notaries often absconded with their clients' money or took kickbacks in shady investment schemes (Suleiman 1987, 63–78).

All attempts to reform or even police the profession to date have essentially failed. Suleiman asserts that the state, because it depends on the profession to collect taxes on every transaction, is constrained from disciplining the notaries severely, and above all from threatening the conditions of their monopoly. Even when a Socialist government (Mitterrand's of 1981) had a major interest in deemphasizing the notaries' role, on ideological and practical grounds, they ultimately had to back down on any real attempt at change; the Ministry of Justice ultimately wound up recommending a *raise* in the fees that the state allowed them to charge. The notaries played one part of the state against another, in an environment where the financial and banking sectors favorable to keeping the notarial monopoly had more power than the Ministry of Justice, which held the formal tutelle relation with the profession (Suleiman 1987, 234–35).

The Vichy regime consolidated the legal status of the notariat by establishing its national ordre—the Conseil supérieure des notaires—and a network of regional and local ordres. During the Vichy years, the notariat was heavily involved in transferring property from Jewish to non-Jewish hands and in invalidating marriage contracts between Gentiles and Jews. Jews even today are a minuscule minority in the profession, which remains known for its systematic anti-Semitism (Suleiman 1987, 161n). After the war, the DeGaulle provisional government allowed the notaries to keep their institutions, although they could no longer enforce the anti-Semitic regulations of the Vichy regime.

The state today continues to allow notaries to sell their office and present to the state the candidate to which the notary wishes to sell. This *droit de presentation* is the modern form of the venality of offices, for the state routinely approves the candidate put forth. The system of national, regional, and local ordres is supported by a percentage of each notary's income. The money is used to maintain the national office, to lobby and do studies to refute from the notary's viewpoint every attempt by the state to curb the profession's privileges.

When the Socialists came to power in 1981 and the Ministry of Justice for the first time opposed the continuation of notarial privileges, the profession upped its level of activity and enlisted the support of two other branches of the state—a powerful state bank (the Caisse des depots et consignations) and the Ministry of Finance. The Caisse des depots was a natural ally of the profession; it held deposits of billions of francs of the notaries' clients, paying a very low interest rate and a 1% fee to the notaries on all the money deposited. The Ministry of Finance, which wanted a lower fee for the notaries' services, nevertheless depended on the taxes that the notaries collected. All of these elements worked informally against the Ministry of Justice's attempt to weaken the notary's monopoly. Finally, the Ministry of Justice acknowledged that a strictly profession libérale notariat would be bureaucratically distanced from it instead of remaining an integral part of the state and directly under its regulatory tutelle, and it fell into line as well. The profession, meanwhile, had begun to modernize in the 1980s, using computers to store information, keep records, and process the reams of regulations that it consulted in advising clients. Once again, it had thwarted an attempt by the state, in this case one run by Socialists, to impinge on its turf. In the end, the Ministry of Justice recommended an increase in notary fees (Suleiman 1987, 132–47, 256–74).

It is principally the notariat's direct state function—which in turn allows the profession both a public and a private status—that makes it powerful and hard to attack. The notaries' ability to neutralize the state's efforts is not available to either those wholly in the private sector, like the avocats or the conseils fiscaux et juridiques, who are more independent of the state, or those strictly in the public sector, like the magistrats, who are only in a position to strike or to beg from the state. In a type of institutional jujitsu, notaries have used the strength of one part of the state (the financial arm) to neutralize the power of another arm (the judicial ministry). This is not to say that clientalism does not exist elsewhere in France—for example, with the medical professions and such groups as the farmers. But its extreme form with the notaries is precisely due to their combined public and private status—a sociological position they share with very few other groups. Thus they are hardly typical, as Suleiman suggests, of cliental relations in France. The French state remains stronger than most professions. But the notaries— a small, politically conservative, sexist, racist, and predominantly anti-Semitic profession—are in control of their monopoly and their relation to the state. They are the exception, however, not the rule.

Magistrates: An Impoverished Profession Under State Domination

To understand the lack of independence of the French magistrature, it is necessary to begin with one critical fact: the profession has been purged seven times by the states that existed between the time of the monarchy and the time of Vichy and once more at the end of World War II (Larivière 1987, 69–76). With the advent of Napoleon, the structure of the magistrature was set in its present form: a hierarchical corps, arranged in a military fashion, presided over by the Minister of Justice, who is named by the state. The majority in this corps are enlisted men or junior officers. Promotion is granted by one's superiors, who are also one's graders—and these actual grade reports were not made available to the junior magistrates until the Mitterrand era (Larivière 1987, 123–25). Naturally, this meant that the younger members would put up with privation and refrain from making controversial decisions for fear of offending their seniors. Boigeol (1988, 54) points out that "in the absence of explicit rules concerning advancement, the career strategy required not alienating the hierarchy and the Chancellery by a radically unseemly public demand. The apparent docility is not a sufficient, but certainly a necessary condition of every promotion [class of students]. In this context, the putting in place of collective strategies of claims is very difficult."

About the same size in proportion to the population as the American judiciary, the French system of magistrates is vastly different in its structure and functions. The key difference is that there is no integrated whole, no single court at the top of the system, although the Cour de cassation and more recently the Cour constitutionnel come closest. At the bottom of the system are the local criminal courts, with their juges d'instruction, whose role combines investigatory and accusatory functions. Larivière calls the juge d'instruction "demi-juge, demi-flic"—half judge, half cop; the office includes the right to investigate an accused person and then either to acquit him or to bind him over for trial—a role which combines that of American prosecutors with that of American judges. The siège judiciary includes 70 percent of all magistrates, including ordinary criminal court judges, as well as family court judges and juvenile court judges. Prosecuting judges, representing the Ministry of Justice, are part of the parquet judiciary, as are judges involved in occupational safety cases and certain other areas concerning state benefits, along with judges who work in the Ministry itself in administrative roles (Chammard 1985, 65–95; Larivière 1987, 258–68).

The typical route of promotion is to become the head of a local and then progress to one of the thirty-eight regional courts. Beyond the local and regional system, with its bureaucratic four-grade model, there is the "supergrade" of the high magistrature, where commensurately higher salaries are paid. Given that this is a French system, it should not be surprising that the vast majority of supergrade positions are in Paris, at the Cour de cassation and the Cour constitutionnel. Several important courts are literally outside the magistrature—the Cour de comptes, for example, and the Conseil d'Etat, which are staffed primarily not by magistrates but by graduates of the grandes écoles, particularly the Ecole nationale d'administration. Occasionally the Ministry of Justice appoints a magistrate for these positions, but these courts, which deal with the majority of questions involving French corporations, are generally outside the areas of magisterial expertise and interest. It is as if the French state considers corporate business issues too important to be left to the judiciary to decide.

French magistrates were overwhelmingly male until the late 1960s, when ten years of increasing female applications to take the Concours for the magistrature began finally to be rewarded. Only one in five students at the Ecole nationale de la magistrature in Bordeaux was a woman in the last four years of the Fourth Republic (1954–1958), and only 25% at the time of the educational reforms in 1968. After that, though, the representation of women grew to 45% in 1974, 55% in 1978, and 63% in 1985 (Applebaum 1990; Bodiguel 1981, 31–41). By the late 1980s about 40% of all magistrates in practice were women, and it has been estimated that by the turn of the century they will be a majority (Applebaum 1990). Applebaum regards the history of the female inroads into the magistracy as a triumph of feminism, but Larivière sees it as an example of the way that the magistracy has been further marginalized in a sexist society (1987, 240). Both authors document the difficulties women have had in entering the profession—in the 1950s they already constituted the majority of applicants to the Ecole nationale—and rising through the ranks. By the late 1980s, however, a woman headed the Cour de cassation, and the Socialist government of Mitterrand had begun to work with the Ministry of Justice to amend the structure of the magistrature, making it easier for married couples in the profession to live and work in the same part of France (Larivière 1987, 244–59).

The posting of married magistrates to vastly different regions was a favorite tactic of Gaullist governments in the 1950s and 1960s to discourage females from joining the profession. But by the late 1980s, the proliferation of female magistrates had led to liberalized family leave. Still, the magistracy is in danger of coming to resemble other French professions that keep the majority of women in the lower ranks and become progressively more male at every step up the hierarchy. Given overall French social values, the feminization of the magistracy is a sign not that women's power is increasing, but rather that the magistracy is in decline.

The magistracy in the mid-1980s was still markedly split on political lines between a group of men in their sixties and early seventies—often the senior regional judges and the various members of the different high courts—and another large group of men and women in their thirties, forties, and early fifties. The former group, many of them trained before the national magistrates' school was instituted, tended to be politically conservative; the latter were all products of the school and were likely to be much farther left on the political spectrum, to have wider interest in the issues of law in society, and, as noted, to be female (Larivière 1987, 210–11). What was missing was a generation of judges in their late fifties and early sixties. This gap in age is the result of the government's repatriating colonial judges after the decolonization of the French empire—judges who were of the same age and political position as their colleagues in the upper branches of the magistracy already in France. The middle-level positions of the courts were thus filled by the same conservatives who filled the upper bench, and a massive split in the ranks resulted—between the generation of 1968, whose prospects of advancement were nearly hopeless, and the older enemies of reform who populated all of the desirable positions in the profession (Bodiguel 1981, 35). The younger judges (and a few older leftists) formed the first judges' trade union, the Syndicat de la magistrature, in 1969 in response to this crisis.

In terms of social class, the magistrature recruits from exactly the same backgrounds as the Ecole nationale d'administration: 57% from the liberal professions and the upper cadres, 12% from middle-level cadres (Bodiguel 1981, 40). The majority of the upper-middle-class students come from professional families, often with a background in the law. In terms of their region of origin, one finds the ratios changing, from a primarily provincial background to one where Paris and the north are more equally represented.

The Syndicat de la magistrature is an example of successful solidarity by the younger faction of the magistrats. Born in reaction to the shortage of jobs and to profession's loss of status under the Fifth Republic, by the 1980s it organized about 20% of the profession (Lyon-Caen 1981; Larivière 1987, 183–93). DeGaulle's new constitution in 1958 had further degraded the roles and responsibility of an already weak profession and system of justice. As Applebaum (n.d., 4) observes,

> The specific formation of the Gaullist constitution substituted the term *autorité* [authority] for *pouvoir* [power] as a symbolic downgrading describing the French judiciary which prescribed the activities of courts and limited access to justice. The devalorization of magistrates was associated with an increase of executive power within the *conseil supérieur de la magistrature,* the institutional force that controlled all personnel decisions among magistrates. Symbolic and real political subordination of magistrates took place at a moment when French magistrates were already considering the creation of a labor union.

The Syndicat de la magistrature consolidated its influence when the Left came to power in 1981. Several of its leading members were put in charge of divisions in the cabinet of Robert Badinter, the Socialist minister of justice, replacing the conservatives of the previous administration. The Conseil supérieur de la magistrature, whose members were all appointed by the government under DeGaulle, won some measure of independence (Larivière 1987, 216–17). The Syndicat has generally taken stands in favor of legal reform, championing individual rights and protesting state curtailment of political and expressive freedoms. But it is opposed by the older and extreme right-wing magistrates of the UNI, the right-wing APM (Association professionelle de magistrats), and the middle-of-the-road Union federale des magistrats. Reforms in general have been limited: the Conseil de la magistrature, for example, still has an appointed majority. Six members are elected by the magistrats, but two each are elected by the National Assembly and the Senate, one is nominated by the Conseil d'Etat, one by the Ministry of Justice, and one by the President of the Republic (Larivière 1987, 216). If this is reform, the system still stands as a weak one.

Finally, the magistrates are weakened by the French state's intervention in the judicial process. The state sometimes orders judicial footdragging or acceleration, depending on the case. The magistrate who dares to proceed full tilt against the corporate sector or such powerful professions as the notariat may be sanctioned or lose any chance at promotion—and the decision will likely be overturned at a higher level of the justice system anyway (Sarda 1981; Troper 1986). On the other hand, the system is very effective at imposing fines and jail sentences on the poor and the working class. France also retains its *jurisdictions d'exception,* special state courts like the Cour de sureté d'Etat (Court for State Safety), presided over by a joint civil and military judgeship to deal with cases of terrorism, of intelligence, and counterintelligence—in short, with any problem that the state thinks threatens its safety and security (Romerio and Hervet 1977, 157–206). These courts, begun in the time of the Algerian war (1954–1962), operate under completely different rules from the standard courts. There is no systematic way that they fit in the French system, save as the state's special weapon against those it defines as its enemies. Leading members of the Syndicat de la magistrature have called for their abolition, but in general the magistrature, divided on grounds of sex, age, political views, and willingness to speak out against abuses, has not taken a position on these issues.

In summary, the French legal professions provide a varied picture. Those professions or parts of professions that work either for the state or in the sector supported by state funding—the smaller avocats working as criminal lawyers for the poor under state subsidy, for example, or the magistrates— have little influence. Avocats who defend large corporations, on the other hand, and the notarial profession, which has a special position both inside and outside of the state, have much greater autonomy. Either working for capitalism or working as an agent of the state (but not directly for the state) are privileged positions. But what remains critical is the relation of one's profession to the state, and the extent to which the profession or the state controls the relation. Avocats maintain their distance, and as a result the state has retained the power to reassign the boundaries of the profession's work and that of related professions. The notaries, with their functions inside the state, have used the contacts they have gained as a result of this position to defend against weakening their guild power. Only the magistrature, totally within the state, is subjected to the state's direct power—to control the careers and prospects of its members. In all the legal professions, the most important variable is the behavior of the state.

Engineering in France: The Demotion of an Elite

In France as in no other nation in our sample, or perhaps anywhere, engineering rose to the top of the professional prestige ladder. The graduates of Ecole polytechnique in the nineteenth century became responsible for the development of the infrastructure of the French state. After a period of postgraduate instruction at the two affiliated schools, the Ecole des mines and Ecole des ponts et chaussées, they fulfilled this role as *ingénieurs d'Etat,* taking positions in the corps of engineers responsible for the roadbuilding, railroad building, canal digging, and other construction activities that created the conditions for the expansion of capitalism in France. Toward the end of the century, Ecole polytechnique graduates had colonized certain of the state ministries and were on their way toward becoming an elite within the private sector as well, rising to the position of président-directeur général (PDG) or chief executive officer in many corporations (Kosciusko-Morizet 1973, 45–69, 95–127).

With the generalized expertise of the Polytechnique graduates generally unavailable for run-of-the mill engineering jobs, by the turn of the century it became necessary to get most French engineers from another source—the Ecole centrale. These graduates, also given generalized or "polyvalent" training, but with more attention paid to specific fields of expertise, filled most of the engineering positions in the growing fields of steel, chemical, and electrical products (Weiss 1982; Ribeill 1985). From the turn of the century to about 1920, a typical French firm would have only one or two technical experts, working at the right hand of the patron or owner-manager. Addressed as "Monsieur l'ingénieur," this expert was clearly a member of the upper middle class (in terms of ideology and eventual job possibilities) and in symbolic alliance with management (Thépot 1985). The working class was far below the engineer in status, with completely different viewpoints and goals.

To understand the development of French engineers after 1920, it is necessary to recognize the strict hierarchy of status among the engineering schools in the nation, and the way that management has always respected this hierarchy in planning, from the day of entrance to the firm, the career patterns of individual engineers. The Polytechnique is at the top of the prestige hierarchy. A candidate is admitted only after a two- to three-year period of postlycée cramming classes and after passing a concours (special exam), which the vast majority fail. This grande école is followed in status by the Ecole centrale and several of the most advanced technical schools, such as Sup élec (Ecole nationale supérieure d'électricité) and Sup télécom (Ecole nationale supérieure des télécommunications), and then the provincial generalized schools.

Gradually the prestige hierarchy shades off from these grandes écoles to the petits écoles, which do not require as much preparation or a special concours, and which are even more applied in nature: such schools as Tannerie (the Ecole francaise de tannerie in Lyon) or Mines Nancy (not to be confused with the prestigious Ecole des mines of Paris). These schools actually give students more explicit practical training than do the major grandes écoles. This is an advantage for the hiring firms but not for the graduates of the schools, because France remains a nation where the generalist has much more career mobility than the specialist (Bourdieu 1989, 185–264). Ranking below engineers from the petits écoles are the graduates of the university system, for these degrees, in applied math, in science, and in engineering, are not worth as much in French industry, regardless of the empirical content of the training. For the firms rank and promote their engineers, and their technical graduates, according the status scheme given above. Because the students do not have to compete to get into the universities, hirers may assume that they are not as disciplined as those who graduated from a grande école. The whole system creates a kind of self-fulfilling prophecy, in which the expertise of an engineer is never judged by his job performance, but rather by the school at which he was trained; graduates of the prestige schools occupy the upper positions in the organizations and work to promote their fellow alumni, often at the expense of those who had the misfortune to attend a school of lesser prestige (Crawford 1989, 67–68).

The university-based programs in engineering existed in the 1930s but did not grow in size and importance until after World War II. These schools, which offer lower-level engineering degrees or technical diplomas, have come to graduate the majority of French engineers—74% in 1958–1959, 72% in 1978–1979 (Crawford 1989: 57). But a university engineering degree confers almost no upward mobility within the French corporation. Polytechnique graduates spend only a few years as engineers, moving rapidly into management. Some Centraliens and the graduates of the few prestige elite specialized schools, such as Sup élec and Sup télécom, go into engineering management and the lower ranks of general management per se, but not as often as Polytechniciens into the ranks of the PDG and upper management of the company, even if the company was originally started by someone without these credentials. Graduates of petits écoles and universities almost never make it to upper management.

Only in the 1970s and 1980s did this system begin to change, and then it changed so as to devalue *any* engineering degree. In recent years, graduates of the commercial grandes écoles, like the Haute école de commerce (HEC) and Ecole supérieure des sciences économiques et commercials (ES-SEC), are beginning to replace Polytechniciens in the director positions in some areas of industry, as French firms shift their emphasis from production to sales. As the same time, engineering credentials have lost value as the market has become flooded with graduates of the second- and third-rank schools (Bourdieu 1989, 265–304, 411–86). In addition, the sons of the businessmen who own these companies are much more likely to attend HEC and ESSEC than the Polytechnique, and room is often made for these graduates in upper management by their fathers and relatives (Bourdieu 1989, 241). As a result, every engineer is pushed down a notch in prestige and the chain is further compressed:HEC graduates replace the Polytechniciens, who in turn replace Centraliens in middle management, leaving even less room for the university graduates (Nouschi 1988, 232–51). Engineering in France is thus a wide status group rather than a unitary profession. As Morsel (1985, 260) sums it up, "It is a hierarchized group. determined by its function in the enterprise (for example, between engineers of management, engineers of research, and engineers of production) but also by status (even if all the diplomas of engineers are supposed to be equivalent), and finally, by the wages and the modes of revenue."

Bourdieu adds another dimension to the analysis when he examines the effects of social class background of the students on their likelihood of applying to any grande école and to specific grandes écoles. Applicants to the Polytechnique and to the Ecole normale supérieure, he notes, are predominantly the sons of the upper middle class (the profession is overwhelmingly male) whose fathers have jobs in the public sector at the upper levels and themselves attended the public prestige lycées. By contrast, applicants to such schools as HEC are predominantly the sons of upper-class businessmen and corporate owners, who have more often had a private school education (Bourdieu 1989, 411). Thus the replacement of Polytechniciens by the graduates of HEC and the Ecole nationale d'administration in the upper administration of French companies can be seen as the owning class itself reclaiming the positions of management as France leaves the technocratic era of the 1950s and 1960s and enters a period of capitalist consolidation.

Historical Developments in French Engineering

French engineering is closely involved with the development of French society in a manner that makes it impossible to discuss the profession separate from the class conflicts that began in earnest in the 1930s and continued throughout the postwar period. We can isolate at least four periods in that history: the economic crisis of the 1930s, the Vichy regime from 1940 to 1944, the immediate postwar period (the so-called Thirty Glorious Years), and finally the slowdown of the later 1970s and 1980s. In each of these periods the status of engineers shifted, along with their relation to the state. The group also grew during this span from a minuscule number of graduates of a few grandes écoles to the graduates of more that 140 grandes and petits écoles and another 70-odd special programs affiliated with universities.

The worldwide economic depression of the 1930s was slow to reach France, but by the mid-1930s it had reduced the salaries and threatened the futures of the French middle class. Both the petit bourgeoisie and the salaried engineers were affected by the devaluation of the franc and the cutback in business. Few engineers took part in the growth of radical activism and the activities of the Confédération générale du travail (CGT), the communist labor union. They were much more likely to be on the side of the Catholic activists in the social Catholicism movement, which formed the Syndicat des ingénieurs salariés and the Union sociale des ingénieurs catholiques. These movements were initiated by graduates of the Ecole centrale and the Ecole polytechnique—though they enlisted the support of a large faction of the industrial engineers—and worked to counter the radical activism of the working class (Descostes and Robert 1984, 57–91). The working class, meanwhile, formed officially recognized bodies to carry out strikes that left the engineers as the middle men of industry, caught between labor and capital, out in the cold. The government of the later 1930s, the Popular Front, recognized the engineers' associations but did little else to improve the status of the profession. Standing up for the interests of the engineers (and other middle-class employees), the early engineering unions began to develop a politics of the middle way, between capital and labor. One major byproduct of this first period was a 1934 law recognizing the title *ingénieur diplômé,* which included graduates not only of the few grandes écoles but also of the myriad of second- and third-ranked programs (Grelon 1986, 7–32; Goutmann 1986).

The Vichy regime favored tripartite division of the work force into labor, skilled middle-level cadres, and management. The Nazi-supported conservative government dissolved the labor unions but supported the engineering organization. Engineers became an integral part of the committees that ran each French factory, working and voting with management and against the labor representatives. The Charte de travail, Vichy's main document governing industry, outlined the responsibilities of the engineer as a critical feature of modern capitalism (Descostes and Robert 1984, 119–21). The Charte heralded the postwar role of the engineer as middleman in industry—a change from his status in the 1920s and before, when M. L'ingénieur was clearly on the side of the old-style patron. Although some leaders of the engineering societies were accused of collaboration after the war, others joined the Resistance. The group received a general amnesty after the war because of its critical role in production.

In the postwar period, engineers focused on winning a legal endorsement of their elevated status. Boltanski shows in great detail how a prewar conservative Catholic movement of engineers was replaced after the war by a campaign for official status as cadres, with which would come special benefits and retirement privileges, as well as tax breaks not available to ordinary workers (Boltanski 1987, 37–96). He also notes that cadre status required the inclusion of various middle-level nonengineering employees who had lent necessary political support. Cadre status has since become more important than identity as an engineer to most of the French profession. According to Boltanski, the cadre movement grew to major proportions by the late 1960s, and by the mid-1980s the term effectively stood for the French employed middle classes. Cadres after the war became organized into the Confédération générale des cadres (CGC), the major bargaining group for employed engineers, although there are minority groups of engineers affiliated with labor unions, both communist and socialist (Boltanski 1987, 37–96, 145–83).

Finally, the period of the later 1970s and 1980s has led to a massive explosion in the public education, both in universities and in technical lycées, of a majority of present French engineers. They have no more chance than before to move up in the French corporation, for middle- and upper-management jobs continue to be reserved for graduates of the grandes écoles. But the proliferation of university graduates blocked upward mobility and often even job security in the French corporations. There is an increased willingness, especially in the high-technology areas where job security is limited, to join labor-affiliated unions, rather than the CGC (Crawford 1989, 181–84). The majority of French engineers today have more in common with the technical staff—the graduates of the technical lycées—than with the management-destined graduates of the grandes écoles. The most significant difference is the engineers' cadre status, which is unavailable to the technicians. Still, most French workers in engineering are not unionized, largely because management considers membership in any organization more aggressive than the CGC as automatic grounds for denying promotion.

Guild Power and the French Engineer

The possibility is slim that such a varied and status-ranked group as French engineers would act in concert against the interests of the employing capitalist firms or the state. French engineers as a group do not belong to any overall professional association and do not have an ordre. Their associational power, such as it is, is through the alumni associations of each grande école, who provide job placement and counseling and co-ordinate social events for graduates of each of the major schools. Only a minority of French engineers are in any sense unionized, those primarily through the relatively passive CGC, and group professional activity is min-imal. Still, their weak associational power does not mean that French en-gineers have no control over the workplace. There, in the manner of their colleagues in the United States and Britain, they control both their im-mediate tasks and the evaluation of those tasks—within limits set by man-agement, which is also responsible for setting the goals of the activity. Most engineers accept management's role and aspire someday to promotion into it. But if this upper management in many companies is composed of former engineers, it nonetheless acts in the interests of the corporation, not of the engineers, in controlling the market for services. Finally, the state is im-portant as the funder if not also the owner of most of the prestige elite grandes écoles, as well as being the locus of employment of a small per-centage of the graduates of the most prestigious grandes écoles. The state, though it approved the title ingénieur diplômé, has resisted any attempt by engineers to require a license to practice, and corporate management can and does use the title "engineer" for certain of the higher-level technicians and some of those trained in science programs in universities. In summary, the group has no market control, and the state, working with capitalist firms, prevents the development of engineering as a unitary profession.

Associational power, in the broadest sense, means control by the profes-sion of the training and of the activities of the graduates of the training programs. The extent of the profession's control over training is the ability to keep the numbers low: Polytechnique graduates no more than about three hundred per year, for example. Engineers successfully resisted pressure by the Mitterrand government in 1984 to double the number of graduates from the grandes écoles. Many leaders of French industry are alumni of these schools, and these powerful allies forced the government to back down within days of submitting the bill. At the same time, the attempt led to the creation of an association of the grandes écoles, committed to thwart-ing a Socialist government's determination to undermine their elite status. The association, with all of its ties to French industry, represented capitalism as a whole, not just engineering, and ultimately proved more powerful than the government (Crawford 1989, 189).

The anciens élèves or alumni associations of the five or six top-ranked grandes écoles represent another form of associational power. New grad-uates of Polytechnique, for example, may join the Anciens élèves de l'X and mix with the older graduates of the school at several social functions per year; many of these senior alumni are the PDGs of their companies. It is the rule among Polytechnique alumni to address one another by the familiar *tu*, which helps break the ice not only at alumni gatherings and sports clubs but also in the workplace (Kosciusko-Morizet 1973, 134–35). Centrale, Sup aéro, Sup télécom, and Sup élec also have alumni associations, but their networks are not as wide as those of the Polytechnique. Of course, nine-tenths of French engineers are not members of these associations and resent the special advantages they provide their members. Neither the universities nor the petits écoles have such associations, so their graduates must fend for themselves in the workplace and try to overcome the prejudices against promoting them.

Other associations are open to almost all engineers. The leading prewar association was the Union sociale des ingénieurs catholiques. Although run by the graduates of Polytechnique and Centrale, the USIC was open to all openly Catholic engineers, and in 1935 at its peak it enrolled about nine thousand (Descostes and Robert 1984, 81–88). Other smaller associations, for the technicians especially, were affiliated with the communist and socialist labor movements. After the war, the largest professional association was the Confédération général des cadres, but from the start it organized not only engineers but all sorts of middle-level personnel. Furthermore, organizational power implies the ability to oppose higher managers and owners, something that the CGC seldom if ever does. Many professional groups have struck to protect their interests, but not the eminently "respectable" CGC.

Yet in spite of this "respectability" the majority of French engineers do not belong to any union, much less the CGC. In the older of the two factories studied by Crawford in the mid-1980s, a mechanical metalworking plant, 42% of the engineers belonged to unions, but at the more modern electronic plant only 10% did. The majority held that membership in any union might "damage their career" (Crawford 1989, 185). Membership in professional associations was even rarer—13% at the metalworking plant, 8% at the electronics company. Crawford (1989, 186) concludes: "Even among those who had published articles, membership in professional societies was rare and of little significance. At neither firm did any ingénieur diplômé express a view of his professional society as a group to which he looked for help or protection of himself or his occupation." Because the leaders of the professional associations of engineers are typically graduates of Ecole polytechnique or Centrale who have become successful in management, the average engineer shares very little with them and has little incentive to join. But conversely, the rate of professionalization is low among engineers, and they exist within a system that focuses exclusively on promotion within the corporation. But the majority of the working engineers are denied these promotions because they did not attend the right grande école. And the employer, not the profession, decides who will be called an engineer at the work site. Corporations thus keep nearly half of all those with the title ingénieur (but not ingénieur diplômé) completely dependent on the management for their status, including cadre privileges. This group cannot appeal for help to the professional associations, which are reserved for ingénieurs diplomés. These lower-ranking engineers are often unwilling to jeopardize their cadre status by complaining of blocked mobility.

The French engineer has somewhat more control over the workplace, the second guild power. Crawford observed for French engineers what Whalley did for their British counterparts and Zussman for Americans, that they are "trusted workers" who are left free to control their work as they see fit (Crawford 1989, 131–35). This freedom in part represents corporate confidence in the engineers' training. But many French corporations, because they value loyalty, dependability, and conformity, spend considerable sums of money and time on psychological testing and screening before hiring anyone as a cadre. This approach became common after World War II with the importation of American industrial management techniques. As Whyte reported of U.S. corporations in the early 1960s, this concern for internal conformity replaced an earlier emphasis on external controls (Whyte 1956). The tendency to give graduates of the politically conservative grandes écoles the positions tracked for upward mobility instead of the graduates of the more Left-leaning universities also reflects the corporate preference for a relatively apolitical engineering staff (Crawford 1989, 214).

Autonomy on the job is displayed in the nature of the work that an engineer does. French engineers have more specialized expertise than their immediate superiors, they have freedom of movement on the job floor, and they receive the information they need horizontally, from other departments, rather than vertically from their bosses. But their autonomy has strict and understood limits. Upper management decides whether an activity or a project is to be expanded or curtailed. At the same time, an engineer may prefer a job with less autonomy and more supervision, as was the case in the metalworking plant, because these jobs had a higher rate of promotion into management. Autonomy is related in complex ways to job security, which was higher in the metalworking plant than in the high-tech company that Crawford used for a comparison case. In the latter, where the work autonomy was higher, insecurity was much greater. Here he found that those few who did join unions were affiliated with the CGT, which was in turn affiliated with Communists, or the Confédération française démocratique du travail (CFTC), which was broadly socialist in orientation. In the metalworking plant, where the rate of unionization was much higher, the majority of those in unions joined the conservative CGC. In general, French engineers have limited job autonomy, but the majority accept those limits and the prerogatives of management. Of course, those who feel otherwise are not likely to get hired in the first place (Crawford 1989, 103–4, 106–13, 184–86).

Control over the market is in the hands of the corporations. Until recently graduates of elite schools who work in the state sector were an exception; the top graduates had control of top jobs in the Ministry of Finance, the Ministry of Transport, and the other applied ministries. But as the slots reserved for the best graduates of the Polytechnique begin to diminish, as they have since the mid-1970s, when ENA graduates began to supplant them, the percentage of Poly graduates going directly into industry increased (Kosciusko-Morizet 1973, 128). Because the profession does not have any monopoly power over the jobs in industry, and because management can designate anyone it wishes as an engineer, the control of the title engénieur diplômé is significant only because it is necessary, along with graduation from a top-rank grande école, for promotion into upper management. But even in industry the graduates of the top rank engineering grandes écoles have gradually come to be supplanted by graduates of HEC and ESSEC, the two leading commercial grandes écoles. As a result, the status of the elite of the profession has declined in recent decades, and the graduates of the petits écoles and the university programs have suffered comparably.

The state avoids direct regulation of the engineers as a group, preferring to work with the existing system of grandes écoles, most of which are state supported if not state run. About 140 national engineering schools existed in 1985, but only about five or six of them were truly elite schools or grandes écoles. There are also hundreds of small private schools, below the level of the ones in the group of 140, called petites écoles, that provide some job-related training. These are of little significance to French industry, however, and are not properly called engineering schools, whatever they claim in their brochures. When a graduate of any of them applies to a French firm, he is likely to be hired as a technician, not as an engineer (Lucas 1990). No ordre has been developed for engineers on the model of the ordre des médecins or the ordre des avocats. Engineers, especially members of the prestige elite, are ambivalent about the prospect of an ordre, for it would undercut the prestige system that underlies their power as a subgroup within the vast mass trained in engineering. Every five years or so, the French state sets up a commission to study the problems of the profession; the commission typically recommends increased university training and gives some lip service to the principle that university graduates should have upward mobility within the corporation. Yet calls to democratize the profession are infrequent, for the commissions are invariably staffed by graduates of the leading grandes écoles. When such recommendations do come—as when Mitterrand proposed to double the size of the graduating classes of the grandes écoles in 1984—the elite schools shout them down. The state cannot force the corporations to change their internal status systems, which are intimately connected with the status systems of the grandes écoles themselves. And according to the grande école graduates and the corporations, elitism is necessary for the survival of technical excellence in France.

The result is that the state is basically used to fund the existing system and to swell the number of technicians and lower-level engineers coming out of the university training programs without changing the nature of the system itself. As capitalism gains more control of industry, it demotes the elite of the profession, replacing them with the sons of capitalists themselves and, at the same time, swelling the ranks of the professional mass. That this continued throughout a Socialist administration is testimony to its deeply ingrained character. Engineers are not a profession libérale and are not likely to become one. The fate of each engineer can still be predicted according to the school from which he graduated and his standing within that school. But even the top schools do not get the engineers the placements they used to, in either the state or the private sector. The period of about 1975–1995 has thus been a time of demotion for the elite and a swelling of a mass profession that never had, and never will have, the opportunities that that elite once possessed.

University Professors:
From Cluster Control to Union-State Bargaining

During most of the nineteenth century, the concept of individual French universities did not exist. Universities had been destroyed by the French Revolution. The system that eventually replaced them, initiated by Napoleon, focused primarily on the lycée degree—the passing of the baccalauréat exam—and the institution of a national system of lycées and university faculties. But there was an important proviso: engineering and technical subjects would be taught not at the university but at the grandes écoles. Napoleon and all succeeding regimes in France put their hope in these elite schools; they viewed the university primarily as a place to train the next generation of teachers. One grande école, however, the Ecole normale supérieure, was reserved for teachers. By the beginning of the twentieth century, the ENS provided the vast majority of the senior professors in the university, in addition to preparing teachers for the lycées; 76% of the Sorbonne professors and 63% of the provincial professors were graduates of the Ecole normale supérieure by 1900 (Verger et al. 1986, 362). The teachers in the most important (Parisian) lycées and universities were ENS grads, and the rest came from the universities. Eighty years later the trend was still clear: for promotion to full professor, graduation from the ENS is key because so many academics who have done so are clustered at the senior rank (Bourdieu 1988, 230–31). The overall system of 1990, however, had changed both quantitatively and qualitatively from that of 1900. The changes in that span contributed to the low degree of guild power by the French professoriate. In strong state where education is considered primarily a government function and where extensive political divisions exist within and between the faculties, it could not be otherwise.

Historical Perspectives on the French Professoriate

By 1930, the beginning of our research period, the French university had assumed its current outlines, but most of the modern developments were just beginning. There were three major faculties, in medicine, law, and arts and sciences. The student population represented only 1–2% of the French of the age grade. Most youth had dropped out before the final years of the lycée and had not taken the baccalauréat exam to enter the university. The elite professors were located in Paris, and gathered around them were their disciples—their current graduate students and their former ones as well, teaching elsewhere in France but returning occasionally for seminars by the master. Each major Parisian professor controlled a series of teaching jobs and research appointments and was the first reader on his candidates' thesis for the Doctorat d'Etat, a kind of super-Ph.D., usually written after years of teaching at the junior ranks, that the French system required for promotion to a full professorship.

Positions within the university system were organized by what Terry Clark calls a cluster leader, who worked with his protégés and the senior scholars of his group to foster his ideas and ways of looking at a field of knowledge. Clark shows that in such disciplinary fields as sociology at the turn of the century, or in history in the Annales school in the 1920s and 1930s, a strong cluster leader—Emile Durkheim in sociology or Marc Bloch in history, for example—could not only dominate the entire field or subfield but could propagate its ideas beyond the university into the general culture. But as happened with Durkheim and sociology, a field could wither if the leader died leaving no suitable successor (Clark 1973, 66–92, 162–95).

The most successful academic track, followed by most cluster leaders themselves, was to graduate from the Ecole normale supérieure, form a university relationship with a powerful older cluster leader, pass the agrégation—mandatory for any teaching position—after a number of years of graduate study, and finally work on the Doctorat d'Etat under the direction of the cluster leader for a period of about eight to ten years. The cluster leader would during this time find a job for the candidate at a lower rank in a provincial university. With the completion of the Doctorat d'Etat, the candidate, usually 35–45 years old by now and still under the sponsorship of the cluster leader, would take a full professoriate at a provincial university. The peak of a career would be a recall from the provinces to Paris, to a post at the University of Paris, but this apex was available only to a very few (Clark 1973, 84–92).

Journals were the property of the cluster, and the group took its lead from the cluster leader, who decided when and what one should publish. If one's ideas differed too much from the master's, publication was denied. Because most fields had only a few journals, each reserved for the students of a particular cluster leader, exclusion from a journal had permanent consequences. Natural and social sciences remained weak in France until well after World War II partly because of this stultifying monopoly by cluster leaders. Research institutions marginal to the university, such as the Ecole pratique des hautes études, were the only other outlets for scholarship, but clusters soon began to develop at those institutions as well. Book publishing was essentially under the same controls, with the cluster leader acting as a consultant to a publishing house and editing a series for those whose ideas he approved of. Publication of articles and books was necessary for promotion, and those without sponsors could seldom develop an adequate publication record; they spent their careers as junior professors in provincial universities (Debray 1981, 60–78).

By the late 1930s a second dimension to the academic profession had begun to develop: the state-funded research units that after World War II eventually became the Centre nationale de la recherche scientifique (Friedberg and Musselin 1987, 97–100). CNRS research staff are in effect tenured full-time researchers who work in a wide network of research laboratories, which in the 1930s were separate from the university. By the 1990s two-thirds of all CNRS research labs were affiliated with universities, but the affiliation remained loose; only 2.9% of the research staff also taught at the university in 1976, although graduate students were often hired by individual units for short-term work (Friedberg and Musselin 1987, 100). A career in the CNRS, combined with, if possible, a position in the successor to the Ecole Pratique des Haute etudes, the Maison des sciences de l'homme-Ecole des hautes études en sciences sociales, provides those who prefer research with an alternative to a teaching career. The EHESS is a research institution with a graduate-level faculty specializing in modern history and in economic, political, sociological, and anthropological studies. It is not a part of the Universities of Paris. Neither is the Collège de France, a prestigious center for innovative academics. Some modern cluster leaders, like Pierre Bourdieu, are based at the EHESS or the Collège de France and, through membership on advisory panels at CNRS, play a major role in the allocation of research funds (Bourdieu 1988, 84–90). It is as helpful in the 1990s as in the 1930s to have a powerful sponsor if one is to rise in the research hierarchy; publication is required for promotion in the CNRS, as it is within academia proper.

The biggest change that World War II and the Vichy regime wrought on French academia was the expulsion of Jewish professors from the university. Jews such as Bloch were were executed for Resistance activity, while others such as Maurice Halbwachs perished in the concentration camps (Clark 1973, 234). The majority of French academics kept silent during this period and did little to help their Jewish colleagues. After the war, when DeGaulle established a framework for the new French state, few academics or publishers were punished for cooperating with Vichy. And few Jewish academic leaders who survived the war reasserted their authority to the same degree after it (Assouline 1985).

Otherwise, though, early postwar French academia was essentially a replica of the prewar profession. From 1945 to 1960, the period of maximum economic growth, the most powerful academics were graduates of the grandes écoles, not the university. But as French industrial productivity improved and the standard of living rose after 1960, the university gradually became the locus for the ambitions of a larger and larger student body—most of whom applied after being unable to get into a grande école. Growth of the university in turn amplified the split in function, with the grandes écoles training the elite in both the public and private sectors and providing most of the education in technology and in business administration that led to real success in France. These subjects remain the primary responsibility of the grandes écoles (Verger et al. 1986, 370–74).

The split became more pronounced in the late 1960s. The university had to accept all students who had passed the baccalauréat, so it was increasingly flooded with students. But it could not place all its graduates in teaching jobs in the lycées and primary schools of France and could no longer even get them jobs in the public sector, where the competition had increased from the newer grandes écoles in the provinces. Enrollment in the French university system, which had risen gradually from 70,000 in 1930 to 125,000 in 1945 and 210,000 in 1960, surged to 661,000 in 1970, to 898,000 in 1978, and was nearly a million by 1983. Most of these students since 1970 were middle and upper middle class; 18% were the children of owners of industry and commercial establishments, 16% were from middle-level cadres, and 48% were the children of members of the liberal professions and upper-level cadres. Faculty were added to accommodate this increase, often from the lycée staffs. There were 10,000 teachers throughout the system in 1960–1961, 26,000 in 1967–1968, and 40,000 in 1973–1974, and finally to 41,300 in 1981–1982. The vast majority since the enrollment increase have been hired at the junior ranks; only 10% of the faculty were full professors until the last time period, when the percentage rose to 25% (Clark 1973, 35; Schwartz 1987, 25; Verger et al. 1986, 397, 403, 406).

Right in the middle of the surge of enrollment, in 1968, came *les événements de mai*—the events of May—a student uprising centered in Paris that divided French society. Recommendations made afterward by the government led to some (primarily cosmetic) changes in the nature of the French university system and the professoriate. The events of May had no single precipitating factor. Student unrest was political but unfocused, and the attempt by students to unite with French workers in a revolutionary alliance and to bring down the regime was futile (Verger et al. 1986, 378–84). DeGaulle held a parliamentary election in June 1968, won by a large margin, and bought off the workers with moderate pay raises and talk of participation in the management of factories. Then with Fauré as minister of education he instituted minor reforms to the university system while leaving the grandes écoles untouched. DeGaulle's aim was to reduce the power of the cluster system with its "mandarins" and to set up a set of independent universities at which junior faculty would have the right to vote on reforms—universities divided not by faculties but into interdisciplinary *Unités de l'enseignement et la recherche,* units of education and research (UER). But the changes led to widespread unionization of university faculty in reaction to greater control by the state in the running of universities and the day-to-day operations of university faculty (which were not, in fact, made financially independent of the Ministry of Education). The cluster system prevailed, though the new mandarins ruled smaller clusters and shared control over the career of academics both with the state and with the junior academics' union, the leftist Syndicat des enseignements supérieure, SNESUP (Cohen 1978; Verger et al. 1986, 385–89).

University reforms in 1969–1970 included changes in courses and programs and increased students' options in both. Thousands of junior professors were hired, and many of them unionized in the SNESUP, which changed the politics of the French university by forcing the state to bargain with them instead of with the professorial elite over promotion. Research branches of the CNRS were also massively expanded, providing jobs for some of the many new graduates. And the universities, though they dragged their heels, began to prepare students in some professional and technological programs; the Instituts universitaires de technologie (IUTs), for example, have become moderately successful small programs that students can enter either after the baccalauréat or with a two-year general diploma (the DEUG). Continuation in academic programs leads to the master's degree (matrice) and then, in academic fields, to the "third-cycle doctorate" (less difficult to earn than the Doctorat d'Etat.) But the business world still prefers the very specific training of the grandes and petits écoles to that of the university, which produces five times as many graduates. Businesses have direct involvement in the programs in the grandes écoles and prefer the conservative political values taught there to the more leftist politics of the university system (Gruson 1978, 264–97).

Under the new, larger university system, a single cluster leader in Paris cannot control a whole academic field. Now rival clusters develop, and provincial centers of expertise in some fields are beginning to challenge Parisian predominance. Still, the Universities in Paris—there are now thirteen—have reclaimed their predominance numerically, registering 34% of all students in 1976 (Verger et al. 1986, 402). Much of the basic research and most of the independent CNRS labs remain in Paris, along with most of the medical research institutes of INSERM and the economic-survey agency of INSEE and many other public and private research agencies. But the clusters cannot any longer foster their own candidates for promotion with the same success as before 1968.

The state has always set up committees to screen candidates for positions throughout the academic system and has always deferred to some degree to professors on the advisory committees. But now the SNESUP union demands promotions for candidates on the basis of years served, regardless of their degree of expertise, so publication records have become less valuable. Because the influence of SNESUP is gaining and the influence of individual professor-consultants is not, a candidate is often chosen who has the "right" political values, even though he may not be the candidate with the best qualifications for the senior position. Political loyalties often divide faculties on issues relevant to individual universities, with medical and law schools relatively conservative and the arts and sciences faculties tending toward the left. But most important decisions are made by the central Ministry of Education, not at the level of the UER departments or at the level of individual universities (Gruson 1978, 296–97).

Finally, to some extent the autonomy of the French professoriate is influenced by the milieu in which it operates: the intellectual field in general, or what is called the "tout Paris" phenomenon. Paris is the center of national intellectual life in France to an extent inconceivable in the United States, Italy, Britain, or Germany, and the newspapers, especially the intellectuals' favorites, like the *Nouvelle observateur* or *Le monde,* and such television book review shows as *Pivot* can catapult a French academic to stardom, and then drop him or her a few years later, just as suddenly.

Because intellectual fashions in France often value the new and flashy over the substantial and scholarly, and because journalists have found a foothold in some branches of the university, the different fields are often divided between serious scholars and media stars. The former have positions in the university and responsibility for graduate students in the cluster system, while the latter, who often have marginal positions within the university system, provide facile criticism and the latest approach to the novel or to social problems. The world knows of the media stars, but they often have little weight within academia (Debray 1981, 79–94). Some of the best researchers, in the Ecoles des hautes études en sciences sociales, are similarly marginal to the university and may also have an influence on the general public but do not participate to the extent that one might expect in training the next generation of French academics.

Guild Power and the French Professoriate

To summarize, in terms of our variables of guild power, the French university professoriate changed markedly from the 1930s to the 1990s. Professors in the 1930s were a small elite who controlled their own association through the cluster system, in a state-funded and state-run program. They controlled promotion to senior ranks completely, and they influenced their relations with the state through their work on consultative committees and in the Ministry of Education, whose positions were reserved for academics. This control was not at the disciplinary level, however: there were no national associations of historians, sociologists, chemists, and so on. Nor were journals refereed in the American sense; articles were invited and academics outside the cluster that controlled a journal were not asked to write for it. Cluster leaders chose their own successors. By 1990 the profession had lost almost all of its guild power. Disciplinary associations have still not been formed, although the number of periodicals has increased in many fields and the kind of cluster loyalty required for publication has been somewhat relaxed. Still, journals belong to their editorial board in a way that their American or British counterparts do not, and scholarly arguments between scholars from different clusters tend to become overheated vendettas. Associational power, such as it is, is not seated in the profession per se but in the two major unions, the SNESUP and the Syndicat autonome, which represents conservative senior professors, especially in some fields of literature, and the medical and legal faculties (Bourdieu 1988, 105–12).

Union action, however, rarely deals with individuals but rather with categories of faculty and tends to reinforce the bureaucratic criteria of promotion through seniority rather than productivity and ability (qualities that, in any case, are judged through the filter of politics and cluster loyalty).

Because the different unions represent different interests before the Ministry of Education, they can be mediated and thus controlled to some extent by the Ministry itself, further weakening faculty power. Research committees of the CNRS are, as in 1930, controlled by leading academics who usually foster the research projects of their younger cluster members. But the state, not any segment of the profession, decides on the size of the research pie and whether the advice of a particular group of academic consultants (and the clusters that they represent) is to be followed or refused. Because the state ultimately controls the majority of the research funding, it can ultimately determine whether a particular cluster will rise or fall in power and authority.

Academics' control over the workplace has decreased markedly since the 1970s; most faculty carry heavier teaching loads, and less money is spent on plant upkeep for a much larger population of students. Again, most decisions on spending are made at the ministry level, and individual universities have little influence over them. Control has increased to some extent for the junior faculty in the UER or departmental systems. But these controls extend only to such matters as the course syllabi or degree requirements; the number and type positions, and to some extent promotions as well, are decided by bargaining between the SNESUP and the Ministry of Education, rather than on the basis of academic excellence alone.

Since the state has decided to install new programs within the university (like the Instituts universitaires de technologie) and set up different standards for hiring these faculty members that are not under the control of the overall university faculty, the professoriate is losing one of its most important guild powers, the monopoly over who practices in the field. Most of these programs give degrees different from the university's, however, and university professors can claim some victory in this distinction. Finally, the state is reasserting its control on the funding process in research and maintaining its traditional control over the faculty. Although some faculty have both research and teaching appointments, this is still rare except informally; the CNRS research units often give seminars to graduate students, but not for credit in any academic sense, and the majority of those in research have no teaching career. Furthermore, funding for research is dependent more and more on the economic needs of the nation, or on the politics of the moment, not on the interests or the successful completion of research by a particular academic or researcher in a cluster. Whole fields can be de-emphasized by changes in research policy.

The overall result is that academics are more divided than ever, and less able to represent their needs as a group to the state. Guild power—the ability of academics to act as a unified group—is at a new low, with the junior faculty in SNESUP fighting in the opposite direction from the senior, more conservative faculty in the Syndicat autonome, with the leftist arts and sciences professors fighting the rightists in the faculties (or departments) of medicine and law. The Socialist government of Mitterrand, while on the whole supportive of universities, was discouraged from any major changes by fiscal constraints as the French economy began to level off in the postexpansion phase. Rather than one academic profession, there are several, sharing little with one another and vying for the attention, and the support, of the state.

5 | ITALY: PARTITOCRAZIA AND POLITICIZED PROFESSIONS

Italy is a nation of contrasts, of puzzles, and of institutions that do not work as they do in most other western European nations. For example, the line that we have been drawing thus far between the state and the private sectors, which is blurred somewhat in France, becomes almost irrelevant in Italy. The state is so large, and includes so many of the corporations, that the economy cannot be seen as an independent force (Spotts and Wieser 1986, 61–63, 83–85). But the state itself is hardly independent; it is controlled directly by the political parties, which also control the professions and determine who rises to the top in the private sector. Italy is an example of an almost totally "politicized" social environment, and this environment is the key to understanding the development of the professions.

Lapalombara, following Italian usage, calls this system *partitocrazia,* rule by parties. All elements of life are politicized, and every person must belong to a political party, and have a sponsor, in order to succeed. Partitocrazia

> creates in Italy a singular relationship between civil society and its institutions, on the one hand, and the state and its institutions on the other. In effect, neither the state nor civil society is independent or autonomous. It is not so much that the line between these two sectors is blurred. It is that the line itself is irrelevant because both sectors are dominated by the parties. This makes Italy a *parties-centered* democracy . . . an established multiparty government, meaning that the political parties are not just the prime instruments of representation but also the

major institutions of policy-making, policy implementation, and much more that transpires in society. (Lapalombara 1987, 271)

Political parties make the policies and arbitrate among themselves, then instruct their representatives in Parliament on how to vote. But governments fall with great regularity, as factions within parties disagree on policies. Still, cabinets often re-form with the same names in reshuffled positions. Italy possesses a clearly delineated group of politicians, a "political class" that carries out the arbitrations that make government possible; in spite of continual "crises," these politicians manage to work together, across party lines, when major legislation has to be passed (Lapalombara 1987, 144–65).

Another key to understanding the political process in Italy is *trasformismo,* the carrying out of policies with the support and participation of the parties not in power, which is made possible by *lottizzazione,* the parceling out of jobs both in the government and in the private sector by the political party of the job candidate, a process that reserves some jobs for the parties not in power (Lapalombara 1987, 77). Thus the large Communist Party and the smaller Socialist Party have established footholds in the state, and even to some extent a presence in private industry, even though they never have been in power. Cooperation is needed among all parties in order to have any major change.

The attitude of the people toward the state itself is marked by cynicism. Large sectors of the society avoid paying anything like a full share of their income tax, and professions are among the most common offenders, along with most small employers (Lapalombara 1987, 48–50; Spotts and Wieser 1986, 156). The state prosecutes few of these wrongdoers, for the costs are high and the chances of success small (Haycroft 1987, 108). In addition, the small firms or *microimprese* are the most profitable sector of the economy, free for the most part from unions and heavy political interference. Most Italians suspect the legal system itself of inefficiency if not corruption, and the judiciary is politically polarized. The university is also politicized, by departments and by faculties, with some departments and universities in the hands of the Christian Democrats, others in the control of the Communists or the Socialists.

Partitocrazia was probably first practiced by Mussolini. From the time when the Fascists officially took power in 1924, they strove to put their representatives in control of every ministry and in positions of power everywhere in private industry. When the Italian economy was affected by the Depression in the early 1930s, Mussolini ordered the state to buy up the failing industries and to make them available for Fascist Party patronage (Lapalombara 1987, 75). After World War II, the two leading political parties, the Christian Democrats (working closely with the Catholic Church) and the Communists began to replace the one-party rule of Mussolini with multiparty rule. The Christian Democrats got the majority of positions in the government and the semipublic corporations, with some positions parceled out to the Communists: a percentage of the positions in the hospitals, the universities, and the bureaucracies are given to members of each political party, based on party strength in the most recent election.

The professions we are concerned with here emerged at different times in Italian history. Physicians, lawyers *(avvocati),* and notaries practiced as early as the Renaissance (Park 1985; Martines 1968). These professions were an important part of the guild system in Florence in the later 1500s. In modern times, the state regulates professions through *ordini,* professional bodies that regulate intellectual professions. Ordini were formed for avvocati and notaries in 1874, shortly after Italy became a nation, and for the doctors (along with pharmacists and veterinarians) in 1910. Engineers were recognized in the early 1920s. Professors have never had an ordine, for theirs is not considered to be a liberal profession (Tousijn 1987b, 178). During most of the period of Fascism the professional ordini used political connections to survive Mussolini's attempt to dismantle them. His regime established a single comprehensive association, the Confederazione fascista dei professioni e degli artisti, but did not at first abolish the existing ordini, which continued with diminished functions, sharing power with the Confederazione. Finally the ordini were formally abolished in the late 1930s (Tousijn 1987a, 47–48). Mussolini fostered capitalism as well; he allowed prospering firms to thrive while abolishing the union movement.

After the war, the ordini were reestablished. There were minor modifications in their administration, such as direct election of their governing councils, as before the time of Mussolini. Speranza believes that the survival of ordini, from before to after Fascism, shows that they were generally unaffected by shifting political orders (Speranza 1987, 215). But this invulnerability was not absolute, and was soon to change.

What is critical, in understanding how a profession was formed and what segments of each profession were successful or not, is the political affiliation of each professional, and of the university department in which he or she was trained. Because the regions of Italy are colored politically in different ways—the North, the industrial regions, and many major cities have been Communist since shortly after the war, while the South and Sicily tend to be heavily Christian Democratic—the path to individual professional success, and the nature of the professional associations that dominate a region, are related to the political party in control of the university and the community. Although Italy has slowly been developing a rule of law, and provisions of the Italian postwar constitution have been finally enacted since the 1970s, the political parties still dominate the economy and the public sector. Finally, because many professionals are involved with the public sector—many doctors work for the National Health Service, lawyers for the state and in legal services programs, engineers for such giant state-owned or-managed conglomerates as the groups around the Istituto reconstruzione italiana (IRI) or the Ente nazionale idrocarburi (ENI), and the academics as full-time civil servants—all are involved in the politics that permeate the public sector and the society as a whole. But, as noted before, here professions are not unique. As Spotts and Wieser observe, "The ultimate impact of partitocrazia is that almost everyone is sucked into this partisanry. Whether an industrialist, judge, typist, general, professor, ambassador, novelist, scientist, or factory worker, every Italian has a clear party connection or at least 'belongs to the area' of a party. As a consequence the shadow of politics falls over industry, culture, academics, the law, and almost every other area of society" (Spotts and Wieser 1986, 6–7).

Italian Doctors and the Struggle for Power

The Italian medical profession from its earliest times was nourished by the state, growing because of it and partly within it. Each of the powerful city-states of Renaissance Italy—Tuscany, Veneto, Rome, and others— had a small number of physicians working in support of the community's poor (Cipolla 1976, 87). They also worked to stem such epidemics as the bubonic plague, although smaller communities within a region sometimes delegated clergymen, if physicians were not present, to deal with these problems (Cipolla 1982). These community physicians, in publicly contracted or *condotto* status, had job security. In an age when the vast majority of those trained could barely make a living unless they could become house physicians for wealthy families, a state job as a doctor was a prized possession. It could provide a small but dependable income for treating the poor, to be used as a base while one expanded one's practice and began to treat paying customers on the side—customers from the crafts and eventually the new middle class.

The Italian university has trained doctors and lawyers continuously since the Middle Ages. Thus, Italy did not go through the apprenticeship professional model of England. Italy has always depended on the formal (often very formal) model of classroom training in medicine, with little supervised practice (Perkoff 1984, 59). Until very recently an internship was not required for general medical practice but was the badge of the elite, who would go on to become specialists. As in all Continental nations, Italian universities have always been almost completely public. Tuition is relatively inexpensive, and the state pays most of it. Most Italians tend to live at home and attend the closest university. The ticket for admission to the university has always been the *liceo* degree, similar to the French baccalauréat, meaning entry at the approximate equivalent of our second year in college. One goes directly into professional training from the liceo, as one does in France from the lycée or in Germany from the gymnasium.

In the late 1800s and early 1900s, and to some extent even today, many professionals who have degrees for which there is no demand and lack the political connections to get state jobs have chosen to emigrate (Barbalgli 1982, 26–33, 36, 117–88, 148–54). Until the twentieth century, public employment was often the only alternative for many doctors. In 1889, for example, almost half of the physicians in Italy were on the public payroll (Piperno 1983, 149). The development of a state-regulated professional monopoly came in Italy at about the same time as it did in the United States. The creation of the ordini for doctors in 1910 was a major step (Tousijn 1987a, 42). Every doctor with a medical degree must belong to his or her regional ordine in order to practice. The Italian ordini have licensing functions similar to those of a state board of registration of medicine in the United States, and like their American counterparts they regulate professional practice. Each profession has a national ordine in Rome, and medicine's is the powerful Federazione nationale ordini medici or FNOM. Medical ordini are run by the profession, but the FNOM retains legally trained staff to deal with questions related to legislation. The ordini attempt to enforce a professional monopoly, and in the years since the technological and scientific revolution, they have usually succeeded. The ordini largely define the division of labor in health care, although in recent years paramedics in Italian hospitals have been demanding a greater voice.

Mussolini created Fascist syndicates for most professions, but because the state had special need for the aid of the medical profession, he did not completely suppress the medical ordini. He allowed them to function in parallel with the state syndicate until 1939, several years after Hitler had abolished similar medical organizations in Germany. The ordini maintained their registration and disciplinary functions, while the Fascist syndicate was responsible for bargaining with the state. But Mussolini could do little to control medical unemployment. A reform introduced by Giovanni Gentile reduced the supply of new medical students from 1923–1924 to 1927–1928, but the number exceeded 2,000 per year by 1933 again, more than the previous high. Twenty thousand new doctors flooded the market from 1930 to 1940, while only 33,000 were practicing professionally in 1931. Although there are complications in measuring such factors, most authors, citing the contemporary medical press, point to an oversupply (Barbalgli 1982, 181).

After World War II the primary task of the Italian profession was to find employment for the growing number of medical graduates. Between 1900 and 1945, the growing *mutualità* or private health insurance associations came to provided additional income for the Italian profession, primarily for in-hospital care. Thus, the profession became more hospital based. The elite corps of hospital-based specialists also had community offices. They received public payments and mutualità payments, as well as extra charges from the wealthy, who paid out of pocket for special treatment.

Neither before World War II nor in the first two decades afterward did Italy move toward the kind of universal, comprehensive health insurance systems found in Germany or France, or toward the development of a national health service on the British model. The percentage of the population given some partial private coverage nonetheless increased through the gradual proliferation of thousands of private health insurance plans for different groups—for unions, for professional groups, for farmers, for craftsmen, for civil servants of different political parties. The percentage covered in some way grew from 3% in 1929 to 40% in 1940 (Bocci 1944). The trend continued after a slight postwar decline, with 38% of the population covered in 1950, increasing to 82% in 1966 and to near total inclusion (in noncomprehensive plans) by 1970 (Piperno 1983, 157).

But these plans were poorly managed, and they encouraged hospitalization in a system where almost no medical equipment existed in the understaffed general practitioner's office. In 1980, for example, many offices had no blood pressure devices, fewer than 9% had paramedics, and only 10.5% had secretaries (Piperno and Renieri 1982, 73). A shortage of diagnostic equipment fed a crisis of confidence in outpatient care by patients, and hospitalization became the only route for all but the most minor illnesses. And most general practitioners were poorly trained in general clinical work; their fear of making a mistake aggravated the trend to massive overhospitalization in the 1950s, 1960s, and early 1970s (Perkoff 1984, 46).

Finally, as length of stay for most illnesses grew to triple the length in most other western European nations and the costs of care escalated, the entire system of private insurance went bankrupt. This fiscal crisis of the 1970s finally led the Christian Democrats and the Communists (the Partito communista italiana or PCI), along with the Socialists, to create the Italian National Health Service (Servizio sanitario nazionale, or SSN) as a cost-control measure in 1978. With some exceptions, the private plans would be replaced by a national public fund. The central management of the SSN would be in a position to cap costs through global budgeting of funds to be distributed to regional offices and then to each service area. This system would begin to ease the crisis, at least in the public hospitals that constitute two-thirds of Italy's hospitals, including many of the prestigious university-related research centers. According to the plan, all hospital doctors were to be put on full-time salary and prohibited from supplementing that income through private practice. Costs in the community were supposed to be controlled by putting the general practitioners on a patient-panel payment system.

Before proceeding to the history of the power struggles involving the Italian medical profession after 1978, it is necessary to review the structure of the profession. The SSN has not diminished the tremendous polarization in the profession between the mass of doctors and the elite—the 15% or so who are successful specialists attached to university teaching hospitals. Nearly all of the remainder are either in multispecialty practice or are family physicians, combining a community practice while attempting to develop a specialty market. About 35% of all Italian doctors are in general practice and another 30% in nonelite public hospitals; the vast majority of these are also generalists (Bompiani 1984, 154). Some general practitioners and specialists have their own small hospitals, which they own and control, and to which they divert patients from the SSN for their own profit rather than sending them to the regular public hospitals. (This practice is legal, though frowned upon).

The massive expansion of the Italian university system in the 1970s— and no numerus clausus has yet been imposed—has made Italy's ratio of doctors to patients one of the highest in the world. The ratio fell from 180: 100,000 in 1936 to 124:100,000 in 1951, then rose to 185 in 1971, 253 in 1978, and 352 in 1985 (Bompiani 1984, 116; CENSIS 1985, 81). Italy has almost three times as many doctors per person as England, which has a much higher standard of medical care. Italy, with 26 medical schools, admitted seventeen thousand medical students in 1980, while the United States, with 124 medical schools and a much larger population, admitted nineteen thousand students in the same year (Bompiani 1984, 145–46). About 20% of these students drop out or continue only part-time. Thousands of medical students every year graduate to unemployment (CENSIS 1985, 195). The sex ratio of the profession, meanwhile, is changing; by the mid-1980s only one of every ten doctors in their fifties was a woman, but four of ten recent medical school graduates were female. The women, as in other nations, tend to concentrate in general practice. The profession is overwhelmingly concentrated in urban areas, with two-thirds of doctors working in one hundred urban centers in the early 1980s and the remaining third in eight thousand small towns and villages (Perkoff 1984, 65). Finally, in political affiliation, almost all specialists were Christian Democrats and most general practitioners were Socialists or Communists (Piperno and Renieri 1982, 82).

For the vast majority of these students, no real bedside clinical training exists in medical school, and a year of internship is not required before beginning practice in the community. The political power of the physician elite has not been mobilized against this low-quality educational system. To massively expand clinical training or to establish a numerus clausus is beyond the capacity of the state and the universities. The medical elite might also make less money if some of their time were devoted to training students. Thus, in spite of major studies and exposés, little has changed since the 1950s (Freddi 1984, 213–91).

Doctors and the SSN Since 1978

The Italian National Health Service does not, in practical terms, exist. A careful reading of the critiques and studies since Law 833 creating the SSN on paper was passed in 1978 reveals that it is neither a service (it is a funding mechanism and an attempt at cost control), nor national (varying in function according to each regional government's implementation); it is oriented toward payment for services (not preventive medicine, which is specified as the main goal of the bill), and it does not reorganize the existing system of services.

The SSN may have been doomed from a political-historical standpoint. It was instituted at a time when Communist power was at its height. The slow ebb of PCI power after Law 833 was passed allowed the Christian Democrats to renege on their agreement to work with the Communists in implementing the new law. As is true of many national human service and welfare laws in Italy, the goals of 833 are couched in broad generalities, with the details to be worked out by each new (since 1974) regional government. Some regions (especially but not only Communist strongholds) have attempted to change the system along the lines of the original legislation. The Italian medical profession, divided by political parties and the class gap before passage of the law, has developed more power and solidarity due to the law's provisions that professional groups must contract collectively with the state for fees and payments.

Intense regionalism—with different dialects and even different languages spoken by the older generation—is a fact of Italian life. Regional governments were finally officially recognized in the mid-1970s, and the regions have attempted, especially in social welfare and health, to take decision-making powers away from the central government, therefore setting up a new series of struggles between center and periphery (Bassanini 1976). Establishment of the regional governmental structure made it almost impossible for a uniform health care system to be set up under the provisions of the SSN, for each region could set up its own part of it without any restrictions from the central government. Consequently, governments in "red" regions, where the PCI was strong, such as Tuscany or Emilia-Romagna (Bologna), attempted to set up health care systems with citizen participation and area planning along the lines of the new law but with boards packed with Communists. But in "white" or Christian Democratic regions, such as the Veneto, the funds were used primarily to expand the network of church-related and Christian Democratic–brokered hospitals, which further expanded the power of the party and the income of the physician elite. In Sicily and Naples, both Christian Democrat and very corrupt, a large share of the SSN funds—some say up to 15%—simply disappeared. In an interview in 1987, one physician told me that the SSN was visible in Palermo only in the building of new and unstaffable hospitals (projects that produced cash for friends of the Christian Democrats and the Mafia) and in a small office with two secretaries.

Ironically, the attempt of the state to nationalize and rationalize the health care system and to control costs has forced the Italian medical profession to organize strongly against this state effort, giving them as a result more solidarity and unity than they had before passage of the law. Italy's doctors thus become a special case in our history of professional power, but the future of the profession still depends on shifts in the balance of power among sectors of capitalism, the state, the political parties, and the profession itself (Vicarelli 1986; Krause 1988).

On paper the SSN looks like a cross between the British National Health Service, with its nationalized public hospitals (though technically in Italy the funding is nationalized rather than the health settings) and aspects of health planning found in the United States under Public Law 93-641. This U.S. law set up health systems agencies (HSAs) to plan for services for every 100,000 to 200,000 people; each state has its own State Health Planning and Development Agency (SHPDA), and a national federal headquarters oversees the system (Krause 1977b, 223–59). Italy has a similar three-tiered system. Like Britain and unlike the United States, the Italian central government has the money as well as the planning capacity, which it passes on down the line to the regional governments and then to the individual health region or USL (Unità sanitaria locale).

As with the SHPDAs and HSAs in the United States, the regional and local agencies have boards with voting power. These boards were occupied in 1978 by citizens, consumers of services, and politicians, but not physicians. Partitocrazia dictated that each board was staffed with people loyal to the governing party of the region. Across the nation, the percentage of board members in each political party closely matched the percentage of that party's vote in the last election and its representation in the parliament. The board hired the staff of the USL by political party affiliation and not necessarily by ability, with the result noted by Perkoff (1984, 30) that:

the administrative personnel of the USLs seem to be less than adequately trained, overloaded with work, and in any case, not at a level to supply the required services, and as I observed were slowed down by activities of a financial sort as well as those of "monitoring." The resulting situation is made much worse by the fact, repeatedly mentioned in our interviews, that the personnel of the collegial directive organs, as well as the administrative personnel, seem to be chosen under criteria which are almost exclusively political.

Until the medical profession organized in 1981 for revisions in the law, it was not represented directly on the local boards or at the regional decision-making level. It is an index of the growth and power of the profession that doctors now co-manage the USLs and have strong representation on the regional and national boards that oversee spending. But here, as before, the doctors are chosen at least in part according to their political party affiliation, which means that a plurality are Christian Democrats, followed in numerical strength by Communists and Socialists.

While the 1978 law had hoped to put physicians on full-time salary both in the hospitals and in the community, the compromise worked out in the first three years produced a contracting system in which medical unions (syndicati) affiliated with each major labor union (and with the nonaffiliated doctors' unions) signed three-year contracts with the SSN for their panel reimbursement or hospital salaries. This need to organize to bargain for better contract terms was the political-economic impetus that led to greater solidarity for the profession after 1978. The role of the ordini is critical here. As semipublic professional regulatory and licensing bodies, they had historically some prestige and some minor national political role. As the only bodies to which all doctors had to belong, they became increasingly important after 1978 as advisers to the doctors bargaining with the USLs, with regional governments, and with the SSN administration in Rome. Even the Communists, who opposed the continuation of a private liberal medical profession after 1978, realized that the doctors had the power to frustrate the new law, given the weak state and the Communists' own loss of power. As Vicarelli puts it: "The PCI believed that a more efficacious outcome would be guaranteed by maintaining their professional group autonomy, and guessed that contracting with the medical profession would assure not only their approval of the new law but also its *legitimation* and its practical *enactment*." She also notes that since "the PCI now agreed with the Christian Democrats about letting up on the doctors, this created a profession with greater power after 1978 than before. This recognition of the 'contracted free profession' signified, in fact conceded to the general practitioners, a 'private government' within limits, one in which they would be required to contract periodically in terms of a 'specific agreement,' without 'giving them a formally recognized role in political planning [concertazione]' " (Vicarelli 1986, 110).

The next step was predictable. Once the general practitioners—the vast majority of Italian physicians—could contract, they could bargain, and if things were not going well at the end of the three-year contract periods, they could threaten to strike on a national level and shut down the health system of the nation. This was a new and very real power. The general practitioners, after many years of trying, finally formed their own political association in 1982: the Società italiana di medicina generale. It would probably never have been formed had the state, by enabling general practitioners to form bargaining units, not forced them to see their common interests as a profession, regardless of party affiliation.

The role of the ordini was critical in translating the law into practice. In my interviews at FNOM headquarters in 1987 it became clear that the lawyers who are the actual operating staff (leading doctors make up the FNOM board, with heavy representation by general practitioners) worked very closely with the parliamentary committees that write changes in health legislation, giving their reactions or "consultations" before and not after passage. This is particularly important in Italy, where parliamentary committees can legislate many of the details and the regulations of large laws (such as the framework law that set up the SSN, Law 833), and the law can become valid without a vote of the entire Parliament. Because the enactment lies in the details, and the FNOM has a heavy impact on these details, the medical profession can be said to participate fully in its own regulation and control (Federazione nationale ordini medici 1988). The edge of reform has thus been blunted.

The victory of the physicians, organizing to frustrate some of the original aims of the SSN, was possible because in Italy the central state remains quite weak and must bargain with special interests. The victory made the FNOM a political model for other professions in Italy. Exaggerating a little, but nevertheless noticing a possible trend, Camusi speaks of a return of professional guild power as the political parties begin to weaken their grip on the state and civil society (Camusi 1986). The creation of a cross-national, cross-professional federation of ordini known as the Federazione nazionale degli ordini is a step in this direction. Yet when I visited the Federazione in 1988, it appeared to be a shell organization, and its tiny staff directed me to what they described as the real professional power center in Italy: the Federazione nationale ordini medici.

Meanwhile, the state is striving to offset the impressive gains of the medical profession in terms of solidarity. The state is finally becoming less passive vis-à-vis the health care cost crisis. The average length of stay has dropped by 40% in public hospitals covered by the cost cap of the SSN—from twenty days to twelve—since the SSN, regional governments, and USLs introduced global, fixed-amount budgeting into the hospital system (Stirpi and Dirindin 1985). The length of stay has not decreased in private hospitals (outside the SSN) with a high balance of chronic patients and mental patients who can afford to pay. The average SSN hospital length of stay figure, while long by U.S. and most western European standards, reflects the assertion of real power, for perhaps the first time in this area, by the state. If physicians have become organized, they are now for the first time forced to deal with an organized state. But the power of the state, though increasing in the health field, is still quite weak compared with other nations in our study.

Profession, Party, State, Capitalism: Future Configurations

Most policy-related discussions of the future of the SSN in Italy, and the role of the medical profession within it, tend to be practical and technocratic. Analysts point to the need for better accountability, for better data collection, for greater cooperation among medical profession, health workers, and the politicians that dominate the USLs, and, above all, for experiments in cost control. These improvements are needed, but, as Donati notes, the SSN cannot be treated as a closed system, independent of Italian attitudes toward freedom and social control, toward the state, and other factors (Donati 1985).

The general trend in welfare states since World War II has been for the state, supported until about 1970 by parties of the Left, to assume control of social spending. As greater percentages of professional graduates work for the state or under contract to it, the state, allied with large capitalist sectors, begins to exert leverage over professional group power, which slowly erodes. In western European states of this type—France is a good example—the state challenges professional group power. Professions then begin a rear-guard action against these attempts to rationalize the work in public sectors or against attempts by the state to let its underpaid professionals compete after hours with colleagues in private practice (Association nationale des avocats de France 1974).

But Italy, as we have seen, does not have France's strong state, the reasonably unified capitalist class, and the cooperation between capitalist sector and state directed against professional group interests. In Italy political parties, through partitocrazia, colonize capitalism, the state, and the professions, with a particular focus on controlling the action and the resources in welfare-state service programs. So future alternatives in Italy can be viewed under at least two sets of assumptions. The first is that Italy will finally, after a fifty-year delay since the time of Mussolini, begin to develop modern capital-state politics similar to those of other western European nations and will develop a stronger state. Under this set of assumptions, crisis in the SSN will force these adjustments despite resistance from the political parties, which will lose influence to the state.

This first scenario gains credibility as old party leaders in PCI, Christian Democratic, and Socialist sectors give way to newer, younger, and more technocratically oriented officials, who recognize the seriousness of the crisis for the Italian state. Large corporations and the unions, which foot most of the bill for the SSN—in effect, subsidizing the endemic tax evasion by small business, the professions, and service sectors—may also put new, more effective pressure on the state to modernize. Or political parties may simply begin to relax their direct involvement in state decision making. Implementation of more effective cost control of hospital spending from 1983 to 1988 provided evidence of this impulse.

Italian statistics are sometimes unreliable, but if this trend really exists and continues, the medical profession will be forced from a position within the state or contracted to it into a more rationalized and industrialized set of working conditions. Tousijn predicts that "because of the concomitant processes being brought into play, the medical profession may be progressively losing its position of supremacy." He lists as causes of its decline the growth of health expenses (and the reaction of the state to them), growing doubts about the efficacy of medicine, the "revolt of the patients" (here quoting American and not Italian sources), the political action of other health workers (especially the unions of paramedics, which are challenging medical authority in hospitals), and the ever growing gap between the elite and the mass of the profession (Tousijn 1987b, 195, 201). But he does not discuss the reaction of the profession to the SSN. Finally, he is optimistic about the state's strength once a welfare state is constructed: "In Italy, and in other European nations, there prevails . . . a further tendency, toward the enlargement and the consolidation of the role of the state, historically relevant from the beginning of the professionalization of the health professions" (Tousijn 1987b, 201).

But, this being Italy, other scenarios are possible. Camusi believed that the political parties were in the mid- to late 1980s finally losing their tight grip on the state precisely because that tight grip had paralyzed the state, brought chronic fiscal crisis to Italy, and caused problems for capitalism. As partitocrazia weakened, professional associations could be expected to gain power to become "le nuove gilde Italiane," the new Italian guilds (Camusi 1986, 2). Her findings on professional actions in the Italian parliament "indicate[d] that the professional organizations are approaching a true and proper transitional phase. While they have not yet acquired a complete financial and normative autonomy, one is no longer able to say that they are completely submerged by political [party] goals or administrative bureaucracy. Rather, we are dealing with associations that alternate moments in which they control and determine their working conditions with moments of incapacity and fragility in this regard" (Camusi 1986, 5).

Clearly, if the hold of partitocrazia weakens, both the state and civil society (professional groups and sectors of capitalism) will become better able to deal directly with the politics of professional authority and control. But the decline of partitocrazia remains an open question. Since Camusi's study the state has endured several national strikes and entered into several comprehensive contracts with the medical profession, contracts that gave the profession, helped by the Christian Democrats and the Socialists, a substantial raises in pay.

What does our case study of the Italian medical profession reveal for standard conceptual models of professional group power and professional autonomy? If political power and control over work came from medical expertise, then surely the Italian medical profession would have begun to dominate the workplace and its relation to the state before 1981. Only a knowledge of the historical relations between professional group political solidarity and power, on the one hand, and state solidarity and power, on the other, can begin to show why doctors rose in power and influence over their workplace. Capitalist rationalization of workplaces is somewhat irrelevant to the primarily public Italian system, yet the increasing pressure by capitalists on the Christian Democrats and the Socialists may have already helped to push the SSN toward cost control. Yet the pharmaceutical industry, a major capitalist sector in a nation where ill-trained general practitioners continue to overprescribe, continues to fight by fair means and foul against attempts to control the prescription of drugs or to reduce funding for them. The industry—in the hands of the Christian Democrats—intervenes consistently on the side of the physicians in their continuing fight against the state.

Thus neither the functional, nor the interactionist, nor the neo-Marxian model of professional power and its changes predicts the central role of political parties in the relations among the state, capitalism, and the profession of medicine in Italy. Partitocrazia is almost a system unto itself. Long-term capitalist rationalization of the economy—and even support for a stronger state in this process—may indeed be the future in Italy, but only because the political parties have decided to move in this direction, and the medical profession will once again lose power in the process. But the short-run outcome is rather the reverse. The state, in attempting to control the medical profession, has strengthened and begun to unify a weak profession.

Avvocati and Magistrates: The Politicization of Justice

Partitocrazia has deeply affected the legal professions in Italy. In a system where no neutrality is possible, the legal system, which is supposed to have some neutrality, is marked by the same divisions that characterize the rest of the society. This has led to a history of decreasing respect for both lawyers and judges and to a lack of autonomy for both groups with respect to the state, which is itself paralyzed by political factions.

Italian lawyers helped shape the Risorgimento—the unification of Italy in 1861–1870. As with many nations in periods of rapid change, the lawyers in Italy were instrumental in applying the values of a new national society, a renewed and more rational social order. Lawyers were very active in the new Italian parliament, supplying 74% of the 1891 legislature and 41% of the 1913–1916 legislatures. As the nation became established, however, lawyers became active less as political leaders and class representatives and more as technical professionals. As in France, lawyers occupied a smaller—though still significant—percentage of the seats of Parliament, 21% in 1953–1962 (Olgiati and Pocar 1988).

In contrast, the judiciary was quite passive, coming from and consistently representing the interests of the upper class in the years after unification, in the first twenty years of the twentieth century, under Fascism, and until about 1965. At that point the judiciary began to split between the elite and the lower court judges; most of the former remained conservative, but the latter group, which included many younger judges, took more radical political positions on issues affecting both the courts and their own careers. Leftist groups such as Magistratura democratica radically reinterpreted the law to favor working-class interests over those of the upper class, creating a major crisis in the judicial system that still continues.

The ongoing clashes within the magistrature have led to much confusion and even greater alienation of the Italian public from the court system. Uncertain of the political leanings of a particular judge, the majority simply avoid the legal system whenever possible. The average lawyer thus has few cases to argue in court, concentrating instead on providing legal advice. Only those who cannot avoid court appearances—businesses in fraud and contract cases, for example, or those accused of crimes—can be found with any regularity in the courts. The general population has contempt for lawyers, judges, and the legal process. We will consider the history and structure of the legal profession first, then of the judiciary, and finally the relation of the two in the legal process. (There are virtually no studies of Italian notaries; they have far less power than their counterparts France and do not contribute significantly to legal activity.)

Italian Lawyers: Elite and Mass Professions

Napoleon was the primary instigator of the formation of the Italian system of ordini, a legacy of the short period when he conquered much of Italy in the early 1800s. The Italian ordini represent each professional group as a body within the state but are almost completely run by the profession itself. As Olgiati and Pocar observe (1988, 340), "The Napoleonic law was in force only briefly, but it was enough—at the time of the Restoration—to revive among Italian lawyers the ideal image of the French ordre, according to which lawyers were *maitres de son tableau* (masters of their own roll) and, more particularly, the ancient and strong Italian tradition of *free* law societies, colleges, associations, chambers and councils, which, in each preunitary state, often derived from medieval and Renaissance municipal institutions." After independence, the decentralized ordini provided whatever order there was in the Italian legal profession. Membership was mandatory in order to practice law, and leading lawyers in each area controlled the local ordine, independent of the weak central state.

A major change in the function of the legal ordini came with the rise of Fascism in Italy. Olgiati believes that the majority of lawyers neither resisted the rise of the regime nor were actively involved in supporting it, but rather used the regime to gain their own ends. The Fascist constitution has continued to be enforced by postwar regimes, yet it included clear elements of arbitrariness. The actions that the Fascist Party took to get rid of its opponents were considered "legal" by the regime, for example, and the courts were not allowed to oppose them. This interpretation left lawyers in a difficult position. The majority, tending politically toward the right, submitted to the new system but tried to moderate Fascist extremism—sometimes successfully, sometime not. They acted as a loyal opposition within the Fascist scheme. Mussolini responded by granting the lawyers a numerus clausus in 1927, but on the other hand he set up a national centralized body in Rome, the Consiglio superiore forense. Half of the Consiglio's members—and all of the executive staff—were appointed by the government, which could thus begin to exert state power against a traditionally local and decentralized profession. Enrollment in the Fascist Party, viewed as an avenue of rapid upward mobility for young avvocati, became widespread (Olgiati 1989).

On the other hand, those lawyers who announced that they were the regime's opponents suffered violence and death at the hands of Fascist thugs as early as 1924 and 1925. To this minority, the regime was implacably hostile, persecuting them as political scapegoats for the entire group (Olgiati 1989, 29–30). The ordini remained until 1933, when the regime replaced them with forensic trade unions, state-run organs that had to affirm the positions of the Fascist state. In addition lawyers were represented as members of occupation-based "corporations" which were found elsewhere in the fascist regime. But the result was not what the regime had intended: "The regime itself had to face, operate and control *three* normative systems—professional, trade-unionist, and corporatist—which were not only different by origin, function, etc. but due to political contrasts within the P.N.F. [Fascist Party] itself also were kept apart and often opposed each other" (Olgiati 1989, 23). As noted, the complexity of the Fascist system allowed lawyers who were willing to work within it to enjoy its advantages and evade its penalties by working its inconsistencies.

Thus even the Fascist state, stronger than those that preceded and post-dated it, did not succeed in gaining total control over the legal profession. The Consiglio nationale was replaced at the end of the war by a return to the decentralized prewar system of ordini. The next step was a series of intermediate organizations overseeing special areas of the law. Finally, in 1964, the Federazione dei sindicati degli avvocati e procuratori italiani was founded. But even this group, which organizes seventy professional associations with six thousand members, still represented only 12% of Italian lawyers in the mid-1980s (Olgiati and Pocar 1988, 342). In effect, what the Italian lawyers have is a continuation of the decentralized system of prewar times, which leaves them little national group power.

The number of avvocati has grown only slowly since 1880. At that time 12,885 lawyers were enrolled in the registers of the ordini, though only about two-thirds of them were probably practicing. The number grew to 25,660 in 1921, to 33,059 in 1958, to 39,415 in 1965, and, in contrast with the rapid increase in France, to 46,491 in 1982, still with only two-thirds in active practice. The lawyer-to-population ratio went from 45:100,000 in 1880 to 82:100,000 in 1982. One reason that lawyers have never proliferated rapidly in Italy is that a candidate must endure a very long apprenticeship—at least three years after the law degree and usually four to five—in the office of an avvocato, then pass an exam to become a *procuratore praticante,* a sort of junior lawyer. Only after six years in this rank is the candidate promoted to the rank of avvocato. Many apprentices earn no wages and procuratori scarcely any, so the profession is effectively closed to working-class or poor students, even those who complete the law degree at the university. The system favors established avvocati and their friends and family, for no lawyer is compelled to take a student as an apprentice, and most will do so only as a favor to his family, a friend, or his political party (Olgiati and Pocar 1988, 346, 358).

Two studies by Prandstraller give the most accurate picture of the Italian avvocato profession, which has more in common with the consolidated

American equivalent than with the specialized British and French ones. The first of his studies analyzed a national sample in 1967, and the second focused on Lombardy, including Milan, in 1981 (Prandstraller 1967, 1981). Several other scholars have replicated the results of Prandstraller's studies, which can serve as an introduction to the Italian profession, its operation, and its political and social attitudes. The vast majority of avvocati have traditionally been male (96% of the national sample, 89% of the Lombardy sample, where a group of female avvocati was found at the youngest age range). Because of the long years spent as an apprentice and then as a procuratore, most avvocati begin practice in their early thirties; 6–7% start by their late twenties. The age range of the profession is thus skewed toward those in their forties, fifties and early sixties; 14% of the 1967 national sample and 9% of the 1981 Lombardy sample were sixty-five years of age or older. Their social background ranges from lower to upper middle class; the fathers of 28% of the lawyers in the 1967 national sample were themselves avvocati or members of other free professions, while 24% of the fathers worked for the state, as magistrates, in the army, or in other state branches. In the 1981 Lombardy sample the figures were similar, with 31% coming from the liberal professions and 23% from government employment, including teachers, military men and judges. Those from the upper ranks of business accounted for only 9% of the national sample and 14% of the Lombardy group. Employees in the nonstate sectors were 10% of the national sample and 13% of the Lombardy sample (Prandstraller 1967, 28–34; 1981, 32–36).

The apprenticeship period is characterized by long hours and little or no pay: 62% of the national sample worked for free during this period (supported by their family), and another 18% were paid only token wages. Most took the exam to become procuratori between the ages of twenty-four and twenty-seven. The transition to practice as a procuratore was easier for the 19% who stayed in their original place of training than for the 81% who set up on their own or with a few friends (Prandstraller 1967, 50–53, 56).

The modal type of practice is solo, with a secretary (48% of the avvocati in 1967, 51% in 1981). But other arrangements are found: most of those who share office space practice in two- or three-person groups. Almost a third have no special area of practice, whereas a third practice primarily civil law, 13% are experts in commercial law, 7% in penal law, and 6% in labor law. In 1981, 29% claimed to practice seven to eight hours a day, 35% said they worked eight to nine hours a day, 14% ten hours a day, and 7% more than ten. First clientele came from relationships with relatives (15%), through friendships (39%), and with the aid of colleagues (9%); another group started with casual off-the-street business (27%). Young avvocati try to get themselves appointed as defense counsel in criminal cases, hoping to establish a relationship with a particular judge who will ask for them again (Prandstraller 1967, 67, 82; 1981, 40, 53, 69).

Italian avvocati were asked in 1967 to estimate what percent of offices gave fees for referrals of cases—an unethical practice that happens all the time. Seventeen percent said less than 5%, 20% thought the figure was more like 5–10%, 16% said between 10 and 20% of offices paid for such referrals, and 13% thought the practice was common among 20–30% of their colleagues. Another 5% put the number at between 30 and 40%, and another 5% felt it was more than 40%. Clearly the difference between what ought to be and what happens, especially among the half of the lawyers who are struggling to survive, is quite wide (Prandstraller 1967, 125).

An upper-class elite of avvocati in Milan, Rome, Genoa, Turin, and Bologna—about 5% of the profession—work in large American- and British-style commercial law firms, but most Italian lawyers are in the lower middle class, except for those who have a second job to supplement their income. Fully 37% of the Lombardy survey said that they would leave the profession for a job that paid 1,666 1981 dollars per month. On the other hand, 54% said they would not leave the profession for another job under any circumstances. About 27% said that they lived modestly, 35% that they lived well without making investments, another 22% said they made very small or small investments, and only 0.1% reported making large investments. Almost half owned their own home. Most lawyers try to develop some relation to a political party or a union affiliated with one as a source of business; some become the counselor (consigliere) for a business, serving that client exclusively. The vast majority in individual practice have clients referred to them by middlemen, typically court officials or officers in political parties or unions, and avvocati therefore stay on close terms with these people (Prandstraller 1967, 157–58; 1981, 100).

The lack of professional unity is clear from the political affiliations of lawyers. Because political organizations often represent an important source of clients, it is not surprising that approximately 32% of lawyers in 1967 had some type of political position—usually a paid one—in the House or the Senate, in regional or local administration, in the political parties, in state run industry, or in the public service, arrangements that are all compatible in the Italian context with working part-time as a lawyer. The percentage involved in this way in Lombardy in 1981 was 18%. Again, no one gets any of these jobs without political connections. Those in top-rank commercial firms have ties to the Christian Democrats, those with union connections rely on the Communist and Socialist parties, and those in local, regional, and national government depend on affiliation to the party in power in that particular context. This situation could be compared with the American system, under which some lawyers choose to get involved in politics, perhaps to be named as a judge. In Italy, all lawyers must be involved politically, both to gain clients and to get the other jobs, which allow them to supplement their legal income and, in a few cases, to prosper (Prandstraller 1967, 157–58; 1981, 100).

In the national sample, 7% of the lawyers described their political choices as tending toward the right, 17% toward the center-right, 22% toward the center, 24% toward the center-left, and 9% toward the left. Twenty-one percent of the respondents refused to characterize their political tendencies. Because the survey sought no party choice but described a broad political spectrum, there is no way to gauge from this sample the relative strengths among lawyers of each specific party. But the neofascist and other right-wing splinter parties would be ordinarily be considered rightist, the Christian Democrats would be described as center-right and center, the Socialists would be the center-left, and the Communists and extraparliamentary left would be at that extreme. According to those assumptions, the Christian Democrats and other parties of the center-right have a clear advantage in the profession over those to the left and center-left, but it is nonetheless remarkable that 33% of the sample said they were left or center-left. In 1981 in Lombardy the figures were 2% to the right, 8% to the moderate right, 27% to the center, 28% to the moderate left, and 20% to the left, giving the left and moderate left 48% of the lawyers in the region. These political affiliations reflect the increasing strength of the Communist and Socialist parties in Milan and represent further evidence that lawyers choose political parties partly on a vocational basis. Lawyers' responses to the surveys—along with the large numbers who actually occupy political positions—provide an index of the profession's involvement in politics, though as we have noted lawyers still do not play the leading role that they had before the Fascist era (Prandstraller 1967, 150; 1981, 95).

Even the limited legal aid that exists for the poor and working class is politicized. Before unification each Italian state had a public defender for the poor. But after unification these defenders were not retained by the impoverished central state. Individual judges can appoint local members of the bar to defend the indigent, and many who need work volunteer for this poorly paid duty as a chance to get some experience in court. These appointments, too, often depend upon shared politics between judge and lawyer. Labor unions have large legal departments to deal with the needs of their members, but the unions are also affiliated with political parties.

In sum, the Italian bar shows the same polarization between the elite and the mass found in the other nations in our sample, though the elite is much smaller and is concentrated in a few major cities. The mass profession was a much larger percentage of the whole than that found elsewhere, with most lawyers scratching out a living, practicing in hundreds of small regional courts, and doing the minor everyday work of the bar, limited by the vast mistrust which the citizens have for the entire legal process.

Italian Judges: The Politicization of Justice

The judiciary in Italy, as in France, is a fully bureaucratic profession. Like lawyers, judges must first obtain a degree *(laurea)* in jurisprudence, after which candidates must pass a rather difficult test. Many aspirants to the bench take the examination each year, but because few pass, the number of judges remains low. A massive increase in the judicial caseload has thus resulted in an overloaded judicial corps. The judiciary is undermined by political divisions, as well: the Unione dei Magistrati Italiani (UMI) represents the conservative upper magistrature, while three factions within the other major judges' union, the Associazione Nazionale dei Magistrati Italiani, represent moderate, center-left and left wings, and disagree not only over judicial philosophy but also over the very nature of the judicial process.

Since long before Mussolini, judges tended to be from an upper-middle-class or upper-class social background and politically conservative. But a few did not cooperate in Mussolini's ascent to power and refused to administer the Fascist laws. Mussolini responded as follows, in 1925:

> There are within the ganglion nerves of the state administration certain immovable individuals whom it is no longer possible to tolerate for moral reasons. And these individuals, not many, fortunately, are also in the magistrature. . . . Today it is urgent to proceed with their purging because the government is not a government but a regime. . . .I am able to document that urgent provisos are stagnating on the tables of bureaucrats, fixed with the intent of sabotaging the executive intent of the government. With all of this we ought to be finished. (quoted in Pappalardo 1987, 56)

The magistrature was put on a military footing—uniforms were issued with an insignia on each to designate the rank of the judge. A starting pretor was given the rank of lieutenant, for example, a judge of the court of appeals that of colonel. By 1929 the Fascist minister of justice was able to report that "Nothing is forbidden to the citizens in interesting themselves in the political life of the nation, and the only thing that is prohibited is to hold up the work of reconstruction of the Fascist government" (quoted in Freddi 1979, 40–41n). By this time the judges who wished to stand in the way were gone; most who did not leave the bench voluntarily were imprisoned.

It is critical to understand that Italy, unlike France, did not purge its judicial ranks after the end of World War II, and former Fascist judges ruled the upper courts in Italy until well into the 1960s. Although some changes were made in the laws after the war, many of the Fascist provisions dealing with law and order remained and were still being slowly removed in the 1980s. This background helps explain why the younger judges, nominated after the war, reacted against the system and changed the way that judges were promoted. Breaking the control of the upper judiciary, with its sizable Fascist contingent, the younger judges instituted a strictly bureaucratic system of salary incrementation in place, through thirty-six stages up to retirement, along with promotion in rank based on objective, nonpolitical criteria. Politically the ex-Fascist and conservative higher judges inspired a radical opposition, the Magistratura Democratica leftists. Since the 1970s politically moderate judges have become a minority in the major judges' unions.

The judiciary is grouped into three main levels: the magistrates of the tribunal level (local and regional courts), the magistrates of the appeals level, and the magistrates of the Court of Cassation (the highest level). Under the tribunal level are courts run either by lawyers or by laypersons temporarily deputized as judges in cases involving small claims and minor offenses. Before 1958, promotion depended solely on the evaluation of the senior upper-rank judges, and candidates with radical or even liberal views were scarcely considered. Between 1953 and 1963, four of every ten positions in the appeals courts were reserved for the winners of a national competition, one in which records of cases decided and overall reputation for fairness were considered as factors. The rest of the positions simply went to the oldest judges who applied. In 1963 the basis for the system of promotion in salary in place by age was instituted, along with a fairer system of evaluating which judges should be moved up the ranks, but there is still, inevitably, a fair amount of politics left in the process. For example, when a 1958 poll by the National Association of Italian Magistrates called for abolition of the career aspect of the magistrature—which empowered senior judges to control courtroom behavior (essentially delegitimizing the values behind the decisions of the younger magistrates)—the older magistrates withdrew from the organization and set up the UMI. This defection changed the composition of NAIM, the magistrates' association's governing body: from 25% younger tribunale judges in 1958 to 45% in 1960 and 67% in 1967. And once the senior judges had left the association, the program became far more democratic (Aquarone 1955, 242–45).

Meanwhile, the Superior Council of the Magistrature was established in the early 1960s to nominate judges for the higher ranks. This institution, composed of jurists elected from all ranks and of parliamentary members chosen by the different political parties, is responsible for disciplining the magistrates—promotion in salary is now automatic, by years of service. The president of the republic is the president of this institution—which presented a problem in the late 1980s when the president disagreed with the judges on issues of legality and the constitutionally guaranteed independence of the judiciary.

Judicial independence in Italy is not compromised by the other state organs but by the interests and activities of the judges themselves. For example, a judge can take a leave of absence from the bench, with no penalty in salary or rank, to run for political office or to serve in government or even in the private sector. In 1981, two hundred of the seven thousand Italian magistrates were in full-time government employment outside the judiciary, and another two thousand were employed part-time in the highly political milieu of the state, even while sitting on the bench for the rest of the time (Freddi 1979, 122, 136–43). Not only does this arrangement tend to bias them in favor of their part-time employers and the political parties that gave them the state jobs, but the very contradiction of being at the same time an "independent" judge and a state bureaucrat or a politician tends to color their interpretation of the law itself (Volcansek 1990, 324). Naturally dissension within the judiciary is aggravated by the involvement of some in extrajudicial politics. The conservative magistrates tend to think of the judge as an interpreter of norms in a closed and complete system, whereas those on the left think of the judge as one who creates and researches the law, in an open and flexible system of norms.

The UMI represented most of the conservative judiciary in the mid-1970s, while the National Association of Italian Magistrates split into three factions: the moderate to rightist Association of Independent Magistrates (Right), the center-left Impegno Costitutionale (Zeal for the Constitution), and the leftist Magistratura Democratica (Barcellona and Cotturi 1974, 73). At a meeting of the Magistratura Democratica in Milan in 1973, the members noted that "Our alternative role is founded on a conscious choice of a field of content opposed to that which informs the bourgeois jurisprudence of authoritarian or reformatist-rationalizing inspiration, a choice not more politicized, but politicized in an inverse and contrary sense, that which is oriented not toward the defense of the capitalist order but rather toward the emancipation of the subaltern classes" (Barcellona and Cotturi 1974, 75). Magistratura Democratica led the fight against the application of the Fascist laws against free assembly and imprisonment without trial for up to ten years (used by right-wing judges to imprison those suspected of radical action against the state in the late 1960s and 1970s). The organization spoke out against those police who were suppressing the extraparliamentary Left and demanded punishment for those who brutalized and murdered political prisoners. Other members of the group went further, calling themselves *pretori di assalto*—assault judges—and singling out manufacturers they deemed guilty of maintaining poor working conditions and of polluting the environment. Naturally, judges on the right felt that these pretori were acting illegally and often reversed their decisions in the higher appeal courts that the conservatives still controlled (Barcellona and Cotturi 1974, 76; Volcansek 1990).

Defendants needed to vary their strategy, approach, and interpretation of the law, depending on whether they stood before a right-wing or a left-wing judge. The same suspect might be convicted and sent to prison for ten years or set free by a judge who blamed his employer for the impoverishment that led to his crime. The majority of Italians find in this intra-judicial conflict another reason to mistrust the courts. The clash in values and approaches between the two groups still prevails, though moderated somewhat by changes in the Italian legal system, especially in the criminal code. These changes, all of which undercut the authority of the right-wing judges, included new standards of proof, based on the American legal system, that put the burden of proof on the state; elimination of the French-style system of judges of instruction who combine police and judicial powers; and limitations on the period of detention without charges (Volcansek 1990, 324–25). Legislation passed by referendum in 1989 has lifted the protection of judges from damage suits against them in the lower courts.

But the changes have not banished chaos and unpredictability. In cases involving the Mafia, for example, physical violence and death continue to be the reward some judges get for prosecuting; political corruption involving judges and the legal system is widespread. Propaganda Due, a secret Masonic lodge that was planning a right-wing coup in the late 1970s, included several highly placed judges, and right-wing judges continue to find many excuses for not prosecuting right-wing terrorists, while arresting and imprisoning those suspected of left-wing terror. Such episodes, along with the extremely slow pace at which the legal system functions—average small cases take three to five years, major ones up to ten years—contribute to the system's low status (Volcansek 1990, 324–25).

In the interaction of the avvocato and the judge is encapsulated all the politics that characterize the Italian legal situation. From the Fascist repression of the 1920s and 1930s to the vestigial Fascist sympathies in the dominant upper courts of the 1950s and early 1960s to the violence and chaos of the 1960s and 1970s and on to the 1980s and 1990s, the main approach of the avvocato has been to keep cases out of court, to act as an arbitrator for business and private parties. Once a case enters the court system, the cycle of trial and appeal, retrial and reappeal, can go on for years. And at no point can the pleader be assured of a fair trial or an unbiased judge—cases that are decided one way by a left-leaning judge at one level are often reversed by a right-leaning one at the next. The result is a legal profession and a judiciary that are both mistrusted and avoided whenever possible by the majority of Italians. Thus the autonomy of both the bar and the bench have suffered drastically over the years, and there is little sign that either will soon regain the support of the community.

Italian Engineers: A Profession in Formation

The first Italian engineers designed and refined military and civilian works in the late 1500s and early 1600s: defensive structures and sophisticated arms and war machines as well as streets, canals, and water courses. In the 1600s, their close relation with the early state made them one of the first bureaucratic professions, a group actually working within the state itself (Parsons 1939, 43–93; Bugarini 1987, 308; Macry 1981). In 1773, Maria Theresa of Austria, who had conquered part of northern Italy, imposed new statutes on the profession, as well as upon architects, *geometre* (urban surveyors), and *agrimensori* (rural surveyors). Yet these early state rulings did not have much effect, for none of these groups had clearly established divisions of labor and no one group had the power to prevent another from poaching on its territory. There was, however, both an educational and a class difference between the architects and engineers on the one hand and the surveyors on the other, with the latter group much more of a trade at the time (Bugarini 1987, 308–9).

The era before, during, and after Napoleon's rule in the North was a time of change and expansion for the engineers. As Bugarini (1987, 310) put it, "With the rapid technological transformation at the midpoint of the 18th century the professions (architecture, engineering, and surveying) were integrated in a deep way in the growing industrial development and in the military, administrative and political systems of the bourgeois state." Napoleon's influence on Italy during the short period of his conquest was to bring the model of the Parisian Ecole polytechnique to Italy. "Schools of application" were set up in Naples in 1811, in Rome in 1817, and by 1830 in Florence, Modena, Milan, Venice, and Turin. These schools graduated the first diplomaed engineers. The schools of application were for architects and engineers, not for surveyors, who were developing their own programs concurrently. Surveyors' training was more practical, and candidates received the title of agricultural surveyor after two years in an architect's or engineer's office, agrimensore after three years, and engineer-surveyor after four.

Yet the marginal surveyor occupation, much like the solicitors in England, was in fact more modern and timely in its development, establishing institutes in Rome, Florence, and Turin from 1800 to 1852, each offering applied coursework in relevant subjects. Surveyors also worked to develop the canal systems of northern Italy and the new building trades, the first modern industrial sector in preunification Italy. But their status was never as high as the university- or institute-trained engineers and architects, because they came from a lower-class background and generally lacked university or institute programs (Bugarini 1987, 310–11, 317).

From the Unification of Italy to the First World War

The Casati reform law of 1856 left the educational model almost untouched, establishing royal schools of application in the chief city in each region: Milan and Turin between 1856 and 1859, Palermo in 1860, Naples in 1863, Padua in 1876, Pisa in 1913. These schools, writes Bugarini (1987, 315), "were later named Polytechnics and from them came diplomaed engineers and architects, after a two-year period of attending the scientific faculty (physics-mathematics branch). Left untouched were the old Academies of Fine Arts and the Schools of Fine Arts from which came diplomaed architects who had attended previously, for three years, the new Superior Technical Institutes." This mixture of types of training would persist for quite a long time, and it would lead to the virtual inability to distinguish the training of architects from the training of engineers. To a degree this occupational blurring reflected public reluctance to consider these occupations as separate. In a long tradition of virtuosity going back to Leonardo da Vinci, many skilled Italians were in effect, both. From another point of view, this difference paralleled that between the old academies of fine arts and the new polytechnics and also between the political Right, which supported the academies, and the growing liberal Left, which favored the polytechnics. In the 1860s the architects lost graduates to the engineers, who had a clearer training path and identifiable image than did the architects, and in struggles between the two occupations for work, the engineers began to win.

In the the 1880s, in the first phase of Italian industrialization,

> a determined role would be played by the new ranks of engineers and technicians coming from the Polytechnics and from the State Technical Institutes and who would be inserted into heavy industry—steel and shipbuilding—sustained and supported by the state, coming therefore to create a consistent "technocracy" conscious of its own power. Only later, in the first twenty years of the twentieth century, in synchrony with technical and commercial innovations in sectors such as metallurgy, autos, in chemicals and cement, in electricity and precision machinery did one see the maturing of the ranks of the technically trained, in particular those coming from the Milan and Torino polytechnics and who combined, in many cases, the role of engineer and that of entrepreneur. (Bugarini, 1987, 317)

In this period, engineering became a way for the upper middle and upper classes of the provinces to place their sons in positions of prestige. The field was not a way for those of working-class background, or even those of the middle and lower middle classes, to advance, for the Italian university of the time was quite elitist. The political philosophy of the universities was by and large conservative, as in France. As Sapelli (1981, 694) observes, "Engineering was used to expropriate the ability of the working class to organize itself, primarily through the manipulative techniques of 'scientific management.' " As elsewhere in Europe and in the United States, engineers became experts in the new organizational culture of the factory. And in this early period they lobbied successfully to eliminate the state title *agricultural engineer* to designate a position held by surveyors and not engineers.

Architects did not revise their complex systems of training until the end of the First World War. Then they established, through the work of the National Committee for Schools of Architecture and the Roman architects in particular, a Higher School for Architecture (Bugarini 1987, 319). That done, their professional track becomes gradually less relevant to our analysis of the engineering profession, except in the building industry, where the rivalry remains. The engineering profession has thus not been able to get the support of the state to delineate its area of expertise in a way that clearly separates it from the architects, at least in the areas where they both are working.

The Fascist Period: Professional Identity and Unemployment

The Fascist period was for the engineers characterized both by professional recognition and by professional deprivation. At the depths of the economic depression after World War I, various parochial organizations combined to form the Associazione Nazionale degli Ingegneri Italiani (ANII the National Association of Italian Engineers). In these years the task was twofold: to protect the role of engineering in industry by holding back the proletariat's attempt to win the economic war that it was beginning to wage with capitalism, and to block the attempt of technicians and architects to develop the same expertise as engineers. Engineers also developed an organization to mediate between capital and labor, a Confederation of Intellectual Labor, which was in fact a protofascist organization, similar in many ways to those we have already discussed for France (Chiodi 1920, 26). The rise in unemployment was another force behind the next step, the creation of ordini for engineers and architects in 1923.

The primary advantage that the Fascist regime offered to the architects and the engineers came with the Gentile reform, a conservative educational program that further diminished the opportunity for members of the working class and the lower middle class to attend the university (Barbalgli 1982, 102–41). Before the reform, some of these students had been able to get into the university without following the rigid and socially selective route of the classical or the mathematics–physics liceo. In theory the reform would limit the number of engineers and architects trained, for the students at the technical institutes could not go from them to the polytechnics or to the Higher School for Architecture. Instead, the Fascist regime provided a lower track for these individuals, creating technical institutes for land surveyors and implementing a law in 1929 that created a register of geometri. The plan was to carefully delineate the division of labor in industry and in the public sector of these three professions. But the attempt failed, both because of the economic crisis (which pitted the groups against one another) and because their areas of expertise were not clearly differentiated.

The Fascist regime, in other words, could not deliver on its promises to these groups. The state, although it centralized power and changed the relations between state and society, could not make what Bugarini (1987, 322) calls a "scientific organization of labor" and could not guarantee a "constitutional government of technicians and technocrats" nor a lever to rationalize the factory system, but created instead a system for the upping of productivity of workers and a simultaneous compression of salary levels. And in this process of salary compression, the engineers suffered greatly. For the Fascist state lumped them with the workers on salary issues, while giving them special status in licensing—a concession that cost the regime and the capitalists nothing. The ordini were instituted in 1923 and a state exam was mandated in 1933, but because the engineers were guaranteed neither the development nor the direct control of the forces of production these apparent successes counted for little. The establishment of the huge semipublic Italian Institute for Reconstruction (IRI) was a source of some jobs, starting in 1929, but was not a solution for many engineers. The supply continued to exceed the demand.

Barbalgli has assembled examples of the conditions of the profession in the Fascist years. In 1920 and 1921, before the advent of Fascism, engineers became the focus of attacks by workers, who considered them tools of the capitalists:

> Placed as usual between the conflicting demands of capitalists and workers, they felt role conflict acutely at the moment when class conflict most polarized Italian society. Unable to make the class leap, to pass over to the other side of the barricades, the engineers became the object of bitter attacks by workers, and, with the occupation of the factories, many of them were "made the target of personal violence, and of abductions." On the other hand, the feeling that the

service they rendered government and industry were not valued and repaid in adequate measure spread within their members. (Barbalgli 1982, 123)

Meanwhile, the Gentile reform reduced enrollments in the secondary schools that were the feeders to the universities and had an impact on engineering in particular. Enrollments in the field went from 11% of the total of new university students in 1896–1897 to a high of 26% in 1917–1918, dropping slowly to 23% in 1921–1922, then diving to 11% in 1931–1932 and 8% in 1936–1937. Furthermore, with each additional year the students were more upper class, eventually resembling those who enrolled in medicine and law. Yet the unemployment problem persisted for several reasons. First, far fewer engineers were emigrating; a solution to the problem of professional overpopulation in earlier years, emigration was less useful in the years of worldwide economic depression. Second, the depression was affecting employment in most sectors of Italy's economy. Finally, any change in incoming students takes years to work through the system. The result was overwhelming unemployment: according to one source, 50% of all engineers were unemployed in 1935. Even Fascist sources, known to underestimate such statistics, admitted 12% unemployment (Barbalgli 1982, 134, 136, 177, 180).

The Fascist regime took other steps to diminish any organizational power by engineers: it dissolved the new ordini of 1923 and replaced them with Fascist unions to represent all engineers, even those who did not join them. The rate of membership in these organizations, considered necessary in order to work, was 75% by 1940. Barbalgli (1982, 180), describes the situation for various professionals, not just engineers:

> The end of their organizational autonomy and the fitting into organizations rigidly controlled from above led to intellectuals' loss of the capacity to exert pressure externally on the government and other state organs as well as to exert internal control such as over access to the professions and over the behavior of those who practiced. In spite of this, the difficulties of unemployment . . . were so great that they ultimately created more tension and conflict within the corporative fascist organization than one might have thought possible.

In other words, Fascism was not a cure for unemployment in Italy. As a nation, it did not have the productive capacity of Germany and thus the ability that the Nazis and German capitalists did to employ the unemployed of the post–World War I years. The engineers tried to influence demand as well, requesting of the government that every *commune*—every village, town, and city—have its own resident engineer as well as its own doctor, paid for from state funds, and that Italian industry modernize and hire engineers instead of technicians for key functions (Bugarini 1987, 324–25).

Although the former venture met some success, the second did not, and the unemployment continued throughout Mussolini's tenure. By 1943, a numerus clausus was established as a final measure to control unemployment, but the Fascist regime had begun to fail. During this period, unemployed engineers often took jobs away from surveyors, with whom they successfully competed. Thousands of others worked as foremen in industry, for during the Fascist years the unions were crushed and therefore could not protect these jobs for workers.

The Postwar Period: From Unemployment to Professional Status

The early postwar years were not a relief for the engineers. Between 1945 and 1951, there were three times as many applicants as positions for the state competitions for jobs. Only with the advent of the Marshall Plan and the postwar growth period did the situation begin to stabilize. From about 1955 to 1970 Italy had its period of greatest economic growth, and expansion of opportunities for engineers in building and industry began to catch up with the supply of graduates, new and old. Furthermore, between 1951 and 1961 the growth curve of new laureates in engineering was virtually flat, while the demand increasingly rose (Barbalgli 1982, 218, 224).

The changed political climate of the 1960s tore down the still high barriers to the university in Italy. The postwar Left was gaining power, and it worked to liberalize access to the university by the members of the lower middle class and working class that were its constituents. By 1969 it was once more possible for graduates of the technical institutes to attend the university, and the university degree became virtually the only pathway to a career in engineering. Although the number of engineers continued to grow, the struggles between the technical fields did not abate: "The industrial development of these years saw the engineers and technicians— salaried in the industries of North Italy (Olivetti, Fiat)—realize important objectives in research and planning. At the same time the strong development of building, the enlargement of the demand for services, and urban planning developed the market for these professions without, however, settling the conflicts between the three professions [engineers, architects, and surveyor/planners], in particular in the civil area" (Bugarini 1987, 326).

The number of engineers increased slowly in the early to late 1950s, then at an increasing rate in the later 1960s and especially in the 1970s and 1980s because the barriers in the university system had fallen. In 1958, there were 30,316 engineers registered on the rolls of the order. This number grew to 41,703 by 1967, to 50,844 in 1973, to 70,619 by 1978, and to 80,021 by 1984. Statistics on how many of these were employed are less certain. Full-time engineers registered in the profession's Cassa di previdenza (retirement fund) constituted 26% of the total in 1977, diminishing to 20% by 1983. But this simply reflects the percentage who are working in *professione libere* status, not necessarily the percentage employed part-time, unemployed, or working on salary. A significant proportion of the younger engineers combine a state job with part-time private practice or have "black" or illegal employment. According to both Barbalgli and Bugarini, the problem of unemployment remained significant into the 1980s, and turf battles between engineers and architects—over the design and construction of buildings, for example—have continued (Barbalgli 1982, 318–27; Bugarini 1987, 326).

Faculties have also grown in size, from about sixty professors in the 1970s to more than three hundred in the 1980s, with the proportion of underemployed or unemployed in practice among the recent graduates somewhat higher than in the 1950s and early 1960s (Bugarini 1987, 324). Without reinstatement of an unpopular numerus clausus or major (and politically unlikely) change in the university system, a large group of graduates will not find jobs as engineers. But unemployment as an engineer does not necessarily mean unemployment in industry or in the large semipublic sector or within the state itself.

In these areas a political party sponsor may help a graduate get a job, even if it is in management or sales instead of as an engineer. The problem for our study lies in the sectoral nature of the data: we have excellent studies of electrical and electronic engineers, but not studies of equal depth of the other subfields of engineering. It is impossible to go from information on those employed to information on the ratio between those employed in the field and those who actually graduated and became members of the ordini. To do so would require the identification of a total sample, of graduating engineers and then following them up to see what percentage actually enlisted in the ordini, what percentage passed the state exam, and what kind of employment, if any, they have one year after graduation.

Although this is not practical, we can say something about two cohorts of students who graduated with the laurea in electrical and electronic engineering in 1970 and in 1979 and who did go into engineering work (but not into other fields). This survey study, by CENSIS, a private research firm in Italy, indicates that the nature of the students' social background changed from 1970, when the university reform was just a year old, to 1979, when it was well under way. The evidence indicates that the classical liceo, the primary pathway to college for the children of the upper class, remained the main route to engineering in 1970. But by 1979, the modal avenue was the scientific (math-physics) liceo, with the IMI technical institutes in second place. These latter are where lower-middle-class students traditionally go for career training as technicians, not as engineers, but with the university reform of 1969 they became a pathway to college and thus to a career in the field. Thus engineering has become a field in which lower-middle-class students can pursue social mobility (CENSIS 1987, 32).

Naturally, trying is not succeeding. The greater number of students accepted after 1969 produced much greater competition for engineering jobs, a competition in which those from powerful and established families with close ties to the political parties have an advantage. One of the least rewarding aspects of engineers' work, in both the 1970 and the 1979 samples, was income; only about 35% of the 1970 sample and 29% of the 1979 sample were satisfied. Thirty-three percent of the electronic engineers and 27% of the electrical engineers thought they were adequately paid. Career possibilities were satisfactory to 48% of each group. In both years covered, 85% felt satisfied with their relations with their colleagues, and 65% with their supervisors. When asked what factors made for a satisfactory work experience, one of the most frequent responses (63%) was professional autonomy. The possibility of learning more at their job was cited as being very important by 53% of the 1970 group and 63% of the 1979 group. Good wages were also important to their considerations of an ideal job (58% of the 1970 group, 53% of the 1979 group). Because they considered wages important yet the majority felt shortchanged, it is clear that they were more satisfied with the noneconomic rewards of their jobs than with the economic (CENSIS 1987, 180–82).

But these engineers were confident (whether rightly or not) that their economic complaints would be addressed: 68% of the 1970 group and 79% of the 1979 group felt that they would improve their professional position within two years. The majority of them felt that this was possible in their own factory (65% of the 1970 group, 64% of the 1979 group). As to the type of improvement they expected, 54% thought it would be a higher salary, 27% better professional qualifications (which no doubt could be used to gain a higher salary). In general, then, the engineers were happy with their colleagues, supervisors, and subordinates, felt that professional autonomy was important (but did not complain of its absence), were not satisfied with their wages, but felt that their wages or professional position in general would improve in the next two years (CENSIS 1987, 183–85).

The survey asked questions as well on the relation between training and work. Some were very simple—the percentage of engineers who used a pocket calculator—which tended to bring rather low responses in many areas except for teachers in the university. Conversely, other questions showed that the majority of these engineers felt that the university education was overly theoretical, and unrelated to the workplace (CENSIS 1987, 65). Note that the Italian system, like the American, routes everyone through college (which tends to be theoretical), while the French system routes its best students into the elite grandes écoles, where they learn to be management-level engineers. The French train ordinary engineers in a range of programs, from minor grandes écoles to applied university programs to a myriad of technical training programs. But the Italian engineers, conversely, can, like the American ones, move up into management, whereas French engineers, except for those who graduated from elite grandes écoles, are kept at the lower levels.

Less is known about the Italian engineers, from the viewpoint of social science, than about practically any other group in any of our nations. But the evidence we have suggests a group similar in many ways, since 1970, at least, to the American profession. Engineers have tended to come from the upper and upper middle class (and, since 1970, the middle and lower middle class), to work under conditions of short-range autonomy and loose control—as "trusted workers" in Whalley's sense (Whalley 1985). Although in some time periods a small segment has become radicalized and worked with the left—as in the early 1920s and the late 1960s—most engineers tend to be relatively passive politically, while carefully cultivating a political allegiance of some sort to facilitate employment and promotion. Only a minority, at least in high tech-industry, are in unions (Consoli 1988, 87). Most engineers are dissatisfied with their wages, but many expect to better their position. In recent years the theoretical possibilities for upward mobility have encountered the reality of greater competition. The unity of engineers as a group seems nil, with the associations acting at best as employment agencies for industry or as cheerleaders for capitalists, doing little to advance the interests of the profession, except in turf battles with rivals in the division of technical labor.

University Professors: Barons in a State-Based Guild System

Perhaps no other profession has as much power in Italy as the university professoriate. This power has been modified and somewhat restricted since the legal reforms of the late 1970s and early 1980s, but it remains remarkable for a group that is nominally state-based and part of civil service. As in France and Germany, the Italian professors are the peak of a pyramid, one in which personal patronage and guild power count for more than membership in a discipline-wide profession. In Italy, modern professional forms are still quite weak, and fiefdoms are built up by professors who are at the same time directors of their own research institutes and editors of their own unrefereed journals. Some sit on research committees that vote the money to support their institutes, and some are even members of Parliament, where they serve on education committees that vote on changes in the university system.

Professors also have a broad range of outside jobs—in industrial firms, as doctors in private practice, as lawyers, as consultants to industry, and as members of the editorial boards of publishing firms or regular contributors to newspapers and magazines. New jobs in the system are under the control of the professoriate as well, working through nationwide recruiting committees that consider the political membership of an individual candidate as important as his or her abilities, for new positions are distributed in proportion to the influence of each party. The politics of the membership of a hiring committee will usually tell more about the finalists for a position than the number of articles published by the candidate in first place. In Italy, "Not only does the structure permit little competition for individual talent and institutional status based on talent, but in addition the Italian fusion of academic oligarchy and state bureaucracy is virtually the ideal system for suppressing competition among operating units. . . . In economic terms, higher education in Italy may be seen as a system strewn with barriers to competition: a monopoly controlled by an oligarchy through a bureaucracy" (Clark 1977, 125). The system was developed under Fascism and was changed little after World War II.

The power the system gave to the professors (who sat on parliamentary committees and could veto any changes) remained unchanged during the period of increased enrollment in the 1960s and 1970s. In the late 1970s the state—through these same education committees—finally increased faculty size, adding new levels of tenured associate professors and tenured researchers, but even then the basic structure was untouched. We can consider the system in broad outline, relying primarily on the work of Clark and Giglioli, then consider the changes that have occurred since the late 1970s and the implications they may have for the power of the professoriate in the future.

The history of the Italian university goes back to 1088, the founding year of the University of Bologna. The university was run by student guilds in its first century, but the professors gradually assumed control; in Paris, as we have noted, the professors were in control from the start (Rashdall 1936). As elsewhere in Europe, the professor was the guild master and the students the apprentices. This form still essentially prevails, and the faculty chooses the dean and rector of the university. In modern times the state provides the majority of the money and sponsors competitions for new positions, with the successful candidates chosen by committees of professors. As in France, these are positions within a national system, for the individual universities do not have the power to hire their own full professors, although they may informally influence the choice if they have power in the selection committees.

Before Mussolini and Fascism, control of the universities was less centralized. In the early Fascist period, Gentile tried to reform the universities and make them part of a centralized state system. But this reform was not completed until the mid- to late 1930s. From that time the system was essentially run from Rome, through the Ministry of Education and specifically the Ministry of Public Instruction (Clark 1977, 52–53). During the Fascist period, the Ministry of Education assumed control over the university, including selection of university deans and rectors, but these privileges were restored to the faculty after the war.

Until the 1970s, almost all courses throughout Italy were prescribed by the ministry, and lists published throughout the nation specified which university offered a particular course. Not all universities offer instruction in all subject matters. The smaller universities are often limited to one or two fields, such as commerce or law, while the larger ones—such as Milan, Bologna, Rome, Naples, Palermo—offer courses in nearly every field. But this central form of organization does not mean centralized control, for several reasons. First, the professors, not the state, choose who will teach in the university, and they choose from among themselves who will be dean of the faculty and rector of the university. Second, although the money comes from the state, there is no centralized inspection corps to visit all the individual universities, and no one investigates how a professor spends his time. This lack of oversight allows the loose scheduling of courses and the substitution of associates and researchers for professors, even in the basic required courses. The result, as Burton Clark notes, is a kind of balkanization of the administrative system: the center publishes rules and regulations, which the professoriate obeys or ignores as it chooses. The central state is weak and paralyzed by the politics of partitocrazia, the education ministry is often run by former or even current professors, and professors are prominent on the education committees of Parliament, so restrictions on the freedom of the professoriate are unlikely. In fact, given the multiple roles of professors, who are determined to build empires or simply to protect their interests and develop contacts in order to provide jobs for their best students, the system could not continue if they were restricted to their narrower university responsibilities. And because the prestige of the university professor is high in Italy, no political will exists in Parliament to curb the freedom of the profession (Clark 1977, 67–71, 103–6).

Giglioli notes the same division of faculties in Italy that occurs in other nations between the "professional" faculty—those in law, medicine and engineering, for example—and the "nonprofessional" contingent in arts and sciences. He characterizes the professionals as being highly involved in extrauniversity professional affairs. (For most of Italian academic history there has been no limitation on time for these activities, no one-day-a-week consulting rule, as is common in American universities) Their academic involvement and social integration in the academic community is minor, their style of life similar to that of other professionals. In terms of academic style, they tend toward one-person institutes with strict control of subordinates, who are given minor teaching responsibilities. Divisions along ideological grounds are minor. By contrast, in the nonprofessional or arts and sciences sectors, Giglioli finds much lower involvement in extra-university activities, major academic responsibilities and a major integration in the academic community, and a style of life that is intellectually oriented (with the typical Italian intellectual's apartment of book-lined walls). This group tends to work in multichair institutes, and their subordinates often have major teaching responsibilities. The nonprofessionals are usually grouped along ideological lines. Christian Democratic sociologists, for example, often will not invite their Communist colleagues to a conference, and vice versa. But if the same split exists as in Italy as in other countries between the professional and nonprofessional disciplines, the disparity in prestige and salary between professors and practitioners does not. Professors of medicine and law are not only the stars in academia but also the highest money earners in private practice—the heads of the practicing profession. This unity between academics and practitioners is a sign of the strength of the academic guild, and of the concurrent weakness of the state (Giglioli 1979, 83–109).

The differences between professional and nonprofessional faculty extend to other areas. For example, rules in the early 1970s that required at least fifteen hours a week on campus for full-time faculty found far more favor among the nonprofessional faculty than among the professional. Although nearly all categories of faculty were in favor of some type of numerus clausus, support was stronger in the professional fields (87%) than in the nonprofessional fields (69%). The numerus clausus is a perennial issue in Italy, yet it almost never is adopted. In recent years, however, a modification is being worked in the professional faculties: all applicants are accepted for the first or second year toward a law or medical degree, after which a test eliminates a specified percentage of the students, much as in France (Giglioli 1979, 170). The percentage accepted is changed from year to year.

In the early 1970s there was a major difference between the professors and the assistants and *incaricati* (who became associate professors after the reforms of the early 1980s), on the issue of the democratization of the university. Faculty members from a lower- and lower-middle-class background were only slightly more interested in democratization than those of higher ranks. But assistants and incaricati were twice as likely to favor democratization. In the more professional faculties, 36% of those professors from medium and medium-high class standing wanted democratization, whereas 91% of their assistants did; for the lower- and lower-middle-class professionalized faculties, 40% of the professors wanted it, whereas 93% of their assistants did. The differences were almost as great among the non-professional faculties. Among the professors of upper- and upper-middle-class background, 47% wanted democratization, whereas 89% of their assistants did. Among those of lower social class background, 49% of the professors wanted democratization and 92% of their assistants did. When the state began to reform the university, the assistants and incaricati (the new associate professor rank) were given tenure and voting power in the faculties, though the professors retained control over promotion to that rank (Giglioli 1979, 108).

The political coloration of the faculties has changed over the years. During the era of Mussolini, leftist professors, a minority to begin with, were soon purged from the faculties, whose members typically belonged to the so-called lay parties (Liberal, Republican, Socialist); not a small number were also Freemasons. Jews, somewhat rare, were not discriminated against until the late 1930s, when Mussolini's policies first became overtly anti-Semitic, partly under the influence of Hitler, partly on his own. Remembering that the state from Mussolini's time on had great control over curricula in certain fields, it is not surprising that the postwar constitution affirmed many of Mussolini's educational reforms—the national system in which professors had a major role and control over their local units—while striking down the barriers he had erected to higher professorial autonomy (Clark 1977, 105–6).

After the war regional power bases began to develop and increasingly to engage the central administration, which in the early postwar years remained somewhat Fascist in orientation. The lay liberal parties lost their commanding control of the university faculties, replaced by the one large postwar party, the Christian Democrats. The Christian Democrats and to a much smaller extent the Communists—who were strongest in the northern "red belt"—controlled most of the professorships in Italy in the 1950s and 1960s. As more younger faculty were added, especially after the 1970s and early 1980s, and the new rank of associate professor was created, the professoriate expanded and turned to the left. When Giglioli did his survey in 1972, before these changes, 63% of his sample of academics classified themselves as on the extreme left, the left, or the moderate left, while 24% placed themselves in the center (usually the Christian Democrats) and 13% on the right—this in a nation where 38% of the general population was on the left, 42% in the center, and 20% on the right. In fact, according to Giglioli's charts, the Italian professorial distribution of political affiliation is similar to the English and the American ones (Giglioli 1979, 140).

The professional disciplines had higher percentages on the right, but even here the balance was shifted to the left, including the engineering, medical, and the law faculties. This tendency was more important for the forming of collegial relations and the reservation of future chair opportunities than in the running of the university, where the professors' desire to hold onto their privileges was apolitical in nature, and cooperation was more common than interparty conflict (Giglioli 1979, 165).

Guild Power and the Italian Professoriate

Guild power, as we have been defining it, involves control over the association, the workplace, the market, and the relation with the state. The Italian professoriate has nearly total control over three of the four dimensions and a major influence in the fourth. To begin with, the professors—including, in recent years, the associate professors—have control over the association, defined as the faculty group; they vote for members of their faculty councils and elect not only the deans but also the university rector. There is no private board of directors to interfere with the faculty decisions.

The only figure in the administration not chosen by the faculty is the administrative director, or business manager, who is chosen by the state to oversee matters of university finance. But the faculty gets its salary directly from the central state, and research grants to support the institutes come directly to professors from the central government or private industries without the intervention of the administrative director, so this figure of the central administration has little direct influence within the university. He does have the power to sign off on requests to the central government for various kinds of academic funding—to support institutes, for example. As the chief representative of the central state education ministry on site, he can also call for investigations of improper use of funds. Still, an administrative director is more likely to build power by working with his faculty, not against it—for it is in both of their interests to get money and new positions for the university (Clark 1977, 100–103).

Associational power in Italy does not include control over the disciplinary associations, what Clark calls the "professional" associations—groups of scholars who share a field, such as medicine, chemistry, or sociology. Disciplinary fields are weak in Italy precisely because given the combination of bureaucracy and oligarchical guild control, they would be a threat to the power of individual professors. A scientific field typically presupposes the free exchange of information in refereed journals, where articles competing for publication are read "blind" by anonymous judges. But in Italy, as in France, articles tend to be read by the professor in charge of a journal connected with his institute. Publishable articles are those that reflect the viewpoint of the professor or his delegated assistants; membership (or former membership) in the institute that supports the journal is virtually required for publication. This naturally limits the quality of the articles submitted, as each professor or institute essentially runs a vanity press. In the social sciences and to some extent in the humanities, the author—and the content of the article—must also share the political outlook of the institute director-professor. The same is true of the publishing firms, whose boards of editors accept or reject monographs, especially in the social sciences and the humanities, based on their political content. This is not to say that good work is not done in Italy—simply that it is done in spite of the system rather than because of it (Clark 1977, 81; Giglioli 1979, 135–38).

Lacking genuine nationwide professional associations, the system also lacks genuine interchange of ideas at national meetings where all—students, assistants, associate professors, and professors—are free to make contributions and to comment on each other's work. These meetings, standard in American academia, are absent in the Italian scene, as they are in Germany and France. In the absence of true disciplinary associations, there is no objective system for ranking the expertise of professors. It is not surprising, therefore, that international agencies rating university systems comparatively, especially in the sciences, rate the Italian system low. Professors in the sciences have admitted that their journals are primarily composed of articles rejected by the international scientific community (Clark 1977, 99).

But if associational power does not extend across disciplines in the Italian professoriate, colleagues can agree in private across party political lines in the faculty committees that run each university. They also exert control over the graduates of the university who want careers in academia; and such aspirants must get a job as a paid or an unpaid assistant working for a professor. The professors have power as well over who is chosen to join their ranks. State-run national competitions determine promotions, but the committees that choose the winners are made up of professors in the field of the new professors. Competition for a position on a particular team to choose a new professorship or associate professorship is thus a contest among the different subgroups in a field, often decided by personal rivalries and political party membership. After the late 1970s, new rules mandated by the state specified that these committees be chosen by lot within designated fields, which has alleviated—but not eliminated—the political element. For each field usually has a high concentration of members from one political party, so that party typically dominates the committee. Committee members often communicate before officially meeting and predetermine which candidates will be ranked highly. And cronyism still thrives. Committees have been known to ignore the best candidate for a job and give it instead to a son or a son-in-law of a particularly powerful individual in the field.

Nobel prize winners in Italy do not necessarily have the best professorships but may languish at smaller universities because they do not have enough friends in the field (Clark 1977, 140).

Professors can move within the system from one university to a vacancy at another without enduring this formal selection process. But again, a professor is not likely to be hired unless he belongs to the same political party and faction as those doing the hiring. Expertise and reputation carry some weight, but reputation, especially in the non-professional fields, can be colored by personal and political alliances.

If the definition of associational power for the Italian professoriate is limited, power over the workplace is unequivocal. The state gives strict deference to the expertise of the professoriate and involves itself only in cases of outright fraud or overt rulebreaking. (An entire architectural faculty in Milan was fired in the late 1960s for being too radical and for giving all the students the same grade, and cases of fraud involving large sums of money are eventually dealt with by the central administration, but these are rare examples.) On the other hand, the state supervises the spending of research funds and has the right to audit the professors who have the grants. Supervision can range from close scrutiny to benign inattention, and the capriciousness of the state oversight has continued. Professors have to teach within the broad framework of a national curriculum, with required courses set by a central board of professors that tends to be somewhat conservative. But each university determines optional courses in each field and can specify that a certain number of them are required for the laurea. Professors enjoy the academic freedom to set examination questions, which vary from university to university and are graded by each professor and his assistants. Examinations are universally oral and can, under the pressure of increased enrollments, last as little as ten minutes. The professor has nearly total control over his own workplace and his own research institute, deploying his staff to substitute for him in lectures, to do research and institute paperwork, or to give final examinations. Because there is no national inspection bureau to check up on the professoriate, there is no real national control of what he or she does on a daily basis (Clark 1977, 55–56, 65–74).

Control over the academic marketplace is securely in the hands of the profession as well. Each new opening—proposed either by the Ministry of Education or by a university with the ministry's acceptance—is filled by a competition controlled by the professoriate. Furthermore, the university is the only system of higher education in Italy—there is no broad network of polytechnics, as in England, no grandes écoles, as in France, no system of technical universities, as in Germany. The university laurea is the only higher education degree—and the professoriate is in control of the placement of those who pursue an academic career.

The normal career pattern for a successful professor is to begin as an unpaid research assistant for a professor, then take a tenured, paid assistant-ship, continuing at this job at the home research institute while taking a position as an instructor or junior professor at a smaller university away from the home base. The aspirant then becomes an assistant and—by open competition or concorso—an associate professor at this or another univer-sity at which the sponsoring professor has ties. Finally, at the appropriate time he puts his name into contention for a chair or professorship—usually at one of the smaller universities. Eventually, if successful, he can move back to a major city and a major university; at Milan, Bologna, Turin, Rome, and Naples, more consultation opportunities are available with busi-nesses and political parties. At every step of the way, the young professor's career is fostered by his mentor. The senior mentors, in turn, move on to Parliament or become members of the Consultative Committee of the Min-istry of Education or the National Research Council; many take jobs as editors in the major publishing houses. Until very recently, there were few women professors at any rank, though many women have joined the new permanent research staff. A small number of women had reached the rank of associate professor by the late 1980s.

The influx of students in the 1960s and 1970s put great stress on the system, and the government, while increasing the number of professors from 1,928 in 1959–1960 to 3,568 in 1969–1970 and 5,209 in 1975–1976, also created the major new tenured associate professor rank (Giglioli 1979, 34). In the short run this expanded patronage, increasing the number of openings for the former students of each professor and creating a new system of professorial superbarons and minor barons. These new tenured positions will not need replacements for quite some time, however, so the long run holds little opportunity for young scholars to work their way up in the academic ranks, just as in France after the reform of 1969. The strategy of the state was thus an ill-considered quick reaction to a long-term problem.

The Italian state, specifically the Italian Parliament, could not effect more comprehensive reform, for each political bloc vetoed one part of such a plan. Ross documents the haggling in committees of the two branches of Parliament over a series of reform plans in the 1950s and 1960s, and even in the early 1970s, before passage of the partial reforms that led to the massive expansion of the tenured rolls in the university (Ross 1987).

It is in the fourth area of guild power, the degree to which the profession can control its own relation to the state, that the Italian system shows the extent of professorial power. Although nominally the Ministry of Education controls the allocation of funds, it first consults the Administrative Council, on which the university faculty is well represented. Each branch of Parlia-ment—the Chamber of Deputies and the Senate—has an education committee, and these committees, controlled by educators, write most laws concerning the university. Furthermore, a fair number of Italian prime ministers over the years have been professors, some of whom kept their university seats while serving. Senior professors can use their membership on the National Research Council to help their colleagues and hurt their opponents, thus furthering political as well as scientific goals. Moreover, with Parliament itself paralyzed between political parties and relying on a succession of coalition governments, the committees staffed by the representatives of the education establishment tend to make the rules for the universities. They can be expected to follow similar policies in the future as in the past, tenuring new categories of university personnel but not by making significant changes in the system (Clark 1977, 100–105).

The changes that have been made since the late 1970s and early 1980s are attempts to rationalize the Italian system in a Continental fashion, with some overlay of American models, such as the creation of academic departments:

> The traditional supports of the system of chairs has been weakened, the increase in the number of professors has favored the breaking up of monopolistic and oligolopolistic control which one or two schools exert over many disciplines, the academic "parties" are destined to fragment and their boundaries to become more confused, the junior teachers are much more secure, and the relation of "clientela" (dependency), often humiliating, between the "capo" and his academic court have been attenuated, as in all bureaucratic systems. (Giglioli 1979, 210)

The ties between junior and senior faculty have been diminished but not removed, for one professor is responsible for giving the young academic his first job, and usually one or a small group are responsible for advancement of the candidate (and these groups are identified with specific political parties). Changes since 1980 have left the professoriate in charge, not in the specifically oligarchical way of the past but still in a hierarchical way in which ties of personal sponsorship drive a highly politicized system. In addition to the political parties the unions representing the junior faculty (in the era of change) and all faculty (since 1980) create further potential for political manipulation, for the faculty cannot stand up and publicly oppose the stands of the union, which in turn is somewhat influenced by the political parties. Partitocrazia thus remains, within the professoriate, the governing principle that lies behind who is advanced or not, and where and when advancement occurs (Froio 1969; Matteuci 1978). The professoriate has evolved from an oligarchically run guild, to another part of the broader political system, responding to external loyalties as well as their own internal political schools and factions.

6 | GERMANY: CORPORATIST SYSTEM, PROFESSIONS INCLUDED

Our final case study involves a nation that has gone through periods of radical change, yet one in which certain basic institutions, such as the universities and the professions, have had remarkable continuity. Professions were taken over by the Nazis in the early 1930s and emerged from World War II basically unchanged—a stability that carried serious moral implications when the large role the professions played during the Nazi years finally came to light in the 1970s. Only in the 1980s did a new generation finally begin to achieve positions of leadership in these professions—the first generation in the period of our study not to be tainted by any relation to the Nazi regime.

The Prussian state was the model for the unified German state in the Bismarck era of the late nineteenth century. Prussia had depended heavily on the goodwill of the aristocracy, and key positions in that state and the subsequent unified German state were reserved for members of this group (Craig 1983, 22) The majority of the bureaucrats, however, were upper-middle-class graduates of the university. The Prussian state helped to foster and organize capitalism, which did not grow independently as in Britain or the United States. The tradition of the Prussian and German professional civil service, and the high status that this status group *(Stände)* maintains in German society, is a key to understanding the status of professional groups both before and after World War II. A second key is the growth and centrality of the German university system as a state organ, with a key role in creating the modern doctorate and specialization in the Bismarck era. The tenured professoriate became defined as civil service in this period (Fallon 1980).

Capitalism in Germany after the turn of the century encountered strong opposition in the Marxist and socialist parties of the Left. After Germany was defeated in World War I, economic and social crises encouraged political polarization that destabilized the society in the Weimar era and led ultimately to the rise of Hitler. Economic depression, combined with uncontrolled inflation, helped Hitler to gain adherents. Jews, prominent especially in professions and in the ranks of the Left, served as a target for people's frustrations. Although only a few capitalists were officially Nazis, the majority played along once the regime came to power, especially after Hitler eliminated trade unions and the Sozialdemokratische Partei Deutschland political party (SPD), which represented moderate socialists and endorsed the labor movement. Leaders of the unions and the SPD were often sent to concentrations camps, along with the Jews (Shirer 1984, vol. 2).

Both continuity and change can be seen through the Nazi period. The power of the state was even further centralized, and the traditional civil service continued its function while separate and parallel Nazi state organs were set up in some areas, such as the judiciary. Laws were passed to expel Jews and leftists from the professions. A *Gleichschaltung*—reorganization under a hierarchical order—placed all professional organizations, including the *Kammern* or professional state-sponsored bodies, under renamed or newly created Nazi ministries (Jarausch 1990a, 125–66). This centralization of power united the professional subgroups, welding them together in greater unity, while at the same time subjugating group independence to Nazi will. Those critical of the profession or the regime were expelled, along with Jews and other "racial minorities." The central state did not nationalize industry, though in the years just before and during the war certain Nazi bureaus began to plan the economy, as well as the new road system. Turner (1985) argues that only a small minority of manufacturers helped Hitler into power. But most benefited from the elimination of the trade unions and the institution of slave labor.

Defeat in World War II led to a brief and somewhat ineffective period of reform of prewar institutions. The Allied forces were eager to reestablish the German university, the German professions, and the German economy, especially but not only in the American zone of the partitioned and occupied state. Denazification ended early and incompletely in the western zones (Tent 1982). Many Nazi professors of medicine, law, and science-engineering were mildly reproached and then allowed to keep their professorships (Proctor 1988, 300). Only in the 1980s, with a new generation approaching senior ranks, was the Nazi era frankly reevaluated. Recent documentation on the role of each profession during the Nazi and postwar eras shows more continuity than change in the professional institutions, professional status positions, key professional actors, and even the political perspective of the professions in West Germany until the 1970s.

The major difference between pre–World War II Germany and the postwar era was in the structure of the state itself. After the ineffective polarized new democracy of the Weimar Republic and the centralized and totalitarian Nazi state, the postwar West German model, continued in reunified Germany, blends pre-Bismarckian regional government and regional states with the American federal model. Even more decentralized than the modern United States, the system structures responsibility, power, and funding regionally to prevent the growth of a new, strong central state. The result is a "semisovereign state" whose governmental organs and bureaus are decentralized, in contrast with a centralized set of social institutions: the capitalists are organized in large complexes of holding companies, labor is organized into strong national unions, and the professions have a peak association—the Bundesverband der freien Berufen—which represents all professions in political and governmental matters (Katzenstein 1987, 58–80; Arnold et al. 1981, 190). Universities are regionalized—as with all aspects of culture, they cannot come under central state control. This organization of society, the wish of the Allies, was acceded to and built upon by the Bonn government. The political parties mediate between the decentralized state and the centralized corporations, unions, and professional groups, involving in the process the large semipublic organizations that in Germany are given functions of public law, working under state supervision while remaining in the private sector. Katzenstein (1987, 8) concludes: "West Germany's coalition governments, intergovernmental relations, and its parapublic institutions are political, territorial, and functional forms of representation that constrain broad policy initiatives. In their interaction these three components of the policy network impose restraints on the exercise of state power that makes intelligible why policy change in the Federal Republic in incremental even when a new government is voted into office."

The postwar structure can be described as an interlocking system of power centers: capitalist industrial, party, labor, and professional interests bargain around a table, while the central government and the ruling political party are checked by the power of regional interests, including regional political parties. This form of government prevents radical change and thus keeps any group from pushing Germany in any direction quickly—thus providing insurance against any rerun of the Nazi era.

In the postwar structure, capitalism is organized through central associations that represent employers, lobbying for the interests of business at all levels (Katzenstein 1985, 25–26). The labor unions are equally centralized in sixteen major union federations (Katzenstein 1987, 26–29). But the capitalist firms are in turn controlled to some extent by three giant merchant banks, who own shares in the major corporations (prohibited under U.S. law). The banks also vote by proxy much of the stock of individual owners, who often deposit their stock. This makes the banks major players in German industrial policy, able to control the direction of industry. The national bank, which is almost totally independent of the German government, works to stabilize the currency, as well as affecting indirectly the policies of the three giant merchant banks (Hall 1986, 234–36). In this respect, capitalism and labor are centralized while the state itself is relatively decentralized.

Professions, traditionally organized in regional Kammern before the Nazi era, were combined with Nazi organizations during the Hitler era as part of the Gleichschaltung. Each group was required to remove all Jews from their governing boards. The Kammern were restructured after the war, and their anti-Semitic clauses rescinded, but most of their leading personalities stayed in place. Every practicing professional must belong to a Kammer, just as they must belong to an ordre in France or an ordine in Italy. As corporations of public law (Körperschaften des öffentlichen Rechts), the Kammern are important members of the group of parapublic institutions that play a key role in running modern Germany (Katzenstein 1985, 29–30). In terms of health-service payments, the prewar system of health insurance funds, which was restricted during the Nazi era, was reestablished, and the doctors were given more power over them than before the war, when the labor union–backed sickness funds were more powerful than the medical profession. A defense bar, essentially destroyed by the Nazi regime, was reestablished. Engineering training, which is always supported during war in any nation and which thrived under Hitler, was further accelerated after the war in the major modernization and expansion of postwar industry. And in spite of Allied pressure, especially from the United States, the university remains an elite institution, though less so than under Hitler, with additional, if restricted, pathways to higher education not available before.

Each profession experienced political polarization under Weimar, and each was forced to expel Jews and others under Hitler. Doctors, lawyers, and engineers actively cooperated with the Nazis; in the case of medicine, Nazi policy had the support of many leading professors. Early postwar reform was mild, and denazification was limited. The strong unity within the professions, created by Hitler, aided in their resistance to postwar change. Not until the late 1980s and early 1990s did professions confront for the first time challenges to postwar status, group power, and control over work. In the conservative structures that run the German professions, it was only in the late 1980s and early 1990s that the leadership was taken over by those whose values were not formed during the Nazi era. The story is complex and varies from profession to profession, but the outlines are the same in each.

In comparing Germany with France, Italy, the United Kingdom, or the United States, one difference in popular values must be understood, and it is as relevant to the power of German professions in the 1990s as in the 1930s: the endurance of German status values, the continuing deference to the university-educated class or *Akademikers* in the state and in the professions (Kahlberg 1983). Professional training is still markedly less available for the working class than in the other nations studied, preserving a real class gap between the doctors, lawyers, engineers, and academics on the one hand and the general population on the other (Jarausch 1990a, 235). Postwar Germany thus retains to some extent the values and some of the structures of a late medieval *Ständestaat* with respect to bargained representation of interests, the importance of status groupings, and the limits on the power of the central state by decentralized interests. Although many have called this corporatism, and certainly Germany is one of the best examples of that phenomenon, the status value dimension—status, Ständestaat support, deference to authority—is not really grasped by the corporatist model. Of all the cases we have considered, the status value dimension provides the reason why the professions in Germany, as acting political groups and as guildlike, have lost less ground vis-à-vis the state, capitalism, and the two forces allied, than they have elsewhere. Both traditional values in the population and the structure of the postwar state have let professional guild forms persist longest in that nation in western Europe that shows the most continuity in societal institutions—after the hiatus of the Nazi period— from late Medieval times.

This is all relative, of course, and I will not make the argument that modern Germany is medieval. Simply put, however, the Federal Republic's limits on the power of the central state give more room for professional guild forms to play an important role. Rationalization of professional work, and the resultant loss of professional group power, is at an early stage. As the central state slowly continues to regain the power it lost after the war, and as each new generation respects the stände values and the interactional rules of deference a little less than the previous one, professional group guild power may gradually erode (Kahlberg 1983, 20). But in the waning years of the twentieth century, that nation in my sample that has come the shortest distance, in structural and value terms, from the precapitalist era is the most supportive at present of the neomedieval guild form that we call organized professions.

I can only briefly consider the case of each profession here, and the data are recently gathered. Only the most recent generations of social historians and sociologists in Germany, and those in the United States and other western nations studying them, are helpful and objective; before the 1960s studies of professions by professional members are quite suspect because of the generational legacy of the Nazi era. Monographs on individual German professions, and even sociological or historical articles, are rare. But we will make an initial attempt, building on the work of these scholars, to assess directions in the development of the relations between German professions, the German state, and capitalism.

German Doctors: From Progressive Experiments to Professional Racism to the Modern Social Insurance System

The German medical profession was a world leader in the era of 1880–1915. The post–World War I profession maintained most of its scientific standards and continued much legitimate research right through Weimar and even in the Nazi era. But the eugenics movement in Germany, advocated from the podium of the most prestigious professorships, took a heavily racist direction even before Hitler (Proctor 1988, 46–63).

From Weimar to the Nazi Regime

When Hitler came to power in the early 1930s, the medical profession was an active supporter. Doctors joining the SA and the SS in proportions ten to fifteen times that of the *Rechtsanwalts* (defense attorneys) or engineers and seven times that of the general public (Proctor 1988, 89–94; Lifton 1986, 34). Many German doctors supported Hitler's racial theories, and Hitler counted on the prestige of the medical profession—the support of the family doctor as well as the medical professor—for his actions against the retarded, the mentally ill, and, from 1938, Jews, gypsies, and leftists, all groups considered by the Nazis "life unworthy of life" (Proctor 1988, 177–222). At every concentration camp physicians, usually members of the SS, determined who was to live and who to die (Lifton 1986, 163–92). Furthermore, at every point in the death camp experience physicians singled out individuals or whole groups for the gas chambers, decided when to evacuate the dead from the chambers afterward, and considered which inmates might be material for experiments to further "German science" (Lifton 1986, 254–302). As Proctor (1988, 293) noted, "The Nazis 'depoliticized' problems of vital human interest by reducing these to scientific or medical problems conceived in the narrow, reductionist sense of these terms. The Nazis depoliticized problems of crime, poverty, and sexual or political deviance by casting them in surgical or otherwise medical (and

seemingly apolitical) terms. Confronting crime with the knife of the surgeon, justifying genocide on the grounds of quarantine, racial hygienists
allowed a reductionist biologism to obscure the political character of social
problems."

Only the small socialist contingent—which included many Jewish doctors in the larger cities—resisted the Nazis; most were outlawed and either
emigrated during 1933 or were arrested subsequently. The profession got
much support from Hitler in return—support for general as well as "racial"
research, support for German scholarly journals, support for preventive and
public health programs for the remaining "Aryan" population (Proctor
1988, 76). Proctor shows in chilling detail that many of the leaders of the
profession and most ordinary doctors escaped prosecution at Nuremberg
and retained community, professional, and professorial posts (Proctor 1988,
306–7). The average German doctor profited from the Nazi regime: his
competition was limited by deportations and a numerus clausus applied to
the medical schools, and his salary rose to equal that of the lawyers by 1935
(Proctor 1988, 93) Professor Otto von Verschauer, director of the Kaiser
Wilhelm Institute for Anthropology, Human Genetics and Eugenics, sent
"interesting specimens" to Doctor Josef Mengele, his research assistant at
Auschwitz. Verschauer retained a prestigious professorship in medicine after
the war, despite his career of active support of Nazism (Lifton 1986, 339–
41; Kater 1989, 233).

The Left was decimated. It had supported the sickness funds in bargaining
against the doctors but lost this battle under Nazism. The medical profession, on the other hand, was the recipient of much support from the Nazi
regime. First, the regime formally gave the medical profession a monopoly
over medical practice, slowly tightening controls over those who practiced
"natural medicine." In 1939 the Natural Healers law required membership
in the Association of German Healers, which was made subsidiary to the
medical profession (Proctor 1988, 247). Irregular practitioners, who had
been tolerated by the Weimar government, were slowly deprived of legal
authority, although Hitler himself was not averse to patronizing such "healers" (Liebfried and Tennstedt 1986, 127–34). Second, Hitler and the Nazi
regime eased severe medical unemployment in the 1930s by forcing Jews
and socialists out of practice. Most of these doctors had practiced in the
larger cities of the North, especially Berlin, so their banishment gave young
doctors—especially those who were members of the Nazi Party—new opportunities (Light et al. 1986, 78–84; Proctor 1988, 146–48). Third, the
Nazi regime undermined the social insurance system of the Weimar period.

The pre-Nazi system involved a number of independent sickness funds,
which were supported by the workers (who contributed two-thirds of the
funds) and employers and which directly hired doctors to work with the

patients who belonged to each fund. Workers, who represented the majority of members, ran the funds. For the Socialist Party (the SPD), positions in fund management provided avenues of upward social mobility to workers who were unwelcome at the German university. The doctors who worked in the funds were paid a salary, and each saw a panel of patients. Most doctors in these funds, especially in the major cities of northern Germany, were Jewish. The majority of German physicians resented the fund doctors' state employment, disapproved of the deviation from fee-for-service medicine, and mistrusted their religious and political affiliations. The independent doctors continued to practice fee-for-service medicine and treated primarily the middle class and the wealthy. But many recent graduates were unemployed and were thus attracted to Hitler's campaign against socialism and "the Jewish menace," which were often equated by the Nazis (Light et al. 1986, 79–81).

But long before Hitler, private practitioners organized opposition to the sickness funds. A doctor Hartmann of Leipzig set up a union in 1903, the Leipziger Verband or Hartmannbund, to stem the growing power of the funds. The membership grew from 6% of all doctors in July of 1903 to 31% a month later, to 53% in 1904, 63% by 1907, 75% by 1913, and 90% by 1919. Stone (1980, 47–48) describes the movement's rise:

> The Leipziger Verband enjoyed enormous success in its first years. Between 1900 and 1911, it engaged in about two hundred conflicts per year and won about ninety percent of them. The main tactics of the Verband were the strike and the boycott. When an employer refused to grant conditions demanded by the physicians, or treated a physician unfairly, the LV organized a collective strike. If necessary, a boycott was also organized to prevent the employer from bringing strikebreaking physicians in from outside, and the names of blacklisted employers were publicized through the medical newspapers.

By 1913, the conflicts between the sickness funds and the medical profession forced the government to broker a treaty between the sides. The medical profession was represented by the Hartmannbund and the German Medical Association (the Deutsche Ärztevereinbund) and the funds by the Union for the Defense of the Interests of Factory Sickness Funds, the General Union of German Sickness Funds, and the Union of Local Sickness Funds. The importance of this treaty was that it set the model for future relations between the sickness funds and the medical profession—equal representation by each side, mediated by the state, which acts as referee. In the postwar system, the state is the final arbiter (Stone 1980, 51–53). Emergency orders by the Weimar government in 1923, 1930, and 1931 consolidated the physicians into large bargaining units and helped the sickness funds control the use of services. As Stone (1980:, 52) observes, "Consolidation of physicians' power occurred through two means. First, the regulations mandated the formation of regional associations of insurance doctors (AIDs), with the status of bodies of public law. Physicians who were admitted to insurance practice were required to join their regional AID. Second, the new regulations eliminated individual contracts between sickness funds and physicians and substituted a system of collective contracts between the funds and the AIDs."

Once in power, Hitler dissolved the directorship of the sickness funds and replaced the commissioners of each fund. These commissioners in turn fired thousands of employees—Jews and those suspected of leftist political sympathies. The young doctors who replaced them, and much of the new staff, were Nazis. In fact, staff jobs were often given to "old fighters" in the Nazi party—mainly untrained working-class recruits with no administrative ability; many drank on the job and carried loaded weapons to work. This chaos in the early years of the regime once produced a backlog of two hundred thousand unprocessed sickness fund forms in the Berlin office until more experienced administrators took control. Workers no longer had majority representation on the boards; the boards, in fact, were effectively eliminated, as all policy decisions came to be controlled by the Nazi Party. Thus ended a major era of experimentation, as many of these funds were in effect labor-controlled Health Maintenance Organizations, which owned a series of clinics, hospitals, and dental clinics in each major city and provided quality health care at a reasonable price to thousands of workers (Light et al. 1986, 81).

The progressive, prolabor direction of the funds had been replaced by a promanagement and pro-Nazi philosophy. Moreover, when the sickness funds were reconstituted after the war, the prolabor direction was not reestablished. Labor and management contributed equally to the funds, depriving the workers of the control that they had once exercised. The result has been a series of conservative funds, one in which election for the boards are not often even held, and a medical profession that has become even stronger after the war than before it, though it has become part of a government-organized bargaining system of sickness funds and the Association of Insurance Doctors (Light et al. 1986, 82).

Postwar German Medicine: Toward a Specialist, Hospital-Based Model

Beyond the prosecution of a few of the chief criminals in the worst concentration camps, there was little postwar effort to denazify the German medical profession. The entire profession, implicated as it was in the actions of the Nazis, refused to speak of its wartime role throughout the 1950s, 1960s, and 1970s—nor did the postwar government force it to do so, any more than it did the other professions. What amounted to absolution was granted the medical profession by the allies, who were eager to get the nation back on its feet, and not until the 1970s and early 1980s was the research done that clearly implicated the entire profession—including many of its leading professors—in the crimes of the Nazi era. By then, most of these individuals were near retirement, although some still held important official positions in the profession. For example, when a thousand medical students attended a two-day conference in 1980 in West Berlin on the topic of the origins and the legacy of Nazi medicine, the representative to the conference from the West Berlin *Ärtztekämmer* or doctors' chamber—elected by his peers—was Dr. Wilhelm Heim, a former brown shirt and SA *Standartenflrer*. The 60 percent of physicians who were forced out of their jobs in Berlin by the Nazis were represented by exiles who returned for the conference. Only in the early 1990s did this older generation finally retire from German medicine (Proctor 1988, 298–312).

Immediately after the war the German doctors' Kammern were reestablished, along with approximately fourteen hundred sickness funds. As occurred late in the Weimar Republic, doctors' charges in the office are negotiated between the Association of Insurance Doctors (which is a corporation of public law and to which all those who wish to participate in the insurance scheme must join) and the organization representing all of the sickness funds. The price of each office procedure is determined by agreement between these two groups; in the case of unresolvable disagreements, compulsory arbitration by the regional or *Länder* governments settles the issue. Both sides have the right of appeal to the courts, but it seldom goes that far (Stone 1980, 75–103).

About half of those in office practice in the early 1980s were in general practice and half in specialties. The bargaining concerns all office procedures but tends to reward physical procedures and diagnostic tests more than the general practitioner's long and time-consuming interviews, a distinction that has fostered the growth of a highly technological office medicine. Only half of all German physicians, however, are in office practice. The postwar years have been characterized by an increase in hospital-based, salaried physician. In 1955 there were slightly more than twice as many office-based physicians as hospital-based ones in West Germany, but by 1978 the distribution was virtually identical, about 59,000 of each; the hospital-based sector had almost tripled in size. In addition, an administrative sector—those in public health, in bodies of public law, in agencies that monitor the expenses of the profession and validate or challenge the charges for service, as well as those in research institutes and in private employment, including those in occupational health—had grown to about 11,800 by 1978 (Stone 1980, 58–59).

The doctor-patient ratio in West Germany in 1978 was higher than in the United States and Britain but lower than in Italy. Nor has the profession grown at the staggering rate of Italy's, rising gradually from 137:100,000 in 1955, to 212:100,000 in 1978. The largest jump during that span was between 1973 and 1974, with most of the new doctors going into the hospital sector (Stone 1980, 59; Arnold et al. 1981). The division of labor in Germany between office-based doctors and hospital-based ones is typical of the Continent. Once a patient is referred to the hospital, he becomes its "property." Hospital doctors cannot do outpatient work, which is the monopoly of the community doctor. Only hospital chiefs of service are exempt from this restriction; they can take a load of outpatients and carry out a private practice or an insurance practice in addition to their hospital position. Generally speaking, those in office practice make slightly more than those in hospitals, except for hospital chiefs of service. In addition, practitioners of some specialties—pediatrics, obstetrics, and ear, eye, nose, and throat for example—can see their patients both in the office and in the hospital. One further restriction prohibits a doctor who has declared a specialty from practicing general medicine, as one can in the United States. No German specialist can supplement his income with general practice patients if the demand for his specialty dries up (Stone 1980, 64).

The insurance funding scheme and the attempts to regulate the costs of care are closely related. In the late 1970s about 90% of the German population was covered by the sickness funds, with another 9% or so covered by private insurance (Stone 1980, 77–78). Unlike the prewar system, under which the funds often directly hired their own physicians and paid them a salary, the present-day funds agree to arbitrate the cost of each office procedure, on a yearly basis, with the Association of Insurance Doctors. This is an essentially inflationary fee-for-service system of payment, one that is overseen by the *Prüfartz* or economic monitor doctors. The Prüfartz are paid by the Association of Insurance Doctors to review cases that stand out from the average charges for a procedure. Thus "cost control" is governed by doctors monitoring doctors for the doctors' association. Decisions by the Prüfartz can be reviewed in turn by the monitor committee of the insurance doctors' association or by the sickness fund. Prescriptions, which are also reviewed by the sickness funds, are another major source of cost, as the powerful German pharmaceutical industry sets the prices. Nevertheless, until recently, there were no limits on a physician's prescription charges, which must be paid by the sickness fund (Stone 1980, 122–33).

Runaway costs of health care in the 1960s and especially the 1970s led to the passage in 1977 of the Health Cost Containment Act. It aimed to deal with two problems of the funds: competition between different types of funds, in which the better-paying funds (those primarily for middle-class employees) established a level of service that the other funds then strove to match, and especially the lack of direct control by the sickness funds over expenditure. The most important change was a set of expenditure ceilings— on physicians' and dentists' services and on prescription drugs. These ceilings are tied in turn to economic indicators: the wage base of subscribers and the costs of medical practice. Administration of the act is the responsibility of a single national commission, the Concerted Action on Health Affairs. When this committee cannot come to an agreement, expenditure ceilings are set through compulsory arbitration. Yet even this setup is not foolproof, given the representatives of the various health interests on the committee (Stone 1980, 151–59).

Hospital costs are a second area where action has become necessary in recent years. Hospital costs were essentially unregulated from the 1950s to the 1980s. Several acts were passed in the 1980s—the Hospital Cost Containment Act of 1981, the KHNG act, which abolished joint funding of hospital expansion by the federal government and the Länder in favor of regional funding by the Länder, and finally, in 1986, a new Federal Regulation on User Charges. This last law changes the method of reimbursing hospitals by introducing prospective budgeting. As Altenstetter (1989, 163) observed: "It dramatically altered the existing method of reimbursing hospitals by introducing a so-called flexible and prospective budget to be calculated on the basis of anticipated occupancy rates in the forthcoming year. . . . Hospitals and sickness funds must agree on the items or rates which make up the budget. If they fail to agree, a neutral and non-governmental arbitration office is called upon to fix them."

These regulations are gradually bringing both the doctors and the hospitals under authority of the Länder (Alber 1988). But the tradition of self-regulation, the strong guild form of the German medical profession, and the political strength of the pharmaceutical industry block any quick solution to the problem of rising costs. Only the crisis of modern German capitalism as a whole—forced to deal first with the slowdown of the 1980s and then with the absorption of East Germany—is finally beginning to reign in the independence of the medical profession. The sickness funds can get little money from either their subscribers or employers, and capitalist power is now driving the changes. Capitalists have strong influence in the circles of the ruling Christian Democratic Party, in the banks, and in the national legislative arena in which these new laws are passed. Doctors, for the first time since Weimar, are losing some direct power over their profession.

But, all that having been said, the medical profession is still strongly organized in corporations of public law, in specialty associations, and in associations of hospital doctors to fight effectively against any threats to their power. Through the Kammern, which have fought against the institution of group practice or the re-creation of the prewar HMOs of the Weimar sickness funds, they have continued the struggle to preserve fee-for-service medicine. The decentralized nature of the German state, and the laws that prevent a central handling of the problem at the federal level, work in the profession's favor—regardless of the results for the consumers of health services.

Thus, in terms of our model of guild power, as it relates to capitalist power and state power, the German medical profession controls its own associations (under state sponsorship and regulation) and controls its own workplace—though in recent years regulation by the state, under capitalist pressure, has begun to rationalize the German workplace. Prices, however, are not set by the physician but by the sickness funds and the state. Finally, the state itself (in which the medical profession is involved through the Kammer system as well as in certain health ministries) mediates disputes between the doctors and the sickness funds, in an atmosphere, beginning in the 1980s, of increasingly strict regulation. This state control is impelled in turn by the needs of capitalism, which along with the consumers themselves has finally come up against an inability to pay much more for services and at the same time maintain a strong German economy. Gaining power during the transition from Weimar to Nazism and maintaining that power unchanged until about 1980, the profession is only now beginning to come more under the control of the state and, indirectly, of capitalism itself. And only with the retirement and death of the last Nazi-era physicians can the profession be said to be rid of the attitudes of racism and inhumanity that characterized it in the past.

German Lawyers: A Judge-Dominated Elite Profession

The German *Rechtsanwaltschaft* or lawyer group is simply one element of an overall professional area that includes judges, prosecutors, and those who work for the state in nonlegal capacities. As in France and Italy, training for all of these groups begins in the German university law schools, which emphasize the viewpoint of the judge. After the first examination at the end of law school, all who wish to become lawyers or judges continue their training for another two and a half years in the courts and, to a much smaller degree, in private practice with a *Rechtsanwalt* or lawyer. After a second examination, composed not by lawyers but primarily by judges and state officials, the candidate chooses a career (Reuschemeyer 1973, 102–4). Traditionally, the prestige career in law is within the judiciary or the higher ranks of the civil service, a second choice is representing a major corporation, and the least desirable option is in independent private practice. This system of prestige—and, to some extent, reward—has roots in the period before World War I, and both the nature of the system and its rewards have essentially survived to the modern era.

From Wilhelmine to Post–World War II Germany: The Dominant Role of Judges

Germany, like France and Italy, is a civil-law nation, with a civil-law system that gives judges more leeway in court while limiting the role of the lawyer. The judge runs the court and asks the majority of the questions, and the attorney who intrudes too much risks insulting the judge. All civil-law systems restrict the attorney's role in court, but the judge in the German system has a special tradition of domination over the Rechtsanwalt. Only since World War II have the lawyers had enough power and control over their own association to begin to counterbalance the power of the court, which in Germany represents the power of the state. All judges are civil servants, members of the higher ranks of the Beamtenschaft. Even today, it is a rare lawyer who criticizes the judiciary.

Jarausch (1990b, 19), writing about the range of professional groups in Germany, observes that "the political orientation of professionals depended on the responsiveness of a particular party, government, or system to their specific desires. Hence during the Empire even liberal professionals were confirmed monarchists, during the Weimar Republic experts remained reluctant about democracy, whereas in the Third Reich many initially welcomed the Nazis until jolted from their illusions by the loss of the war. German professionals preferred an apolitical brand of politics that prized specialized expertise over public struggle." The lawyers originally had a liberal orientation, at least in the later years of the empire and in the earlier period of Weimar. It was considered a victory when lawyers won "free profession" status in 1878; before then they had essentially worked for the court system (Jarausch 1990b, 8–13). Even after the establishment of a free profession, however, the lawyer was essentially very much controlled in court by the judge. For example, in a 1926 decision by the German Supreme Court, an advocate was disqualified from representing a client who was a Communist because the lawyer himself was a Communist; at issue was whether a lawyer who was of this political persuasion could also be a Member of the Court and act "in the interest of the public good" (Reifner 1986, 109). Thus even in the middle of the Weimar Republic, the judiciary began to chip away at the recently won rights of the lawyers, noting that their primary role was not to defend individual rights but rather to "pursue objective social goals."

This attitude on the part of judges encouraged lawyers to split into a liberal wing, the majority of whom were Jewish and practiced in the larger cities of the North, and a conservative wing, who practiced primarily in the smaller cities of middle and southern Germany. Leading members of the bar and the German Bar Association, which was founded in 1871, were Jewish, and often ran the annual meetings of the association. In 1932 about 60% of the lawyers in Berlin were Jewish, as were 11 of 25 members of the General Council of the German Bar Association. The relation between religious origin and politics was clear (Reifner 1986, 109). As Reifner (1986, 109) observed, until 1871 the Prussian bar was a government organ and admission to practice was granted only by the state. But "when advocates finally succeeded in making the law a liberal profession, free of absolute state control, they effectively opened the profession to Jews. It is thus not surprising that Jewish lawyers came to defend not only political liberalism, but also the principle of a liberal legal profession. This, in a sense, made them natural allies of democracy and political liberalization, as well as logical opponents of the ruling coalition of the Second Reich."

This political tendency among Jewish lawyers prevailed throughout the period of the Weimar Republic, but outside of the larger cities, the bar tended to be politically conservative and anti-Semitic (Reifner 1986, 109). So after Hitler came to power in 1933 and carried out a series of measures over the next five years that escalated from eliminating Jews from the bar to shipping them to concentration camps, there was little outcry from the rest of the bar. Antidemocratic in spirit and submissive to the restrictive attitudes of the judiciary, conservative lawyers accepted the removal of their Jewish colleagues without public protest.

The Nazi regime practiced a kind of legal terrorism, with the acquiescence of the bar. In 1933 a law to "restore" the civil service gave the Nazis the power to eliminate any judges who were Jewish or politically liberal; in the same year the president of the German Bar Association asked the Jewish members of the council to resign. In 1934 the Nazis purged the remaining socialist and communist lawyers from the bar, and in 1938 all the remaining Jews. The bar itself was absorbed into the Nazi system (gleichgeschaltet), and individual lawyers were totally subjected to the power of judges, who controlled what the prosecutor and the defense lawyer said and did in court (Jarausch 1990a, 116–19, 127–28, 131–32; Reifner 1986, 116–20).

In the first year of the Nazi regime, women were denied entry to the bar, along with Jews and other "undesirables." Although only a tiny percentage of all lawyers (less than 2% in 1933), women made up about one-quarter of the law school classes in 1932, the last year of the Weimar Republic (Jarausch 1990a, 243). For younger lawyers—those who were Aryan, male, and conservative—the purge of the bar was a windfall, for it opened jobs in the key cities of Germany in a time of depression and unemployment. In addition, the regime gave lawyers a monopoly over all legal advisory services, eliminating competition from lay advocates and labor union advisers. But for anyone who opposed the regime, or whom the regime opposed, the court system became a mockery of justice:

> The structural consequences of political and personal racism which led to the identification of the Jewish element with liberal, democratic, and socialist positions turned the bar from a guardian of individual rights into a shelter for legal terrorism. The desire for personal enrichment on the part of most members of the German bar made these lawyers collaborators of the Nazi state. They relinquished their solidarity with their colleagues as well as their role as independent advocates for their clients. They accepted an increasing integration into the Nazi system, even to the point of demanding the death sentence for their own clients. (Reifner 1986, 120)

During the Nazi regime the police, the SS, and the Gestapo were completely outside the legal system, exempt from the law and the courts as they rounded up and murdered millions of people. The state itself controlled criminal law and administrative activities, and industry's treatment of Jewish and foreign workers was likewise outside of the Nazi court system.

In spite of the lawyers' rush to join the Nazi party once Hitler came to power, World War II and the Nazi regime inhibited the legal profession. In 1933 there were 19,276 lawyers and 9,943 judges; by 1943 there were 12,000 lawyers and 16,000 judges (Jarausch 1990a, 238). Law school enrollments declined under Nazism, and the role of the lawyer was compromised by the ideologies and the laws of the new state. The courts could function almost without lawyers, and even the business of the legal clinics declined. Representation of organized labor was now unavailable, for the labor union movement had itself been crushed by Nazism. Doctors, psychologists, and engineers profited organizationally from the Nazi regime, but lawyers did not share the gains. As Jarausch (1990a, 199), in speaking of *all* professional groups, concludes, "Advances in the knowledge, wealth or organizational power of professionals between 1933 and 1945 were fragile, often to be reversed by the Second World War, which cannot be dissociated from Hitler's policies. Moreover, professionals could only prosper individually or collectively as long as they did the bidding of their Nazi masters—a favor that could be revoked at a moment's notice when conflicts arose. Finally, the ethical price for such gains was appalling."

After World War II the Nazified legal profession was barely touched. Although the chief Nazi figures were prohibited from practicing law, the vast majority of German lawyers, most of whom had cooperated with the Nazi regime, were allowed to resume practice, as were the judges. Even in the mid-1980s, the journal of the major bar association in West Germany would not print Reifner's article; it was published instead in a critical legal studies journal. Through most of the postwar period, the basic stance of the bench and the bar has been unrepentant silence, unwillingness to consider their past. Even the "scholarly" studies on the Hitler-era role of the judges have been carried out primarily by Nazi apologists. As with the doctors, not until the end of the 1980s and the beginning of the 1990s did the wartime generation finally fade from the profession. The younger generations of lawyers, and in particular the organizations of defense lawyers, have begun to make the profession's accommodation under the Third Reich a major issue at annual meetings.

The postwar legal profession was built on the ashes of the Second World War and the re-created institutions of Weimar and Wilhelmine Germany, with the major difference of a decentralized state structure. The postwar profession was studied extensively by Cohn (1960), by Reuschemeyer (1973), and by Blankenberg and Schulz (1988). What is immediately striking about the profession during this period is its lack of basic changes. What Cohn says in observing professional trends and customs in 1960 can be repeated almost verbatim in 1989, though the profession became more crowded after 1970, and especially after 1980, as universities in Germany opened to the masses.

In size, it is important to remember that the defense bar (or *Rechtsanwalten*) includes only one contingent (about a quarter in 1972) of law school graduates who take the second state examination (Reuschemeyer 1973, 32). Some lawyers work as notaries; 85 percent of all notaries in Germany are lawyers, but eligibility rules for the notariate vary from Land to Land (Reuschemeyer 1973, 40). Another group, about a quarter of the profession in 1972, worked as advocates in business, some as members of in-house law firms. A third group, another quarter or so in 1972, worked as judges or prosecutors in the extensive court system. A final group—about a quarter of all law graduates in 1972—did not practice law at all but used their legal credentials for entry in to the upper levels of the civil service, primarily to work as administrators (Reuschemeyer 1973, 32). One small segment of the civil service group, the legal professoriate, has the most prestige. Law professors can argue cases in court directly as if they were a member of the Rechtsanwaltschaft, as well as providing legal opinions in the appeals courts at the Länder level and in the Supreme Constitutional Court (Blankenberg and Schultz 1988, 134–35).

From 1974 to the late 1980s, the primary variances in these patterns are increases in those who work as lawyers and those who do not practice law at all but leave it; the court system and the state civil service have dried up as sources of employment for all but a few law graduates, and jobs in the business world have begun to level off as well. The most prestigious position in the legal profession, and the first choice of many law graduates, remains the judiciary. This is hardly surprising given the law schools' emphasis on the role of the judge and the training after the degree in the court system. Only about five to six months of the two-and-a-half-year postdegree program is spent in a lawyer's office; the majority of the time is spent as an assistant to a prosecutor or a judge (Reuschemeyer 1973, 104; Blankenberg and Schulz 1988, 132).

We can at this point begin to make an assessment of the nature of guild power of the Rechtsanwalt group. The profession has little associational power—control over its own training and its numbers. Except for the Nazi period, there has been no numerus clausus for the group. Lack of a numerus clausus did not lead to overcrowding except in periods of major economic downturn, but it has left the profession relatively helpless when large numbers apply to join the profession, as they have since the 1970s. The increase in college attendance in Germany, while less than in France or Italy, much less the United States, has nevertheless begun to challenge the training system and limit opportunities in the Rechtsanwaltschaft. The court system, moreover, can hardly cope with its share of training for all of the extra law students.

After the successful passage of the second examination, an additional apprenticeship of another year is strongly recommended before a lawyer begins to practice. But this last year of apprenticeship depends more upon the acceptance of a particular lawyer than does the required period, which is carried on essentially under state supervision. This last period effectively separates the sheep from the goats among those who wish a career as a Rechtsanwalt. Given the political conservatism of the typical senior Rechtsanwalt, candidates with the wrong politics—or gender—may not be accepted for the apprentice year. Only in the late 1980s and early 1990s did the sex ratio in the profession begin to change significantly. Women made up less than 1% of the group in 1932, were eliminated during the Nazi era, made up 3% of the profession in 1962, 5% in 1972, 9% in 1982, and 12% in 1985, when a third or more of the French and Italian bars were female (Blankenberg and Schutz 1988, 154).

The national Rechtsanwalt association, the Deutsche Anwaltsverein, has played a major and conservative role in maintaining the solidarity of the profession. After World War II it resumed its independent responsibilities for advancing the interests of the profession vis-à-vis the state. A voluntary association, it represents about two-thirds of German lawyers. For several reasons, solidarity is easier to maintain within this profession than, for example, in the French or American bars. First of all, the range of income within the profession is less extreme than for most of the bars we have considered. In 1961 the German Rechtsanwalt earned an upper-middle-class-income, with neither the extremes of riches of the American or French corporate bars nor the near poverty of the small solo practitioner in either nation, and in the decades since then, nothing has changed significantly. Second, the modal form of practice remains either solo or one or two numbers of associates in a law firm, and these partners are often the sons or sons-in-law of the senior partner. In Reuschemeyer's terms, the modern postwar German bar more closely resembles that found in medium and small American cities just after World War II than it does the rationalized "law factories" of the modern American corporate bar. Third, the Kammer system is a regional system. Members of the bar are attached to the appeals court of each area; a Kammer is identified by this area court. Because each lawyer is required to join the Kammer, it provides a focus for socialization and informal group control, all of which can lead to solidarity among the members. Most attorneys are allowed to practice only in the area where they live, their daily interactions are likely to be a source of mutual evaluations. Fourth, as with all university graduates in Germany, the lawyers share a set of cultural values that distinguish them much more from the general population than in other nations in our sample, where the educated strata are far larger (Reuschemeyer 1973, 116–22).

Yet in spite of solidarity that is possible in a profession where all practice together in limited regions and the majority share a common background with university graduates and/or civil servants, and have incomes within a fairly narrow range, the profession has not been able to reach the position where it completely regulates itself. While minor offenses are dealt with by the Rechtsanwaltskammer, the more serious offenses are considered by a court system on which the profession itself has only minor representation (Blankenberg and Schultz 1988, 139–40). More important questions concern the solidarity between those who work full-time in private practice and those who work for corporations. In this latter group are those who work full-time for business (and who are not considered members of the profession) and the so-called *Syndiken* or syndics, those who work for them part-time but maintain small private practices. The syndics do not participate directly in the meetings nor are they very active in the Anwaltskammer. The final group, those who are both lawyers and notaries, have a somewhat divided loyalty to the profession.

The degree of control over the legal workplace varies according to the kind of work. In a typical courtroom exchange, the lawyer does not ask more than two or three questions of the witness. The questioning is organized and led by the judge, not the lawyer, in contrast to the adversary system of the United States. Continental legal systems give far greater leeway to the judge and forbid attorneys from coaching or preparing witnesses ahead of their court appearance. Germany maintains an extreme version of this system: the lawyer's function is simply to help the judge with his work. Outside of the courtroom the lawyer has more control, but advice to business clients, a common part of the practice for a British solicitor, an American corporate lawyer, or a French elite avocat, is in Germany much more likely to be in the hands of the house counsel, for German corporations are much less likely than others to hire outside firms (Reuschemeyer 1973, 36). And in the appeals court and Supreme Court, court cases are likely to be argued by law professors. The result is much narrower control by the German lawyer over his work than in other nations in our sample. Nor can the lawyer charge whatever he wants, for fees are set by the state, with extra charges beyond that only if mutually agreeable to client and lawyer. Overcharging the client is a much more serious offense for a German lawyer than for an American one, for an "honor court" deals with professional misbehavior. (Blankenberg and Schultz 1988, 139–40). On the other hand, the ethical rules of the German system allow a lawyer to quit a case after it begins if he believes that the client is guilty or has misled him in the process of preparing the case. The lawyer thus has some autonomy, but as a result some clients have difficulty getting someone to defend them on serious charges, especially serious political charges (Reuschemeyer 1973, 127).

With respect to control over the market for legal services, nonlawyers have come to compete for any kind of activity except arguing and advising in court cases, over which lawyers still have a monopoly. As Blankenberg and Schultz point out (1988, 136), "Solo practitioners generally concentrate on litigation, but in larger firms the bulk of the work is advice. Here lawyers face vigorous competition from tax consultants and chartered accountants, who combine advice on business strategies, tax strategies, and management. Tax consultants increasingly form their own partnerships offering comprehensive business advice, including the drafting of contracts and wills. By concentrating on the forensic areas in which they have a monopoly, advocates have lost much of the growing consultantcy market." Lawyers in the Weimar period were far more interested in business work and consultation. But the majority of the experts in this specialty were Jewish, and when they were eliminated, the Nazi Party began to control the economy in ways that discouraged legal response by business (Jarausch 1990a, 66–67). After the war, the proliferation of tax consultants and chartered accountants and the increasing use of the law professoriate for important cases continued to lower the profile of the lawyers in this area of work. The tendency of most larger German corporations to use their own house counsel more frequently than in the other nations of our sample has further diminished the market for legal services since World War II—at least the market for services by the freely practicing lawyers.

Competition between lawyers has also intensified with the rapid growth of the profession in the 1970s and 1980s. In Wilhelmine Germany, the supply of lawyers was kept in check by the very low percentage of students attending the university. Both in absolute and relative terms, this changed after World War I, and especially in the later 1920s and early 1930s, when the numbers of law graduates began to rise markedly for the first time. The number of lawyers was nearly identical before and after World War I— 12,297 in 1913 and 12,030 in 1919. Then slow growth to 13,578 in 1925 and rapid growth to 19,276 in 1933 was interrupted by the Nazi regime, which was not only anti-Jewish but generally antilawyer and antilaw. The numbers shrank to 18,712 by 1935 (by which time the majority had joined the Nazi front organizations) and to 14,800 by 1939. Yet because the Nazi regime discouraged citizens from using courts to settle disputes and reduced the fees that lawyers could charge, the smaller number of attorneys could not capitalize on reduced competition with higher income, although inflation had less effect on their real earnings than under the Weimar government. Slow and steady growth characterized the early postwar years, from a low of 12,844 in 1950 to 26,854 in 1975. At this point the numbers began to grow rapidly—a gain of more than 9,000 by 1980, to 36,077, and nearly 11,000 more by 1985, to 46,927 (Blankenberg and Schultz 1988, 150).

Thus in one ten-year period, from 1975 to 1985, the bar grew far more than it had in the previous sixty years. Naturally the increase in the size of the bar meant a decrease in the opportunity for younger lawyers. But what has made this a far more striking problem has been the inability of the bar to widen its market to other kinds of legally relevant work. Because of the growth of the competition from other professions in the general legal area, and the disinclination of the elite to change the rules to allow the bar to operate in these areas, the bar faces a troublesome future. Even the creation of a new numerus clausus, which the bar strongly opposes, would provide little short-term relief. More and more lawyers are chasing less and less work.

There is of course an elite in the German bar; in the larger cities of northern Germany and in Munich firms of ten to twenty partners specialize in working with larger corporations and in international work. But these firms represent an infinitesimal percentage of the bar in Germany (Blankenberg and Schultz 1988, 140–41). A large minority still practices law alone and a larger group practices in law firms of two to three partners in unspecialized work, in a civil-law system in which the law is less complex than in a common-law system. Many academic professors of law, moreover, serve as consultants to the system at the upper level. As a result, the bar appears to have no room to grow.

The state's role is all-pervasive within the German legal profession. Although law is technically a free profession, its role in court as an *Organ der*

Rechtspflege or organic member of the administration of justice, is taken more seriously than in nations such as France or Italy, where the advocate works solely for the client. The judiciary supervises the fees that attorneys charge, the disciplinary system above the bottom level, and courtroom practice, including the number of questions a lawyer asks his client. In the criminal courtroom, the state prosecutor sits on the bench at the level of the judge while the attorney and his client sit in a box at a lower level— an unmistakable symbol of the relative importance of the judge and prosecutor and the relative unimportance of the attorney (Blankenberg and Schultz 1988, 139–40). Yet activists within the legal profession who attempt to change the situation come up against a wall of professional conservatism. Even attempts to broaden legal education—to give the student more exposure to social science and more experience in court, more exposure to clinical work in law—have been rejected by the legal profession as recently as the mid-1980s (Klausa 1981). Because the German bar lacks a strong activist tradition and remains unwilling to criticize the role of the judiciary, it is being overwhelmed by thousands of new graduates in a field where the competition from nonlawyers is increasing.

Legal Professionals and the Civil Service: Judges and Bureaucrats

In Germany, at least in the twentieth century, the civil service has been considered a place of honor, an occupation of high status if only moderate pay, primarily for those of the upper class who had an independent family income. Legal training—right through the postgraduate period in the chamber of judges and prosecutors—is considered necessary for a position either in the judiciary or in the higher civil service (Reuschemeyer 1973, 34–35, 76–77). This legalistic approach to the civil service was shared with Italy but not with France or Britain; in France the graduates of the Ecole polytechnique, an applied engineering school, or Ecole nationale d'administration are preferred for civil service, in Britain the graduates of Oxford and Cambridge with a general education in humanities. What all these system shared, of course, was a screening system that ensured an upper-middle-class or upper-class civil service. In Germany judges and upper-level civil servants were characterized by their political conservatism, and both groups expressed their distaste for the wide-open politics of the Weimar Republic, as well as the increasingly important role of capitalists in the affairs of the nation. Neither group mourned when Hitler replaced the Weimar regime, although those civil servants in charge of personnel were taken aback by the extent to which Hitler, once in power, replaced or pushed aside career civil servants to provide patronage jobs for some of the Old Nazis, incompetent though they were at carrying out their tasks (Wünder 1986, 138–46).

The inflation of the Weimar period cut the effective salary of the judges and the career civil servants drastically—another reason why they hoped for better under Nazism. About 14% of the judges were Jewish in 1933 before Hitler had them removed, but Jews made up only a tiny percentage of the wider civil service. The role of the judge expanded under the Nazi regime, and their numbers began to grow. The judge became all-powerful, in effect a *Richter-König* or judge-king (Reifner 1986, 103–4, 110–11; Hirsch et al. 1984). Leading judges later tried to whitewash their role under Hitler—two major studies of the Third Reich judiciary were written by former judges under the regime—they were even more involved than the Rechtsanwaltschaft in deciding who would be defined as handicapped and therefore sent off to be killed as "life unworthy of life" (Reifner 1986, 101n).

After the war, at least up to the mid-1970s, judges and lawyers affected a belief in the democratic process, even while behaving in many court cases as if Nazi traditions (or even pre-Nazi ones) were still in force. The German judiciary was never purged, though it was intimately involved in enforcing the Nazi laws. Unlike in the French and especially the Italian system, no radical wing exists in the German judiciary, no younger branch of judges who wish to reform the old system. As before the Second World War, or for that matter the First, the judges represent a kind of authoritarian element within the German state. Thus the Supreme Constitutional Court upheld the law passed after the upheavals of the 1960s and 1970s that forbids Communists and ex-Nazis from positions within the German state—in the judiciary or the civil service as a whole, including positions in the university. This law, the *Berufsverbot,* has never been effectively enforced against members of the Nazi Party, past or present, the way it consistently has been against the Left (Reifner 1986, 123–24).

The careers of German judges depend on the seniority rules of the German civil service—and on the conformity that senior judges press upon any junior judge who threatens to deviate from the rules of the system or to render controversial opinions. The normal career, after completing the apprenticeship and receiving high enough marks on the second examination to qualify for a position, begins with a position at the district court, or very rarely at the Court of the Land. After a period of years, it is possible for some judges to move up in the hierarchy to the appeals courts, of which there are several, divided by their function within the court system. Finally, some lateral mobility is possible into nonjudiciary positions within the government, usually civil service positions but also occasionally high appointive positions. Return to a court position is always possible, even advancement if the nonjudiciary position was high enough. But unlike in the Italian or French systems, few judges take this path toward advancement. Conformity was even more essential in the first thirty years after World War II, when many senior judges were ex-Nazis, with a absolute horror of any judge who espoused radical or even liberal viewpoints. Their attitudes stamped the next generation, who have finally begun to establish themselves in these senior positions in the judiciary. Although this generation does not share the values of the ex-Nazis, these younger judges still tend to be much more conservative than the population as a whole.

In general, therefore, it is impossible separate the political attitudes of the judiciary and the Rechtsanwaltschaft from the social classes that they represent—the upper middle and the upper class. They have always been politically conservative, resisting change that would make the court system more fairly represent the attitudes of the German population. Every plan to modernize legal training in the mid-1980s was defeated. Innovative law schools like the University of Bremen, which has an excellent faculty by any standard, are consistently rated by the profession at the bottom of the scale (Blankenberg and Schultz 1988, 155n; Klausa 1981). The increasing irrelevance of much legal education, combined with the unwillingness to change it, signifies as nothing else might the function of this education as a rite of passage rather than as training for the practice of law or for being an objective judge. A nineteenth-century elitist bench and bar prevail, with a new overlay of impoverished law graduates who will never be judges or civil servants and who cannot make a living as Rechtsanwalten.

German Engineers: A Profession Integrated into Capitalism

From the very beginning, the German engineering profession was split between a technical educational elite and a mass profession trained on the job or in a series of schools that were not related to the university. These latter schools eventually became secondary schools well integrated into the capitalist system, with close relations between the workplace and the school—the so-called higher and lower machine-building schools of the late nineteenth and early twentieth century. Gispen (1989, 37) observes that this split,

> the dividing line between *Bildung* and *Besitz* [cultured education and property], between status and class, came to run right through the middle of the engineering profession. At the "production end" of the profession, an industrial "shop culture" emerged that was organized toward practice, business, and the substantive-functional dimensions of technical knowledge: it rested largely on private initiative and was oriented toward "society." . . . At the other end of the spectrum, a status-seeking "school culture" grew up that inclined toward theory and

"pure science" and was joined to the complex of academic-bureaucratic officialdom.

The early capitalist German entrepreneurs, though themselves often graduates of the Technische Hochschule or technical colleges (comparable to MIT or Rensselaer), preferred to hire the products of the practical programs. The latter did not claim to possess the sheen and polish of the graduates of the Technische Hochschule graduates or demand wages and benefits beyond what the new capitalists thought engineers deserved. Far easier to take the rising sons of the working class who had some practical technical education, and to train them further on the job, than to deal with the status-conscious (and arguably less competent) graduates of the higher technical schools (Gispen 1989, 160–86). The Technische Hochschule achieved university status around 1900, although the German upper class and most members of the state elite bureaucracy (typically graduates of the law school) did not consider them properly educated, possessed of the characteristic values and ideals of a humanistic education summed up by the term *Bildung*.

Three organizations formed in the late 1800s and early 1900s characterized the nature of the splits within the engineering profession. The first, the Verein Deutsche Ingenieure or VDI was run by those engineers who had become capitalists and senior managers of their industries. These members insisted that the association take positions of strict neutrality on labor-management issues, and also on issues surrounding the creation of an engineering profession analogous to the medical and legal professions. The labor-management neutrality was more theoretical than practical, of course, for most of the officers of the association were themselves essentially capitalists. The VDI, founded in 1856, gradually built up an empire of technical subsocieties for each specialty and created a publishing empire as well. It did much of the technical publication before and after World War I, with a natural market for the journals comprising not only engineers but also capitalists with an interest in productivity and profit. The VDI organized scientific sessions as well, and it did not bar those who had not graduated from the technical universities from participation or membership. But by ignoring such issues as patent rights of engineers to products that they had developed, and by denying support to those engineers who struck to protest brutal and selfish policies of their capitalist employers, the organization supported the status quo (Gispen 1989, 187–219).

In reaction to the VDIs unwillingness to act on workplace or professional issues, two organizations developed in the first years of the twentieth century, the VDDI or Verband Deutsche Diplom-Ingenieure, and the Bund der technischen-industriellen Beamten (BtiB). The first, a professionalizing group of engineers with the diploma from the Technische Hochschule, was formed in 1909. Its organizers hoped to monopolize the higher functions within the engineering profession and to limit upward mobility within the field—and use of the title engineer—to graduates of the Technische Hochschule. The VDDI was never as successful as the VDI in gaining the support of a majority of Diplom-Ingenieure; at its highest point of popularity, it organized barely a fifth of them (Gispen 1989, 223–54). Far more popular was the BtiB, which emphasized the class conflict in engineering, allowed membership to all engineers regardless of training (though not to the working-class foremen, who had their own large and successful union). In fact, more Diplom-Ingenieur joined the BtiB than joined the VDDI, for the wages of the engineers were in most cases lower than those of the foremen. The VDI opposed violently the formation of both groups. It condemned as needlessly elitist a professional association limited to graduates of the higher technical school and opposed as well the BtiB union, observing that class conflict would get the engineers little. When the Nazis came to power in 1933, they immediately abolished the BtiB, which had grown in size and power since its foundation to be the major organization representing the interests of a large proportion of the engineers. A few years later, in irritation, they abolished the VDDI as well, though the majority of Technische Hochschule graduates were by that time well represented in the Nazi movement (Jarausch 1990a, 115–42).

The depression of the early 1930s and the overproduction of engineering graduates lowered salaries, and engineers began to ask the state for special measures to curb the increase in graduates. When Hitler came to power, he did help the engineers, but he did not give them a Kammer or professional rights. More importantly, the revival of the German economy led to full employment as engineers were caught up in rearmament. Engineering salaries began to rise for the first time. Engineers in the mass tended to be passive and grateful for work, but the elite tended to be actively pro–Nazi. Significantly, Hitler believed that the VDI should not be forced to disband in the process of Gleichschaltung, and the majority of the journals of the VDI, and its scientific meetings, continued throughout the Nazi regime. Hitler approved the VDI's designation of a Nazi as the head of the organization throughout the war period and interfered with the plans of other party leaders to destroy the organization. Deeming the profession essential for war work, he made most engineers ineligible for the German draft, but he eventually disbanded the VDDI, for efforts to professionalize were considered too elitist and selfish in the *Völkisch* value system of Nazism. Of course, Nazi anti-Semitism made Jews, already a tiny percentage of German engineers, ineligible for VDI membership after 1933. The majority of Jewish engineers moved to England, Palestine, or the United States, and many became involved in war work for the Allies (Jarausch 1990a, 131).

Hitler also abolished the BtiB, for unions also violated the Nazi ideal and tended to hamper the capitalists from producing large numbers of weapons and goods at low prices. Although the majority of the members of the BtiB were probably not Social Democrats, their antagonism toward management could not be tolerated by the regime; many union leaders were imprisoned and perished in the concentration camps. Engineers who were members of neither the VDDI or the BtiB could continue to attend the scientific meetings of the VDI and its constituent societies, and they earned higher wages than ever before. Nazism was rewarding their long years of keeping their noses to the grindstone (Jarausch 1990a, 150–51).

Most engineers remained unideological. But many who were politically active embraced what Herf calls "reactionary modernism," an ideology that predates Nazism but blossomed with Hitler's rise. This philosophy combined the reactionary politics of the Nazi cause with a kind of technological romanticism, a mythology of technology as essentially German, an attempt to create a kind of "humanist technological idea" to compensate for what engineers keenly felt they did not have, even in the 1930s—a classical education or Bildung based on literature and literary ideas (Herf 1984, 156–57). Right-wing political ideologues who were no longer antitechnology could be very attractive to engineers searching for meaning and not finding it in the Weimar Republic, run as it was by capitalists feuding with Social Democrats:

> National Socialism promised them the possibility of combining self-interest and service to the *Volksgemeinschaft*. The cultural politicians among the engineers came to believe that National Socialism would silence the critics of technology from the so-called cultivated world and would also wrest technical development from control by commercial interests. Nazism's appeal to the engineers was not an antimodernist attack on technology but a promise to *unleash* modern technology from the constraints the Social Democrats placed on it. (Herf 1984, 160–61)

If the majority of engineers remained unideological, this philosophy provided their politically active colleagues with reading material and something to think about during the period of the Third Reich, while their labor union and their professional association were outlawed.

In general, the Nazi state forced engineers even further into the arms of the capitalists than they were under the Weimar Republic. The state, which had, with the support of capitalism, maintained the two-tiered educational system set up in the nineteenth century through the first three decades of the twentieth, was taken over by a group that was not interested in legal rights to self-determination of any group, no matter how essential they were to the short-run and long-run aims of the regime. What is fascinating about the postwar story is that the state has worked with the capitalists and the capitalist-oriented VDI to set up an official, licensed, two-tiered engineering profession. But since the war there has been little support among engineers for either of the Weimar alternatives—a strong nondiscriminatory and broadly professional labor union, or a professional association exclusively for the Technische Hochschule graduates.

The Postwar German Engineering Profession

Much of Germany's infrastructure was destroyed in the bombing and the battles of World War II. The engineering profession, which had been intimately involved in the war effort, soon became intimately involved in the work of reconstruction. And of all the professions we have considered, the engineers were the first, starting as early as 1947, to begin a moral reexamination of their professional activities under Nazism. A "credo of the engineer," presented at the VDI meeting in Kassel in 1950, included "respect for the dignity of human life." A series of conferences dealt with the moral implications of the use of technology (Jarausch 1990a, 209). Although most engineers were and are in the employ of capitalists and cannot choose the ends of the projects on which they work, these gestures nevertheless stand out in admirable contrast to the steadfast refusal of the medical profession, the legal profession, or the university professoriate to acknowledge their complicity in the Nazi period.

The structure of the postwar German engineering profession is similar to that under Weimar, with the marked absence of either a strong professionalizing association like the VDDI or a unionist group like the BtiB. The VDI was reconstituted in 1950, with new headquarters at Düsseldorf. As before the war, it opposed the elitist plans of the Diplom-Ingenieur, but it agreed to support a plan to restrict the title of ingenieur to the graduates of the technical universities. This restriction was overruled in 1968 when the current system was instituted, recognizing two classes of engineer: the Diplom-Ingenieur or graduate of the technical university, and the Ingenieur-Grad or graduate of the *Fachhochschule,* special engineering schools not quite at the university level (Hutton and Lawrence 1981. 13–33). These latter schools are the descendants of the old machine-building schools, and preparation for them does not require a Gymnasium degree but rather attendance at a sequence of secondary schools that are more practically oriented. There are also general universities in a few Länder, which students without a Gymnasium background can attend and study engineering for a Diplom-Ingenieur degree—primarily in SPD-dominated areas where the distinction between the different degrees is itself considered excessively elitist. Industry, as before World War II, pays little attention to the differences between the various degrees (Hutton and Lawrence 1981, 13–33).

Modern German engineers are overwhelmingly male (about 97% in the early 1980s), from the middle to upper middle classes (typically from engineering or lower level bureaucratic families), and employed in the private sector (about 90%) (Hutton and Lawrence 1981, 35, 119). Those with the Diplom-Ingenieur ranking are much more likely to work in research and development, those with the Ingenieur-Grad ranking in general production (Hutton and Lawrence 1981, 46–54). Those with the Diplom-Ingenieur ranking are more likely to work for small companies after their first job, while the majority of all engineers continue to work for companies with more than five hundred employees (Hutton and Lawrence 1981, 48). Because of the close ties that the universities share with technical schools on the one hand and industry on the other, some vocational training or placement is included in the programs of both degree programs, and the typical graduate of a German engineering school has much more practical knowledge of his work than do his British or French counterparts. In fact, the Ingenieur-Grad programs, with their inevitable striving for upward mobility, are reducing the work requirement and becoming more like the Diplom-ingenieur programs, making the graduates less acceptable to industry (Lutz and Kammerer 1975).

Politically engineers tended, at least in the mid-1970s, to be slightly left of center politically (Kogon 1976). This was particularly the case with the younger engineers, probably because of their sympathy with the broader social values of the time, but many older engineers are also moderate leftists or members of center parties (Hutton and Lawrence 1981, 181). On the other hand, only a small minority of engineers join associations of any kind, including professional ones. This pattern is in marked difference to the prewar position of the profession, where the mass was likewise politically inert but the leadership elite was pro-Nazi, with half of the engineers elected to Parliament in 1931 being members of the Nazi Party (Jarausch 1990a, 70). This conversion from right to slightly left is a consequence of the war experience and the generational shift.

In terms of our variables of guild power, the modern German engineer has achieved a kind of professional status without the combination of engineers into a strong association, for the VDI does not represent the interests of engineers per se. The engineers have never directly controlled membership but have tried, outside of and inside the VDI, to influence the state authorities, in postwar Germany at the Land level. The prewar DATSCH or Deutsche Ausschluss für technisches Schulwesen (German Society for Technical Education) battled with the state and included representatives of the old VDI, VDDI, and BtiB (Gispen 1989, 210, 219), but no such nation-wide association exists today. In the absence of such a group, no numerus clausus has been established for postwar engineering students. While this was not a pressing issue during the gradual growth of the 1950s and 1960s, it assumed more importance in the late 1970s and especially in the 1980s. As the German university has expanded rapidly in recent decades, the technical universities have borne most of the burden. In 1989 there were 1.5 million students in a German system that had room for 800,000 (Kirk 1989, 1427). This expansion threatens the future of engineering students in particular, for as the German economy has leveled off, openings in industry have rapidly diminished. Engineers are demanding a numerus clausus with increasing urgency.

Studies of German engineers' control over the workplace are limited, but they do tend to indicate that the "trusted worker" model of Britain applies in the German case. The engineer benefits from the high valuation that German culture puts on technical expertise *(Technik)*. They earn promotion into the ranks of management faster than in Britain or even the United States. A larger percentage of German engineers serve in management and on boards of directors than in most other Western nations, except for France, where graduates of the Ecole polytechnique (but not other engineering schools) are often found on the boards and in higher management. These engineers on the boards and involved in the day-to-day direction of the company understand the role of the engineer on the workplace—although, as with any capitalist enterprise, they keep their eye on the bottom line concerning costs. A comparative study indicates that German engineers had more secretarial help than British ones in the mid-1970s, enjoyed salaries almost double those of the British, and were generally better educated and more likely to write scientific articles and have more patents on their work—activities that are impossible in industry without the support of management. Furthermore, although the VDI is not an engineers' lobby, it nevertheless has some influence over corporations that employ many engineers to allow them room and freedom to work (Hutton and Lawrence 1981, 106, 118–26, 129–33).

Recent studies exist on the expected rationalization of engineering work as the numbers of graduates began to crowd the labor market. To some degree this overcrowding of the field will continue to have a negative effect on the salary and the working conditions of many engineers. In addition to this, the Computer Assisted Design/Computer Assisted Manufacturing process (CAD/CAM) lessens the autonomy of the German engineers in the one area where studies have indicated that they prefer to be—in design work. Neef (1982, 195) describes the result: "With the introduction of decentralized work terminals the engineer must be at his workplace in the firm on a 24-hour a day basis, so that the plant can be fully utilized. This means first of all a growing number of overtime hours, then the introduction of shift work for the engineers. . . . Through the CAD machinery the process of the breaking up of the horizontal relations among engineers, which had begun with the centralization of cooperative relationships in the planning department, is finally completed." Given the job market and the lack of an engineering union to fight back, management was safe in carrying out such plans.

As in other nations, the market for engineering services is controlled by the hiring corporations. During the gradual expansion of the 1950s and 1960s, and even into the early 1970s, engineers had some leverage. In practice, though, the majority of engineers studied in the late 1970s did not change jobs often, with the majority either working for the same employer that originally hired them or making only one move. By 1980 their leverage had disappeared.

Few existing studies can predict whether the upward moves of engineers into management will decline from the rates of the mid-1970s as increased numbers of graduates in the business and economics programs head into industry. The possibility of movement into management has been a factor in the profession's failure to reembrace the sort of professional action or unionism that characterized the Weimar era. If German industrialists adopt the American model of assigning business planners instead of technical experts to upper management, the main avenue of upward mobility for engineers will be closed—and engineering unions may make a comeback. But as of 1990 German industry had not made that shift, and a fair number of managers are former engineers.

The role of the German state in the development of the engineering profession has diminished since the mid-1800s. Originally responsible for the development both of capitalist enterprise and the engineering profession (the elite branch or the technical universities), the state began to share its role with capitalism and with the VDI during the later 1800s and especially in the interwar period, when the DATSCH (which was funded primarily by the VDI) began to influence the direction of engineering. Under Nazism the state gave engineers employment but ignored their professional aspirations for autonomy and a closed market (abolishing the VDDI, for example). The postwar government protected the title engineer in the early 1950s and began in the 1960s to make the training pathways of the profession more flexible. Yet the profession remains isolated and controlled by capitalist employers rather than directed by the state. Furthermore, as the state has come to share power with corporate capitalism and, since the war, with the unions, and as the educational system has become decentralized, the modern German society-state complex is difficult to analyze using a simple uni- or bidirectional model. The modern German state clearly does not control the engineering profession, but conversely the engineering profession does not control the state in areas of professional policy. Industry plays a major role in employment, but not in education. As with many other areas of professional life, the recent crisis in the education of the engineering profession is likely to be considered by a commission with representatives of engineers, professors at the university, industry, the Länder and the federal government.

In sum, the engineering profession in Germany remains unable to control its own fate. It made major steps forward in the Weimar period toward the development of both a union for all engineers and a professional association that would build unity among all graduate engineers. But both of these organizations were destroyed by the Nazis and not restored by the postwar society, leaving the capitalist-controlled VDI as the only major association for the engineers. Within this framework, the profession made strides in personal mobility into the ranks of management (including upper management) between 1950 and 1975. The economic realities since then, however, in particular the overcrowding of the university, have led to yet another crisis in the field.

German Professors: From Mandarin Elite to Bureaucratized Mass

German professors have traveled quite a distance from the elite status of the period before 1968 to the mass professoriate of the 1990s. Yet even after this decline, they remain quite privileged in comparison with the *Mittelbau,* the untenured professors and researchers who are the successors of the old Privatdozenten, who lectured at the university without much hope of ever achieving tenure (Fallon 1980, 10–31). The new system shares with the old a tendency to depend on the state for all important decisions on funding and development of programs. The evolution of the German university, and the role of the professor within it, is a complex story. Wilhelm von Humboldt, who is considered the father of the German university, in fact simply used his knowledge and political skill to convince the German bureaucracy and the elite of the importance of a modern university. The University of Berlin, which Humboldt founded, quickly attracted a distinguished faculty and became the flagship of the German system. In this university, the professor was the key to the entire system. As Fallon (1980, 40) puts it,

Developing scholars in an institute were heavily dependent upon the incumbent full professor, not only for such material matters as salary, office space, teaching load, and working conditions, which the full professor negotiated for them with the ministry, but also in intellectual matters. The limited number of full professors in Germany controlled the professional societies, the journals, and the review boards of the publishing houses. Thus an intellectual disagreement with a full professor could easily destroy the career of a developing scholar altogether.

Although the system was formally much like that of Italy and France, the German university clearly put all the emphasis on the professor and little or none on, for example, the different intellectual schools (as in France) or the political party to which the professor belonged (as in Italy). Most if not all professors were politically conservative, both before and after World War I. They were lukewarm at best toward the Weimar Republic, which nevertheless bent over backward to leave the professors with as much independence as was possible in a state-run and state-organized system (Mommsen 1987, 63–64).

The end of the Weimar Republic came with the student uprisings of 1932 and 1933, for the students and not the faculty first jumped on the Nazi bandwagon (Jarausch 1984, 165–99; Mommsen 1987, 67). But the professors, most of them on the right in any case, did little to resist the Nazi power grab, hoping that the obvious crassness of the new party would not affect them. Once in power, however, Hitler moved almost immediately to destroy the intellectual independence of the professoriate, putting Nazis into positions of power in each university and including the universities as well as the medical and legal professions in his Gleichschaltung.

Hitler then moved to simplify the curriculum, reducing the term of study before the state examinations for which most students attended the university and substituting political training sessions for established coursework. (Mandatory Nazi summer camps prepared faculty to teach student indoctrination courses in racism.) University attendance declined even as faculties were purged of such "degenerate Jews" as Einstein. England and the United States accepted the riches that Germany forfeited, émigrés like Einstein, Walter Gropius, Arnold Schoenberg, Thomas Mann, and Bertolt Brecht (Mommsen 1987, 68).

But not all Germans were unhappy with the new Germany. For second-raters on the faculty, the Nazi administration and emigration of the famous meant opportunity. In medicine those who specialized in genetics and eugenics received much support from the government, and the creation of a new class of subhumans after 1938 meant that medical experimentation could go forward, unhindered by morality, eventually depending on the concentration camps for material. Law faculties were decimated, as the profession of Rechtsanwalt became increasingly unrewarding, and the judiciary began to resemble a series of kangaroo courts. Only engineering faculties continued to hold reasonably steady, as their students were exempted from the draft (Jarausch 1990a, 179–80, 237). Because the Nazis were not particularly interested in the arts and the humanities, these subjects tended also to suffer, although an occasional star figure whose work was consistent with Nazi doctrine was lionized—the existentialist Martin Heidegger, for example, was adopted by the party and put in charge of a university (Mommsen 1987, 67). Hitler's demand for a "German physics" resulted in a dismissal of the developing quantum physics and of Einstein's ideas in favor of a resurgence of old-style Newtonian mechanics—a direction that hamstrung Nazi efforts to develop an atomic bomb (Beyerchen 1977, 127). A high proportion of the physics community either was Jewish (and had already left) or sympathized with the plight of Jews and gypsies under Hitler (Beyerchen 1977, 15–39). Thus a fairly small pool of qualified physicists was active in the doomed effort to create a "German physics".

Social science, especially sociology, suffered during the Hitler era, when it was turned from a humanistic and critical discipline into an applied science that no longer asked the big questions—which had already been answered by Nazi ideology. The Frankfurt school, composed primarily of Jewish intellectuals and those who promoted psychoanalysis, was disbanded; the majority of its members relocated in New York. Rammstedt (1986, 142) notes that "in place of sociology as a social philosophical subject, after 1935/ 1936 had been placed the empirical research specialist, with his knowledge wholly in the service of National Socialist business, that is, the Party. The sociologist appeared no more in his professional role as a competitor with National Socialist politicians, only in his role as a social technician."

Not all social sciences were hurt by the advent of Nazism. Psychology, for example, was advanced by the interest in testing for the German army and because of the practical applications of industrial psychology (Geuter 1988). Nonpsychoanalytical psychiatry was also advanced, primarily because a close relative of Herman Göring's led the association (Cocks 1990). But in the main those disciplines (or individuals within disciplines) who questioned the status quo, who developed new approaches and were critical of the Nazis, were diminished or died under the regime—much as they have under all totalitarian systems, such as the Communists or the religious fundamentalists of the Middle East.

The defeat of Germany in World War II and the subsequent partitioning of the nation into West and East Germany had several implications for the academic profession. First, after a brief and half-hearted attempt at denazification, the focus of attention for England, France, and the United States shifted toward building up the western sectors and not "worrying too much about the past" (Tent 1982, 254–311). This attitude led in turn to a wholesale pardon by the new West German government of most of those accused shortly after the war. The new government was eager, as were the allies, to get Germany on its feet again. This meant a revival of the old German university, an elite system of recruitment to it, and the continuation of the previous Weimar forms of professional activity—though without, of course, the Jews who had been exterminated or had escaped the country. Otherwise the only change was in the level of aspiration of the average German middle-class family: far more of them sent their children to the Gymnasium (the German equivalent of the French lycée or the Italian liceo), graduation from which with a successful grade on the *Abitur* or final exam ensured enrollment at the university (Kraul 1984, 206–20).

Beginning gradually in the early 1960s and then more rapidly later in the decade, the shape of the German university changed as the professoriate became overwhelmed by a flood of politically active students. In the winter term of 1950–1951 there were 112,000 students in the university system; by 1960–1961 that number had risen to 217,000. But by 1970–1971 the figure was 605,000, more than five times the enrollment of twenty years before. By 1981–1982 the number was more than 900,000, including the students at the new comprehensive universities. Enrollment has continued to grow, to about 1.5 million in 1989 (Mommsen 1987, 172; Kirk 1989). The turning point, at which a quantitative and qualitative shift in the professoriate became necessary, was the late 1960s, when the small elite university could no longer really operate. The lower ranks of faculty were expanded to accommodate the increased enrollment. These younger faculty members had almost no chance of tenure, and they often sided with the students when the protests against the university rocked the German campuses in 1968 and 1969. The postwar generation of students had been brought up to respect democratic values, yet in the university they saw an archaic, elitist German institution. In effect, a protest that might have been directed at broader national targets was directed against the university itself (German Universities Commission 1978, 103–48).

The government responded in several ways. Even before the protests, the new Wissenschaftsrat, an advisory board to the ministry responsible for the universities, had suggested the expansion of existing universities and the conversion of part-universities (special schools) and professional schools to full university status. This meant immediate promotion for a generation of younger academicians. But these measures were "too little and too late to alleviate the dramatic student overpopulation of the next decade [1964–1974]" (Mommsen 1987, 73).

A more radical approach changed the institution of the university itself. The control of the senior professors over all aspects of university life seemed increasingly unfair to the Mittelbau, who did 75–80% of the teaching and research but had no voting rights in the faculties. Because government responsibility for the universities had been decentralized as part of the founding law for West Germany, each province acted independently, but within broad guidelines set by the central government. The result was a law whose main principle was taken from German industry. There *Mitbestimmung* meant codetermination of plant activities between management and labor; in the university, "management" was the senior professoriate and "labor" the junior faculty and the students. In its original form the new law, passed by the SPD when it came into power in the late 1960s, created the German "group university," where senior faculty, junior faculty, and students had nearly equal voting rights. A junior faculty member or researcher was still obligated to work with a senior professor on research projects and to consult with the senior faculty in writing the habilitation—the second piece of work that would qualify the junior faculty member for a senior professorship. Later, the federal Constitutional Court would nullify regulations that gave students or junior faculty rights to decide on such academic matters as tenure or curriculum, but these groups, especially the junior faculty, nonetheless retained far more rights than before—a share of the research funds, for example, and voting rights in new departments like those in American universities (Mommsen 1987, 73–80).

As a result of the change in structure, power moved away from the faculty and toward the government. As Mommsen (1987, 81) observes, "The democratization of university bodies was somewhat fictitious because government authorities retained firm control over financial matters; democratization did not strengthen the autonomy of the universities. They were even less able to decide on future developments, not only because it was difficult to reach consensus within the new representative bodies elected according to rather complicated suffrage regulations but also because governments retained the final say about all new academic positions." The universities had also lost support in the population at large as a result of the campus disturbances. Further "democratizing" changes led to the inclusion of the training colleges, vocational institutes, and schools of art in the same category as the universities, offering their senior faculty the privileges and support of full professors in the university system. This upgraded their status but drastically increased the costs of administering the entire academic system. Other changes included the invasion of academic terrain by the *Hochschulrahmengesetz,* a federal law, passed down to the Länder level for interpretation, which established the rules for university reorganization. Introduction of the numerus clausus in fields like medicine, psychology, English, and German literature meant new bureaucracies to enforce these regulations, and Länder governments often created new positions on the basis of teaching needs and not research: "For the first time the authorities imposed quantitatively stringent teaching obligations, differentiated according to type of class, and all new appointments were made dependent on actual teaching demand. Research was of little importance. Even worse, academic positions not apparently necessary to meet the obligations stipulated in the new Studienordnungen (laws concerning studies) were eliminated. Simply put, teaching requirements became criteria according to which university departments were developed or cut back" (Mommsen 1987, 77–79, 83).

Finally, it became much less possible than before for distinguished scholars to bargain with universities tendering competing job offers because the education ministers at the Länder level were no longer interested in this game. The result has been a degree of academic stagnation, exacerbated by the academic world's loss of an entire generation of scholars until the mid-1990s, when tenured positions again began to open. German professors can still count on fairly good academic salaries and the prestige that a high-level civil service job still has in Germany. But the state has taken a far greater role than before in administering the direct and daily life of the university, reducing the powers and privileges of the full professors.

What about the moral responsibility of the professoriate for the Nazi era? This question finally came to the forefront in the 1980s—again primarily as a result of student action, supported by young faculty. The seniority system in the German university—and the conformity that it tends to enforce on junior colleagues—kept the matter from being addressed earlier. As long as older professors still controlled major chairs in the university, critiques from the Left were generally ignored. Not until the 1980s did the generation that was trained in the first two decades after the war reach senior positions and assume the power and independence to criticize earlier scholarship and attitudes. The same situation applied to the medical, legal, and to some extent the engineering professions. When the *Historikerstreit*—the intellectual debate over the meaning of German history—broke out in West German newspapers in the early 1980s, the Left had already begun to lose some of the power that it had gained in universities in the late 1960s and the 1970s (Maier 1988). A new generation of conservative scholars wished to regularize the German past, to accept the Holocaust as an extreme example of the sort of events that also occurred in Armenia or Cambodia. Leftists like Jürgen Habermas protested violently concerning this attempt to explain away the past in order to have a new future for Germany. Historikerstreit was also an argument over the nature of history itself. No one won or lost the argument, for each side rejected the other's basic premises (Maier 1988, 160–72; Craig 1987, 16–19).

Just as the argument over the past died down, the Berlin Wall toppled and Germany was once again united. But the new united Germany has less money and more students than ever, and less inclination to consider the social and philosophical issues raised by the Holocaust and by the recent resurgence of Nazism. A new and more conservative German state has fired or demoted professors in the eastern provinces based on their politics—specifically, their loyalty to some of the principles of Marxism-Leninism. German universities are recasting themselves in a more technocratic mold, approximating on an expanded scale the French Grandes écoles and deemphasizing programs in the social sciences, especially political science and sociology. The result is a more pedestrian system in which the engineering schools—the Technische Hochschule—are the model that the universities are trying to imitate, rather than the old German university itself.

Even with its clear faults, the older university pursued knowledge for its own sake, with little regard for the needs of capitalism, which seem to drive the modern German university. Those professorial departments in sympathy with the expansion of capitalism will grow—programs in business administration, engineering, and biotechnology, for example. The social sciences and the humanities will recede as less government money is made available for professorships and institutes in these fields. The result promises to be a university system shaped to fit the needs of capitalism and not society as a whole, and a professoriate that increasingly sees nothing wrong with such an aim. This is an exaggeration and oversimplification of a more complex reality, of course. But the direction is clear. The professoriate's influence as a critical force in German society had a brief moment in the sun in the late 1960s and early 1970s, but it has receded and been replaced by the same kind of careerism that is typical of the United States, and to some degree of France, Italy, and Great Britain as well.

7 | COMPARATIVE AND INTERNATIONAL PERSPECTIVES

In a comparative approach, one can compare many things—the individual professions of medicine, law, engineering, and the university professoriate, for example, each across the national boundaries. This is a useful exercise but an impractical one, involving as it does so many variables, as well as data that are both incomplete and not precisely comparable. It also goes against the grain of the book, which is primarily to show the uniqueness of each professional group in each cultural situation, each with its own history. On the other hand, certain general comparisons, more limited in nature, are possible. First, given the same core tasks for each profession across all the nations in the sample, we can pay particular attention to variations in the numbers of professionals trained and in practice—the elemental issue of supply and demand. Second, we must ask how the national context itself has changed from the 1930s to the 1990s, and how this change in context, especially the international relations that have formed since World War II, has increasingly affected the ability of a given profession to perform its tasks more or less independent of the wider forces of the state and capitalism. Third, we will view the international context itself, as it influences national professions, with special attention to the European Common Market.

Is it fair to say that doctoring, lawyering, engineering, and university teaching share enough from nation to nation for us to attribute to each a set of core tasks carried out in each modern nation? I think that the answer for three of the four professions is obvious: for medicine, engineering, and teaching, the core activities are similar enough to do so. Whatever the span and scope of activities that can be included under these three rubrics, they share enough to act as a framework for comparison of the contexts impinging on them. This is not to say that there are not, for example, details of medical work that differ from nation to nation, or varying strategies of diagnosis and emphasis of problems. A whole comparative literature has been developed for medicine, and it shows how French doctors, especially general practitioners, are more likely to attribute certain malaises to the liver than are German general practitioners, who might suspect trouble in another organ. Nor can we say that engineering is exactly alike in the different nations of our sample—variations in the British case come to mind immediately. But regardless of the extent and nature of the training, the social role of the engineer on the workplace remains similar in all of the nations we have considered: they are "trusted workmen" who are given independence, within broad guidelines, to carry out their work for the benefit of the corporation. Academics, too, have the same function in each of our nations: as instructors of students and as researchers of new knowledge. How much teaching or research, and under what degree of observation, is of course a key question.

Only for the lawyers are the differences from nation to nation defining. Lawyers on the continent of Europe work within variations of a civil-law system, one that gives a larger role to the judge and a smaller one to the attorney than either the British or the American systems, whose courts give more weight to case law and precedent than do those on the Continent. Yet the two systems seem to be converging, as Continental courts begin to adopt some of the features of British and American law—bills of rights, for example, or the principle of habeas corpus, or a more generalized role for the lawyer in business—while the American and British system have developed codes that owe much to Continental law. The increasingly international nature of business encourages this greater similarity, for the role of lawyers on the Continent is expanding, and competition everywhere is increasing for the quasi-legal work that is carried out in some nations by accountants or notaries or both. As lawyers begin to compete in these broader areas of work, as Desolay notes, they change from narrow specialists on the Continental model to generalists on the Anglo-American model (Desolay 1992).

References are omitted in this chapter for discussions of comparisons of individual cases; the reader is referred to the case studies. Where new sources are introduced, they are documented as usual.

The Supply and Demand for Professional Manpower

The first issue on which comparison is necessary is the vexed question of the supply and demand for professionals. Defining supply is generally not difficult in the nations of our sample: the number of university graduates in the field and then, at an advanced stage, the number who have gone through graduate training programs. But defining demand is far more difficult, especially for those professions that are primarily in the "free" or profession libérale sector, since those professionals can, within limits, define demand. That is, a doctor who is in need of patients can, in a completely free situation, define a borderline case as one needing service, whereas the same doctor in a market with less competition—and thus enough patients— might persuade the patient that the case is not serious enough to require treatment. So, too, for a lawyer in private community practice, although the average consumer is less likely to allow a lawyer to define the level of problem that needs his services than to accept a doctor's advice. This issue is central because it bears directly on whether a profession is "overproducing" or "underproducing" its numbers. Let us consider this question for the doctors and the lawyers and then look at the variations that come into play when we consider the engineers and the professors.

Physicians. The 1930s was an era of oversupply of medical care, measured against the ability of the population to pay, though not, according to many studies, when measured against the actual need of the population. Because the medical profession was operating in a fee-for-service system (except in large German cities), and because the fees were not in the hands of the patients, the number of physicians who could earn a living was smaller than the number trained. In the United States, the inability of the patients to pay spawned the Blue Cross/Blue Shield model, a third-party scheme whose primary function was to keep the existing medical profession and hospital system solvent. Britain took a far more conservative course before World War II, with a scheme for part of the working class. The charity medicine that characterized this era in both nations went only a short distance toward meeting the needs of the patients, and therefore toward providing a supply of patients for the existing physician pool. Prewar France also had a two-class system, with the wealthy able to get care from the specialists at the university and the mass tied to the local general practitioner. Italy had more of a public system for the poor, with a certain number of salaried positions in each town reserved for doctors who would take care of the poor. Private insurance also increased throughout the prewar Fascist years in Italy, especially for the working class in key industries and for those in the professions. Yet the German system before Hitler was clearly the most progressive one, allowing the workers in most of the larger cities to join HMOs, while in the smaller cities and towns the old fee-for-service system prevailed. Once Hitler took over, the German medical profession gained power at the expense of the consumer, who suffered from the abolition of the urban HMOs. In general, the 1930s were characterized by low demand and low supply, as medical education was an elite activity and medical services were limited to members of the small insurance or HMO plans in each nation, plus those in the upper middle and upper class who had the money to pay the fees.

The advent of World War II had a variety of effects on medical supply and demand. In the United States, the "birth control" rules of the American Medical Association continued to control the numbers of doctors trained, resulting in a shortage of physicians as the majority were drafted and sent overseas. The entire British health care system was nationalized for the duration of the war, and the state directed the distribution of physicians across the map of the nation; this strategy had little effect on the overall number of practitioners, but working class patients in provincial cities could nevertheless find doctors more easily, as could those in the middle and upper middle classes. But, as in the United States, the military draft made a shortage of physicians inevitable. On the other side, the Germans and Italians took different approaches to wartime challenges. Because the medical profession was effectively taken over by the Nazi Party, and because doctors were needed not only for the war effort but also for the administration of the Final Solution, Hitler's physicians who remained at home worked even longer hours than those on the Allied side. There was a modest rise in numbers during the war. In Italy the rise was gradual also, but conditions remained far different in the North, where the supply of physicians was adequate, than in the South, where doctors were in even shorter supply during the war than before it. France presents the case of an occupied nation, with Vichy adopting a conservative stance toward increasing the supply of physicians. In all three of these Continental nations Jewish doctors were first forbidden to practice medicine and then, toward the end of the war, sent to concentration camps. During the war, because politically acceptable physicians were in short supply, their professional leverage actually increased, and they gained guild power at the expense of the state.

The postwar era, through the mid-1960s, was a period of reestablishing prewar ratios of doctors to patients. The medical profession grew modestly in most of the nations, except for Italy, which experienced a rapid increase of medical graduates. But the system into which the physicians graduated was beginning to change in some nations. For the American doctors, fee-for-service medicine was still the primary model, though increased health insurance coverage after the war produced a greater increase in those seeking medical care than in those providing it, for the AMA adopted a policy to limit the size of medical school classes. Demand for medical services soon exceeded prewar levels, and the power of the AMA consequently increased. In Britain, on the other hand, the National Health Service rationalized the distribution of doctors and the funding process through the state guaranteed services for all. This in turn led to an expansion of medical education; existing medical schools, attached to the teaching hospitals primarily in London, accepted more candidates, but an increasing share of the teaching was done in certain regional centers. The latter primarily trained general practitioners, with the London hospitals still training the majority of the specialists. Although the medical profession certainly played a strong role in deciding the size of the postwar classes, the government, which funded the education system increasingly after the war, began to determine the mix between specialists and general practitioners, encouraging proliferation of the latter as the base of the NHS.

France, Germany, and Italy took different postwar approaches to the relation of supply to demand. In France, the major change came with DeGaulle's imposition of a national insurance scheme in 1958. In this early period, although there was some growth in the size of the medical profession, it was limited by the state's control over access to the university through the baccalaureat system, and medical school classes were only slightly larger than before the war. In Germany the situation was similar. In the first years after the war, the return to private practice of a number of the wartime physicians, plus the continuing elite nature of the German university, allowed only slow growth in the size of medical school classes. The situation was quite different in Italy. While Italy shared the Continental system of a baccalaureat-to-university transition, the Italian state was never powerful enough to create any effective barriers within the education system. The result in the late 1940s through the early 1960s was crowded medical school classes and an oversupply of physicians—who were, incidentally, ill-trained compared with those in the other nations in our sample, because they were required neither to take laboratory courses nor to serve a year of internship after graduation. With no curb on oversupply, many Italian physicians failed to earn a living, some of them competing with lawyers instead for government jobs.

The medical profession's experience in the late 1960s and thereafter has depended on its guild power relative to the power of the state. The U.S. profession lost some of its guild power and some of its ability to control the numbers, as the federal government forced expansion over the objections of the AMA. By the late 1960s government had begun to exert leverage on the research grant–dependent faculty. The medical schools were told to increase the size of their graduating classes or lose federal research support. At the same time, the government also gave stipends to the medical schools for each additional student trained. Contrary to the government's intentions, this increase in the number of graduates in the 1970s and early 1980s did not lead to an increase in the proportion of those going into general practice or practicing in rural areas but simply to increased competition in urban and suburban areas. HMOs and other salaried systems developed in part because of the growing oversupply of med school graduates. By the late 1980s and early 1990s, more new doctors were willing to practice in rural areas.

In Britain, the recent period has been a frustrating one, for as medical school classes have grown, increasing emigration from Britain has more than matched the gains, and the number of physicians available to practice within the NHS has leveled off. Some of those graduated—much fewer than Thatcher and the Conservatives would have wished—go directly into private practice, but these are usually the elite physicians with Oxbridge and London connections. The profession has maintained its equilibrium largely through immigration by physicians all too willing to work for NHS salaries that are low by British standards. France and Italy, on the other hand, have not maintained equilibrium at all. In France, until a few years ago, medical school classes grew at the same rate as the rest of the French university system; the number of internships was also increased as a result of university reforms and the development of Centres Hôpitals-Universitaires (university teaching hospitals) throughout France. This led, throughout the 1980s, to rapid proliferation of medical graduates and a decrease in the average wage that these graduates have been able to earn, especially those working as general practitioners in provincial towns. The situation is even worse in Italy. The late development of the Italian National Health Service, and its lack of central controls over medical school class size, has preserved the Malthusian model for physicians that characterized the immediate postwar period. Only in Germany has a reasonable equilibrium been established between the profession on the one hand and the state on the other, testifying to the continuing guild power of the German medical profession. Here the numerus clausus has been reestablished for entry to medical education, with the state and the profession working closely together to avoid both oversupply and shortfall.

In general, therefore, determination of numbers has shifted between the 1930s to the 1990s either from the profession (in the United States and Britain) or from the state working with the profession (in France, Germany, and Italy) to a greater role for the state. Not only is the state more involved in all of these nations—because of its increasing role in the funding and delivery of service—but as the costs of health care have risen, those within and outside of the state have become conscious of the ways in which the deployment of medical expertise affects the use of services by the consumer.

This in turn leads to attempts to affect the nature of medical education (generalists vs. specialists) and also, increasingly, to attempts by the state to redefine the division of labor in health care—to provide more responsibility for nurses and other auxiliary health professionals. In addition, the cost crisis has become an issue for corporate capitalism, which has backed the state in its attempts to put greater controls on the profession. In spite of this, however, weak and disorganized states (Italy is a prime example) have had limited success in changing the behavior of the profession. And when the state in confronted by a massive increase in determination to attend the university (as was true in both western Europe and the United States from the mid-1960s to the mid-1980s), then all previous plans have to be adjusted. For burgeoning enrollments lead inevitably to a rapid increase of medical practitioners, with negative consequences for the profession as a whole—although the elite of the profession tends to suffer less from the oversupply than the mass.

Lawyers. The pattern of professional growth has been similar for lawyers and doctors during our historical period. The pattern everywhere from the 1930s to the 1950s is either one of very slow growth (in the United States, Italy, and France) or stability and even some regression (because of war losses in Britain and deemphasis of the profession in Nazi Germany). Changes in the nature of the educational system (in Britain, the use of the university as a law school preparing for the bar final) and in the number of students completing legal training—in Europe, schooling is simply the first stage of legal education—expanded the pool of lawyers eventually practicing. The American practicing profession, for example, doubled in size between 1970 and 1980; the British profession grew less radically, but more lawyers began to choose a career as a solicitor rather than one at the bar. On the Continent, where the size of the bar had been essentially constant from 1880 to 1950, followed by relatively slow growth in the 1950s and early 1960s, the French profession doubled in size between 1973 and 1983. Control of the size of the profession came to depend less on limiting entering students and more on testing after the last year of law school. The Italian bar grew much more slowly than the medical profession. A growth spurt in the 1970s and early 1980s was less pronounced in Italy than in the other nations of the sample, in part because of the long period (five to seven years after graduation from law school) required to become established as a full attorney, in part because an enormous proportion of university graduates with law degrees, who have chosen not to practice, act as a backlog and as competition for new graduates. Finally, the German profession's growth curve resembles the American and the French. Before Nazism the profession was split between an urban, predominantly liberal, and largely Jewish elite and a conservative, non-Jewish mass. The profession was de-

emphasized under Nazism, then grew slowly i
rapidly in the late 1960s, 1970s, and early 1980s.

After the 1960s, oversupply has ended the tradition
and to a lesser extent France for government to serve as an a
for law graduates. These graduates now crowd the private-pra
of the profession. In Britain, competition is increasingly coming from w
out the profession as well as within, from the chartered accountants. The
American profession, like the others, has been split between a corporate-
practicing elite and a vast practitioner mass. The primary comparative lesson
for both the medical and legal professions, in fact, concerns the split between
the elite and the mass. When the size of the profession is controlled, there
is work for both the elite and the mass. When rapid growth produces oversupply, the mass suffers but the elite continues to thrive—though as we
shall see, the international scene is changing and beginning to affect even
national elites.

Engineers and academics. For our other two groups, the conditions of demand are set by the employers, not by the professionals themselves. Neither
engineers (except for a small minority of consultants) nor academics are
"free professionals." There is, however, a major difference between the
two in that employers can define anyone as an engineer, regardless of academic credentials, whereas professors apply the criterion of the degree to
their colleagues, even though the university or the state actually determines
employment. The levels of skill required for professional status differ ac-
cordingly. Up to 30% of engineers, depending on the nation, do not have
even a college degree; for academics, especially after 1960, a graduate degree, research ability, and a number of years in a probationary status are
necessary to become a tenured professor, and no junior professor, no matter
how talented, is ever guaranteed tenure. During the period of massive university expansion, from the late 1960s to the late 1970s, most of those in
the junior ranks did achieve tenure in the United States, on the Continent,
and to a lesser degree in Britain. But this was a short and exceptional period
in the history of academia.

Engineering has been, in most of our nations, a profession where scarcity
was the rule during World War II and in the decade after it, giving graduate
engineers their strongest bargaining leverage. But beginning in the mid-
1960s, as the university populations in the West began to rise, the supply
of engineers began to outgrow the demand. The Depression limited the
call for engineers by industry in the 1930s, though the rate of those studying
in the field remained relatively constant. With the onset of the war, the
demand began to outrun the supply, and those who were virtually unhirable
during the late 1930s found war work in the early 1940s. Peacetime produced another upturn in production, particularly in western Europe, where

...re engineers than the univer-
...ut. This situation led in turn to
...cians into engineers within post-
...he numbers of undergraduate en-
...iediate wartime era. Britain's lack of
...ne university meant that, even more
...ons trained their own technicians and
...neering status, leaving the university al-
...n France, the Ecole polytechnique and its
...sées and Mines, turned out graduates who
...war effort in occupied and Vichy France.
...engineering students during the war—in part
beca... ...red status—as did Italy, where the increase was
moderate ... ...dards. In both Germany and Italy, and to a great
degree in Franc... ...d, the upper-middle-class nature of the university
system or the major grandes écoles limited the number of graduates. In the
United States, where engineering was never considered an elite profession,
and in Britain, where it was defined as a working-class one, the relation
between university status and engineering was as governing as it was on the
Continent.

In the immediate postwar era, through the 1950s, the status of engineers
improved as part of the boom economy. Even more than during the war,
demand outran supply. The German case was typical. With war losses
among engineers and with the task of building the postwar economy, the
role of engineers was even more critical than in wartime. Germany responded by expanding the Technische Hochschule sector of the university,
and by creating a second-level technology degree, a strategy that led to a
slow expansion of the profession. Italy turned out more graduates from its
engineering faculties—which were combined with the architecture faculties
in many universities—and these provided skilled engineers for the nation's
postwar recovery in manufacturing and housing. In France, during the
Trente Glorieuse—the first thirty years of postwar recovery—the supply of
engineers could not meet the demand. The reform of the French university
system, which led to the creation of many university-related industrial and
technology programs, did not begin to produce graduate engineers in any
numbers until the early 1960s, whereupon in a few short years the supply
began to exceed the demand. (During this same period, an increasing number of graduates of the engineering grandes écoles went straight into management.) The same pattern obtained for Italy, without the complication
of the grandes écoles. The number inscribed on the rolls of the engineering
ordini, which had already grown rapidly by 1970, rose exponentially from
1970 to 1990, producing an inevitable oversupply. Even Germany, which

had found ways to control the growth of the medical and legal professions, could not stem the proliferation of the engineers in the mid- to late 1970s and early 1980s. Only in Britain, with its backward relation between the university and industry, and in the United States, with its notoriously poor science background in most high school programs, has the demand continued to match the supply.

On the other hand, several major technological changes and the growth of capitalism make it unlikely that a new market demand will arise for the engineering graduates of the 1990s. The end of the Cold War, with its stress on new weapons production, has eliminated many engineering jobs, and changes in the nature of production, specifically the emphasis on CAD/CAM techniques, are leading to growth in a few engineering specialties, like robotics and computers, but to stagnation in many others. Finally, as capitalism begins to move more of its manufacturing jobs to developing countries, the corresponding engineering jobs tend also to move. Thus after cycles of boom and bust, in which training and employment seem to be continually out of phase, the oversupply of the mid-1990s shows little sign of mitigation in the short run or even in the long run.

The status of engineering as a profession has be closely tied to the social origins of its recruits—from lower-middle- to middle-class in the 1930s, it became a middle-class profession after World War II and has held this place since. But with the relative loss in productive power of most Western nations since the 1970s and the increase in productive power in the primary and secondary sectors of production in Japan, in the rest of the Far East, and in the developing nations, the loss of engineering jobs appears permanent in the West. Unfortunately, this is occurring at a time when the supply of engineering students in Western Europe already far exceeds the demand.

Professors. The professoriate is doubly involved in the changing professional population. As the instructors of the students, professors influence the numbers for each of the other professions. At the same time, the size of their own profession is related to the increase or the decrease of students. In the 1930s, the only significant deviation from an elite model of education occurred in the United States, where the state university systems were already providing an alternative at the college level. The limited number of jobs available for new recruits to the professoriate came primarily from these systems. During the Second World War, plans for education were deferred in many nations. The postwar recovery led to an upswing in student enrollment, and thus in faculty positions. But the biggest change, especially in Europe, came during the mid- to late 1960s, as the French, Italian, and German university systems became accessible to the masses. Many tenured positions became available, but those positions were soon filled by a backlog of heretofore underemployed academics. Those who had the misfortune to be applying for tenured positions in the late 1970s and the 1980s were faced with a large, entrenched professoriate. The student population, particularly in Germany and Italy, rose still further, but the number of faculty did not, except for a massive increase in the untenured ranks.

In all three of the Continental nations in our sample, the result was the development of a highly bureaucratized professoriate, with much less bargaining power than before the war. In Italy, however, because the state is weak and the professoriate relatively strong, increased funding and the creation of a large number of new tenured positions occurred without new restrictions on the professoriate. The French education ministry and the German Länder governments, in contrast, take a more active position vis-à-vis the professoriate than does the Italian education ministry.

Britain and the United States present two further variations on this model. Even before the upswing in enrollment in the late 1960s and early 1970s, the U.S. system was already open to the masses. The United States responded to the enrollment surge with a hiring phase, at the same time giving more power to the professoriate. By the time enrollment leveled off in the late 1970s and early 1980s, a tenured professoriate was in place; the period since has been characterized by intense competition for the positions that remain, while cost pressures have eroded many of the privileges of professorial life. At all but the most elite private universities, this has strengthened the hand of the administration at the expense of the faculty's autonomy. In Britain, the trend has even been more marked. The Thatcher government responded to the great rise in student enrollment from the early 1960s to the late 1970s by allowing only a slight increase in faculty positions, expanding the polytechnic institutions, replacing the University Grants Committee with a council that was more closely controlled by the government and less responsive to faculty needs, and, most injurious to the autonomy of the professoriate, abolishing tenure for all new hires. This result has been a "decline in donnish dominion" (Halsey 1992).

Clearly, then, in all but the Italian case, the professoriate of the mid-1990s does not have the independence of the late 1960s—a high point that was related in part to the willingness of states to let the faculty have its way, in part to simple supply and demand. Except in Italy and at certain private prestige universities in the United States, the professoriate has since become less autonomous and more bureaucratized.

Regarding numbers, then, the following conclusion pertains to all of our professions. Except in weak and disorganized states, like Italy, professional autonomy has declined between the 1960s and the 1990s—though the elite sectors of the professions have been far less affected by the trend. Among physicians, for example, specialists have retained more autonomy than general practitioners, although the ability of the state to compel changes in the mix varies from nation to nation. The legal profession has become massively oversupplied everywhere, though again the elite practitioners, serving capitalist interests, have managed to hold their own. But the legal profession, particularly the elite segment, also faces increasing competition from other professions that deal with capitalism, specifically accountants and notaries. Increased competitiveness within the elite segment and from without the profession, as well as a loss of the older "gentlemen's ethic," has eroded guild power and autonomy for the profession as a whole. The proliferation of available practitioners has contributed to this situation.

Similar trends apply to engineers and professors. The former, the direct employees of capitalism, are closely connected in their training and placement with the needs of capitalists. The problem has been twofold in recent decades. First, changes in the supply of engineers has always been at least a decade behind changes in the demand; large numbers of engineers have entered the market just as the economy has turned soft or, increasingly, has been transferred from western Europe and the United States to developing nations. A significant percentage of engineering students in the West today are from those nations and can be expected to return to them, but the majority are not. At the same time, the middle-level jobs in administration, a favorite target of engineers ten years after graduation, have disappeared or been filled by people with business backgrounds. As a result, engineers in the West face increasing job insecurity and an oversupply of new recruits.

The situation is similar for academics. Although the production of new Ph.D.s or their national equivalents has finally begun to decline, the number still far exceeds the supply. Some nations have separate research-based organizations for academic graduates—the CNRS system in France, for example, and the Max Planck Institutes in Germany (Bourdieu 1988, 125, 140–42). But in the 1980s and 1990s even this second pathway was becoming blocked by tenure. By the millennium the job prospects may be more hopeful once again for academics—but in very different job settings than those of the late 1960s, settings where faculty power is lessened and state and university administrative power is stronger.

States, Capitalism, and Professions: The Importance of the Context

Changes in the context within which a profession practices are of primary importance to the profession's degree of autonomy. The profession that stood completely outside of the state in the early 1930s—medicine—has changed its position everywhere, and is now much more closely controlled by the state and indirectly by capitalism, which exerts pressure on the state to control costs. Law, primarily a petit-bourgeois profession of local notables in the 1930s, has evolved into a bifurcated profession—the elite dealing with corporate capitalism, the mass with much smaller corporations and with middle-class individuals. Engineering, although much diminished since the 1930s, has changed the least of the professions we have considered—in the employ of corporate capitalism everywhere, and without the kind of guild power that the physicians and lawyers have hung onto to some degree. Academics, including the teachers in each of the other three professions, have on balance improved their position somewhat since 1930, but the improvement in guild power reached a peak in the late 1960s and early 1970s and has been on a downtrend since then, especially for arts and sciences faculties. Different national histories have produced variations in this general progression, though with time and the impact of international factors, the patterns have increasingly come to resemble one another.

United States. Capitalism in the United States differs from capitalism in the other nations of our sample. It has a broader social reach, and its ability to affect other institutions is unmediated by an activist state that consistently acts to counter excesses. Thus the inclusion or exclusion of an institution by capitalists explains much of that institution's history. During the period of laissez-faire capitalism in the United States, the professions began to grow and to develop their university-centered model out of the apprenticeship systems of the nineteenth century. But after World War II a more centralized capitalism worked to influence professional institutions. Unlike engineering, which never had any guild power, medicine, law, and the professoriate began to be reshaped, with much input from capitalism.

Yet the results, which were different for each of these groups, related to the changing history of relations that capitalism had with each of these groups. Medicine, as long as it was irrelevant to capitalist priorities, developed major guild powers. But when these powers began to threaten capitalism in a competitive international system, capitalists began to work with leaders within the professions to limit the degree of professional guild powers. Calls for reform from within academic medicine and from the state were seconded by capitalists, who had a profit motive in rationalizing the health care setting. Lawyers were divided between those who provided direct help to capitalist firms, who were allowed to keep some guild power, and those who were irrelevant to capitalism and were allowed to fight it out in the mass sector. All work primarily to advance the interests of the wealthy and the upper middle class. Engineering has always been the province of capitalists, who recommended coursework in engineering schools, employed the graduates, and offered advancement within the corporation as an alternative to guild power. American academics, when they were more marginal to capitalism, could develop limited security and guild power. But since World War II, as they have become more relevant to corporate profit, they have found themselves, as a group, subjected more and more to capitalist priorities.

Finally, the vexed question of the American state is critical in understanding developments in the professions. As long as the professions could co-opt a small piece of state authority—licensing boards in Massachusetts or New York, for example, which work with the universities, which in turn provide the degrees that are prerequisites for the licensing exam—then the location of state action was "local." But as both capitalism and the state became more centralized, and as Washington, D.C., became more often the focus for action, then federal mechanisms—Supreme Court decisions, regulatory agency rulings, cost reimbursement schemes for medical care—began to co-opt and contain the professions. Washington was in turn co-opted—in all three branches of the federal government—by capitalism.

So the historical shifting of the scene of action—including decisions affecting the independence of professions—has meant a much greater dependence by professional groups on what the state, following the dictates of American capitalism, demands of them. The curbing of professional monopoly power, in the service of conservative and procapitalist ideologies, but also with consumer support, had undercut the leverage of professions and professional subgroups against capitalism. The absence of a political Left has meant that the entire history of professional development has occurred within a context that never developed a true opposition party or a welfare state.

Britain. Clearly the tendency in Britain is also for more state involvement in professional life. Whether this activity is direct, as when the medical profession was included in the National Health Service or when the university budgets were cut back and tenure abolished, or indirect, as when new legal service programs were used to fund the training and employment of junior barristers, the postwar era has been one of increasing state involvement. But there is an enormous difference between the quality and extent of the state's involvement in the pre-Thatcher years and its involvement after Thatcher took power in 1979. In the pre-Thatcher years, regardless of whether Laborites or Conservatives were in power, the professions were respected by government, which sought their input on the shape and nature of reforms before implementing them. Because the professions tended to defend their own interests in this process, change was slow, but when it occurred, it was with the (sometimes grudging) support of the groups involved.

Thatcher introduced an era of direct confrontation. The state has made allies of some professional groups—those closest to and most dependent on business interests, such as accountants—but in general has advocated less government payment for professional services and greater government regulation of professions in the public sector, like medicine and the professoriate. Thatcher's advocacy of a larger private sector for British medicine, combined with a rearrangement of the payment schemes for most British doctors, clearly decreased the autonomy of the individual professional at the point of diagnosis and treatment—the core of medical autonomy as defined by Freidson (1970a). But this was not an example of her laissez-faire ideology, which she saved for the private sector. Neither were her reforms of the legal profession intended to produce more autonomy for lawyers. These reforms, which enjoyed popular support, simply accelerated trends that predated her government. They are likely eventually to produce a situation similar to that in the United States: a two-class bar-and-solicitor profession, an elite serving the interests of capitalism, and a smaller, far less prosperous, and much more female segment serving the needs of the middle class and the poor. Thatcher's deliberate devaluation of the British professoriate and British education generally was combined with micromanagement, by a far more pro-cost control bureau that has taken the place of the University Grants Committee, regarding how the system is to be funded in the future. Yet because the rate of college attendance in Britain is low and relatively few voters identify with the world of universities, this reform was instituted with little more than a ripple from the public. Perhaps this is a result of the original decision of the Robbins Commission to enlarge the system but keep it an elite one rather than to open it to the masses on American or Continental models. Having little stake in the system and little hope of upward mobility within it, many Britons do not care about its slow decline.

The Britain of the 1990s is, in many ways, the result of gradual trends toward greater state involvement and a greater use of state power, at the expense of such institutions as the professions. It is also the result of refusing to extend traditional gentlemanly assumptions about Britain's government into areas where custom—but no laws—prohibited state intervention. The result, as some professions in Britain have discovered, is that long-valued rights and privileges have been swept away by administrative fiat, by governments that do not consult affected interests before acting. The private sector is left freer to succeed or fail on its own. The state has little control or even input into the central bank, and the banking industry does not often finance long-term British industrial investment. Thus, in the case of the engineering profession, which is primarily in the private sector, the world of education and the world of practice remain apart, with credentials gained in the former world of little use in the latter. For the state, while micromanaging the university world, has little leverage over the world of capitalism, while conversely this world still does not respect the credentials of the world of education to the extent seen either in America or on the Continent.

So ultimately the British case is one in which capitalist values, in the personification of the Thatcher and Major administrations, have gained hegemony over the world of higher education and over the moderately progressive wing of the professions. With the help of recent governments, the professions of concern to us here are becoming even more stratified, in the manner if not the form of the 1890s, into elite segments serving the wealthy and the upper middle class, and a vast mass of practitioners serving the working class. This latter group is much more likely to be female and to come themselves from lower-middle-class backgrounds. Britain, never a bastion of social equality—except to some ideological extent when Labor governments were in power—has become more socially stratified than ever.

France. States, capitalism, and professions evolve in relation to one another. The French professions of 1930, confronting the capitalism and state of the time, are vastly different from those of 1990, confronting a state and capitalism that have evolved new ways of relating to one another. The primarily private professions libérales of 1930 have given way to a far more complex set of successors. Although all historical periods are of course important, perhaps three are particularly so for our study: the Vichy period, the early years of the Fifth Republic, and the Mitterrand era of the 1980s. During the Vichy period France modified and extended its conservative system of ordres for doctors and the different legal professions, while giving engineers recognition as cadres but not the independent status of a profession libérale or an ordre. Much of the postwar era was shaped on these changes, which began the modernization of France. Capitalists lost some power in the early postwar years because of their role under Vichy, and the professions were able to continue much as before. Clientalism characterized the relation between the professions and a slightly weaker (in French terms) central state.

This situation began to change in the early years of the Fifth Republic, when DeGaulle and the new and reinvigorated French central state subdued the doctors, and his successors took on the legal professions, rationalizing them to some extent but failing to control the notaries. After DeGaulle's administration, the state worked as more of an equal partner with capitalism, and those professions or subprofessions that could aid capitalism began to pull ahead of those that primarily served the individual. Thus avocats who worked with large corporations gained influence and respect, and an American-style prestige hierarchy of specialties developed. The notaries, meanwhile, continued to make their bargains with the state to preserve their flexibility and their capacity to serve capitalism as consultants. They ensured the security of their monopoly by continuing to serve as the state's agents, and they used leverage available only to them involving certain state banks.

Gradually, however, France began to dissolve the planning system and revert to more straightforward encouragement of capitalism, with its agents gaining more and more leverage over state policy. Capitalist pressure was instrumental in drawing the medical profession into a national system. The Conseils fiscaux et juridiques grew as a special group to serve the legal needs of capitalists and defeated the legal profession's attempt to include them in the 1971 reformed avocat profession. Engineers have always been necessary for the fiscal health of production sectors of capitalism. Because of this, capitalists have always interceded to prevent any attempt on the part of the state to give the profession status independent of the owners of the individual firms.

Finally, capitalists in France have demonstrated their continuing contempt for academics by perpetuating the two-class system of grandes écoles and universities, with the state as a willing participant. Because almost all leading positions in the French state, and in French capitalism, go the graduates of the grandes écoles, and because these institutions maintain close relations with their graduates in the state and in industry, it is almost impossible to change the structure of a system that defines most university education as second-rate. The government after 1968 did not touch the system of elite schools when it attempted to reform the universities. Later, Mitterrand, a Socialist, tried to increase the size of the student bodies at the grandes écoles, a much milder reform, but the leaders of industry (most of them graduates of these schools) and high state officials (also graduates) lobbied successfully to keep the system as it has always been.

Since about 1974, when avocats invited the leaders of the other major professions to a joint conference, the professions libérales have organized to fight back—against what they claimed was unfair competition by state-based professions, against high taxes and Sécurité sociale payments to the state and lower payments from the state, against state policies that guaranteed the unemployment of professionals, and generally against the social devaluation of the French professions. The Union nationale des associations des professions libérales (UNAPL), founded in Paris in 1977, has become active in promoting the rights of all professionals, even to the point of holding a street demonstration in 1980. In the planning for the changes in profession-state relations accompanying the European Economic Community in 1992, the UNAPL also has been instrumental in forming the Union mondiale des professions libérales as an international association to fight for the autonomy of professionals. Yet their need to do so, in a situation where the state and capitalist forces are organizing to further diminish their power, is a sign of weakness rather than of strength. Professions, especially but not only in France, are under attack for their perceived greed and self-interest. Professionals might well reply, especially in France, that those attacking them are not without interests of their own.

Thus the French state has increasingly had capitalism as a partner in its decisions governing the changes in professions. Those changes that further the development of capitalism are instituted, those that might hinder it often are not even considered. That this process continued under a Socialist government is testimony to the power of the capitalist class in France, for Mitterrand was defeated at nearly every turn. French professions, which never developed guild power comparable to that of their counterparts in Britain or the United States, are losing what little they have in the face of joint action by capitalism and the state. By the 1990s, their remaining clientalism was more of a holding action to protect their dwindling power and influence than a strategy to gain more.

Italy. Italy provides an important case for our study of the relations between professions and the state, for the political parties that engage both also tend to diminish the autonomy of both. Political affiliation is paramount in the anomic process of Italian society. Careers are organized around political parties. When the Right is in power, either absolutely as under Fascism or moderately as with the Christian Democrats, social mobility tends to be blocked and the professions become a preserve of the upper classes. When the Left is strong (it has never actually been in power) the university tends to expand, but this brings with it the problem of mass education and contested mobility, as too many compete for too few jobs in the professions. Partitocrazia prevails in any case, parceling to each group a share of the jobs, powerful positions, and career opportunities.

Yet nothing remains unchanged. Even partitocrazia can be modified— as it must be by the fall of the Soviet empire, which has disrupted the unity of the Italian Left and undercut their ability to maintain their share of the spoils of partitocrazia. Parties of the Right have suffered as well, as prosecutors have successfully pressed charges of official corruption. Perhaps as the political parties begin to lose their grip on Italian society, the state might begin to act more independently of these actors. No state can be independent of politics; the only question is the degree of autonomy which it has. Similarly, these recent changes may lead to greater independence of the professions from the state, as well as to greater political solidarity on their part—a rebirth of the Italian guilds. On the other hand, the changes may mean nothing more than that capitalist sectors will gain more direct control of the state as party control weakens. Professors will still control the education committees of the legislature, doctors will still primarily be employees and contractors (albeit powerful ones) of the Italian National Health Service, engineers will still work for capitalist firms or in the broad state sector.

But if the political parties lose their strength, capitalist rationalization may have a more elemental effect on Italy, for partitocrazia has been a preventive factor against stronger capitalist control of politics and the economy. Growing capitalist influence has already led to the enlargement of the private sector in medicine. It widened further the split in the legal profession between the business-related elite in major Italian cities and the mass legal profession of individual-service practitioners. The legal profession, uniquely in Italy, is facing an increasingly leftist senior judiciary as judges of the late 1960s and 1970s move up the ladder. Engineers too, in some major sectors at least, are facing rationalization of the workplace, and with it the elimination of the middle-management jobs that had represented their usual step up from technical engineering.

Finally, if capitalism has gained, so, too, has the Mafia, as it confronts in ever more violent ways the increasingly disorganized state. A state that cannot police its own funds and employees can scarcely control the Mafia. Since the 1970s, in spite of massive attempts to control it, the Mafia has spread to the center and the north of the nation. Mafia members demand and receive a share of National Health Service funds, and possibly a share in the profits of many legitimate businesses. They attack the avvocati who prosecute them and the judges before whom they are brought. In many ways, Italy is behaving as if it were a Third World nation—but one with the problems of a major industrialized power. Welfare sectors are under attack, or degenerating, with obvious implications for the professional groups employed within them.

Germany. The very continuity of German professions throughout periods of tremendous turmoil has itself caused something of a moral problem. The professions have a record of continuous development from the Weimar years right through the Nazi era and into the postwar period. That continuity was never broken because practitioners who participated fully in the Nazi regime became leaders in the postwar practicing professions and in the university system of West Germany. Perhaps it is unfair to hold up the German professions to a moral critique that the others need not endure. Yet this is what made the German professions stand out in our sample: their virtual imperviousness to the consequences of their wartime crimes.

Professions are collective forms, and their aims are not simply self-defense and self-satisfaction. Guilds, whether ancient or modern, are supposed to prescribe a minimum ethical standard for their members. The absence of such a standard distinguished the German professions even from the French and Italian ones, where there was at least a difference of opinion on professional wartime behavior and postwar reconciliation between the majority Right and a healthy, critical Left. In Germany the war obliterated the professional Left, which had quite a struggle reestablishing itself in the postwar period. Perhaps this was due in part to the continuation in their chairs of powerful ex-Nazi and Nazi-sympathizing professors of medicine, law, engineering, and general studies; perhaps it was due to the unequal application by the right-wing judiciary of the postwar Berufsverbot, which barred Communists and other leftists, but not ex-Nazis, from civil service jobs, including university jobs. The student protests in the late 1960s brought about the expansion of the training levels of the professions without significantly changing the political complexion of the practicing professionals. Eventually engineering developed a mildly leftist contingent, but there is little evidence that significant numbers of doctors, lawyers, or university professors share those sentiments.

The role of the German state—in its regional and national structure—is buttressed by the growing strength of German capitalism. Until the 1980s, the medical profession had enough power to maintain a role in the policy process, but this role has diminished since that time as the fight over costs has escalated. German lawyers make up a relatively homogenous profession, but one whose future is threatened by widespread unemployment. It is beginning to develop a bifurcated nature like that of its counterparts in other nations of the sample, with a growth at the top and bottom ends of the pay scales. German capitalism has worked successfully with the German state (and with the education ministry in particular) to partially reform the two-class system of German engineering; in recent decades engineers have become less militant, and the profession has not revived a major professional association like the VDDI or a union like the BtiB. The professoriate, after some protests in the late 1960s and early 1970s, has returned to the quiescence that has usually characterized it, despite much heavier teaching loads and much more state interference in the university; the university setting itself, meanwhile, has been reshaped in a form more acceptable to German capitalism. The result is a set of tamed but entrenched professions, with little activism against the status quo. The aim has become to protect professional prerogatives against an increasingly encroaching state and the European superstate.

We might conclude this comparison of state-profession-capitalist relations with a brief recharacterization of the different "triangular" systems themselves. Until the Second World War, we had the independent American model of private professions co-opting state governments, with professional training at the university, as on the Continent. In Britain, we had the more private model, with professional training and licensure controlled more by the private sphere. Continental systems had stronger roles for the

state, but except for the university professors, the professions we are concerned with here were in the private sector. The rise of Nazism and Fascism
involved the key professions in Italy, Germany, and France in the politics
of the era, giving their ordres, ordini, and Kammern stronger powers while
enlisting them in the cause of anti-Semitism.

In the postwar era, an increased state role brought change. The United
States remained a capitalist-dominant system in which professions had a
minor part. The British system (until Thatcher) was a dissociated system,
with professions separate from the university, capitalism somewhat separate
from the state, and with little relation between capitalists and the university.
France was a state-dominated system, with the grandes écoles far more
important than the university, which trained some professionals but not the
elite that ran both the public and the private sectors. In Italy partitocrazia,
developing out of Fascist one-party rule to include the Communists and
the Socialists, permeated every sector—the state, capitalist firms, the university, and the professions. In Germany, the postwar era brought with it a
bargained state, with regions having many responsibilities, including professional training in the universities. Professions had a significant, if small,
place at the table.

The state's role began to change after about 1965. In the United States,
for example, the federal government for the first time began to act vis-à-
vis the professions, depriving them of certain special exemptions from the
regulatory process. Meanwhile, as the federal government paid a larger share
of the bill for health services and health research, it began to have leverage
over both the academic wing and the practicing profession of medicine. It
had less impact on lawyers, except to enforce laws against discrimination in
graduate applications, thus reducing even further the role of the profession
itself as gate-keeper. The postwar British state maintained the dissociated
model until the late 1970s, but gradually the state began to increase its legal
funding and in the process to reform the nature of that system; in medicine
and the universities the change came in the Thatcher era, toward a much
more active role for the state. In France the dirigiste central state was gradually superceded by a more traditional role for capitalism in guiding state
policies. The grandes écoles continued to provide graduates to staff both
the public and private elite subsystems, effectively holding the system together. The postwar Italian state remained paralyzed by partitocrazia, but a
health-financing emergency and the creation of the SSN gave the medical
profession an opportunity to organize politically and gain strength against
a weakened state. Finally, in Germany, the slow change from Länder control
of professional education and practice to a more explicit role for the central
state has brought this model closer to the French one, though without the
overt clientalism of the latter. The bargaining between the interests de-

scribed by Katzenstein continues in Germany, but the hand of the professions is getting slowly weaker and that of the state is getting slightly stronger.

As the era of major postwar growth leveled off in western Europe, and as economic competition from the rest of the world increased, the role of such superstate organizations as the European Economic Community became more important in understanding these triangular relations. The superstate has begun to further complicate these relations, while further hindering the professions. Professions remain primarily national creations, international conferences notwithstanding. But capitalism, international to some extent by 1960 and to a much greater extent by 1990, began to view professionals as obstacles to economic progress. It is to this latest development that we turn to next.

The Common Market and the Professions: Superstate Dynamics

A major aspect of the context of the professions has been the relation between states and capitalism. Relations were close in some nations before World War II—Italy and Germany come to mind immediately, and the seeds of the association in postwar France were evident as well. But in Britain and the United States the relation was a distant one, except in certain sectors of the economy. In both nations, the shock of World War II brought about a closer direct working relation, and in the immediate postwar era, the military-industrial complex in the United States and the nationalization of the British coal and transportation industries, among others, by the Labor government, exemplified new and closer alliances between capitalism and the state. France's postwar state planned sector by sector with chosen capitalist firms to reinvigorate the French economy, whereas in Italy the overlap between state and capitalist control grew so that in the late 1970s fully 40% of the economy was in this sector. In Germany, the role of the state in industry was more conservative, and much capitalist planning was done by the large investment banks. But throughout western Europe, the state's direct role in the economy increased during the postwar era.

The economic downturn and leveling off since the middle 1970s expanded the role of the state—this time of a superstate, the European Economic Community. Founded by six nations with the Treaty of Rome in 1959 and gradually adding six others, the EEC has worked, with the support of the capitalists (but usually not the farmers or the small businessmen) of member nations toward the goal of "full economic integration." Although this full integration was not achieved by the target year of 1992, the degree to which member nations control certain activities within their own borders has changed. Borders themselves have lost meaning as a result of liberalized customs rules between member nations, which have strived to remove barriers to trade in goods and services.

The EEC has included professional services in its definition of goods and services. Beginning in the 1960s and accelerating into the 1970s, 1980s, and 1990s, the EEC has announced a series of sectoral directives dealing with the training and the rights of professionals in one member nation to migrate and practice in another. The regulatory machinery of individual nations has been used in the past as a barrier to the free migration of professionals—particularly in periods of oversupply of trained professionals, such as have prevailed in recent years in Europe. Sectoral directives covering such professions as medicine and architecture instruct member governments and their affected professions and universities to harmonize training and to reciprocally accept credentials.

National professional associations, reacting to the intent of the European Community to integrate professions across borders without recognizing the vast variances in training, formed liaison committees made up of representatives of professions in member nations. These committees worked with the EEC to modify the directives in the draft stage, to protect professional standards from sinking to a "lowest common denominator" (Orzack 1991). In addition, interprofessional international organizations like the Union Mondiale des Professions Libérales or the European Secretariat for Liberal, Independent and Social Professions (SEPLIS) have also formed to influence the EEC's oversight of professions. The result has been that

> an immense flow of documentary materials moves within and among the labyrinths of the Community, national governments, associations, and liaison committees. Intersecting memberships, consultative arrangements, invitational participation in policy review meetings, journalist coverage, and leaks of confidential materials to interested parties allow for ample and continuing exchanges of ideas, voicing of alarms, and formations of coalitions. Resistance and action strategies receive support from interinstitutional and cross-national blocs and coalitions. Proposals for directives move ahead in the E.E.C. under close observation from other structures. Where interests seem threatened, counteraction can be initiated at many points. (Orzack 1983, 255)

Orzack and others have considered these political forces in great detail in a series of studies of professions covered by sectoral directives that won acceptance of national governments (medicine, nursing, midwifery, architecture) and of others that have not succeeded (engineering, law) (Orzack 1989; Orzack and Calogero 1988; Quinn 1980). The efforts have been more likely to succeed when training is similar from nation to nation, when the relevant professional associations cooperate, and when there is no extreme oversupply of professionals.

Neale, Hurwitz, and Orzack have each considered an inevitable next step on the part of the EEC (Neale 1994; Hurwitz 1990; Orzack 1991). In 1989, the EEC proposed a so-called General Systems Directive to include the professional groups, including law and engineering, that had not been the subjects of individual sectoral directives. The General Systems Directive was discussed in secret, without the participation of the affected professions and their representatives, leading to much anxiety and turmoil on the part of these groups. The directive was designed to preempt the objections of national and international professional associations, which routinely intervened at every step of the genesis of an individual directive, claiming concern for the "vital interest" of the public but in reality protecting the solidity of their national professional monopoly. The general systems directive simply called for mutual recognition of diplomas, without dealing with the minutiae and differences between nations that made the achievement of individual directives such a long and tedious process, one in which national and international professional associations intervened at every step, always claiming that the "vital interest" of the public was at stake, whereas in reality what was at stake was the solidity of their national professional monopoly. Because difference between professions over the qualification for particular tasks varied by nation (midwives in one nation, for example, being allowed to perform procedures that only doctors were allowed to do in another), the sectoral directives and the General Systems Directive have left large areas still to be bargained over. New organizational features include so-called competent authorities in each nation and watchdog committees to see that the new legislation is enacted at the national level. But who will be represented as "competent authorities" and who will be, and watch, the watchdogs (Orzack 1992)?

The enactment of the General Systems Directive promises many future battles between states, national professions, international organizations such as the EEC, and the international professional lobbying bodies. In general terms guild power of individual professions in individual nations has been significantly curbed by this addition of a supranational body whose rulings have the force of law within the member nations. But a particular profession, working with its own national government, can use the EEC as leverage to gain more power and control over work for a particular profession in its jurisdictional battles with a neighboring profession in a given nation.

Several factors enhance state power and further diminish professional power in the EEC nations. First, making professional training "interchangeable" from nation to nation forwards a clear aim of the capitalist mentality that underlies the bureaucratic activities of the EEC to rationalize the professions. Second, national professions and national governments, even if they are allowed to keep considerable autonomy and control over their professional training and practice situations, now have to do so within the context of the EEC. Any national attempts to change professional boundaries will have to be checked with the relevant EEC bureaucracy first, leaving the states and professions much less flexibility. Third, the professions' attention to issues carries with it huge costs in money and time spent in primarily defensive lobbying. In the short run, all of this activity affects between 5 and 10% of the professionals in Europe. And the lobbying could not stop the EEC from instituting the general systems directive.

Clearly both Marx and Weber would view this long-term process as an example of capitalism in action. Marx would see the role of the superstate as once again smoothing the way for capitalist expansion and trade, over the objections of the primarily craft-organized professions. As Marx and Engels stated in the Communist Manifesto (1848, 225), "Independent or but loosely connected provinces, with separate interests, laws, governments, and systems of taxation, become lumped together into one nation, with one government, one code of laws, one national class-interest, one frontier, and once customs-tariff." Substitute the words "European Economic Community" for "national" here—the rationale remains the same. In a sense, the imposition of the EEC is from a Marxian viewpoint another example of the difference between a craft-guild way of organizing a society and a modern capitalist rationalization of an area that had been allowed in past years to remain somewhat untouched by these processes. Weber would agree with Marx on this and would also be concerned with the nature of the bureaucratization involved by bringing the EEC, with its myriad agencies, into the process of professional regulation and control. For one, the entire EEC process can be viewed as an attack on professional status per se. Once professional groups are put into a bureaucratic meatgrinder whose machinations benefit capitalists primarily, what comes out the other end is packaged, homogenized professions that have lost their individuality and much of the status that comes with this uniqueness (Weber 1978, 305–7). Secondly, Weber would view the antiprofessional values of the EEC bureaucrats as an example of the way that capitalist values have seeped into the public sector itself—for the EEC agencies, though they work in the interests of international capitalism, are nevertheless public agencies at a superstate level (Weber 1958, 196–244).

Those who argue that the EEC has had a limited effect on professions can point to individual cases and to the modifications that tend to get in the way of the goals of the EEC. Because the number of professionals who migrate between nations is so low, for example, and because the EEC rules influence primarily only those who do move, the effect is minimal for most professions in most EEC nations. But EEC-mandated modifications in the professional training regimes constitute a permanent change in the ability of a given profession to control its own work in a given nation. The ineffectiveness of the EEC bureaucracy is also cited by those who minimize the effects of the superstate. Not only can it can be neutralized by professional lobbying, but directives that have been accepted de jure by a national government can be ignored de facto, for a while at least, by the profession. A profession can advise its members that they have two options: observe the restrictions and hurdles of EEC directives or reject them, and take their objections to the World Court in Brussels. But in the intervening five to seven years it will take for their case to come to court, they cannot practice in the profession.

A final limitation on the effectiveness of the EEC directives is the nature of the work being done by a particular professions and the credentials necessary for doing it. Evetts (1994), in her study of the effect of the general systems directive on the profession of engineering, describes a supranational engineering organization—the Fédération européenne des associations nationales d'ingénieurs or FEANI—that acts as a credentialing group for engineers who want a title of Euroengineer. She notes that only Britain and Ireland within the EEC recognize this non-EEC title, which the EEC should (but probably won't) accept. But in fact much credentialing activity in this particular profession is irrelevant, for the capitalists who hire engineers do not in many cases even make the distinction between those with a full university background in engineering and those who have shorter, technical training programs. If national credentialing is considered irrelevant or minimally important by the main employers of the profession, international credentialing is unlikely to carry more weight.

Three case studies illustrate the complexities involved in this supranational arena: doctors in Britain, dentists in Italy, and lawyers in France. Stacey (1992) in her study of the reactions of the British Medical Association to the sectoral directive on physicians, noted that in the short run many doctors, including those in positions of power, continued to act as if the directive did not exist. Requiring language exams, expressly forbidden by the EEC, they continued to block the way for many foreign physicians. The EEC objected, and a compromise was worked out whereby the doctor must show competence in English but may not be tested for it. How this will work out in reality is anybody's guess, but Stacey suggested that the BMA might be expected create inventive new ways to block immigration. Another blocking technique was described by Hurwitz (1990, 2), who reported that in Belgium, France, and Luxembourg the request for a migrant doctor's credentials, supposedly an automatic procedure, could be dragged out for months if not years to impede a physician from practicing legally in his new nation. This practice, too, flouts an explicit sectoral directive on the migration of physicians and has triggered an EEC threats to prosecute in the World Court. According to Stacey, the passage of the directive has not led to any major increase in migration by doctors.

The second case is one we have considered several times before—lawyers or avocats in France. The legal profession, working with the French state, got many of its competitor professions included, in 1971, as part of a new avocat profession. But the profession was not successful at that time in getting the conseils fiscaux et juridiques included as avocats, which left the conseils free to advise businesses on legal matters. In 1989 the EEC General Systems Directive was passed but not yet adopted by the individual states. Nevertheless, it acted as leverage on the French state to include the conseils fiscaux et juridique in the legal profession. Foreign legal professionals must now take an aptitude test before practicing in France, one that they previously did not have to pass because the conseils did not have one. Although Speranza cites this as conclusive proof of the power of the French legal profession to manipulate the French state toward its own end of a more unified and inclusive legal profession, he neglects two critical other professions that are part of the legal world in France (Speranza 1994, 5). Both the notaries and the international accountants provide legal counsel to corporations, for the French state still refuses to give the avocats a monopoly over this activity. And, as Desolay indicates, the boundaries between accounting and business law are beginning to fade in France at precisely the time that the legal profession is trying to expand its mandate (Desolay 1992, 165–201). The French notariat is also in a strategic position to counsel all businesses. The result, therefore, is scarcely a clear victory for the French legal profession. In addition, Speranza ignores the issue of those who have already qualified as conseils and who will therefore have to be included as avocats, including many foreign lawyers, in postulating a victory by the avocats.

Speranza (1994, 5) considers a third case, reconsidering and updating the work of Orzack on the Italian dental profession. Orzack had shown that the profession was brought into existence under EEC pressure, for dentistry in Italy had been a branch of the medical profession. An international liaison of dentists, including progressive members of the Italian medical-dental specialties, favored the changes; the majority of the doctor-dentists were against it. The ECC had in 1978 confronted the Italian state and the majority of the medical profession with a demand for the creation, de novo, of a dental profession. Otherwise no Italian dentist could practice elsewhere in Europe, and no dentist elsewhere could practice in Italy (Orzack 1981). Italy created its new profession in 1985. The Italian state, which did not have the strength or the will by itself to oppose the medical profession, could with the EEC's demands as a superstate do exactly that. Speranza (1994, 2) suggests that the dental profession was already evolving in Italy before the EEC mandate. But in fact, without the pressure of the EEC, Italian dentistry as a separate profession would not exist today.

These three case studies highlight the complexities that accompany the imposition of a superstate onto the political field on which professions and states interact. Capitalist interests advocate the complete interchangability of labor from nation to nation and the EEC promulgates directives to that effect. The professions object and form liaison committees that oppose the EEC, arguing that training rules are not the same from nation to nation. The EEC, after a number of years' experience with what it considers professional footdragging, promulgates yet another and more general regulation, this time covering all remaining professions in all EEC nations, and declares that if the professional training period for a given profession is three years long, then for purposes of the EEC all degrees of community members will be considered reciprocally valid. Actions by such groups as British doctors, French lawyers, and Italian doctors achieve mixed results in the battle to retain professional autonomy.

But the general direction is clear. Capitalist rationalization, this time at the superstate level and supported by the EEC bureaucracy, is winning out over the rear-guard actions of professional groups. Whether it is legitimate to consider professions in the same category as other occupations is unquestioned by the EEC, as are the surpluses of professionals in all of these nations, a condition that puts intolerable burdens on national governments that wish to observe EEC directives but must also consider the interests of their own national professions. Because EEC law now supercedes national law in these areas, the professions in Europe can still fight on, winning many small battles but ultimately losing the war, for each "win" will result in new and modified regulations from the EEC. Capitalism is on the EEC's side and helps to steady its hand in the face of professional opposition to its laws and directives.

8 | CONCLUSIONS: GUILD POWER AND SOCIAL CHANGE

At the beginning, we asked a question: has capitalism finally caught up with the last remaining guilds? Throughout this study, we have shown the ways in which formerly self-run professional groups have slowly been losing the ability to control their own associations, to control the workplace, to control the market for their services, and to control their relation to the state. How the world has changed since the early 1930s for the major professions has been the primary story told in these pages. The three-way model that we have used has shown its ability to investigate the professions in radically different nations in the West—all, to be sure, capitalist, but with varying arrangements among professional groups, the state (in its many bureaus that relate to professions), and capitalist corporations. Lobbying by these corporations, within the political process or directly with the state itself, has changed the nature of professional work by enlisting the state in its overall long-term rationalization process. But the process has been shown to be different for different nations.

Our comparison of the United States, Britain, France, Italy, and Germany has shown how different historical developments and different political pressures have had different results for professional groups. Long-term patterns, such as the dominating role of capitalism in the U.S. political economy, the centrality of the French state, the "privateness" of the British professions, the paralysis of partitocrazia in Italy, and the bargained interconnectedness of state, capitalism, and the professions in Germany have been shown to continue during widely different historical periods.

In spite of these continuities, however, some changes have occurred. Both the professions of medicine and law—especially their elites—have increasingly bought the capitalist model itself and have imposed capitalist rationalization upon those lower in the professional pecking order. Engineering has always accepted capitalist values and has therefore never been a profession acting in its own interest in competition with the values and aims of capitalism. The university itself, the source of the professional training, has increasingly been made over in the image of capitalist interests, as programs with little application to capitalism have withered while those that train the foot soldiers of capitalism have flourished. Perhaps this process is a final example of what Weber would have called "die Entzauberung der Welt," the loss of any noncapitalist values within the professions, both because of external pressures we have considered here and because of the surrender of positive guild values—of collegiality, of concern for the group, of a higher professional ethic beyond mere profit—that has eroded the distinction between professions and any other occupation and thus left them together as the middle-level employees of capitalism (Weber 1978).

To what extent have we actually proved the thesis set out here? Much of the evidence is indirect, from studies that may have been fallible. I wish that the professions were more frequently studied than they appear to be outside of the U.S. case, that both the historical and the qualitative evidence were clearer and more directly focused on the issues we have considered. There is also the problem of the abstractness of the model we have used: state-profession-capitalism. Nevertheless, the case studies have gone into the details and dealt with actual political parties, real historical events, and splits between the elite and the mass within each profession—all of the complications and complexities that one has to deal with if one is really concerned with the fate of actual professions in vastly different nations. And as capitalism itself has changed, and gone much more closely into partnership with the state (or controlled it ever more thoroughly from outside), the international context within which professions have always existed has become ever more directly relevant to their daily life within each nation. Thus the concern in the comparison chapter for the growing role of the EEC in professional life in western Europe. The new international world trade agreement will ultimately begin to affect the professions in the United States as well.

We have found the standard interpretations of professional power and change inadequate in dealing with the long-term phenomena considered here, with the possible exception of Weber's concern with capitalist rationalization. Marxian theories of proletarianization, when taken literally, cannot be applied to the major professions at all until the late 1980s and only to a small fraction since then. Before that, professionals in medicine and law, though pressured more and more with each passing decade, were not completely deprived of control over their work. Even in the recent years, and even in the most rationalized settings, these professions maintain some control over their immediate work tasks, although this is coming under supervision in some settings that an earlier generation would feel was intolerable. Engineers are not proletarianized precisely because of their "trusted worker" status, as well as the short-term freedom they have to control their work and their opportunity to move up within the company. Academics complain increasingly about the pressures that interfere with their ability to control the university's work, but neither can their condition be called proletarianization.

Perhaps Weber's concern with the nature of the rationalization of society under capitalism is more relevant than Marxian thought to understanding what is happening to the professions. Weber's concern with the role of examinations as the producers of a special closed status group is of key importance (Weber 1978, 1000). But in our modern era, especially since the 1960s, what Collins called "credentialism"—the use of examinations and school degrees as a method of selecting those who have a chance to maintain their status or to move up the social ladder—reached the crisis point (Collins 1979, 191–95). As the numbers of Ph.D.s and graduates in medicine, law, and engineering began to far exceed the number of jobs available to them, the ability of the professions to control their world hit a new low. As we have indicated, pressures on the state from capitalists have been part of the reason for the increases, while pressures toward proletarianization in the wider society have driven far more individuals to seek the "protection" of professions. At the same time, university programs expanded regardless of the need for their graduates. In a situation of oversupply, when the majority of new positions are not only salaried but also either under direct capitalist control or under the control of "capitalist-thinking" professional managers (particularly in law and to some extent in medicine), the guild powers of the group simply fade into insignificance. The pressures from capitalists and the state to take over areas of guild control are especially successful in a time of overproduction—which is itself an aspect of loss of guild control.

Durkheim had hoped to use professional groups, in particular the French ordres, which supposedly regulated the moral behavior of professionals, as a model for building a transformed and guild-like political system to replace the anomie of his time (Durkheim 1957, 8–13). Regardless of whether he had an accurate view of the true functions of the professional ordres, which then as now served primarily to protect the profession from outsiders, his model is now doubly irrelevant. Not only have the moral functions of modern professions effectively disappeared, but the professions hardly seem to exist as unified entities in their own right, as the "occupational communities" that Goode (1957) called them, in the 1950s. When Freidson, in much of his recent work, still maintains that professions primarily control the state that regulates them, one wonders what world he is observing—certainly not the one described in these pages.

Once again, it is important to emphasize that I am not saying that professions are dying. What is dying is their guild power—as this power is increasingly being replaced by the power of capitalists or the state or both together to control the nature and quality of the professional associations, the professional workplace, the professional marketplace, and the relation of professional groups to the state. This is happening slowly, so slowly that a group of professionals recently interviewed by Derber, Schwartz, and Magrass, themselves citing Derber 1982, take for granted their inability to set goals, perhaps not recognizing that this was once a common privilege of professionals. As these authors note, "Unlike their self-employed 'free' ancestors, modern salaried professionals . . . must ultimately serve their employers' goals and clients. Such loss of control was experienced by other workers in the earliest stages of capitalism. It now threatens the professional's soul, creating 'a type of worker whose integrity is threatened by the expropriation of his values or sense of purpose. It reduces the domain of freedom and creativity to problems of technique; it creates workers, no matter how skilled, who act as technicians or functionaries' " (Derber et al. 1990, 136). To be fair, when asked whether they had some control over their work, the majority of these doctors, lawyers, and engineers said yes. But that response is suspect because their self-respect was on the line; the majority of their complaints indicated that in any time-frame their degree of control was lessening.

If professionals increasingly do not control their own work, and capitalists or the state increasingly do, then what does this mean for the consumer of professional services? That may depend upon whether the reader has faith in the theory that capitalist rationalization of health care and the legal profession is good for them. Certainly the capitalists who control the majority of present day health maintenance organizations in the United States would agree. But their statements are obviously self-serving, and health care in a for-profit HMO is rationed first to take care of profits and only second to take care of consumers. And the consumer who cannot afford to participate in the for-profit HMO can be left with inadequate care in a rationalized system. The same principle applies to the quality of legal services available to the middle and lower classes. As the providers become more rationalized in capitalist fashion, then the cases of this huge segment of the population will be taken only when they can be subjected to formal protocols and computerized procedures, on which profit can be made. Engineers have always been directly subject to capitalist pressures to cut corners, and the stories of the blacklisted engineers who have blown the whistle on employers continues to discourage acts of conscience.

Finally, although the university to date has been remarkably resistant to direct capitalist rationalization, perhaps the days of the professor are numbered as well. Recent advances in in the use of television and videotapes in teaching, of electronic devices to take the place of personal instruction, are ominous for the future of the professoriate. For years it has been commonplace for courses at many universities to be taught by graduate students or part-time faculty. Given the cost constraints on universities, what was unthinkable in one decade may become standard practice in another one. The degraded nature of the teaching environment is evident, as is the increasing inequity in outside funding, which flows much more freely to fields close to capitalist interests than to others.

A series of further questions arises. First, are the processes seen here observable in other parts of the world? In most of the developing world, the distance between social elites and the mass is even greater, and the split between the two is increasing rather than decreasing with the passage of time. Also, the role of the state is if anything even more pervasive elsewhere than in western Europe and the United States. Elite control of states, authoritarian regimes and dictatorships, comprador capitalism, and religious fundamentalism all play a role in determining the future not only of these states but of the professions within them. Future research should be devoted to analyzing the political and social role of professions with respect to states and to capitalism in the developing world, including eastern Europe and the nations of the former Soviet Union.

Second, what is the future role of the consumer of professional services in determining or even affecting the trends that we have inspected? From the 1930s to the mid-1960s, as the guild power of professions was rising, their interest in the concerns of consumers was limited. The professions were motivated to attract consumers to the fee-for-service practices that characterized the medicine and law of this time period, but because they were not overproducing their numbers they had market leverage over the consumer, who valued the professional's relatively rare expertise.

In the transitional era of 1965 to about 1975, an upturn in consumer activism generated a response from younger professionals. Free-standing clinics in medicine specializing in the care of blacks, women, gay people, and (in the United States) non-English speakers date from this time period. Legal education began to stress clinics for the poor, and the consumer movement appeared to have some influence over the way engineers were told to design such projects such as cars and home appliances. In academia, students were either given the rights and responsibilities to evaluate faculty teaching (as in the United States) or given formal responsibilities on the committees that actually ran the university (as in Germany). Professionals vigorously debated the wisdom of much of this activity, which was often carried on against the background, and with the support, of liberal political movements that were not necessarily in sympathy with the guild aims of professional groups.

With the return to power in the late 1970s and 1980s of more conservative political parties, professional groups might have expected more sympathetic treatment and a return of some of their waning guild powers. Instead the parties that took control of national governments were more overtly procapitalist and antiprofessional than the liberal governments that they succeeded. These governments were also less sympathetic to consumers' rights. As capitalists, the states, and the elites within the professions worked to rationalize the services to attain efficiency in the service of profit, the consumer once again became irrelevant. Consumer organizations still existed, and sometimes were formally consulted before actions were taken. Yet in the long run, the strength of the consumer—a potential fourth major force joining the triad of profession, state, and capitalism—has remained minimal. On the other hand, if we count the capitalist firm as a consumer of services—as the corporations often do—the situation looks markedly different. Even nonprofit health plans try to tailor their services to please large corporate buyers; the corporation's desire to have cheaper legal services has led to price-cutting. But the ordinary consumer is little regarded, for his weight is not enough to influence the new and larger professional service bodies. Practically anything that this consumer is likely to want is viewed as an unnecessary cost by the profit-conscious provider of service, be it extra time in the hospital, more individual service in the law firm, or a car that provides the safety and low-cost maintenance. Also, consumers are often listened to briefly by providers, who have their eye on what in their minds are more important things, such as the "bottom line." When minor modifications are made, ostensibly in response to consumer demand, they are trumpeted as major innovations—patients' rights forms, for example, are circulated in many hospitals to new patients, but the staff to explain them and the advocate to defend them have long since been fired on cost grounds.

Consumer activism is thus on the wane at precisely the moment when it is most important. Perhaps the cynicism of the 1990s discourages consumers from trying to influence professions, or even from trying to affect what the state determines is acceptable and unacceptable in the way of professional services. Nursing as a profession is a good example of this. For a brief period in the late 1980s, it looked as if the nursing profession was beginning to improve its salaries and working conditions, even to develop some solidarity and guild power. Just at that point, the latest wave of rationalization hit the profession, and nurses were fired wholesale from some of the most prestigious hospitals in the nation. The result for the average patient may well be poorer-quality care by an even more overburdened staff. Perhaps consumers no longer feel that they can influence the state on their behalf, or even reach the politicians who are primarily responding to capitalist interests and not their own. Perhaps this, too, is but a phase. My guess is that it is not, and that the processes at work here represent a great threat to the health and welfare of us all. The question remains: what can be done to resist what appears to be an irresistible tide?

REFERENCES

Abbott, Andrew. 1983. "Sequences of Social Events." *Historical Methods* 16, no. 4: 129–47.

——. 1988. *The System of Professions*. Chicago: University of Chicago Press.

Abel, Emily K. 1984. *Terminal Degrees*. New York: Praeger.

Abel, Richard L. 1986. "The Transformation of the American Legal Profession." *Law and Society Review* 20, no. 1: 7–17.

——. 1988a. "United States: The Contradictions of Professionalism." In Richard L. Abel and Philip S. C. Lewis, eds., *Lawyers in Society*, 1: 186–243. Berkeley: University of California Press.

——. 1988b. "England and Wales: A Comparison of the Professional Projects of Barristers and Solicitors." In Richard L. Abel and Philip S. C. Lewis, eds., *Lawyers in Society*, 1: 23–75. Berkeley: University of California Press.

——. 1988c. *The Legal Profession in England and Wales*. Oxford: Blackwell.

——. 1989. *American Lawyers*. New York: Oxford University Press.

Abel-Smith, Brian, and Robert Stevens. 1967. *Lawyers and the Courts*. Cambridge: Harvard University Press.

Ackerknecht, Erwin H. 1967. *Medicine at the Paris Hospital, 1794–1848*. Baltimore: Johns Hopkins University Press.

Alber, Jens. 1988. "Regelungsmechanismen des Gesundheitswesens in der Bundesrepublic Deutschland." Paper presented at the Franco-German Colloquium on the Development and Status of Health Care Policy, Grenoble, France.

Alford, Robert R. 1975. *Health Care Politics*. Chicago: University of Chicago Press.

Altenstetter, Christa. 1989. "Hospital Planners and Medical Professionals in the Federal Republic of Germany." In Giorgio Freddi and James Bjorkman, eds., *Controlling Medical Professionals*. Newbury Park, Calif.: Sage.

AMA [American Medical Association]. 1990. Statistics and Membership Divisions, Chicago.

Applebaum, Paul. 1990. "Feminism and the Judiciary in Contemporary France." Paper presented at the International Sociological Association conference, Professions and Public Authority, Weston, Mass.

———. n.d. "The Syndicat de la Magistrature and the Art of Living Contrary to All Forms of Fascism." Unpublished paper.

Aquarone, A. 1955. L'Organizzazione dello stato totalitario. Turin: Einaudi.

Arnold. M., H. P. Brauer, J. F. V. Deneke, and E. Fiedler. 1981. Der Beruf des Artztes in der Bundesrepublik Deutschland. Cologne: Deutscher Artzte-Verlag.

Ashby, Eric. 1970. The Rise of the Student Estate in Britain. London: Macmillan.

Association nationale des avocats de France. 1974. Le "defi" de la profession libérale. Paris: Dalloz.

Assouline, Pierre. 1985. L'epuration des intellectuels. Brussels: Complexe.

Auerbach, Jerold S. 1976. Unequal Justice. New York: Oxford University Press.

Azéma, Jean-Pierre. 1979. De Munich à la liberation, 1938–1944. Paris: Seuil.

Badie, Bertrand, and Pierre Birnbaum. 1982. Sociologie de l'Etat. Paris: Grasset.

Bancaud, Alain. 1989. "Une constance mobile: La haute magistrature." Actes de la recherche en sciences sociales 76–77: 35–48.

Barbalgli, Marzio. 1982. Educating for Unemployment. Trans. Robert Ross. New York: Columbia University Press.

Barcellona, Pietro, and Guiseppe Cotturi. 1974. Stato e giuristi tra crisi e riforma. Bari: Laterza.

Bassanini, Franco. 1976. Le regioni fra stato e communità locali. Bologna: Mulino.

Becker, Howard S., Everett C. Hughes, Blanche Geer, and Anselm Strauss. 1961. Boys in White. Chicago: University of Chicago Press.

Becker, Jean-Jacques. 1988. Histoire politique de la France depuis 1945. Paris: Armand Colin.

Ben-David, Joseph. 1984. The Scientist's Role in Society. Chicago: University of Chicago Press.

Berger, Suzanne, ed. 1981. Organizing Interests in Western Europe. Cambridge: Cambridge University Press.

Beyerchen, Alan D. 1977. Scientists Under Hitler. New Haven: Yale University Press.

Bezat, Jean-Michel. 1987. Les toubibs. Paris: Clattes.

Birch, Anthony H. 1967. The British System of Government. London: Allen and Unwin.

Birnbaum, Pierre. 1988. States and Collective Action. Cambridge: Cambridge University Press.

Black, Antony. 1984. Guilds and Civil Society in European Political Thought from the Twelfth Century to the Present. Ithaca: Cornell University Press.

Blankenberg, Erhard, and Ulrike Schultz. 1988. "German Advocates: A Highly Regulated Profession." In Richard Abel and Philip S. C. Lewis, eds., Lawyers in Society, 2: 124–59. Berkeley: University of California Press.

Bledstein, Burton J. 1976. The Culture of Professionalism. New York: Norton.

Bocci, M. 1944. *La mutualità in Italia*. Milan: Ascoli Piceno.

Bodiguel, Jean-Luc. 1981. "Qui sont les magistrats français? Esquisse d'une sociologie." *Pouvoirs* 16: 31–41.

Boigeol, Anne. 1988. "The French Bar: The Difficulties of Unifying a Divided Profession." In Richard L. Abel and Philip S. C. Lewis, eds., *Lawyers in Society*, 2: 258–94. Berkeley: University of California Press.

Boltanski, Luc. 1987. *The Making of a Class*. Trans. Arthur Goldhammer. Cambridge: Cambridge University Press.

Bompiani, Adriano. 1984. "La formazione del medico: Breve commento al 'Rapporto Perkoff.' " In Giorgio Freddi, ed., *Rapporto Perkoff*. Bologna: Mulino.

Bourdieu, Pierre. 1988. *Homo academicus*. Trans. Peter Collier. Stanford: Stanford University Press.

———. 1989. *La noblesse d'Etat*. Paris: Minuit.

Bowen, Howard R., and Jack H. Schuster. 1986. *American Professors*. New York: Oxford University Press.

Brentano, Lujo. 1870. *On the History and Development of Gilds and the Origin of Trade Unions*. London: Trübner.

Brown, E. Richard. 1979. *Rockefeller Medicine Men*. Berkeley: University of California Press.

Bugarini, Fabio. 1987. "Ingengneri, architetti, geometri: La lunga marchia delle professioni techniche." In Willem Tousijn, ed., *Le libere professioni in Italia*, 305–35. Bologna: Mulino.

Calhoun, Daniel. 1965. *Professional Lives in America*. Cambridge: Harvard University Press.

Camusi, Maria Pia. 1986. "Le nuove forme della rappresentanza professionale." *CENSIS: Quindicinale de note e commente* 15–16 (August): 1–12.

Caplow, Theodore. 1954. *The Sociology of Work*. Minneapolis: University of Minnesota Press.

Caplow, Theodore, and Reece McGee. 1958. *The Academic Marketplace*. New York: Basic.

Carlin, Jerome E. 1962. *Lawyers on Their Own*. New Brunswick: Rutgers University Press.

Carr-Saunders, Alexander M., and P. A. Wilson. 1933. *The Professions*. Oxford: Oxford University Press.

Carswell, John. 1985. *Government and the Unions in Britain*. Cambridge: Cambridge University Press

CENSIS. 1985. *Indagine sulle condizioni socio-professionali e gli spazi occupazionali dei medici italiani*. Rome: CENSIS.

———. 1987. *I nuovi ingengneri*. Milan: Franco Angeli.

Chammard, Georges. 1985. *Les magistrats*. Paris: Presses universitaires de France.

Chiodi, C. 1920. "Per una confederazione del lavoro intellectuale." *Giornale dell'Associazione nazionale degli ingengneri Italiani*, Feb. 10: 26.

Cipolla, Carlo. 1976. *Public Health and the Medical Profession in the Renaissance*. Cambridge: Cambridge University Press.

———. 1982. *Faith, Reason and the Plague in Seventeenth Century Tuscany*. Cambridge: Cambridge University Press.

Clark, Burton R. 1977. *Academic Power in Italy*. Chicago: University of Chicago Press.

Clark, George N. 1966–1972. *A History of the Royal College of Physicians of London*. 3 vols. Oxford: Oxford University Press.

Clark, Terry. 1973. *Prophets and Patrons*. Cambridge: Harvard University Press.

Cocks, Geoffrey. 1990. "The Professionalization of Psychotherapy in Germany, 1928–1949." In Geoffrey Cocks and Konrad H. Jarausch, eds., *German Professions, 1800–1950*, 308–28. New York: Oxford University Press.

Cohen, Habiba S. 1978. *Elusive Reform*. Boulder: World View.

Cohen-Tanugi, Laurent. 1985. *Le Droit sans l'Etat*. Paris: Presses universitaires de France.

Cohn, E. J. 1960. "The German Attorney: Experiences with a Unified Profession, I." *International and Comparative Law Quarterly* 9: 580–99.

Collins, Randall. 1979. *The Credential Society*. New York: Academic.

Committee on Higher Education (Lord Robbins, Chairman). 1963. *Report*. Command 2154. London: Her Majesty's Stationery Office.

Consoli, Francesco. 1988. "Esplorazione delle ricerche e problematiche emergenti." In Enrico Cecotti, Francesco Consoli, and Sergio de Lazzari. eds., *I professionisti dell'innovazione*, 83–90. Turin: Rosenberg and Sellier.

Coorneart, Emile. 1968. *Corporations en France avant 1789*. Paris: Editions ouvrières.

Craig, Gordon A. 1983. *The Germans*. New York: Meridian.

———. 1987. "The War of the German Historians." *New York Review of Books*, January 15: 16–19.

Crawford, Robert. 1989. *Technical Workers in an Advanced Society*. Cambridge: Cambridge University Press.

Curran, Barbara. 1986. "American Lawyers in the 1980s: A Profession in Transition." *Law and Society Review* 20, no. 1: 21–52.

Dagnaud, Monique, and Dominique Mehl. 1988. *L' elite rose*. Paris: Ramsay.

Damien, André. 1987. *Les avocats en temps passé*. Paris: LITEC.

Davis, Fred. 1963. *Passage Through Crisis*. Indianapolis: Bobbs-Merrill.

Debray, Regis. 1981. *Teachers, Writers, Celebrities*. Trans. David Macey. London: New Left.

Debré, Jean-Louis. 1984. *Les républics des avocats*. Paris: Librarie Academique Perrin.

Derber, Charles. 1982. "Professionals as Workers." In Charles Derber, ed., *Professionals as Workers*, 37–63. Boston: Hall.

———. 1983. "Sponsorship and Control of Physicians." *Theory and Society* 12: 561–601.

Derber, Charles, William A. Schwartz, and Yale Magrass. 1990. *Power in the Highest Degree*. New York: Oxford University Press.

Descostes, Marc, and Jean-Louis Robert. 1984. *Clefs pour une histoire du syndicalisme cadre*. Paris: Editions ouvrières.

Desmaze, Charles S. 1975. *Metiers de Paris d'apres les ordonnances de Chatelet*. Geneva: Slatkin-Megariotis Reprints.

Desolay, Yves. 1992. *Marchands de droit*. Paris: Fayard.

Doan, Bui Dong Ha. 1984. *Les médecins en France*. Paris: Centre de sociologie et de demographie medicales.

Domhoff, G. William. 1979. *The Powers That Be*. New York: Vintage.

Donati, Pierpaolo. 1985. "Il sistema socio-sanitario come apparato di controllo dei bisogni di salute nel Welfare State: I limiti della attutali strategie di razzionalizzazione." In Vittorio Ghetti, ed., *La regolazione sociale del sistema socio-sanitario,*: 43–71. Milan: Franco Angeli.

Durkheim, Emile. 1957. *Professional Ethics and Civic Morals*. Trans. Cynthia Brookfield. London: Routledge and Kegan Paul.

Eckstein, Harry. 1958. *The English National Health Service*. Cambridge: Harvard University Press.

——. 1960. *Pressure Group Politics*. Stanford: Stanford University Press.

Ehrenreich, John, and Barbara Ehrenreich. 1979. "The Professional-Managerial Class." In Pat Walker, ed. *Between Labor and Capital*, 5–48. Boston: South End.

Engel, Arthur. 1980. "The English Universities and Professional Education." Davis Center Seminar Paper, Princeton University.

Evetts, Julia. 1994. "The Internationalization of Professional Regulation: Engineering in Europe and Beyond." Paper presented at the International Sociological Association conference, Regulating Expertise, Paris.

Fallon, Daniel. 1980. *The German University*. Boulder, Colo.: Associated University Press.

Federazione nazionale ordini medici. 1988. Staff interviews.

Fein, Rashi. 1967. *The Doctor Shortage*. Washington, D.C.: Brookings Institution.

Fellmeth, Robert. 1970. *The Interstate Commerce Omission*. New York: Grossman.

Field, Mark G. 1957. *Doctor and Patient in Soviet Russia*. Cambridge: Harvard University Press.

——. 1988. "The Position of the Soviet Physician: The Bureaucratic Professional." *Milbank Quarterly* 66, supplement 2: 182–201.

Fielding, A. G., and D. Portwood. 1980. "Professions and the State: Toward a Typology of Bureaucratic Professions." *Sociological Review* 28: 23–53.

Finniston, Montague (chairman). 1980. *Engineering Our Future*. Command 7794. London: Her Majesty's Stationery Office.

Fleming, Donald, and Bernard Bailyn, eds. 1969. *The Intellectual Migration*. Cambridge: Harvard University Press.

Flood, John A. 1983. *Barrister's Clerk*. Manchester: Manchester University Press.

Foner, Philip S. 1972–1975. *History of the American Labor Movement in the United States*. New York: International.

Freddi, Giorgio. 1979. *Tensione et conflitto nella magistratura*. Bari: Laterza.

——. 1984. "Conclusioni: Il servizio sanitario come sistema politico-organizzativa." In Giorgio Freddi, ed., *Rapporto Perkoff*, 213–91. Bologna: Mulino.

Freidson, Eliot. 1970a. *Profession of Medicine*. New York: Dodd, Mead.

——. 1970b. *Professional Dominance*. New York: Atherton.

——. 1975. *Doctoring Together*. New York: Elsevier.

——. 1986. *Professional Powers*. Chicago: University of Chicago Press.

Friedberg, Erhard, and Christine Musselin. 1987. "The Academic Profession in France." In Burton R. Clark, ed., *The Academic Profession*, 93–122. Berkeley: University of California Press.

Froio, F. 1969. *Università*. Florence: Cultura.

Fry, Geoffrey K. 1985. *The Changing Civil Service*. London: Allen and Unwin.

Galbraith, John K. 1967. *The New Industrial State*. New York: New American Library.

Garceau, Oliver. 1941. *The Political Life of the American Medical Association*. Cambridge: Harvard University Press.

German Universities Commission. 1978. Report on the German Universities. *Minerva* 16: 103–48.

Geuter, Ulfried. 1988. *Die professionalisierung der deutschen Psychologie im Nazionalsozialismus*. Frankfurt-am-Main: Suhrkamp.

Giglioli, Pier Paolo. 1979. *Baroni e burocrati*. Bologna: Mulino.

Gill, Derek. 1980. *The British National Health Service*. Washington, D.C.: USDHEW, Public Health Service, National Institutes of Health.

Gilson, Martine. 1990. "Quand le prestige fout le camp." *Le nouvelle observateur*, 8–14 February.

Gispen, Kees. 1989. *New Profession, Old Order*. Cambridge: Cambridge University Press, 1989.

Glaser, Barney, and Anselm Strauss. 1965. *Awareness of Dying*. Chicago: Aldine.

Glover, Ian, and Michel P. Kelley. 1987. *Engineers in Britain*. London: Allen and Unwin.

Goffman, Erving. 1961. *Encounters*. Indianapolis: Bobbs-Merrill.

Goldthorpe, John. 1980. *Social Mobility and Class Structure in Britain*. New York: Oxford University Press.

Goode, William J. 1957. "Community Within a Community: The Professions." *American Sociological Review* 22: 194–200.

Goutmann, Pascal. 1986. "La genèse parliamentaire de la loi sur le titre d'ingénieur." In Andre Grélon, ed., *Les Ingénieurs de la crise*, 171–76. Paris: Ecole des haute études en sciences sociales.

Grelon, Andre. 1986. "L'evolution de la profession d'ingénieur en France dans les années 1930." In Andre Grelon, ed., *Les Ingénieurs et la crise*, 17–31. Paris: Ecole des haute études en sciences sociales.

Gritzer, Glenn, and Arnold Arluke. 1985. *The Making of Rehabilitation*. Berkeley: University of California Press.

Gruson, Pascale. 1978. *L'Etat enseignant*. Paris: Mouton/EHESS.

Hall, Peter A. 1983. "Policy Innovation and the Structure of the State: The Politics-Administration Nexus in Britain and France." *Annals of the American Academy of Arts and Sciences* 466 (March): 43–59.

——. 1986. *Governing the Economy*. New York: Oxford University Press.

Halliday, Terrence. 1986. "Six Score Years and Ten: Demographic Transition in the American Legal Profession, 1850–1980." *Law and Society Review* 20, no. 1: 53–78.

——. 1987. *Beyond Monopoly*. Chicago: University of Chicago Press.

Halpern, Sydney A. 1987. "Professional Schools in the American University." In Burton R. Clark, ed., *The Academic Profession*, 304–30. Berkeley: University of California Press.

Halsey, A. H. 1992. *Decline of Donnish Dominion*. Oxford: Oxford University Press.

Halsey, A. H., and Martin Trow. 1971. *The British Academics*. Cambridge: Harvard University Press.

Hart, Julian Tudor. 1971. "The Inverse Care Law." *The Lancet* 7696: 405–12.

Haskins, Charles. 1923. *The Rise of the Universities*. New York: Holt.

Haskins, George L. 1960. *Law and Authority in Early Massachusetts*. New York: Macmillan.

Hatzfeld, Henri. 1963. *Le grand tournant de la médicine libérale*. Paris: Editions ouvrières.

Haycroft, John. 1987. *Italian Labyrinth*. London: Penguin.

Hazell, Robert. 1978. "Pupillage." In Robert Hazell, ed., *The Bar on Trial*, 82–98. London: Quadrangle.

Health Manpower References. 1974. *The Supply of Health Manpower, 1970 Profiles and Projections to 1990*. Washington, D.C.: DHEW, Public Health Service, Health Resources Administration.

Heilbut, Anthony. 1983. *Exiles in Paradise*. Boston: Beacon.

Heinz, John P., and Edward O. Laumann. 1982. *Chicago Lawyers*. New York: Russell Sage and American Bar Foundation.

Herf, Jeffrey. 1984. *Reactionary Modernism*. Cambridge: Cambridge University Press.

Herzlich, Claudine. 1973. "Types de clientele et fonctionnment de l'institution hospitaliere." *Revue française de sociologie* 14 (special number): 41–59.

——. 1982. "The Evolution of Relations Between French Physicians and the French State from 1880 to 1980." *Sociology of Health and Illness* 4, no. 3): 239–53.

Higgins, Joan. 1988. *The Business of Medicine*. London: Macmillan.

Hirsch. M., D. Majer, and J. Meinck, eds. 1984. *Recht, Verwaltung und Justiz im Nazionalsozialismus*. Cologne: Burelli.

Hirschfield, Daniel S. 1970. *The Lost Reform*. Cambridge: Harvard University Press.

Hoffman, Lily M. 1989. *The Politics of Knowledge*. Albany: State University of New York Press.

Horowitz, Morton J. 1977. *The Transformation of American Law, 1780–1860*. Cambridge: Harvard University Press.

Horsky, Charles. 1952. *The Washington Lawyer*. Boston: Little, Brown.

Hughes, Everett C. 1958. *Men and Their Work*. Glencoe, Ill.: Free Press.

Huppert, George. 1977. *Les bourgeois gentilshommes*. Chicago: University of Chicago Press.

Hurwitz, Leon. 1990. "The European Medical Profession and 1992: The Role of Regional Interest Groups in the Implementation of EEC Decisions." Paper presented at the International Sociological Association conference, Professions and Public Authority, Weston, Mass.

Hutcheson, C. Allan. 1989. *Critical Legal Studies*. Totowa, N.J.: Rowan and Littlefield.

Hutton, Stanley, and Peter Lawrence. 1981. *German Engineers*. Oxford: Oxford University Press.

Immergut, Ellen. 1987. "The Political Construction of Interests: National Health Insurance Politics in Sweden, France and Switzerland, 1930–1970." Ph.D. diss., Harvard University.

——. 1992. *Health Politics*. Cambridge: Cambridge University Press.

Jarausch, Konrad H. 1984. *Deutsche Studenten, 1800–1970*. Frankfurt-am Main: Suhrkamp.

——. 1990a. *The Unfree Professions*. New York: Oxford University Press.

——. 1990b. "The German Professions in History and Theory." In Geoffrey Cocks and Konrad H. Jarausch, eds., *German Professions, 1800–1950*, 9–24. New York: Oxford University Press.

Jencks, Christopher, and David Riesman. 1969. *The Academic Revolution*. Garden City, N.Y.: Doubleday.

Johnson, Terrence. 1972. *Professions and Power*. London: Macmillan.

——. 1990. "Thatcher's Professions: The State and the Professions in Britain." Paper delivered at the World Congress of Sociology, Madrid.

Jones, Philip. 1981. *Doctors and the British Medical Association*. Farnsborough, England: Gower.

Kahlberg, Stephen. 1983. "German and American 'Deep Customs': One Level of Structured Misunderstanding." Unpublished research proposal.

Karpik, Lucien. 1985. "Avocat: Une nouvelle profession?" *Revue française de sociologie* 26: 571–600.

——. 1986 "Democratie et pouvoir au barreau de Paris: La question de la gouvernement privé." *Revue française de science politique* 36: 490–517.

——. 1990 "Technical and Political Knowledge: The Relationship of Lawyers and Other Legal Professionals to the Market and the State." In Rolf Torstendahl and Michael Burrage, eds., *The Formation of Professions*, 186–97. London: Sage.

Kater, Michael H. 1989. *Doctors Under Hitler*. Chapel Hill: University of North Carolina Press.

Katzenstein, Peter J. 1985. "Policy and Politics in West Germany: A Semi-Sovereign State." Paper presented at the Center for European Studies, Harvard University.

——. 1987. *Policy and Politics in West Germany*. Philadelphia: Temple University Press.

Kearney, Hugh. 1979. *Scholars and Gentlemen*. Ithaca: Cornell University Press.

Kennedy, Helen. 1978. "Women at the Bar." In Robert Hazell, ed., *The Bar on Trial*, 148–67. London: Quadrangle.

Kerr, Clark. 1967. *The University in America*. Santa Barbara, Calif.: Center for the Study of Democratic Institutions.

Kett, Joseph. 1968. *The Formation of the American Medical Profession*. New Haven: Yale University Press.

Kevles, Daniel J. 1971. *The Physicists*. New York: Knopf.

Kirk, Don. 1989. "German Universities: Bursting at the Seams." *Science* 2431, no. 4897: 1427–28.

Kissam, Philip C. 1983. "Antitrust Law and Professional Behavior." *Texas Law Review* 62 (August): 1–66.

Klausa, Ekkehard. 1981. *Deutsche und amerikanische Rechtslehrer.* Baden- Baden: Nomos.

Klein, Rudolph. 1983. *The Politics of the National Health Service.* London: Longman's.

Koenig, Thomas, and Michael Rustad. 1985. "The Challenge to Hierarchy in Legal Education: Suffolk and the Night Law School Movement." In S. Spitzer and R. Simon, eds., *Research in Law, Deviance and Social Control.* Greenwich, Conn.: JAI.

Kogan, Maurice, and David Kogan. 1983. *Universities Under Attack.* London: Kogan Page.

Kogon, Eugen. 1976. *Die Stunde der Ingenieure.* Dusseldorf: VDI Verlag.

Kornhauser, William. 1963. *Scientists in Industry.* Berkeley: University Press.

Kosciusko-Morizet, Jacques A. 1973. *La "Mafia" polytechnicienne.* Paris: Seuil.

Kramer, Stella. 1929. *The English Craft Guilds.* New York: Columbia University Press.

Kraul, Margaret. 1984. *Das Deutsche Gymnasium, 1780–1980.* Frankfurt-am-Main: Suhrkamp.

Krause, Elliott A. 1977a. "Giant Hospitals Enter Cost Control Fray." *Hospital Progress* 58 (December): 50–52.

———. 1977b. *Power and Illness.* New York: Elsevier.

———. 1988. "Doctors, Partitocrazia, and the Italian State." *Milbank Quarterly* 66 (supplement 2): 148–66.

Krieger, Joel. 1986. *Reagan, Thatcher, and the Politics of Decline.* New York: Oxford University Press.

Kuisel, Richard F. 1981. *Capitalism and the State in Modern France.* Cambridge: Cambridge University Press.

Lapalombara, Joseph. 1987. *Democracy, Italian Style.* New Haven: Yale University Press.

Larivière, Daniel S. 1982. *L'avocature.* Paris: Ramsay.

———. 1987. *Les juges dans la balance.* Paris: Ramsay.

Larson, Magali S. 1977. *The Rise of Professionalism.* Berkeley: University of California Press.

———. 1980. "Professionalization and Educated Labor." *Theory and Society* 9, no. 1: 131–75.

Layton, Edwin T., Jr. 1971. *The Revolt of the Engineers.* Cleveland: Case Western Reserve University Press.

Lebrette, François. 1990. "Diagnostic alarmant: Les médecins sont malades." *Figaro-magazine,* January 20: 54.

Leonard, J. 1977. *La vie quotidienne de médicin de province au XIXe siecle.* Paris: Hachette.

Lesson, Robert. 1979. *Travelling Brothers.* London: Allen and Unwin.

Leys, Colin. 1989. *Politics in Britain*. London: Verso.

Liebfried, Stephen, and Florian Tennstedt. 1986. "Health Insurance Policy and Berufsverbote in the Nazi Takeover." In Donald W. Light and Alexander Schuller, eds., *Political Values and Health Care: The German Experience*, 127–84. Cambridge: MIT Press.

Lifton, Robert J. 1986. *The Nazi Doctors*. New York: Basic.

Light, Donald, Stephen Liebfried, and Florian Tennstedt. 1986. "Social Medicine vs Professional Dominance: The German Experience." *American Journal of Public Health* 76: 78–81.

Lucas, Yvette. 1990. "An Interface Evolutive Category: The Technicians." Paper presented at the International Sociological Association conference on Professions and Public Authority, Weston, Mass.

Lutz, B., and G. Kammerer. 1975. *Das Ende des graduierten Ingenieurs*. Frankfurt-am-Main: Europaische Verlaganstalt.

Lyon-Caen, Pierre. 1981. "L'experience du syndicat de la magistrature: Temoignage." *Pouvoirs* 16: 55–67.

MacMahon, Arthur W. 1972. *Administering Federalism in a Democracy*. New York: Oxford University Press.

Macry, Paolo. 1981 "I professionisti: Note su typologie e funzioni." *Quaderni storici* 48, no. 3: 922–43.

Maier, Charles S. 1988. *The Unmasterable Past*. Cambridge: Harvard University Press.

Marmor, Ted. 1970. *The Politics of Medicare*. London: Routledge and Kegan Paul.

Marrus, Michael, and Robert O. Paxton. 1981. *Vichy et les juifs*. Paris: Calmann-Levy.

Martinelli, Alberto. 1978. *Università e società negli stati uniti*. Milan: Einaudi.

Martines, Lauro. 1968. *Lawyers and Statecraft in Renaissance Florence*. Princeton: Princeton University Press.

Marx, Karl. 1867. *Capital*, vol. 1. Trans. by B. Fowkes. Harmondsworth, England, 1976.

Marx, Karl, and Friedrich Engels. 1848. *The Communist Manifesto*. In David McLellan, ed., *Karl Marx: Selected Writings*, 221–47. Oxford: Oxford University Press, 1977.

Matteuci, Nicola. 1978. "Università e potere: Le basi culturali per la riforma dell'università." *Il Mulino* 256 (March–April): 281–97.

Mayer, Martin. 1966. *The Lawyers*. New York: Harper and Row.

McKinlay, John. 1982. "Toward the Proleterianization of Physicians." In Charles Derber, ed., *Professionals as Workers*, 37–63. Boston: Hall.

McKinlay, John, and John Stoekle. 1988. "Corporatization and the Social Transformation of Doctoring." *International Journal of Health Services* 18, no. 2: 191–205.

Melosh, Barbara. 1982. *The Physician's Hand*. Philadelphia: Temple University Press.

Metzger, Walter. 1987. "The Academic Profession in the United States." In

Burton Clark, ed., *The Academic Profession*, 123–208. Berkeley: University of California Press.

Miller, Stephen. 1970. *Prescription for Leadership*. Chicago: Aldine.

Millerson, Geoffrey. 1964. *The Qualifying Associations*. London: Routledge and Kegan Paul.

Mills, C. Wright. 1956. *The Power Elite*. Oxford: Oxford University Press.

Mitteis, Heinrich. 1975. *The State in the Middle Ages*. Trans. H. F. Orton. Amsterdam: North Holland.

Mommsen, Wolfgang J. 1987. "The Academic Profession in the Federal Republic of Germany." In Burton Clark, ed., *The Academic Profession*, 60–92. Berkeley: University of California Press.

Monopolies Commission. 1970. *Professional Services*. Command 4463. London: Her Majesty's Stationary Office.

Morsel, Henri. 1985. "Debat sur statuts, pouvoirs et contraints." In André Thépot, ed., *L'ingenieur dans la société française*, 260–61. Paris: Editions ouvrières.

Mumford, Emily. 1970. *Interns*. Cambridge: Harvard University Press.

Murrow, James G. 1963. *AMA: Voice of American Medicine*. Baltimore: Johns Hopkins University Press.

Navarro, Vicente. 1976. *Medicine Under Capitalism*. New York: Prodist.

———. 1978. *Class Struggle, the State, and Medicine*. Oxford: Martin Robertson.

Neale, Pauline. 1994. "European Qualifications: Harmony or Discord?" Paper presented at an International Sociological Association conference, Regulating Expertise, Paris.

Neef, Wolfgang. 1982. *Ingenieure*. Cologne: Bund-Verlag.

Nelson, Robert L., and John Heinz. 1988. "Lawyers and the Structure of Influence in Washington." *Law and Society Review* 22, no. 2: 237–300.

Noble, David. 1977. *America by Design*. New York: Oxford University Press.

Nouschi, Marc. 1988. *Histoire et pouvoir d'une grande école: HEC*. Paris: Laffont.

Olgiati, Vittorio. 1989. "The Law 'In Motion' and the Role of Lawyers During the Fascist Dictatorship in Italy." Paper presented at the World Conference on the Sociology of Law, International Sociological Association, Caracas, Venezuela.

Olgiati, Vittorio, and Valerio Pocar. 1988. "Italian Legal Profession: An Institutional Dilemma." in Richard L. Abel, ed., *The Legal Profession*, 2: 336–68. Berkeley: University of California Press.

Orzack, Louis. 1981. "New Profession by Fiat: Italian Dentistry and the European Common Market." *Social Science and Medicine* 15A: 807–16.

———. 1983. "International Authority and National Regulation: Architects, Engineers and the European Community." *Law and Human Behavior* 7, nos. 2, 3: 251–64.

———. 1989. "Engineers in Europe: 1992 and Beyond." *Technology Studies* 7 (Spring): 6–8.

———. 1991. "The General Systems Directive: Education and the Liberal Professions." In Leon Hurwitz and Christian Lequesne, eds., *The State of the European Community, 1989–1990*, 137–51. Boulder, Colo.: Lynne Riener.

———. 1992 "International Authority and Professions: The State Beyond the Nation-State." Jean Monnet Chair Paper, European Policy Unit at the European University Institute. Florence.

Orzack, Louis, and Caroline Calogero. 1988. "Midwives, Societal Variation, and Diplomatic Discourse in the European Community." In Helena Lopata, ed., *Current Research in Occupations and Professions* 5: 43–69.

Pappalardo, Sergio. 1987. *Gli iconoclasti*. Milan: Franco Angeli.

Park, Katherine. 1985. *Doctors and Medicine in Early Renaissance Florence*. Princeton: Princeton University Press.

Parsons, Talcott. 1952. *The Social System*. Glencoe, Ill.: Free Press.

———. 1954a. "The Professions and Social Structure." In *Essays in Sociological Theory*, 34–49. New York: Free Press.

———. 1954b "A Sociologist Looks at the Legal Profession." In *Essays in Sociological Theory*, 370–85. New York: Free Press.

Parsons, William. 1939. *Engineers and Engineering in the Renaissance*. New York: Williams and Wilkins.

Perkin, Harold. 1969. *Key Profession*. London: Routledge and Kegan Paul.

———. 1989. *The Rise of Professional Society*. London: Routledge and Kegan Paul.

Perkoff, Gerald. 1984. "Efficienza et efficacia del servizio sanitario: Condizione professionali e organizzativo-istituzionali. In Giorgio Freddi, ed., *Rapporto Perkoff*. Bologna: Mulino.

Perucci, Robert, and Joel E. Gerstl. 1969. *Profession Without Community*. New York: Random House.

Peterson, M. Jeanne. 1978. *The Medical Profession in Mid-Victorian London*. Berkeley: University of California Press.

Piperno, Aldo. 1983. "Medici e stato in Italia." In Pierpaolo Donati, ed., *La sociologia sanitaria*, 141–92. Milan: Franco Angeli.

Piperno, Aldo, and Alberto Renieri. 1982. *Il medico generico nella medicina di base*. Milan: Franco Angeli.

Podmore, David. 1980. *Solicitors and the Wider Community*. London: Heinemann.

Poggi, Gianfranco. 1978. *The Development of the Modern State*. Stanford: Stanford University Press.

Prandstraller, Gian Paolo. 1967. *Gli avvocati italiani*. Milan: Communità.

———. 1981. *Avvocati e metropoli*. Milan: Franco Angeli.

Prandy, Kenneth. 1965. *Professional Employees*. London: Faber and Faber.

Proctor, Robert N. 1988. *Racial Hygiene*. Cambridge: Harvard University Press.

Quinn, Sheila. 1980. "The Nursing Directives in the Context of the Major Health Professions." In Sheila Quinn, ed., *Nursing in the European Community*, 168–76. London: Croom, Helm.

Raguin, Catherine. 1972. "L'independence de l'avocat. Reflexions sur deux réforms récents: La rénovation de la profession et l'aide judiciare." *Sociologie du travail* 14, no. 2: 164–84.

Rammstedt, Otthein. 1986. *Deutsche soziologie, 1933–1945*. Frankfurt-am-Main: Suhrkamp.

Ramsey, Matthew. 1988. *Professional and popular medicine in France, 1770–1830.* Cambridge: Cambridge University Press.

Rashdall, Hastings. 1936. *The Universities of Europe in the Middle Ages.* Oxford: Oxford University Press.

Reader, W. J. 1966. *Professional Men.* New York: Basic.

Reifner, Udo. 1986. "The Bar in the Third Reich: Antisemitism and the Decline of Liberal Advocacy." *Mcgill Law Journal* 32, no. 1: 96–124.

Rendel, M. 1970. *The Administrative Functions of the French Conseil d'Etat.* London: Weidenfeld and Nicholson.

Reuschemeyer, Dietrich. 1973. *Lawyers and Their Society.* Chicago: University of Chicago Press.

———. 1986. "Comparing Legal Professions Cross-Nationally: From a Professions-Centered to a State-Centered Approach." *American Bar Foundation Research Journal* 1986: 415–46.

———. 1988. "Comparing Legal Professions: A State-Centered Approach." In Richard L. Abel and Philip S. C. Lewis, eds., *Lawyers in Society,* 3: 289–321. Berkeley: University of California Press.

Reverby, Susan. 1987. *Ordered to Care.* Cambridge: Cambridge University Press.

Ribeill, Georges. 1985. "Profils des ingénieurs civils au XIXe siècle: Le cas des centraux." In André Thépot, ed., *L'ingenieur dans la société française,* 111–25. Paris: Editions ouvrières.

Richmond, Julius B. 1969. *Currents in American Medicine.* Cambridge: Harvard University Press.

Robson, J. 1973. "The N.H.S. Company Inc.? The Social Consequences of the Professional Dominance in the National Health Service." *International Journal of Health* 3: 413–26.

Romerio, Francôis, and Robert Hervet. 1977. *Le metier de magistrat.* Paris: France-empire.

Ross, Robert. 1987. *Reform Politics and Elite Perceptions in the Italian Transition from "Elite" to "Mass" Higher Education.* Ph.D. diss., Yale University.

Roth, Julius. 1963. *Timetables.* Indianapolis: Bobbs-Merrill.

Rothblatt, Sheldon. 1981. *The Revolution of the Dons.* Cambridge: Cambridge University Press.

Royal Commission on Legal Services. 1979. Summary Report. London: Her Majesty's Stationery Office.

Ruscio, Kenneth P. 1987. "Many Scholars, Many Professions." In Burton R. Clark, ed., *The Academic Profession,* 331–38. Berkeley: University of California Press.

Sampson, Anthony. 1971. *The New Anatomy of Britain.* London: Hodder and Stoughton.

———. 1982. *The Changing Anatomy of Britain.* New York: Random House.

Sapelli, Giulio. 1981. "Gli organizzatori della produzione tra struttura d'impresa e modelli culturali." *Storia d'Italia,* annual 4, "Intellectuale e potere": 590–696. Turin: Einaudi.

Sarda, François. 1981. "L'intervention au pouvoir dans les instances judiciares." *Pouvoirs* 16: 69–78.

Schrecker, Ellen W. 1986. *No Ivory Tower*. New York: Oxford University Press.

Schwartz, Laurent, ed. 1987. *Ou va l'université française?* Paris: Gallimard.

Seligman, Joel. 1978. *The High Citadel*. Boston: Houghton Mifflin.

Seron, Carroll. 1988. "The Professional Project of Parajudges: The Case of U.S. Magistrates." *Law and Society Review* 22: 557–74.

Sewell, William H. 1980. *Work and Revolution in France*. Cambridge: Cambridge University Press.

Shirer, William L. 1984. *Twentieth Century Journey*. Vol. 2. Boston: Little, Brown.

Sialelli, J. B. 1987. *Les avocats de 1920 à 1987 (ANA-RNAF-CSA)*. Paris: LITEC.

Skocpol, Theda. 1985. "Bringing the State Back In: Strategies of Analysis in Current Research." In Peter B. Evans, Dietrich Reuschemeyer. and Theda Skocpol, eds., *Bringing the State Back In*, 3–37. Cambridge: Cambridge University Press.

Slaughter, Sheila. 1980. "The Danger Zone: Academic Freedom and Civil Liberties." *Annals of the American Academy of Political and Social Science* 448 (March): 46–61.

Smigel, Erwin O. 1964. *The Wall Street Lawyer*. New York: Free Press.

Sofer, Cyril. 1970. *Men in Midcareer*. Cambridge: Cambridge University Press.

Spangler, Eve. 1986. *Lawyers for Hire*. New Haven: Yale University Press.

Speranza, Lorenzo. 1987. "Agronomi e veterinari: Azione collectiva e struttura del mercato." In Willem Tousijn, ed., *Le libere professioni in Italia*, 203–44. Bologna: Mulino.

———. 1994. "The Consequence of EEC for National Professions: Big Brother's Syndrome and the Sociology of Action." Paper presented at the International Sociological Association conference, Regulating Expertise, Paris.

Spotts, Frederick, and Theodore Wieser. 1986. *Italy: A Difficult Democracy*. Cambridge: Cambridge University Press.

Stacey, Margot. 1992. "Europe and the British Regulation of Doctors: The Experience of the General Medical Council." Paper presented at the International Sociological Association conference, Professions in Transition, Leicester, England.

Starr, Paul, and Ellen Immergut. 1987. "Health Care and the Boundaries of Politics." In Charles Maier, ed., *Changing Boundaries of the Political*, 221–54. Cambridge: Cambridge University Press.

Steffen, Monika. 1987. "The Medical Profession and the State in France." *Journal of Public Policy* 7, part 2: 189–208.

Stephen, Jean-Claude. 1978. *Economie et pouvoir médicale*. Paris: Economica.

Steudler, François. 1973. "Hôpital, profession médicale et politique hôpitalière." *Revue française de sociologie* 14 (special number): 13–40.

———. 1986 "La pratique de groupe." *Prospective et santé* 37: 103–21.

Stevens, Robert, and Rosemary Stevens. 1974. *Welfare Medicine in America*. New York: Free Press.

Stevens, Rosemary. 1971. *American Medicine and the Public Interest*. New Haven: Yale University Press.

Stirpi, S., and N. Dirindin. 1985. *Publico e privato nella tutela della salute*. Riva del Garda, Italy: Fondazione Smith, Klein.

Stone, Deborah. 1980. *The Limits of Professional Power*. Chicago: University of Chicago Press.

Suleiman, Ezra N. 1974. *Politics, Power and Bureaucracy in France*. Princeton: Princeton University Press.

———. 1978. *Elites in French Society*. Princeton: Princeton University Press.

———. 1987. *Private Power and Centralization in France*. Princeton: Princeton University Press.

Tent, James F. 1982. *Mission on the Rhine*. Chicago: University of Chicago Press

Thépot, André. 1985. "L'union sociale des ingénieurs catholiques durant la première moitié du XXe siecle." In André Thépot, ed., *L'ingenieur dans la société française*, 217–27. Paris: Editions ouvrières.

Thrupp, Sylvia. 1965. "The Gilds." *Cambridge Economic History*, 3: 230–80. Cambridge: Cambridge University Press.

Tocqueville, Alexis de. 1838. *Democracy in America*. New York: Knopf, 1945.

———. 1856. *L'ancien regime et la revolution*. Paris: Michel Lévy-Freres.

Tousijn, Willem. 1987a. "Tra stato e mercato: Le libere professioni in Italia in una prospecttiva storico-evolutiva." In Willem Tousijn, ed., *Le libere professioni in Italia*, 13–54. Bologna: Mulino.

———. 1987b. "Medicina e professioni sanitarie: Acesa e declino della dominanza medica." In Willem Tousijn, ed., *Le libere professioni in Italia*, 169–201. Bologna: Mulino.

Troper, Michel. 1986. "Fonction juridictionelle ou pouvoir judiciare?" *Pouvoirs* 16: 5–15.

Tuckman, Howard P., Jaime Caldwell, and James Gapinski. 1978. "The Wage Rates of Part-Timers in Higher Education: A Preliminary Survey." Proceedings of the American Statistical Association.

Turner, Henry A. 1985. *German Big Business and the Rise of Hitler*. New York: Oxford University Press.

Ullmann, Walter. 1966. *Individual and Society in the Middle Ages*. Baltimore: Johns Hopkins University Press.

USDHEW [U.S. Department of Health, Education and Welfare]. 1971. *Report on Licensure and Related Health Professions Credentialling*. Washington, D.C.: DHEW.

U.S. Supreme Court. 1980. "NLRB vs Yeshiva University." 444 U.S.

Varaut, Jean-Marc. 1986. *Le droit au droit*. Paris: Presses universitaires de France.

Verger, Jacques, Laurence W. B. Brockliss, Dominique Julia, Victor Karady, Jean-Claude Passeron, and Charles Vuillez. 1986. *Histoire des universités en France*. Toulouse: Bibliotheque historique Privat.

Vicarelli, Giovanna. 1986. "Professioni e Welfare State: I medici generici nel Servizio Sanitario Nazionale." *Stato e mercato* 16: 93–122.

Volcansek, Mary L. 1990. "The Judicial Role in Italy: Independence, Impartiality and Legitimacy." *Judicature* 73, no. 6: 322–27.

Walker, Mack. 1971. *German Home Towns*. Ithaca: Cornell University Press.

Walsh, Mary R. 1977. *Doctors Wanted: No Women Need Apply.* New Haven: Yale University Press.

Weber, Max. 1958. "Bureaucracy." In Hans Gerth and C. Wright Mills, eds., *From Max Weber,* 196–244. New York: Oxford University Press.

——. 1978. *Economy and Society.* Ed. Gunther Roth and Klaus Wittich. Berkeley: University of California Press.

Weiss, John H. 1982. *The Making of Technological Man.* Cambridge: MIT Press.

Whalley, Peter. 1985. *The Social Production of Technical Work.* New York: Macmillan.

Whitehead, John S. 1975. *The Separation of College and State.* New Haven: Yale University Press.

Whyte, William H., Jr. 1956. *The Organization Man.* New York: Simon and Schuster.

Wiebe, Robert H. 1984. *The Opening of American Society from the Adoption of the Constitution to the Eve of Disunion.* New York: Knopf.

Wilensky, Harold L. 1964. "The Professionalization of Everyone?" *American Journal of Sociology* 70, no. 2: 137–58.

Wilke, Arthur S., ed. 1979. *The Hidden Professoriate.* Westport, Conn.: Greenwood.

Wilson, Logan. 1979. *American Academics, Then and Now.* New York: Oxford University Press.

Winks, Robert W. 1987. *Cloak and Gown.* New York: Morrow.

Wright, Erik O. 1978. *Class, Crisis, and the State.* London: New Left.

Wrigley, Christopher. 1976. *David Lloyd George.* New York: Barnes and Noble.

Wünder, Bernd. 1986. *Geschichte der Bürocratie in Deutschland.* Frankfurt-am-Main: Suhrkamp.

Zeldin, Theodore. 1979. *France, 1845–1945,* vol. 1. Oxford: Oxford University Press.

Zussman, Robert. 1985. *Mechanics of the Middle Class.* Berkeley: University of California Press.

INDEX